# COMMUNITIES OF THE CONVERTED

A VOLUME IN THE SERIES

## Culture and Society after Socialism
Edited by Bruce Grant and Nancy Ries

*A list of titles in the series is available at www.cornellpress.cornell.edu*

# COMMUNITIES
## OF THE CONVERTED

*Ukrainians and Global Evangelism*

**CATHERINE WANNER**

*Cornell University Press*
*Ithaca and London*

First published 2007 by Cornell University Press

First printing, Cornell Paperbacks, 2007

Printed in the United States of America

Library of Congress Cataloging-in-Publication Data

Wanner, Catherine.
    Communities of the converted : Ukrainians and global
    evangelism / Catherine Wanner.
       p. cm.— (Culture and society after socialism)
    Includes bibliographical references and index.
    ISBN 978-0-8014-4592-7 (cloth : alk. paper)—
    ISBN 978-0-8014-7402-6 (pbk. : alk. paper)
       1. Evangelicalism—Ukraine.   2. Evangelistic work—Ukraine.
    3. Church and state —Ukraine.   4. Secularism—Ukraine.
    5. Ukraine—Religion.   I. Title.   II. Series.
       BR16442.U38W36 2007
       280'4094770904—dc22

                                    2007018966

Cornell University Press strives to use environmentally responsible
suppliers and materials to the fullest extent possible in the publishing of its books. Such materials include vegetable-based, low-VOC
inks and acid-free papers that are recycled, totally chlorine-free, or
partly composed of nonwood fibers. For further information, visit
our website at www.cornellpress.cornell.edu.

Cloth printing        10  9  8  7  6  5  4  3  2  1

Paperback printing   10  9  8  7  6  5  4  3  2  1

# Contents

# ACKNOWLEDGMENTS

One of the most rewarding aspects of writing a book is the opportunity it creates to express your gratitude to the people who have shown you extraordinary generosity by sharing their thoughts, time, and energies along the way. It is a genuine pleasure for me to name them here.

I have conducted research in Ukraine since 1990, and these early experiences inform my choice of topic. Most of the research for this book, however, was conducted from 1998 to 2005 and was generously underwritten by a grant from the National Council for Eastern European and Eurasian Research, a National Endowment for the Humanities Collaborative Research Fellowship, a grant from the National Research Council's Twinning Program, and an International Migration Fellowship from the Social Science Research Council. This support made a critical difference in conducting this research and in its timely publication. I offer my thanks to each of these agencies.

Portions of this research were presented at Stanford University, the Max Planck Institute, Harvard University, and the Kennan Institute. I thank those who invited me as well as the commentators and audience members who asked incisive questions.

I am very grateful for the thoughtful reading, enthusiasm, and ongoing support over the years that I have received from the editors of this series,

Bruce Grant and Nancy Ries. The book is far better thanks to their insightful comments and encouragement. I thank Peter Wissoker at Cornell University Press and Martin Schneider and Karen Laun for thoughtful advice and for improving the overall clarity of this book. Others have read and commented on the manuscript and have added immeasurably to what this book has become. Most of all, I would like to thank Melissa Caldwell, Heather Coleman, Roger Finke, Sarah Phillips, Annie Rose, Serhii Plokhy, and Mark von Hagen. I am hugely indebted to these friends and colleagues for years of conversation, exchange, and friendship. Other friends and colleagues have contributed more to this book than they know: I would like to acknowledge Dominique Arel, Greg Eghigian, R. Po-chia Hsia, Roman Ivashkiv, Philip Jenkins, Van Kuno, Hiroaki Kuromiya, Sally McMurry, Michael Naydan, Maggie Paxson, Gregg Roeber, Blair Ruble, Sophie de Schaepdrijver, Mark Steinberg and all the participants at the Kennan Institute Religion workshop, and Frank Sysyn.

My debts to friends and colleagues in Ukraine were already enormous before I began this research, and they have only continued to grow. This is particularly true of Olga Filippova, Valentyna Pavlenko, and Svitlana Shlipchenko. They have my profound thanks for the hours of inspirational conversation that only fed my fascination with Ukraine. Mykola Polyuha, Tatyana Ilina, and Ksena Lvova transcribed many interviews and were helpful with other aspects of the research process. Other friends have influenced my thinking about Ukraine over the years in ways too numerous to recount, including Olena Yahodovs'ka, Andrii Alexandrovich, Ludmilla Asmalovskaia and her entire extended family, the Patlay family, and Yuriy Mykytenko. I must also offer my profound gratitude to the nearly two hundred people who were formally interviewed for this project. They graciously gave of their time in responding to my numerous inquiries and were willing to trust a stranger with their most intimate experiences, fears, memories, and dreams. They might disagree with some of my interpretations, but I hope that they at least will recognize themselves on these pages.

Lastly, I wish to thank my husband, Adrian Wanner, for years of inspiration and the good cheer that has sustained me through this project and through so much else that we undertake together. It is to him that I dedicate this book.

# Note on Transliteration

I use the Library of Congress system of transliteration from Ukrainian and Russian when rendering quotations, except when another spelling has become accepted usage in English ("Chernobyl" rather than Chornobyl, "Gorky" rather than Gorkii). I have indicated whether the translation of quotations and citations was from Ukrainian or Russian. All place names in Ukraine have been transliterated from Ukrainian (Kyiv rather than Kiev, Odesa rather than Odessa), but the names of Soviet government agencies have been rendered in Russian. All translations are my own.

# COMMUNITIES OF THE CONVERTED

# INTRODUCTION

Ukraine was called the Bible Belt of the Soviet Union.[1] It was home to over half of the 1.5 million registered Baptists in the USSR, making Soviet Ukrainians the largest Baptist community in Europe, and one of the largest in the world outside of the United States. As early as 1954, however, Soviet Baptists estimated their ranks to be nearly three million, reflecting the significant number of unregistered believers and children who participated as well as numerous underground communities.[2] If the growth of evangelical communities during the Soviet period was steady, since the collapse of the USSR it has skyrocketed. Already by 2000, one quarter of all registered places of worship in Ukraine were Protestant, and in southeastern Ukraine, the number of Protestant churches nearly equaled the number of Orthodox churches.[3] Today, the largest evangelical megachurch in all of Europe is an independent Pentecostal church that was founded in Kyiv in 1994 and now has over twenty-five thousand members.

Not only has Ukraine become home to some of the most active and robust evangelical communities in all of Europe, it has also rapidly become a center of evangelical publishing, seminary training, and missionary recruiting that aims to serve all of Eurasia. Hundreds of Ukrainian missionaries travel to Russia and throughout the former Soviet Union every year to evangelize. These staggering changes in the religious landscape have largely taken root since the late 1980s.

Many scholars were taken by surprise when a religious renaissance flourished during the final years of Soviet rule. The Soviet regime's vision of modernity and of a "bright future" enlightened by science and free from superstitious belief rendered religious communities and religious practice anathema. To a stunning extent, antireligious agitation beginning in the 1920s managed to chase religious sentiment, symbolism, and practice from the public sphere. This retreat, compounded by an ongoing barrage of antireligious propaganda and waves of repression against active believers over the following decades, led many analysts to conclude that Soviet society had indeed become secular, if not outright atheist.

Yet during the Soviet period, evangelical communities in Ukraine and throughout the USSR not only survived, they thrived. Whether one speaks of the Revolution of 1905, the Revolution of 1917, or the collapse of the USSR in 1991, during each of these periods of jarring political reform, widespread social change, and extensive moral questioning, there were seismic shifts in the religious landscape that led to the growth of evangelical communities. These social and political crises, which were to some degree predicated on alienation from Orthodox authorities, led to extensive legal reform concerning the status of minority religious organizations. Affiliation with nontraditional religions carried decisively different political and national implications. During these periods of tumultuous change, evangelical believers constructed alternative cosmologies, philosophies of life, and moralities as self-conscious traditionalists within the confines of religious communities that were branded as "foreign."

The broad religious renaissance that flourished throughout the region in the 1990s suggests that repressive conditions did not altogether eradicate religious belief and practice and produce only secular worldviews among Soviet citizens. Although communist policies secularized the public sphere to an impressive extent, the Party's propaganda often made use of religious sensibilities, in the process reaffirming them. Antireligious legislation chased the expression of religious sentiment and practice into private, atomized domains, where knowledge of religious practice and doctrine was often, with each passing generation, replaced by ignorance or indifference, even if the sensibility often remained. For some Soviet citizens, however, religion became a refuge, a meaningful identity and mode of living in an alternative moral universe, in defiance of the numerous risks and penalties involved. These communities constitute further evidence of a vibrant and resilient form of "civil society" that existed during the Soviet period.

This book explores individual motivations to convert to evangelicalism and the strategies these communities employed to survive and grow. There have been tremendous shifts from the sensibilities, beliefs, and practices these evangelical communities embraced during the Soviet period to those they advocate at the dawn of the twenty-first century. In analyzing these shifts my intention is to provide an analytical framework for thinking about the historical experience of Soviet secularism to better understand the religious renaissance that occurred after 1991. How does a state foster the secular? How can individuals and groups respond? For this reason, I have privileged evangelical responses to state policies rather than focusing on the formation of the policies themselves.[4] It is not my intention to provide a comprehensive historical account of secularization or of the evangelical experience from 1905 to 2005. This century was punctuated by world wars, revolutions, famines, collectivization campaigns as well as sweeping urbanization, industrialization, and mass mobility. While these events and dynamics form the backdrop of the evangelical experience, they are not directly depicted here. Rather, I situate the processes of secularization, the debates about moral agency, and the spread of global Christianity within these tumultuous periods of transformation.

These dynamics and processes reached far beyond Ukraine and affected much of the former Soviet Union. Although there were of course local specificities of culture and history that affected how these dynamics played out in Ukraine, much of what Ukrainian evangelicals encountered and experienced pertained to other believers in the former Soviet Union as well. So along with a broad, overarching framework of how Soviet secularism and evangelism have intersected, I also illustrate the specifics of how dynamics of change affected religious practice in Ukraine by providing an ethnographic profile of selected communities over time in Kharkiv, a major industrial center that was once an early Bolshevik stronghold as well as the first capital of Soviet Ukraine.

When I speak of "evangelicals," given the Soviet and post-Soviet contexts, I am referring to Baptist, Pentecostal, and charismatic believers. State policies have lumped these denominations together, both legally and administratively. In spite of some doctrinal differences, these are all evangelizing Protestant faiths. They share a belief in the inerrancy of the Bible and in the necessity of a "born-again" experience in which one confesses one's sins and accepts Christ in order to receive eternal salvation. All believers are encouraged to evangelize, or spread the "good news of the Gospel." Clergy are not assumed to have a privileged relationship with the divine, so there is extensive lay participation in ritual and congregational life. Unlike Baptists, Pentecostals draw on a theology of Pentecost and a belief in spiritual gifts, yielding an experiential knowledge of God through baptism of the Holy Spirit as evidenced by glossolalia, also called "speaking in tongues." Beginning in the late 1980s, charismatic communities appeared that melded Pentecostal doctrine to an experiential piety and particular modes of ecstatic worship.

The prominence of evangelical communities in Ukraine is often overlooked because of the multiple and vague terms that others use to refer to them—and that they use to describe themselves. This opaqueness can partially be explained by evangelicals' beginnings in the Russian Empire as unwanted "sectarians" (Ukr./Rus. *sektanty*). They called themselves "Evangelical Christians" or "Baptists," but in the southwest of the Russian Empire, in what today is largely Ukraine, they were called "Shtundists," to reflect the influence of Germans and German Anabaptist theology.[5]

The arrival of Protestantism in the eighteenth century introduced the possibility that religious practice did not have to be an ascriptive attribute of identity bestowed at birth, as was historically the cultural and legal norm throughout the Russian Empire.[6] Protestant proselytizers proposed that religious identity was a personal choice, a conscious decision based on conviction developed after a spiritual encounter. Civil and ecclesiastical authorities found Protestantism threatening, even "dangerous," to the established social and political order because it represented the decoupling of nationality and religion as an organic entity.

Evangelicals were persecuted, initially under the Russian Empire and later under the Soviet regime, because they were accused of embodying alien worldviews and values.[7] Especially during the Soviet period, accusations of illegitimate financing from the exploitative capital of "Brother Rockefeller" served as the justification to stigmatize and persecute evangelicals.[8] Soviet authorities clearly recognized the power of religion to transcend state boundaries, even their own formidable ones, and forge bonds of allegiance among coreligionists of different social backgrounds and political systems, and they attempted to prevent this.[9]

Religiously motivated migration to evangelize and missionize underlined the greater global community to which believers shared a connection. This movement also exposed comparatively small and isolated communities to practices and values embraced by believers in other parts of the world. The desire to evangelize motivated Ukrainian immigrants to the United States to return to their homeland in the 1920s to proselytize. Similarly, religiously persecuted Ukrainian refugees who emigrated to the United States after 1989 today play a critical role in missionary efforts to open churches and provide charitable assistance to the needy.

My focus on the evangelical religious renaissance that took root after the collapse of the Soviet Union reveals how these formerly sequestered religious communities with an ascetic, pietistic, and legalistic ethos have evolved. The dynamics driving religious change squarely situate Ukraine within the socialist experience. There is no denying the simultaneity of the resurgence of religion and the demise of socialism. Furthermore, most religions thriving in the region tend to be conservative and doctrinal, suggesting a germane connection between socialist ideology and fundamentalist religions, likely a product of their shared eschatological visions, a readiness to identify an evil Other, authoritarian tendencies in leadership, and a disciplined core of true believers.

Religious communities have also become powerful globalizing forces that help Ukraine move beyond its socialist past. The enormous traffic of evangelicals relocating and traveling after 1991 quickly ushered Soviet believers into a far wider transnational religious field that brought images, knowledges, and connections to people from other places. At the same time, congregational membership, with its commitment to active participation in a specific neighborhood church, simultaneously intensifies connections to the local and immediate. The creation of an independent Ukrainian state that has embraced legal codes and legislative policies promoting religious pluralism, unlike most of the other countries in the region, has radically altered the religious landscape in Ukraine. In other words, religion is a sphere that makes tangible the shared experience of socialism and at the same time unleashes dynamics that create difference on a multitude of levels—between Ukraine and its socialist past, between Ukraine and the former countries of the Soviet bloc.

My interest in religious practice in the Soviet Union crystallized in the early 1990s. At the time, I was interested in how the politics of revisionist historiography affected nation-building. Yet I could not help but notice that efforts to "nationalize" Ukrainians had to compete with a vast spectrum of religious affiliations that promised to connect them to communities that were decisively transnational. This was particularly true of the "national" churches. The Ukrainian Orthodox Church-Moscow Patriarchate has pronounced political and cultural links to Russia. The Ukrainian Autocephalous Orthodox Church has strong connections to Ukrainian diaspora communities in Canada, the United States, and Australia. The Ukrainian Greek Catholic Church recognizes papal authority and links this denomination to the "universal" Catholic Church and Catholic believers worldwide.

Ukraine was a preferred destination for a plethora of missionary groups from around the world, especially evangelical Protestant groups from the

United States. They saw the end of the Cold War as a chance to reclaim for Christ white Europeans from the atheist upbringing that an "evil" communist state had foisted upon them. I lived in Ukraine from 1992 to 1993 and again in 1995; I have since returned at least once nearly every year. During these journeys, I often felt that I might be the only person on the whole jumbo jet who was not "on mission." Plane after plane bound for Kyiv carried missionary, youth, and medical mission groups sponsored by individual churches or religious organizations.

Once on the ground, the Mormons, with their signature black pants and white shirts, could be seen tag-team missionizing in pairs along with pantomime street theater groups of young Americans unable to speak Ukrainian or Russian but nonetheless trying to enact scenes from the Bible with gestures in an effort to church the unchurched Ukrainians. After so many trips seated next to eager missionaries, I began to wonder why so many Americans agreed to spend their annual vacations—indeed, often their annual savings too—to witness to Ukrainians. What did Ukrainians make of these efforts to shake their "atheist upbringing" when they had just commemorated the millennium of Christianity in Kyivan Rus' in 1988?

At the same time that such questions were distracting me from my research, many people I had interviewed immigrated to the United States. With stunning frequency, they told me of the Ukrainian Baptist they had found in Evansville, Indiana to repair their car, the Ukrainian Pentecostal children who were taking art classes taught in Ukrainian in Lexington, Kentucky, or the wonderful Ukrainian Baptist carpenter who was remodeling their home in Everett, Washington. These cities are hardly typical immigrant destinations. Yet significant Ukrainian and Russian-language congregations of evangelical believers were forming there. Indeed, by the mid-1990s, the largest *Ridna Shkola,* or Ukrainian school that teaches Ukrainian language, culture, and history, was located in Sacramento, displacing the historic predominance of the Ukrainian Saturday schools in Philadelphia and New York that serve the children of the Ukrainian diaspora. Who were these Soviet Ukrainian evangelicals and how did they adapt to life in the United States? Would they follow the path of the post–World War II Ukrainians who had crystallized into a diaspora and closely followed Ukrainian politics even as they laid down roots in America? Or would they be like the Jewish refugees from Ukraine, largely secular, professionally successful, and culturally Russian?

Caught in the middle of the enormous movement of American evangelicals to the former Soviet Union and Soviet evangelicals to the United States, I began to think about why evangelicalism would have held out such appeal to Soviet citizens and now Ukrainians. I realized that converts found the alternative moralities that evangelical communities advocated in the face of secularizing tendencies relevant and meaningful to their daily lives.

## Secularizing and Desecularizing

I have taken inspiration from Talal Asad's recommendation that the process of secularization be approached indirectly.[10] The secular is thrown into relief when one studies its counterpart, namely the religious and the sacred. Through a diachronic exploration of evangelical communities, I identify the dynamics that fed processes of secularization and sacralization and how they were experienced by individual believers. I use this to explain the more general resurgence of religion that set in as the Soviet system collapsed and the particular tenor that evangelicalism has since taken in Ukraine.

The twentieth century offered two vivid examples of secularization, the Soviet Union and Western Europe.[11] In some respects they exhibit similar attributes, and yet there are key differences. Secularization of the public sphere—that is, diminishing religious observance and the retreat of religion from certain domains of social life, such as education and government— evolved gradually and voluntarily over time in Western Europe whereas it was imposed in the Soviet Union. When coercive mechanisms in the USSR against religious practice were lifted, for example during World War II, religious communities rebounded with tremendous agility, suggesting that secularization in the sense of an eradication of religious belief did not have deep roots in Soviet society, in spite of state policies that vastly reduced the presence and influence of religious institutions and overt religious practice. When Gorbachev relaxed antireligious policies in the late 1980s, there was a popular outpouring of interest in spirituality. This is why scholars have always referred to "European exceptionalism" when discussing issues of secularism.

Still, there are important parallels between the European and Soviet experiences of secularism. Most European countries have a traditional state church or churches. In explaining why religious participation has steadily declined over the course of the twentieth century in Europe and now even appears irreversible to some, José Casanova suggests that it may be because these state churches refused to compromise on their dominant, privileged, and protected status and resisted the breakdown of the alliance between throne and altar.[12] The established churches in most European societies refused to accommodate the modernist processes of functional differentiation that relegated secular and sacred affairs into different spheres, leading to a steady decline in affiliation and allegiance to traditional churches in modernizing European societies. The failure of such churches to change with the tide cost them their credibility, and they eventually ceased to play a meaningful role in individuals' lives.

A parallel dynamic of sorts was operating in the Soviet Union. The ideological project to realize socialism involved the institutionalization of a secular, materialist, and rationalist worldview. Yet just as European state churches refused to allow the emergence of social and political spheres devoid of religious content, Soviet leaders also barred secular communist ideology from being sequestered in the political domain and insisted that it permeate all aspects of social life. Although Soviet ideology was also upheld and protected by the state, its ability to provide sufficient and sustainable levels of meaning over time waned. As a result, not only the ideal of Soviet secularism but also the ideology behind it became tarnished as a viable component of modernity. In other words, the socialist ideological project itself was subject to a process of secularization in the sense that it suffered a steady decline in belief and allegiance.

Yet the conditions of socialist modernity opened up what Danièle Hervieu-Léger has called "utopian spaces," an existential quest for answers and certainty believed to be recoverable from a distant past. Indeed, the Marxist view of socialism was a utopian response to the ills of modernity and industrial capitalism that took inspiration from the communalism of small-scale indigenous societies. Bolshevik and Soviet ideology embodied expectations of equality, solidarity, and prosperity. To make this secular ideology meaningful, paradoxically, religious sensibilities were used in Soviet commemorative rituals and devotional cults of various leaders and "heroes of labor." Fundamentally religious concepts, such as transcendence, resurrection, and deliverance, were harnessed to mobilize the population behind the Soviet project to build socialism.[13] For some time, these sacred practices helped generate legitimacy for the state. But over time the Soviet Union's sacred vision of worldly salvation became something of a Potemkin village, something citizens nodded to in a gesture of ritualized behavior, even though they recognized that it penetrated no deeper than the public facade.

If one considers processes of secularization not just in the narrow terms of "religion," as measured by a linear decline of overt religious practice and the number of religious institutions, but also in terms of the "sacred," meaning those objects, practices, and symbols imbued with a mystical aura of grace and power, a very different picture emerges. Sacralization occurred in the Soviet Union in many nonreligious spheres and served, I argue, to keep alive religious sensibilities and dispositions. Soviet efforts to secularize society concentrated on eliminating the "religious" and, as far as it goes, did indeed succeed in vastly reducing the infrastructure, authority and power of religious institutions and sharply restricting all forms of public religious practice. Over decades, this bred widespread ignorance of religious doctrine and ritual practice. But it would be a mistake to equate this assault on religious institutions and the ignorance it produced with the actual elimination of belief in the supernatural and reverence for spiritual beings.

On the contrary, thanks to an ongoing presence of the sacred in Soviet society in political ritual, folklore, and in everyday social and cultural practices, I argue, religious sensibilities were kept alive and this paved the way for a resurgence of organized religion once it became politically feasible. Reversing secularism amounted to recreating a religious infrastructure, a process that was swiftly set in motion in the late 1980s. The evangelical communities I analyze reaffirm socialist moral dispositions of equality, solidarity, and prosperity and offer reassurances of continuity. They have attempted to fill the "utopian spaces" left vacant by first the failings and later the collapse of socialism by promoting disciplining practices and discourses of salvation that offer a sense of deliverance and transcendence.

Ukrainian evangelicals resisted the elimination of the religious and the sacred in Soviet society, and their efforts reveal the cycles and reversals of Soviet religious policies. They defied mandates to force religious practice into an invisible, privatized domain. It is precisely this dimension of their experience that they seek to reverse in their efforts to broaden the presence of the "religious" and the "sacred" in contemporary Ukrainian society. The evangelical quest for a more public role for religion is justified by a belief in the need for moral renewal.

## Remaking Self and Society

Many studies situated in formerly socialist states have taken up the issue of morality, noting that basic belief in right and wrong has come under question and is no longer widespread.[14] The transformation that has beset the region has destabilized basic understandings of the self, of an individual's relation to the collective, and of the mutual obligations shared by citizens and their state. Yet many authors trade on an undertheorized notion of morality that stems essentially from the difficulties in defining it. What is morality and how does it relate to the concepts of culture and religion? What is the significance of referring to moralities?

Morality suffers in an analytical sense from some of the same criticisms that have been leveled against the concept of culture. Many anthropologists have shifted their study of culture to practice, discourse, and other forms of observable behavior, refusing to speak of an American, Soviet, or Ukrainian culture as if it is a totality or a bounded, identifiable whole. In the same vein, to speak of "moralities" instead of "morality" is meant to avoid the false sense of unitary notions of consensus, as there is no single Morality, no totality of moral codes, in Ukraine or elsewhere.[15] The multidimensionality of morality is manifest in the articulation of moral principles on a social level, their enactment on an individual level, and sanctions against their violation on a collective or legal level.

The elusiveness of the concept is exacerbated when moral principles are exclusively conceived as emerging *sui generis* as a result of social interaction. Morality so conceptualized can rarely connote more than a tautology of ideas about virtue encapsulated in a universal projection of a judgment of a person as "good" (Ukr. *dobra liudyna,* Rus. *khoroshii chelovek*) or "respectable" (Ukr. *poriadna liudyna,* Rus. *poriadochnyi chelovek*) because they are seen as moral. These social commentaries on a person's social and moral worth are tremendously important because they bespeak evaluations of an individual's ability to behave in a predictably virtuous way in unpredictable circumstances. They also indicate who can be trusted, the bedrock of all economic transactions and the law itself. We need to trust the person with whom we make an exchange, be it labor for wages or goods for cash. In order for the law to be respected and obeyed, there must be trust that the law is sufficiently predicated on justice, that its basic principles are ethical and fairly implemented. Precisely because these moral judgments are so important, it is not analytically insightful to cast the concept of morality as one that indicates a "good" person or practice or some other tautological notion such as a "proper" or "virtuous." To move beyond the "good/bad" binary, which inevitably casts the Soviet Union as immoral and bad, the concept of morality needs to be refined to provide insight.

One of the ways Signe Howell suggests conceptualizing moralities is as obligations, as duty to respect certain core values or practices.[16] I would refine this and suggest that the core of morality is *commitment* to particular practices and beliefs. According to this framing, the difference between, for example, the obligation to engage in reciprocal exchange and the *moral* obligation to do the same is the level of commitment, the intensity of felt emotion. The use of "moralities" indicates that in every society there are multiple core sets of values and practices to which certain individuals or groups feel an intensely strong commitment. References to post-Soviet moral quandaries, as I have written elsewhere, usually do not reflect moral indecision and paralysis of action, as some have interpreted it to mean.[17] Rather, individuals generally have a moral compass that gives clear indicators as to what is "right" for them to do in a particular situation. Yet those same individuals might disagree with the moral choices others make. Hence, there are multiple moralities in play as individuals or groups, each with their own understandings of morality, interact.

Scholars have used such analytical tools as the "diagnostic event," the "primary orienting symbol," and "transcripts" as windows into understanding what is truly most culturally meaningful.[18] Arguably, one could say that morality, by codifying those beliefs to which commitments are most fervently held, offers a similar opening into the web of meaning that forges logic into each cosmology. Religions in general, and evangelical faiths in particular, communicate a fairly explicit, seemingly transcendent moral code. Emile Durkheim was the first to state outright that one of the defining attributes of a religion is that it forms a "moral community," asserting that shared understandings of morality and the project of realizing a moral existence are what hold religious communities together.[19] Returning to this early insight, I use the experience of Ukrainian evangelicals to anchor the concepts of commitment, agency, and authority in religion to trace how such understandings change over time in tandem with the particular socio-political circumstances a group is obliged to confront.

Religious communities are moral communities to the extent that they articulate prescriptions as to how one should make conscious choices to live morally. By focusing on the moral domain as one of conscious decision, religious communities confront cultural change and the contradictions and confusion it produces and attempt to resolve them. The moral domain also provides a means by which religious communities can affect the direction and nature of change by using divine authority to cast judgments on certain values and practices and forging commitments to others. Communal life becomes a vehicle to encourage certain commitments, to reaffirm the righteousness of those commitments with such frequency and conviction that the rules that uphold them ultimately become internalized and part of an individual's disposition.

So while morality indicates commitment to certain principles, it also embodies commitment to a group that helps uphold them through shared discourses and disciplining practices, which, in turn, reflect certain understandings of good and evil, of virtue and vice. By connecting moral understandings to faith-based communities, we see how particular articulations of morality intersect with those of other social groups to shape an individual's commitment to various collectives and how these commitments change in tandem with particular socio-historical contexts.

The born-again conversion experience (Ukr. *navernennia* or *navertannia*, Rus. *obrashchenie*) carries with it a newfound commitment to personal holiness and spiritual perfection. This leads believers to draw sharp boundaries between themselves and the world, between the saved and the lost. These boundaries are symbolized by the morally prescribed practices of strict asceticism affecting sexuality and gender roles as well as commitments to charity, strong family life, nonviolence, obedience to laws, and personal evangelism. These commitments are evidenced by a forfeiture of alcohol, tobacco, dancing, card playing, theatergoing, and other worldly amusements. This usually results in the denigration and even condemnation of secular culture (sometimes including even the religiously infused novels of Tolstoy and Dostoevsky) in the name of realizing a higher moral calling. Evangelical communities in Ukraine support such understandings of morality. Through evangelism, they forge social relationships across the globe and introduce particular understandings of agency, commitment and divine authority that underpin their moral visions for cultural and political change.

## Global Christianity

To study the emergence of evangelical communities in Ukraine in the wake of socialism, I have departed from the traditional pattern in historical and anthropological research of conducting a sited study of a village, congregation, or denomination, opting instead to give greater consideration to travel and movement. Soviet evangelical communities have been shaped by the twin processes of extensive evangelizing and displacement. My intention is to signal the effects that movement has had on the deterritorialization, even despatialization, of identity and culture. By focusing on religiously inspired movement in and out of the city of Kharkiv, and Ukraine more generally, it becomes clear that the study of religious communities—particularly evangelical ones, with their moral mandates to evangelize—increasingly makes it incumbent on researchers to design multi-sited research. For, as I will argue, these are not only "religions that are made to travel."[20] They are religions that make people travel too. The doctrinal belief that "every believer is a missionary" plants migratory potential in every evangelical.

After the fall of the Soviet Union, the reception of Western missionaries was somewhat different in Ukraine than it was in other postcolonial regions around the world. First, many Ukrainians already considered themselves Christians, even if they did not express this identity in the same way as the arriving missionaries. Eager converts were often fierce critics of Soviet culture and championed their turn to religion as part of a process of recovery that they actively pursued. As a result, the embrace of evangelicalism did not produce conflicting portraits of the self as "sinner" through denigration of indigenous culture, as others have documented for missionary activity elsewhere in the world.[21] So, while other studies focus on how colonized peoples resisted Christianity, I have analyzed why Ukrainians were so willing to convert.

As in other colonial contexts, global Christianity was part of a cultural matrix into which economic practices, political orientations, and moralities were integrated. Many converts eagerly learned these practices with the hope that membership in a transnational community would help navigate the myriad forms of dislocation introduced after the collapse of the USSR. Through the construction of local communities, global Christian organizations situate an individual within a particular locale and articulate reciprocal obligations between an individual and the local community by introducing new knowledges, practices, and commitments and reshaping attitudes toward social responsibility, social welfare, and social transformation more broadly.

Even as I stress the transnational nature of these communities, I do not wish to discount the ongoing importance of individual states. Religious practice is grounded in a particular place even as it transcends it. Attitudes and loyalties are deeply rooted in historical experience and remain a point of division among believers. Ukraine has a pronounced history of institutionalized multi-confessionalism and religious pluralism dating back at least to 1596 and the creation of the Ukrainian Greek Catholic Church. As a "borderland" of a multiethnic empire, Ukraine has historically been home to an ethnically diverse population that tended to self-identify in religious terms. Even during the Soviet period, there were two-thirds more Orthodox churches in Ukraine than in Russia although the Ukrainian population was one-third that of Russia. The inability to buttress the nationalist project by delivering a canonically recognized independent Ukrainian Orthodox Church led to disillusionment with Orthodoxy among those Ukrainians who supported Ukrainian nationalist ideals. All of these factors over time contributed to a greater openness to other faiths in Ukraine than in many other regions of the former Soviet Union.

More recently, the diverse policies adopted by the Ukrainian, Russian, and Belarussian states have structured the frequency and intensity of this evangelical encounter and, by extension, the dynamics of religious life in each respective country. As a result of more tolerant policies toward "non-traditional" religious institutions in Ukraine, qualitatively different social and religious institutions now dot the cultural landscape of this traditionally Orthodox land.

## Researching Religion

Doing research on religion poses particular challenges, only some of which I could imagine before I embarked on this project. Religion is often confined to a "cultural red light district, along with all the other unfortunate frailties and vices," as Wilfred M. McClay has written.[22] Evangelicals are especially thrust into this zone because they are usually considered to be "a repugnant cultural 'other,'" writes Susan Harding.[23] I understand where these biases come from, and indeed, I think I shared some of them before I embarked on this project, but now I seek to challenge the impulses that prompt us to dismiss religion and evangelicals from serious engagement. For better or for worse, religion has become a powerful force propelling change on personal, social, and political levels in many parts of the world.

My own religious background and beliefs often arose in the course of conducting this research. The tables would turn, and suddenly I would be the one being interviewed, with an intensity that I had never experienced when I conducted interviews on politics or poverty. Many studies of religion, be they historical, sociological, or anthropological, are conducted by individuals who are affiliated with the religious group they study. An insider's perspective clearly offers invaluable advantages in terms of generating trust when the discussion focuses on topics as intimate as spirituality. I should state from the outset that I have not followed this path. I am not an evangelical, nor have I ever been a missionary. Yet in the course of this research I attended a multitude of services and rituals and participated as a "betwixt and between" outsider in a number of church-sponsored activities at a broad spectrum of evangelical churches. I was an empathetic outsider to the extent that I conceded that the nearly two million Ukrainians who consider themselves evangelicals must do so because it offers them something that they find meaningful. I was there to learn what it was.

I was constantly reminded of the degree to which I have embraced the secular, liberal views that hold that religion is a private affair. I never shed the discomfort of being more than an observer at these events, and I always tried to be as innocuous as possible, to avoid any kind of active role. I announced my interloper, outsider status in numerous ways for all to see. I did not cover my head during services, nor use the familiar greetings between believers, nor cease wearing earrings and other forms of ornamentation that are not encouraged for women. I did not refuse to follow communal norms in a purposeful effort to challenge them. Rather, it was my intention to be honest about who I was—an outsider, an observer, and a critic.

However, my outsider status was frequently overcome in the most spectacular of ways. Upon arriving at a particular community, I would always explain, usually first to the head pastor or someone else in authority, why I had come, always being frank about my own non-evangelical, non-Ukrainian background. With his blessing—literally—I would begin interviewing members. Yet, often those I interviewed would speak of me to others as "Sister Cathy from America." Once I was even presented to a whole congregation this way. For quite some time, I could not understand why people were willfully remaking me into one of their own, when I had gone to such painstaking, soul-searching trouble to impose some clarity on the murkiness of my own religious beliefs and to deliberately announce my outsider status by my choice of dress and other forms of self presentation. Finally, it dawned on me. Most of these believers wanted to talk, to be heard, and to have their sufferings recognized. Any hesitation they might have felt about sharing their biographies, beliefs, and hopes with me, a worldly person, could be more easily overcome if they just turned me into an ersatz believer. For some, misrecognition made it easier to trust me and thus easier to share the best and most painful moments of their lives. Once some people started treating me *as if* I were a fellow believer, which usually entailed generous offers of assistance and hospitality, others mimetically followed. For me, this softened what Lila Abu-Lughod calls feelings of "inauthenticity," of trying to walk the line between keeping communication and trust going while still being honest about the gap in professed piety, morality, and politics between the interviewer and interviewee.[24] Such misrecognition had the advantage of allowing me to keep the conversations focused on the Ukrainian believer and away from efforts to try to save me. It did not, however, soften the radical socioeconomic disparities that separated us.

These factors were not in play for a Ukrainian colleague of mine, Valentyna Pavlenko. I received a grant that had a collaborative component, so we conducted some of the interviews together. The reaction of Ukrainian evangelicals to her, especially among longstanding Soviet-era believers who had emigrated to the United States, could not have been more different. There was a tacit understanding that I, as an American, had my own beliefs, whatever they were, and this provided me a certain respectful distance that precluded dogmatic efforts to proselytize or challenge me on other issues. The same courtesies were not always extended to Valentyna. She stated up front that she was not a believer, and on several occasions, she was aggressively pursued in turn-the-table interviews, driven by the interviewee's sense of urgency that she must be saved. People far more frequently peppered their responses to her with biblical citations, and far more of the interviews she conducted began and ended with prayer. It provided much insight to witness the very different receptions each of us received.

I began this research with a series of informal interviews among Ukrainian refugees in the United States in 1998 and twenty pilot interviews with evangelical believers in Kyiv and Kharkiv in 1999. These exchanges informed the formal research that began the following year. Between 2000 and 2005, I conducted participant observation every summer in evangelical communities in Kharkiv and Kyiv and, together with Valentyna Pavlenko, conducted a total of 183 semi-structured interviews, including 109 in Ukraine and an additional 74 in the United States, primarily in Philadelphia, as well as countless informal interviews. Many of the believers with whom we spoke were able to compare evangelical practice under the Soviet regime with what it had become since the late 1980s. All interviews were conducted in either Russian or Ukrainian, with the exception of some interviews with non-Ukrainian missionaries and clergy that were conducted in English. I conducted approximately half of them. All names of individuals and places and some of the identifying biographical details have been changed to protect the anonymity of those interviewed. In instances where respondents are public figures or have published materials, I have used their actual names.

I chose to situate my research of Ukrainian evangelical life in Kharkiv because it is one of the most secular cities of Ukraine. During most of the Soviet period, the city was the center of academic life in Soviet Ukraine and a key site of military and industrial research. More recently, the majority of the population in Kharkiv was part of the anti-Western, pro-Russian camp that opposed the Orange Revolution of 2004. In March 2006, the Kharkiv city council was the first in Ukraine to subvert the national language law and declare Russian, not Ukrainian, the official language of Kharkiv in order to placate its highly Russified population. With two exceptions, all interviews with Ukrainians in Kharkiv were conducted in Russian.

Such political and cultural factors combine to create an atmosphere of pronounced secularism and a lack of openness to Western missionaries, especially when compared to other regions of Ukraine. For example, less than 50 percent of the population in Kharkiv oblast claims to believe in God, compared to an average of 63 percent nationwide and 90 percent in each of the seven western oblasts (L'viv, Ternopil, Ivano-Frankivsk, Rivna, Zakarpatia, Volynia, Chernivtsi). Less than 5 percent of the population in Kharkiv oblast attends religious services weekly. This oblast, together with neighboring Luhansk and Donetsk oblasts, has only 8 percent of the total number of religious communities but 21 percent of the total population.[25] Some of the communities I visited in Kharkiv were established prior to the Revolution of 1917 thanks to local initiative and others were literally being built before my eyes in large part because of financing and other resources provided by American religious organizations.

The legacy of Soviet secular policies has not only yielded low levels of religious belief and a paucity of religious institutions in Kharkiv, it has also led to negligible participation in religious activities and a suspicion of organized group activities more generally. Numerous scholars have documented that conversion rates are far higher when individuals reaffiliate—that is to say, when they switch from one denomination to another rather than abandoning a life of non-belief to become a believer.[26] Moreover, professing evangelical belief, certainly during the Soviet period and even today to some extent, remains stigmatized.

When taken together, these factors present formidable challenges for those engaged in "church planting" and in the search for new converts. And yet even in Kharkiv, the collapse of the Soviet Union led to a religious renaissance, and evangelicals have thus far been its main beneficiaries. Let us now consider why.

*Part One*

# SOVIET EVANGELICALS

# CHAPTER ONE

# SPIRITUAL SEEKERS IN A
# SECULARIZING STATE, 1905–1941

On Easter Sunday, 17 April 1905, Tsar Nicholas II signed the Edict of Religious Toleration. This edict expanded religious pluralism in the vast multinational empire by affirming the right to be and to become a member of a minority faith. Remarkably, the decree allowed for the free practice of religion by granting the right to build prayer houses, reopening religious buildings closed by judicial and administrative actions, and permitting services to be held in private homes. This represented a significant shift in religious policy that was to have enormous consequences for the growth of evangelical communities in the Russian Empire.

Until the Revolution of 1905, national differences among peoples were recognized in religious terms that were understood to be inherited and unalterable.[1] The state privileged ascriptive religious identity over subjective religious allegiances. As the established church of the Russian Empire, the Russian Orthodox Church asserted that the east Slavic world was its canonical territory, and the church relied on the state to retain the faithful by charging that apostasy equaled treason to the tsar and motherland. Only Orthodox authorities could register marriages, births, and deaths, which meant that practitioners of minority faiths were not considered married and their children were viewed as illegitimate and hence ineligible for admittance to Orthodox-run schools. Prior to 1905, open manifestations of "false dogma," meaning publications, processions, and open-air preaching of a non-Orthodox nature, were criminalized. The hostility to sectarianism in particular was revealed in a 1891 statement made in Moscow by K. P. Pobedonostsev, the procurator of the Holy Synod from 1880 to 1905: "The rapid rise of sectarianism represents a serious danger to the government. All sectarians should be prohibited from leaving their place of residence. All crimes against the Orthodox Church should be tried in ecclesiastical, not civil, courts. The passports of sectarians should be marked in such a way that they cannot find work or a place to live so that life in Russia becomes unbearable for them. Their children should be seized by force and raised in the Orthodox faith."[2]

Not all government officials agreed with such pronouncements. Sergei Witte (1849–1915), the former railway director and minister of finance, argued that the repression of religious minorities was counterproductive to the overall goal of strengthening a weak autocratic government because repression merely created social disorder and alienated groups, such as the Baptists and Old Believers, who would likely support, or at least not overtly challenge, state authority if given a measure of religious freedom. By spring 1905 the autocracy was under pressure from a multitude of groups in virtually all regions of the empire, including Ukraine, to resolve its numerous shortcomings with means other than repression. A series of violent uprisings in 1905, Bloody Sunday and the mutiny on the Battleship Potemkin among the most notorious, represented the culmination of years of peasant uprisings, student strikes, and numerous long-simmering workers' grievances.

Later that same year, Nicholas II's Manifesto of 17 October 1905 offered additional concessions by establishing a national legislature based on universal male suffrage and granting a host of civil rights, such as freedom of conscience, speech, and assembly, all of which dramatically affected the religious landscape in the empire. Thus, among the many changes the Revolution of 1905 triggered was an atmosphere of tolerated religious pluralism and a spectrum of new spiritual possibilities that could be shared through greater freedoms of press and assembly and spread through increased mobility. No longer obliged to gather quietly in private homes or in open spaces, evangelical believers began to build prayer houses and to proselytize their faith more openly.

They were adept at putting in place the infrastructure and administrative means to grow and develop their communities.[3] As early as 1903, evangelicals from the Russian Empire participated in an international congress of European Baptists in Berlin. D. I. Mazaev, the head of the Russian Baptist Union, was keen on forging links with Baptists abroad and on establishing the Baptist faith in the Russian Empire as a distinctly Russian faith.[4] The Russian Baptist Union was incorporated into the Baptist World Alliance at its first congress in London in 1905. In 1911, when the Baptist World Alliance Congress met in Philadelphia, Ivan Prokhanov, graduate of an English Baptist Bible college, employee of the Westinghouse Electric Company in St. Petersburg, and member of a large delegation of Russian believers, was elected one of the Alliance's vice presidents. Upon its arrival in Philadelphia, the Russian delegation was feted by the Slavic Baptist Church, discussed in chapter 3, that had been founded there earlier by Slavic immigrants.

After the Revolution of 1905, the Russian Baptist Union held its own congresses in Rostov-on-the-Don from 1905 to 1907, in Kyiv in 1908, and in Odesa in 1909. In 1906 they issued a general statement of faith and a year later established a missionary society in Odesa with twenty full-time evangelists. All of these initiatives, especially when combined with the growing numbers of peasants and workers choosing their faith, meant that by 1910, just five years after the changes in religious policy were enacted, evangelicals could assert that they had over a hundred thousand believers.[5] Given the origins of evangelicalism as an unwanted "foreign" sectarian movement in the Russian Empire, these were dramatic changes indeed.

## Sectarian *Shtundists* in the South

In the nineteenth century, Baptist communities emerged in Russia among "German colonists," whose ancestors had arrived after Catherine the Great published decrees in Europe in 1762 and 1763 inviting settlers to Russia with offers of free land, deferred taxation, interest-free loans, self-administration, and assurances of religious liberty. The Germans who settled in Ukraine were primarily from Württemberg, Bavaria, Alsace, and Switzerland and often had religious motives for relocating. Although some were Mennonite, most were Lutheran or Calvinist, and their theology drew on a pietistic Anabaptist theological tradition of reformation. Rejecting the rationalist spirit of the age, these pietistic groups advocated introversion, self-imposed isolation, and individualized Bible study. Germans were allowed to practice their own Protestant faiths but were forbidden to proselytize. However, the Orthodox peasants they hired were often included in their Bible study sessions.

The term *Shtundist* refers to the German word *Bibelstunde,* the hour dedicated to Bible study. The Odesa newspaper *Odesskii Vestnik* referred to

"Shtundism" on 14 March 1868 in reference to a German preacher, Karl Bonekemper, who had graduated from a *Gymnasium* in Odesa and later studied in Estonia, the United States, and Switzerland before returning to Odesa to proselytize.[6] The article noted with alarm the growing number of Orthodox peasants in the southwest of the Russian Empire who, having combined work and prayer, were converting to "Shtundism." Initially, many Ukrainians simultaneously attended Orthodox services and Bible study sessions. Some, however, began to criticize the Orthodox Church and refrained from receiving Orthodox sacraments and observing Orthodox fasts. Given Shtundism's German origins and practice among the more successful farmers, it quickly became associated with literacy, industry, and sobriety.[7] Shtundists became Baptists when they were "reborn" and received "believer's baptism" (Rus. *vodnoe kreshchennye po vere*), full-body immersion baptism as an adult believer. Most early converts to the Baptist faith were Shtundists; Mennonite Brethren, a Mennonite splinter group; and Molokans, an Orthodox schismatic group named for their refusal to observe the Orthodox fasts, which meant that they drank milk (Ukr./Rus. *moloko*) during Lent.

Evangelical mythology traces the "first Russian Baptist" to Nikita Isaevich Voronin (1840–1905).[8] It is said that in Tbilisi, Georgia, a German Baptist from Lithuania and a convert from Lutheranism, Martin Kalveit, secretly christened N. I. Voronin, a former Molokan, during the night of 20 August 1867 in the Kura River.[9] Under the leadership of Voronin, a gifted organizer and missionizer, the first Russian Baptist church was created when six Molokans joined in 1867, with Martin Kalveit serving as deacon.[10] Voronin chose to call his community Baptist instead of Baptized Christians (Rus. *Kreshchennye khristiane*) or Shtundist.

The first Baptist community in Ukraine was established only two years later by Efim Tsymbal in Liubomyrka, Kherson province. He was baptized with thirty Germans by a Mennonite Brethren leader. Within a year Tsymbal had converted seventy Shtundists to Baptism, including several men who later became leaders. In the 1870s Baptist communities formed and slowly grew in Odesa, Kyiv, and especially Taurida and Kherson provinces.[11]

The introduction of the Baptist faith coincided with the growing social disorder and political dissent that began after the emancipation of the serfs in 1861. Mounting tensions prompted the state to introduce new laws to standardize the administrative regulation of sectarians, Old Believers, and other religious minorities as part of an effort to shore up national unity and support for an autocratic regime. Evangelicalism was deemed "especially harmful" because it represented a departure from the hereditary and geographic understandings of Orthodox identity. K. P. Pobedonostsev insisted that the designation "Baptist" be exclusively reserved for Germans. As a result, the Baptist faith in this part of the world absorbed the connotations of being a "foreign" faith and became firmly associated with Germans—even though it had originated in seventeenth-century England.

The Orthodox Church charged that emissaries of foreign interests isolated converts from the communities in which they lived and deracinated them nationally as well as spiritually by introducing alien cultural practices. The refusal of converts to honor icons and participate in common cultural practices such as drinking, smoking, and dancing almost always led to conflicts between converts and their kin and neighbors. When home is sanctified by icons and nationality is understood in religious terms, conversion to evangelicalism is a willful rejection of established patterns of lifestyle and identity, which is why evangelicalism became associated with unrest and strife, particularly in rural areas.[12]

## The Preference for Division over Compromise

As the number of converts to evangelicalism grew, two distinct movements emerged, the Evangelical Christians and the Baptists. Their differences can best be explained by the ambitions of the respective groups' leaders, the strain of geography that such a large country imposed, and the socioeconomic status of their respective memberships. Baptists in the south were mostly members of the peasantry, whereas the socioeconomic spectrum of Evangelical Christians in the north was wider, even including members of the aristocracy. Ongoing discussions over the term "Baptist" also contributed to the division. Some noted with regret that as a non-Russian, non-biblical word, Baptist had no meaning other than the negative associations that had grown around it. In the mid-1870s converts in St. Petersburg began to refer to themselves as "Evangelical Christians."

The Baptists, led by D. I. Mazaev and his supporters in the south, countered that "Evangelical Christian" was ambiguous and that other believers, including the Molokans and, later, the Pentecostals, also used a similar designation. They noted that Baptist connected believers to a denomination abroad of tens of thousands of coreligionists and that there was no such corresponding body of Evangelical Christians. Ironically, the theological orientations of Evangelical Christians had more in common with Baptist denominations abroad; the more cosmopolitan Evangelical Christian leadership was more adept at building on those connections.

Aside from the name, two other simmering issues emerged that divided evangelical believers. With legal status after 1905 came the obligation to register with civil authorities. But just how much governmental authority, interference, and oversight should be tolerated? The Baptists were quite guarded about accepting any role for the state in congregational life, and some even refused registration altogether and preferred to continue an illegal, clandestine existence. The Evangelical Christians, more inclined to work with recognized bodies to improve the law, advocated cooperation. The second enduring issue was whether a person had to be baptized to receive communion. The Baptists said yes and the Evangelical Christians said no, but they both agreed that only baptized persons could become members.

These points of disagreement were enough to split them into two groups, with the Baptists, primarily located in Ukraine, shaping up to be more conservative than their northern brethren. Evangelicals the world over, and now in the Russian Empire too, expressed a preference for division over compromise in matters of faith. The Evangelical Christians formed a parallel union, the All-Russian Union of Evangelical Christians, after a congress in Odesa in 1909. I. S. Prokhanov led the union until his death in 1935. Most Baptist believers in Ukraine joined the Russian Baptist Union, which also included German and southern brethren in the Caucasus. Institutionally and doctrinally, by the early twentieth century Baptists in Ukraine were moving away from their coreligionists in Russia.

On the other hand, the prominence of the Russian language forged other powerful connections between Ukrainian and Russian evangelicals. The Bible was widely translated into vernacular languages after the Reformation. It became available in Russian in 1876, making Russian the textual language of Protestantism in the multiethnic, multilingual Russian Empire. Whereas most religious languages required specialized knowledge, such as Old Church Slavonic used by the Orthodox church, Protestantism celebrated a believer's unmediated contact with God and the direct reading and interpretation of key religious texts. The availability of the Bible in Russian over Ukrainian and the centrality of the text and citationalism in evangelical practice inevitably led to Russian becoming the predominant language of prayer and sermon.

## Communal Life in Kharkiv

In many ways, the dynamics and tensions of religious development were magnified in Kharkiv. The city was a significant industrial center along a key north-south axis of transport within Russia. Located in what is today Ukraine but close to the Russian border, communities in Kharkiv revealed divided loyalties. The first evangelical community was formed in 1880 as a branch of the British Bible Society.[13] This community joined the Union of Evangelical Christians when it was created in 1909 in St. Petersburg, but its daughter communities joined the Baptist Union, which was more firmly anchored in Ukraine.

The growth and activity of the first community attracted the attention of the Orthodox Church and police authorities shortly after the turn of the century.[14] By 1902 police efforts focused on arresting the person who lent his home for services. As a result, believers met clandestinely in the woods, often at night, where it was significantly harder to detect their activities. They continually subdivided into small groups to facilitate gatherings, especially in winter, when they were forced indoors. When in a private home, they often covered the windows with pillows from the inside to make the singing and prayer less audible and to protect themselves in case stones were thrown. The modesty of their ritual prescriptions and symbolic accoutrements allowed them to worship at any locality, freed from the necessity of any specially consecrated building, place, or object. This, in turn, made it easier to adapt to varying levels of hostility.

Orthodox rituals, on the other hand, include icons, an iconostasis, incense, and other objects that make improvisation and clandestine activity difficult. In stark contrast to Orthodoxy's formalism and centralized, hierarchical chain of authority, the independent and local orientation of evangelical churches was a by-product of institutional structures built on the principle of the "priesthood of the believer" and the doctrine of three churches: universal, congregational, and familial. Local communities and individual believers had great autonomy and saw themselves as agents of individual and social transformation. Their groups were elastic, stretching to include great numbers when conditions permitted and tightening back to include only family members on other occasions. These forms of ritual minimalism and congregational flexibility, although not designed with such a functional intent, proved fortuitous under repressive circumstances.

As communities formed in Kharkiv, the decision as to which group to join, Prokhanov's All-Russian Union of Evangelical Christians or Mazaev's Baptist Union, was rendered somewhat easier for Kharkivites. Authorities in this part of Ukraine categorized Slavic Baptists as "Shtundo-Baptists," a designation all wished to avoid. This prompted one of the largest communities in Kharkiv to call itself in 1905 the Society of Evangelical Christian Believers.[15] The Union of Russian Baptists declined to support them, claiming that the Society "enticed" away members and ushered in unnecessary divisions. Against the backdrop of such institutional tensions, the lay leadership declared itself a church council and the Society a church. With this act, two groups were firmly established in Kharkiv by 1907, the Evangelical Christians, with M. P. Khoroshilov as head, and the other, older group calling itself Christian-Baptist, or "Pashkhovites," referring to the leader of the Evangelical Christians in St. Petersburg. Eventually both groups joined the St. Petersburg–based Union of Evangelical Christians when it was created in 1909.

Few convictions are held more unwaveringly than religious ones. The relationship between the two groups, the Evangelical Christians and the Christian-Baptists, began to deteriorate over minor theological disputes aggravated by personal hostilities, and the divisions between the two groups became more entrenched. As a result, members of both groups could not participate in communion together, preachers could not preach to the other group, and marriage to someone of the other group was now forbidden. In other words, the strict demarcation believers held between themselves and the "world" now applied between Evangelical Christians and Baptists in Kharkiv as well.

In spite of tensions, squabbles, and ongoing attempts by state and ecclesiastical authorities to shut them down over accusations of proselytizing to Orthodox believers, both groups continued to experience significant growth. The original Christian-Baptist community evolved into the central Baptist church of the city of Kharkiv, which is discussed in chapter 5. The congregation moved from its first rented meeting space on Aleksandrovskaia Street, where members had gathered since 1908, to a larger registered prayer house with its own school on Staromoskovskaia Street in 1910. A third and even larger building was rented in the center of the city on Moskovskaia Street in 1912, where they continued to run a school that often welcomed visiting preachers and officials from both unions. The Evangelical Christians also opened their own school in 1921.

Having a school was a high priority. An enduring problem for evangelicals throughout the twentieth century was that multiple generations received only minimal education. Along with faith, restricted access to education was passed down over generations. Evangelicals were suspicious of Orthodox—and later Soviet ideological—indoctrination in schools and did not encourage education. These attitudes fed assertions that ignorance was the driving force behind religious belief. In Kharkiv, evangelical believers tried to create their own schools to encourage literacy and learning, all in the name of becoming a better Christian.

Literacy also extended into the musical domain. Music played an extremely important role in worship services from the earliest days of Protestant practice; most communities had multiple choral groups (men's, women's, youth, all-congregation, and so on). Believers understood musical performance to be both a reflection and an expression of spirituality. They used the melodies of folk songs to compose their own hymns. They established song festivals and courses to train musical directors, and strove to make all of the choir singers musically literate. The Christian-Baptist community in Kharkiv became known for its choir and for their performance of original compositions.[16]

The two groups, the Christian-Baptists and the Evangelical Christians, were pushed back into a cooperative and defensive mode in 1913 thanks to growing hostility from the Orthodox and provincial-level authorities. Orthodox leaders agitated for the revocation of the status of their buildings as prayer houses and argued that it should become more difficult to legalize new communities. During Orthodox sermons, priests referred to evangelicals as heretics. Orthodox missionaries visited evangelical services for the purpose of disrupting them and discrediting them theologically.

Although ecclesiastical authorities were united in their opposition to evangelicals, there were tensions and disagreements among civil authorities, particularly in the south, about the threat that evangelicals posed to the state. After 1911 Evangelical Christians in St. Petersburg were prohibited from holding annual congresses, although Baptists were able to do so in the south until 1915. The Kharkiv governor warned the Department of Spiritual Affairs in 1913 that Baptists were propagating antimilitary and antistate views and building strong foreign connections.[17] The vice governor, taking a particularly dim view of evangelicals, instructed the deputy head of police to interrogate the clergy, missionaries, and members of the local evangelical communities and, on the basis of the information obtained, to force the closure of the Christian-Baptist prayer house on Moskovskaia Street. The order was specifically not given to the head of the Gendarme Administration of Kharkiv because that official, unlike the governor and vice governor, did not think that Baptists posed a threat and was not in favor of infiltrating their communities. Nonetheless, on 6 March 1913 the governor issued a resolution authorizing the police to close the Baptist prayer house because of the "illegal activity" conducted there and to force an end to the activity conducted in private homes by Ivan Neprash, a visiting preacher from St. Petersburg. The nature of the alleged illegality was twofold, consisting of who was present during services and what was said. The authorities objected that Orthodox believers, children, and young people of military service age were in attendance. The resolution notes that clergy were encouraging believers to violate the laws of the Empire by reaffirming the moral obligation of believers to refuse to take weapons into their hands. Ivan Neprash was also personally charged with criticizing the Orthodox faith and its rituals, urging believers to subscribe to the evangelical newspaper *Gost'* and illegally collecting money, on 3 March 1913, to finance evangelical activity in Russia.[18]

The Baptist Church Council gathered the day the resolution was issued to write an application for a new meeting place. Before it could finish, the police arrived and arrested all of its members. With the church closed and the Church Council under arrest, other members of the community took it upon themselves to request permission for a new meeting place. Permission was denied. For six months in 1913, Baptist communal life was effectively suspended in Kharkiv.

The hostility of state authorities toward evangelicalism was fed by the conviction that dissent in organized religious communities had the potential to become radicalized. The head of the Gendarme Administration from neighboring Poltava province wrote, "Everyone inclined toward protest goes into sectarianism."[19] These sentiments were echoed by the head of Kherson province who wrote that the "sympathy of this sect for the revolutionary movement is not to be doubted since with [the revolutionary movement's] success the Baptists envision receiving full freedom of action in the spreading of their teaching and for unchecked organizational activity."[20]

Although tsarist authorities were suspicious of the antistate and antimilitary attitudes and the political changes evangelicals might advocate, it is important to note that these communities were never terribly active politically, either then or during the Soviet era. Their political goals essentially centered on securing the ability to practice their faith unencumbered, which included the moral obligation to practice nonviolence, to witness about their various encounters with God, and to proselytize the tenets of their faith. Yet this alone was enough to bring them into confrontation with the state, neighbors, and employers.

On the eve of World War I, the Orthodox Church noted with dismay that there were more Orthodox converting to evangelical faiths than there were evangelical believers renouncing their faith and returning to Orthodoxy.[21] The outbreak of the war evoked patriotism, and the widespread association of Baptists as German brethren reignited an inhospitable atmosphere for evangelicals. Baptists were suspected of being pro-German, and their pacifist stance and the refusal of some to serve in the military compounded their perceived disloyalty to tsar and motherland. By 1916 all evangelical churches were shut down in St. Petersburg. To rein in the growth of evangelicalism, state authorities exiled the more active members of evangelical communities and simply closed down their prayer houses. As resented as their intense congregational life and zeal for evangelism were, in the new wartime situation it was their Anabaptist refusal to take up arms that contributed to the virtual banning of the Baptist sect.

## Revolutionary Fervor

Social turmoil accelerated in the period leading up to the Revolution of 1917, and many scholars have documented the religious prism through which political aspirations and values were filtered at this volatile juncture. A sacred character was projected onto the dismantling of the Empire and the creation of the modern Soviet state from the outset. Believers from a variety of faiths argued that it was their Christian duty to participate in building a new country and society. They saw the breaking of the old social and political order as an opportunity for spiritual renewal, even a moral resurrection of the people, that would result in a new encompassing spiritual community (Rus. *sobornost'*).[22]

Anatolii Lunacharskii and Maksim Gorky were two of the main proponents of "Godbuilding" (Rus. *Bogostroitel'stvo*), an effort to impart a religious dimension to socialism that held currency from 1905 to 1917.[23] Lunacharskii and Gorky took inspiration from Ludwig Feuerbach, who believed that God was a projection of the desire for justice, love, and knowledge. Because this desire was projected onto a divine figure and not onto humanity itself, Feuerbach cited religious worship as evidence of humanity's own self-estrangement. This prompted Lunacharskii and Gorky to propose Godbuilding as a means for humanity to realize its own divine power via socialist religion. Socialism would elevate humanity to the status of the divine by allowing it to live virtuously before communism remade individuals and society by shedding greed and egoism, which would deliver a victory over suffering and allow morality to supplant law as a means of social control. Although Plekhanov and Lenin attacked this as a resurrection of traditional religion and mysticism, Godbuilding proved to be an early forerunner of the infusion of Soviet ideology and ideological practices with religious sensibilities.

Debates over the merits of Godbuilding occupied members of the intelligentsia, not the rank-and-file revolutionaries. Yet individuals who experienced revolutionary fervor often expressed it in the sacred, transcendental, and moral terms that Lunacharskii and his Godbuilding project sought to harness. Orlando Figes notes that hundreds of individuals of various denominations sent telegrams to the Provisional Government in which they expressed their views of the events of 1917 in religious terms. They described the tsarist regime as "sinful and corrupt" and likened the revolutionaries to "Christ-like saviors of the people."[24] Religious rebirth became a metaphor for the Revolution, symbolizing the advent of a more just state and more moral people.

Evangelicals greeted the February Revolution of 1917 with great hope. They held up Jesus as an example of a true revolutionary, a champion of the weak and downtrodden and a force for morally infused social justice. In a particularly telling quotation, E. N. Ivanov, one of the most respected members of the Kharkiv Evangelical Christian community, wrote as early as 1902 that "we are all striving for one goal, which is to establish the Kingdom of God on earth . . . the name is different but the goal is the same, the means of battle are different but the goal is the same."[25] The Bolsheviks recognized these sentiments and the evangelical preference for egalitarianism, collectivism, and non-hierarchical organizational structures as "revolutionary potential" and sought to mobilize persecuted religious groups as well as oppressed national minorities, such as Ukrainians, to support the Revolution.[26] It is important to note that although Lenin and the Communist Party were highly critical of organized religion because of its reactionary role in Russian society, they devoted little energy to promoting atheism prior to 1905. Their position, as articulated in the 1903 Bolshevik party program, was to advocate freedom of conscience, secular education, and the separation of church from state, a platform that had more in common with promoting religious pluralism than militant atheism.[27]

Two leaders of the Baptist Union from Odesa, V. Pavlov and M. Timoshenko, were among the eight hundred exiled Baptists allowed to return after the Revolution. They summed up their views on social reform in a document called "Political Demands of Baptists." In it, they advocated the separation of church and state; freedom of assembly, union, speech, and publication; equality for all citizens regardless of nationality; freedom to worship and preach all confessions that do not contradict generally accepted morals and do not defy the government; and the removal of laws designed to chastise certain religions. They also advocated specific initiatives such as civil registration of weddings and the establishment of juridical rights for religious communities and unions. Although they had specific political goals, several factors inhibited evangelicals from realizing their religiously inspired visions for a new social and moral order. During World War I, their unions and organizations were closed down or paralyzed, numerous leaders were in exile, and many congregations had bi-vocational clergy or no clergy whatsoever, all of which compromised their unity and ability to function as concerted political actors at this critical juncture.

Although there was some overlap as to which reforms should be implemented, evangelical understandings of *how* reform should be achieved differed significantly from Bolshevik conceptualizations. Believers argued that neither changes in material conditions nor economic relations would transform individuals or a society. Rather, only *transformed people* could alter the social conditions that might lead to a better society. Politics are incapable of bringing forth the changes that faith can, either in an individual or in a society, and any political program that was not based on biblical principles was destined to fail because it could not be moral. They thought the only effective path to a more just and equitable society was through individual moral renewal, which could only be achieved by adopting a set of biblically inscribed self-disciplining practices. These practices are the bedrock of moral values, which, when used to guide individual behavior, can lead to divinely inspired spiritual transformation of individuals and, on a broader scale, to the transformation of society at large.

Evangelicals rejected the intelligentsia's understanding of evil as rooted in class-based animosities driven by capitalist enterprise as well as their proposed political solutions to suffering that involved orchestrated collective action. Instead, they advocated a code of personal moral conduct and individually tailored, text-based guidelines for faith as a means to understand evil and avoid sin. Evangelical solutions to poverty included communal workshops, agricultural collectives, and study circles that celebrated equality, labor, and commitment to the collective, all of which echoed Bolshevik initiatives. However, believers embraced such forms of social and economic activity not out of a commitment to political engagement but rather because their conversion carried with it certain moral principles of charity and grace that were realized through collective endeavors of mutual assistance.

In keeping with a Marxist materialist understanding of teleological social evolution and a European Enlightenment critique of religion, the Bolsheviks viewed religion as an epiphenomenon of economic conditions and assumed that with economic development, increased literacy, and a general improvement of living standards, religious belief would wane in favor of rational, scientific explanation and the need for religious communities would evaporate. They understood the idea of God to be an abdication of individual responsibility for social life because it provided a means to project explanations for problems and expectations of resolution onto an unreal, divine realm. Their reforms of economic relations aimed to reduce such self-alienation. As a result, they anticipated religion under communism would die out as a vestige of the past.

There were also sharp differences in the ways they saw morality. The Bolsheviks cut morality free from biblical, religious, and humanitarian values. Following Marxist-Leninist doctrine, they understood morality and moral judgments to be embedded in social interests, even encased in class-based interests, making morality a form of consciousness whose sources were external to the individual. Marxist-Leninist ethics referred to a "science of morality" because it accounted for the socioeconomic origin and development of morals. The Bolsheviks declared something inherently moral if it helped build socialism because this advanced the destruction of the dominant class's imposition of its (im)morality, which enabled the oppression and exploitation backed by the power of the state and organized religion.[28] Any act was immoral by definition if it impeded this project. Any actions that brought revolutionary fervor to fruition were by their very essence moral.

Figes calls the revolutionaries "civic missionaries" to evoke a comparable level of zeal and certitude among its proponents. He writes, "The democratic intelligentsia set out with the passion of civic missionaries to break down these linguistic barriers [of ideological terminology] and communicate the gospel of their revolution to the peasantry."[29] Yet the revolutionaries were criticized for speaking incomprehensibly at the peasantry, using terms, texts, and citations that they did not readily understand.[30]

Evangelicals, on the other hand, proposed collaborative study of a sacred text with no participant in a privileged position to interpret it. Their strong emphasis on Scripture and its interpretation provided both an authentic, historical tradition and room for local and individual adaptation. Evangelical doctrine was positioned as transcendent, and yet religious practice was tailored to local cultural practices, which made it accessible and meaningful to individual believers. Heather Coleman has studied the narratives of converts to Baptism before and during the revolutionary period. She writes, "These narratives painted compelling pictures of individuals finding the means for self-expression and growth within a new kind of community, one based on a religious rather than on secular and humanitarian ideals. They were the product of groups that wished to be both in the world and not of this world, to be part of Russian culture but also to transcend it."[31] In sum, while there was much overlap in the evangelical and Bolshevik endorsement of such values as egalitarianism and collectivism, the locus of the "salvation" each group hoped to achieve by remaking individuals and society was entirely different. For believers, the new moral practices and forms of social organization aimed to achieve an otherworldly salvation, whereas the salvation Bolsheviks sought was decisively material and earthly.

## Secularization from Above

Bolshevik understandings of progress stemmed from a multifaceted concept of socialist modernity that required the execution of a number of interlinked projects that included secularization. In sharp contrast to the Imperial regime that preceded it, the new leadership rejected the need for a sacred cosmos or public religious worldview and set out to create a secular society. Their efforts demonstrate that secularization should not be conceptualized as a unitary, unidirectional process that pits the simplistic binaries of the "secular" against the "religious." Rather, secularization is a process that involves multiple interpenetrating dimensions.

Western societies have been characterized by a progressively more circumscribed, even compartmentalized, religious domain, which has diminished the ability of religion over time to participate in a meaningful way in multiple spheres of social, legal, and political life.[32] The emergence of these differentiated spheres of social life was the first means of establishing the secular. In Western societies the predominance of secularized domains purged of religious authority became as "natural" as the religious domination of social and political life had once been. A second dimension to the process of secularization was the decline of religious belief and practice, which scholars originally assumed was a by-product of modernization and therefore would affect all "developed" societies. Contradictory empirical evidence, most of it stemming from the acknowledged vitality of religious belief and religious organizations in the United States, has prompted scholars to rethink the interlocking effects of development and secularization as automatically yielding a decline in religious participation and a lack of endorsement for a religious worldview. The final dimension of the secularization process involves the "privatization" of religious belief, which amounts to making the religious less visible in the public sphere. This does not negate the possibility of the religious and the sacred remaining meaningful in the lives of individuals.

To rein in the active social, political, and educational role the Orthodox Church had played, that is, in essence, to impose a dimension of secularization that would evolve over time quite voluntarily in Europe, the Bolsheviks set about recasting the meaning and function of religion in society. Although they sought to eradicate belief in the supernatural, a rather abstract and elusive political goal, they never forged a unified policy on religion or atheism. Indeed, the priority of eliminating religious institutions and religious beliefs wavered over time, as did the strategies for achieving it. Until the Cultural Revolution began in 1928, there were voices in the Bolshevik leadership that advocated restraint, instead of repression, when it came to belief. As a result, policies were initially directed toward separating church and state, the first dimension of secularization, rather than toward addressing the cultural dilemmas of constructing a sense of secular authority by implementing atheist policies.

On 21 January 1918 the Bolsheviks issued a Separation Decree that initially brought relief to sectarians and other religious minorities by stating, "Every citizen may confess any religion or profess none at all. Every legal restriction connected with the profession of certain faiths or with the profession of no faith is now revoked."[33] This was not only the first step in differentiating the spheres in which the Orthodox Church was operative, it also began the process of dismantling the authority of the Church.

The early years of Soviet rule were unlike the 1930s, when dictatorial policy mandates could be implemented by an established chain of command. In the early 1920s, all policy mandates had to be presented and justified at the oblast and local levels. Even then compliance was not assured. One of the first moves was to nationalize the substantial land holdings of the Russian Orthodox Church to limit its economic might, from which it generated other sources of power in society. Second, after nearly ten centuries, all bureaucratic functions regulating marriage, divorce, and births were taken away from ecclesiastical authorities and made the responsibility of civil authorities, dramatically reducing the Church's administrative and regulatory powers over social life.

In a parallel effort to widen the secularization of the public sphere by removing religious authority, all educational institutions, from parish schools to seminaries, came under the authority of Narkompros, the People's Commissariat of Enlightenment. Literacy programs and public education were to be devoid of religious content and would henceforth reflect the new hard-edged differentiation of secular and religious spheres. Not only was an ecclesiastical role in education eliminated, even the teaching of religious doctrine was now also regulated by civil authorities. Access to religious education for children was highly limited; as of 1923, private religious instruction could not be provided to more than three children at a time.[34] Orthodox religious holidays (all ninety of them) became working days, and a series of secular holidays and secular ceremonies emerged to replace religious ones.[35] All in all, the initial efforts to secularize Soviet society centered on vastly reducing the Orthodox Church's economic base and on reining in the public displays of religiosity and religious iconography in an effort to undermine the authority of religious leaders and institutions so as to facilitate the envisioned separation of church and state.[36]

Just when the Church was the target of massive state reform, it was also subject to substantial criticism from within, which facilitated Bolshevik efforts to disempower the Church and contributed to a decline in Orthodox allegiance and a rise in evangelical conversions. The "renovationist" (Rus. *obnovlencheskoe*) movement sought to bring about radical reform in Russian Orthodoxy to renew and revitalize the Church. Even prior to the Revolution, they had made sweeping proposals for church and canonical reform, such as replacing the liturgical language, Old Church Slavonic, with the vernacular to permit lay persons to participate in services, adopting the Julian calendar, and allowing widowed priests to remarry.[37] The activities of the Renovationists triggered an outright split within the Russian Orthodox Church when the Tikhonites, a group of clergy and laity who professed loyalty to Patriarch Tikhon, sought to thwart their proposals for political, ecclesiastical, and liturgical reform. The Renovationist efforts mostly ended in failure, but the split fostered dissent and disillusionment among Orthodox believers and threw the Church's leadership into greater disarray, compromising their ability to spurn the measures limiting the Church's power and presence in society.

The status of the Orthodox Church was even more complicated and conflicted in Ukraine. Following the Revolution of 1917, an autonomous national government formed in Ukraine that existed from 1917 to 1920 and strove to achieve an independent state. Parallel to this, in 1921 the long-simmering unmet demands for the Ukrainianization of the Orthodox Church resulted in the creation of the Ukrainian Autocephalous Orthodox Church (UAOC), a church that was distinctly national and popular in orientation. UAOC clergy proposed reforms that were common practice in evangelical churches, such as using the vernacular and integrating local customs, such as art, music, and literature into church rituals, as part of a greater plan to "Ukrainianize" the church.[38] The UAOC had an adversarial relationship with the Russian Orthodox Church, which, along with all other patriarchates, refused to recognize the UAOC canonically. The lack of canonical status made the church controversial even among adherents of the autocephalous movement. Some believers ceased to support the church when it professed to use "revolutionary," and not canonical, means to wrest Orthodoxy in Ukraine from Russian control. In this way, a breakaway Ukrainian Orthodox group itself splintered into factions. Support in Kharkiv for the UAOC was among the lowest in all of Ukraine. In addition, Ukraine was home to a significant Jewish community. Memories of the 1905 pogroms were still fresh, and the postrevolutionary period saw renewed pogroms against the Jews of Ukraine.

In sum, the predominance of the Orthodox Church in Soviet society meant that it was the first and most sustained target of (often violent) secularization policies. Moreover, the demands for reform within Orthodoxy and the political chaos of the period meant that the leadership of the Orthodox Church was besieged and divided. The weakened state of the Orthodox Church in the 1920s, triggered by Bolshevik secularization policies but compounded by its own intraconfessional disputes and divisions, contributed to Orthodox believers turning to evangelicalism as an alternative form of spirituality and religious community.

### Remaking the Religious Landscape in Ukraine

The goal of separating church from state proceeded differently in Ukraine than it did in Russia. In Ukraine the leaders of the regional and district administrations decided in 1920 that it would be necessary to create special organs to separate the church from the state and to separate the schools from the church in response to the 1919 decree. In Russia this was handled by the People's Council of Justice (NKIu) and the People's Council of Internal Affairs (NKVD). In Ukraine a Liquidation Department, directed by I. V. Sukhopliuev, with Liquidating Commissions (Likvidkomy), was charged to work with provincial and district-level officials.[39] Their goal was to ensure a quick and successful reduction in the power of institutionalized religion by going after its property.[40] Yet, even in Kharkiv, the capital of Soviet Ukraine, the work of the Liquidating Commissions proceeded very slowly. They began by establishing an inventory of buildings and other forms of property owned by religious institutions, which for evangelicals was quite modest, and arranging for religious organizations to rent their own buildings back from the state, often sharing their premises with additional tenants.[41]

By 1922 administrative units created within the Soviet Ukrainian NKVD were charged with overseeing the "registration of the status of religious communities and the preparation of their closure" as part of the "exact implementation and fulfillment of all the instructions and orders of Soviet power."[42] Instructions issued by the NKVD in August 1924 indicated that any religious organization's building could be closed if any one of following circumstances applied: (1) if a government or social organization was in need of housing, the particular religious group could relocate or remain with their new co-tenant; (2) if there was an insufficient number of believers wishing to sign a contract securing the rental space of the religious group, the building could be confiscated; and (3) if the building was declared dilapidated and in need of renovation, it could be closed.

To close a building, a host of signatures was needed, and the final decision was made by the All-Ukrainian Central Executive Committee (VUTsIK).[43] Forty-nine religious buildings were closed in the last six months of 1925. Although the NKVD received many complaints about the closures, it maintained that "excesses were not observed."[44] In 1928 the Secretary of the VUTsIK put pressure on the NKVD to resolve complaints quickly to ensure closure before the upcoming Easter holiday season so that churches could be used to "sing other songs and do other things" in recognition of May Day.[45]

What began as policies that could be characterized as pursuing nonreligiosity during the tumultuous years of the civil war and its aftermath were becoming ones of antireligiosity. Evangelicals were initially spared the harsh measures of secularization that were foisted upon the Orthodox Church because they had substantially less influence, property, and valuables. Their highly decentralized organizational structure and nonconfrontational political posture also made attacks less frequent and less visible when they did occur.

Yet in June 1923 the tide began to turn against evangelicals when the Communist Party of Ukraine issued a statement that said:

> The Extraordinary strength of the sectarian movement has become apparent. The struggle with them is proving to be significantly more difficult than with the official church. Therefore, the question of sectarianism demands deeper study and the elaboration of special antireligious measures of propaganda and struggle. It is necessary to remember that the least repressive measures of all have been applied against sectarians. . . . But they can and will be used in those instances where the activity of sectarians reveals enemy elements against the Soviet state, such as those instances of categorical refusal to pay taxes or refusal to join the Red Army.[46]

The Thirteenth Party Congress in 1924 confirmed a change in antireligious policy: confrontations were to be avoided in favor of propaganda as the preferred means to combat religious belief and practice by enlightening the people. Natural phenomena would be explained in scientific, rational terms, which would reveal the futility of superstitious beliefs and allegiances to reactionary institutions. Antireligious efforts involved debates, lectures, museums, and "godless" corners in factories and village reading huts, all for the purposes of instructing Soviet citizens on how to acquire knowledge that was "true" and "real."

The Society of the Friends of the Newspaper Godless began in 1925 and grew into the Union of Godless with 20,000 members in Ukraine alone by 1928. One year later the union's membership was up to 150,000. In another demonstrative step, the union changed its name to the League of the Militant Godless in 1929 under the new slogan, "The Struggle against Religion is a Struggle for Socialism," signaling that their aim was to spur conversions of the religiously inclined to socialism.

Education became a sphere excised of all religiosity. An antireligion studies center was created at Artem Kharkiv Communist University, the main university of Kharkiv, which, together with the Institution of People's Education, offered pedagogical courses on the "Fundamentals and Methods of Antireligious Propaganda" and the "Criticism of Religious Doctrine and Faith." At technical and trade (Rus. *profsoiuz*) schools, antireligious propaganda was included in historical materialism and other ideological disciplines.[47]

Medical and agricultural students were especially targeted for extra instruction in antireligious seminars with the goal of transforming them into "antireligious propagators" (Rus. *propagandisty-antireligiozniki*). Many of them would later work in rural areas and because medicine and agriculture touched on illness and weather, forces that often left a person feeling powerless, vulnerable, and especially tempted by appeals to the divine.[48] In 1929 the Kharkiv Institute of Agriculture developed an Antireligious Department that had twenty-four students its first year.

The authorities recommended that antireligious circles or discussion groups be created at educational institutions. to address such issues as the comparative-historical study of religion, natural science-based propaganda to discredit religion, and antireligious propaganda from a class-based perspective. A more accessible and simplified program was designed for peasants in order to offer scientific explanations of natural forces. Pamphlets exposed "miracles" as a misreading of science. Educational programs that considered how soil, climate, and weather affected crops were laced with antireligious propaganda with the understanding that if peasants had greater knowledge of science and nature, they would cease to rely on religion. Beyond literacy and educational programs at all levels, antireligious exhibits, and eventually entire museums of the history of religion and museums of atheism, news outlets and theater productions appeared as forms of antireligious educational leisure. All of these educational programs aimed to deliver applicable knowledge and prepare antireligious activists to strengthen the ideological legitimacy of the nascent state.

The "civic missionaries" had competition from evangelicals, who offered their own religious instruction, for the converted and the nonconverted alike. It took the form of pageants, choral groups, orchestras, and a variety of other participatory artistic forms. If the Communist Party's youth league was the Komsomol, the Baptists countered with the Bapsomol, a parallel youth league designed to promote a sectarian worldview.[49] Evangelical missionizing efforts have always targeted the most vulnerable populations for witnessing. With similar goals and strategies, Soviet authorities also targeted orphanages and schools for disadvantaged children for saturated exposure to antireligious propaganda.[50]

## The Arrival of the Pentecostals

Amid the accelerating attacks on religious institutions and beliefs, Pentecostals gained a presence in the Ukrainian religious landscape. Ukraine was to become the seat of the greatest Pentecostal activity, which was largely the doing of I. E. Voronaev. Voronaev immigrated to San Francisco via Harbin, China, in 1911. From there he moved on to New York to serve as a Baptist pastor. While in New York, he converted to Pentecostalism, then still a very new form of religious practice, and founded the first Russian Pentecostal Church on 1 July 1919. In 1921 Voronaev and his family traveled to Odesa as Pentecostal missionaries thanks to the support of two organizations, the General Council of the Assemblies of God and a Chicago-based organization called "America and Russia for Christ." Voronaev began to convert Baptists, Evangelical Christians, and others to Pentecostalism and opened the first Pentecostal congregation in Odesa in February 1922. By 1930 membership at this congregation alone would reach a thousand adult members, nearly half of whom were former Baptists.[51] The name Pentecostal (Ukr. *P'iatydesiatnyky* and Rus. *Piatidesiatniki*) refers to the fiftieth day after the resurrection of Jesus, when the Holy Spirit appeared before the Apostles and they began to "speak in unknown tongues."

Pentecostalism traces its origins to a Methodist healer named Charles Parham, who led a bible school in Topeka, Kansas.[52] He made the radical assertion around 1901 that baptism of the Holy Spirit was accompanied by "speaking in tongues," or glossolalia, meaning the unconscious uttering of unknown sounds, understood to be evidence of the presence of the Holy Spirit.[53] Parham claimed that baptism by the Holy Spirit constituted a third rite as part of believers' salvation following conversion and baptism. These ideas were embraced by an African-American evangelist, William J. Seymour, whose preaching sparked the now-famous revival in 1906 at 312 Azusa Street in Los Angeles. That revival spread to urban centers in the northeast, including New York City, where Voronaev encountered it.

Early Pentecostal missionaries in the USSR were fortuitous in their timing. They were effective in recruiting converts and in establishing a Pentecostal presence during a period in Soviet history that, for all its turbulence, nonetheless granted a certain relaxation of state restrictions on religious minorities.[54] It helped that they could graft onto Baptist communities, just as the Molokans had provided a ready supply of potential converts for the Baptists. Pentecostals worshiped with the Baptists as they built their own communities and gained a critical mass of believers. All of these factors enabled Pentecostal communities to establish themselves quickly after the Revolution. If Slavic Pentecostal missionaries had not begun proselytizing during this period of relative toleration for sects and openness to spiritual alternatives and if they had not had the Baptists to proselytize to, they would never have been able to become established in Soviet society so swiftly.

Voronaev traveled throughout Ukraine opening new churches, training preachers and conducting open-air evangelism with street meetings and revival services, prompting "explosive" growth.[55] Doctrinal differences prompted Voronaev and his followers to create an independent union in 1924, the National Union of Christians of Evangelical Faith, which he led. By 1926, the union represented 350 congregations with seventeen thousand members; had its own newspaper, *The Evangelist* (Rus. *Evangelist*); and proclaimed its loyalty to the Soviet state.[56]

The Pentecostal understanding of "spiritual gifts," namely, the ability to speak in tongues, prophecy, and faith healing, was anathema to the teachings of Baptists and Evangelical Christians. Some called these practices "doctrinal error." Others called them heresy. Baptists accused the Pentecostals of encouraging "shaking" (Rus. *triasunstvo*) and asserted that any Baptist believer who engaged in such emotive forms of worship would be excommunicated. In spite of these tensions, Baptists and Pentecostals were both Protestant religious minorities viewed by the state as "dangerous sectarians"; ultimately, the boundaries between the two denominations were "exceedingly indistinct" because of the high degree of cross-visitation and even intermarriage among believers.[57] From the beginning, the fortunes of Pentecostals were inextricably tied to those of the Baptists.

## The Golden Period in Kharkiv, 1925–1928

Confidence was building in the 1920s as evangelicals practiced their faith, missionized, gained converts, and still enjoyed relatively cordial relations with the state, which remained focused above all on reducing the authority of the Orthodox Church. At the Baptist World Alliance Congress in 1924, the delegate from the USSR, P. V. Pavlov, announced, "We are experiencing an epoch of enthusiasm. Our movement is growing and spreading because the spirit of the ancient apostolic church lives among us. . . . We look ahead cheerfully and boldly; we rejoice for the success of the evangelical movement under the banner of the Baptists."[58] The cultural atmosphere of experimentation of the 1920s extended into the spiritual realm; as a result, the memberships of evangelical communities grew significantly.

Remarkably, the 1927 All-Ukrainian Congress of Baptists began by first commemorating ten years of freedom in the Soviet Union. Only then did the delegates acknowledge the sixtieth anniversary of their brotherhood. In some areas of Ukraine, communities increased by 20 percent annually in the 1920s, the highest rates in the Soviet Union. Most new members were middle and rich peasants, or kulaks, and their conversions were triggered by personalized, one-on-one missionizing.

The period from 1925 to 1928 is characterized by significant growth *and* submission to Soviet power. The city of Kharkiv was at the heart of both projects in Soviet Ukraine. As the republican capital and a major urban center, the Baptist leadership deemed it important to make the city the spiritual center for evangelicals as well. By 1 January 1925, there was one Evangelical Christian church with eighty members and one Baptist Church with 220 members in Kharkiv.[59] These two communities reportedly had "fraternal, friendly relations."[60] The Kharkiv district (Ukr. Okruh) had a total of eighteen Evangelical Christian churches with 478 members and thirty-seven Baptist Churches with 1,845 members. Only Sumy district had more registered believers, with a combined total of 3,540. In the Kharkiv oblast, there was a total of seventy-one Evangelical Christian churches with 4,547 members and ninety-five Baptist churches with 4,223 members.[61]

The fourth All-Ukrainian Congress of Baptists took place in Kharkiv on 1 July 1925 and yielded a new union, the All-Ukrainian Union of United Baptists (Rus. *Vseukrainskii soiuz Ob'edinenykh Baptistov*), whose specific goal was to serve the needs of the brotherhood in Ukraine and advance the twin goals of local evangelization and union-wide missionary work. The coverage of the Congress in the newspaper *Baptist Ukrainy,* which began publication in 1926, celebrated the "full religious freedom that the Soviet government has proclaimed."[62]

By 1924 two trends had become obvious. First, Baptists in Soviet Ukraine were more conservative doctrinally than those in Russia. Second, the Soviet Ukrainian government was more liberal than its counterpart in Russia. The Soviet Ukrainian government, for example, allowed evangelicals to legally organize unions, which was not possible in Moscow, and print and distribute religious literature.[63] The Ukrainian Union published ten thousand Bibles and five thousand New Testaments in Russian thanks to Ivan Neprash, who raised the money from the Federated Union of Baptists in the United States, to which Neprash was the Soviet representative. In 1926 the competing All-Ukrainian Congress of Evangelical Christians also held a congress in Kharkiv, under the direction of I. I. Motorin; launched a publication, *Evangelist*; and sponsored the publishing of a biblical dictionary.

Formal discussions began in 1926, however, as to whether it was better to maintain the existing handful of independent unions or create one powerful union to serve all Soviet evangelicals. The stance on this issue from the All-Ukrainian Union of United Baptists was unequivocal: a federation of unions was the best means of serving the "periphery."[64] An article in *Baptist Ukrainy* (Rus. "Baptist of Ukraine") justified this position: "In relation to Ukraine this question [of federation] has still other associations, the Ukrainian people, like all other peoples, have their own Ukrainian language, which is the language of record of all government institutions in Ukraine. We must also consider the fact that we are living in a moment of national awakening and this affects the life of our brotherhood. Together with this fact, it is necessary to consider that there is truly no need to maintain the old traditions of centralization."[65]

Although such a federated organizational structure was the approved Soviet model for institutional creation and was replicated in other domains such as the arts and education, the author justifies his opinion with direct reference to upholding the thriving policy of "indigenization" (Rus. *korenizatsiia*), which led to a significant period of national awakening and the increased use of Ukrainian language in religious life. Although the language of evangelical publications was still overwhelmingly Russian, the first Ukrainian-language hymnal was published in 1925. *Baptist Ukrainy* carried a large section of articles in Ukrainian. The All-Ukrainian Congress of Baptists combined preaching and singing in Ukrainian with prayers and other songs in Russian. In this respect, evangelicals were in keeping with Soviet political mandates.

The following statutes, which were accepted by both the Ukrainian

Evangelical Christians and Baptists, detail the obligations of believers and illustrate the tenor of communal life, both of which placed a notable priority on evangelism. Those communities that accepted the statutes agreed (1) to feature the reading and explanation of the Word of God, as well as prayer, hymns, and music at prayer meetings and all public gatherings; (2) to preach the Gospel of the Kingdom of God to all people in all places; (3) to publish, sell and distribute pamphlets, brochures, and books of the Holy Scripture and journals and books of religious content at places of worship and wherever else possible; and (4) to establish prayer circles for young men and women, children's services, religious courses for presbyters, schools, libraries, reading rooms, orphanages, almshouses for the elderly and the sick, and other types of philanthropic and charitable institutions.[66] Special activities were also developed for youth, including discussion groups, choirs, and musical performances.[67]

The formal acceptance and institutionalization of these statutes in local communities united them; they served to establish evangelizing as a common, ongoing activity for all communities in the quest to recruit new converts. Even though Soviet authorities were determined to disestablish the authority of religious knowledge and institutions from all spheres of public life, the evangelicals demonstrated their resolve in the mid-1920s to infuse educational, charitable, health, and other social institutions with their own religiously inspired moral vision.

State authorities nonetheless intervened to curtail evangelical activities. Although it was legal to carry out baptismal rituals in an open fashion in the late 1920s, believers were required to obtain written permission from local authorities.[68] Applications required the exact type of ritual to be conducted, the date and place of occurrence, and the number of people expected in attendance. Authorities retained the right to forbid any communal activity that, in their opinion, disturbed the social order or in any way infringed on the rights of other citizens. On this basis, they denied requests for clergy to visit homes to administer final prayers or communion to a sick or elderly person.[69] When several churches requested permission to hold a series of concerts, the Kharkiv District Administration (Rus. *Okradminotdel*), responded that they must request permission for each concert separately and that an individual decision would be made in each instance. As the request in question was for several concerts, it was denied.[70] In this way, bureaucratic tactics were used to frustrate organized activities. In addition, believers complained that the authorities reduced their access to electricity—or even denied it altogether—as well as impeded their efforts to renovate buildings so as to justify forced closure.[71]

In spite of such ongoing bureaucratic interference, a report submitted by the Department of Spiritual Affairs covering the period from 1 May 1925 to 1 June 1926 paints a fairly sympathetic portrait of the twenty-five Evangelical Christian communities and the twenty-eight Baptist communities in the Iz- iumskii district of Kharkiv oblast.The report details the apolitical, noncon- frontational nature of these communities, which, of course, placed them in sharp contrast with the Russian Orthodox Church, which was incessantly locked in a political struggle with Soviet authorities. The report concludes that, unlike what the authors had expected from a cult-like organization, such col- lective activities as working the fields and cultivating vegetable gardens were not obligatory, rather purely voluntary, and happened only under exceptional circumstances.[72] It goes on to conclude that "mutual aid among sectarians is not practiced. There is no noticeable labor exploitation among sectarians."[73] Underlining how self-sufficient, even isolated, these communities were, the re- port states that there was only one instance recorded over the course of a year of a believer traveling from Kharkiv to the communities in this district.

The report also flatly states that no propaganda against the state, against taxes, or against the Red Army was observed. Four believers refused to serve in the Red Army and followed proper procedures to establish themselves as conscientious objectors. Regarding protest or any form of active resistance, it states, "There was no noticeable active agitation by the sectarians. Although the sectarians are against the League of the Militant Godless, they avoid speaking with them and almost never initiate discussions and even avoid an- swering the questions of the Godless. Among village masses, the sects do not conduct any cultural work whatsoever."[74] The report even downplayed evan- gelizing activities, claiming that there was no visible distribution of sectarian literature among other members of the population and that youth groups were primarily concerned with studying Scripture and singing hymns.

Overall, the Mennonites came in for far harsher criticism. They were ac- cused of being rich peasants (kulaks) and were prohibited from receiving higher education. The Mennonites and the Lutherans, both viewed as for- eign ethno-religious groups, responded in the 1920s to the restrictions So- viet authorities placed upon them by massively emigrating from Soviet Ukraine to North and South America.

## Pacifist Patriots?

The issue of military service, however, was a perennial and deep-seated point of contention between believers and civil authorities throughout the

Soviet period. A decree titled "On the Release of Military Service for Religious Reasons," passed on 4 January 1919, allowed conscientious objectors to fulfill alternate military service in a socially useful civil capacity, such as in hospitals or in construction brigades. As an article in *Baptist Ukrainy* reminded believers, "Many of our brothers are unaware that an order exists about universal military training on the basis of which young brothers, owing to their religious convictions, can be exempt from the special military instruction linked with use of weapons."[75] In some places, such as the older, established communities of believers around Kharkiv in Libotynskyi and Valkovskyi districts, believers were released from any service obligations altogether.[76] The evangelical advocacy of nonviolence fostered suspicions that they were not loyal citizens of the new regime and bred enduring resentment among the greater populace—which persists to this day.

In all of Soviet Ukraine, in the early years of Soviet rule approximately 350 to 400 men were freed annually of military service due to religious convictions, most of whom were sent to the Russian north to do forestry work under brutal conditions. In Kharkiv in 1924, prior to a Union-wide law passed on 18 September 1925 reinstating the obligation to serve, only two Evangelical Christians, six Baptists, and three Mennonites refused combat duty.[77] After 1925 far fewer applied. Only 194 applicants in Ukraine were granted conscientious objector status in 1928.[78]

The state made great efforts to get believers to serve. By 1929, the Kharkiv Military Committee (Rus. *Voenkomat*) registered two Baptists who agreed to switch to active combat units and one Evangelical Christian who renounced his faith altogether.[79] Sometimes local authorities would ignore court decisions releasing believers from military service and would send them off to the Red Army anyway. Believers complained that even some who had not been called up for military service by the Military Committee were captured and taken.[80] Evangelicals were suspected of opportunistically manipulating the law to avoid military service. This fed charges that presbyters endorsed the applications of young men for alternative military service when they were not, in fact, members of a church.

The All-Russian Conference of Baptists on 1 September 1923 addressed this issue, noting that there were insincere and mercantile potential converts and advising how to guard against them. One of the proposed solutions was to mandate that young men of military age participate in church activities for a minimum of one year before they could become members of the church. A new republic-wide policy in 1924 required all presbyters and deacons to register with the NKVD of Soviet Ukraine; two years later, members had to register too. As part of the registration procedure, clergy and deacons were asked to provide their residential status (Rus. *propiska*), nationality, social status (class status), education, party status, and so on. They were also obliged to state if they served with the Petlyura or Denikin armies during the civil war.[81] The applicant had to state his position on military service and paying taxes and whether or not he objected to fulfilling these civic responsibilities on religious grounds. If the applicant objected to these state mandates, he was asked how he foresaw the reactions of believers to these policies.[82] The Evangelical Christians were the first to urge their members to complete military service, followed by the Baptists in 1926 and the Seventh-Day Adventists in 1928. The Mennonites never advocated forfeiture of their pacifism.[83]

Once believers were in the army, their questionable loyalty presented another set of issues, namely trying to shake their religious beliefs and prohibit them from proselytizing. A secret instruction for officers written in 1925 indicated how to conduct "successful struggle" with believers that included such statements as: "It is necessary to isolate the most hardened of the Red Army sectarians. Do not conduct special antisectarian work among them, because in the majority of cases, that work is doomed to fail. Do not organize spectators for a debate. It is necessary to isolate them from each other. Study their behavior and control each one separately. For those who appear the most strident, discredit them and, if necessary, legally charge them and use other means of influence."[84] The instruction also warned that although sectarians were against serving in the military, they did not say so openly. The only thing sectarians forthrightly criticized, the instruction cautioned, was the policy of atheism.[85]

Indeed, with the acceleration of both antireligious propaganda and coercive measures against religiously active Soviet citizens, few came in for harsher treatment than those who refused to serve in the military. Already in the 1920s, the Red Army was well on its way to becoming the prestigious institution that it would be in Soviet society. The refusal to serve the motherland was a position that, more than their anti-scientism, dogmatism, and evangelism, caused resentment and suspicion to fester against evangelicals, both among state authorities as well as among the general population.

## Law of Religious Associations of 1929

The forced collectivization of agriculture began in 1928 and dealt the first blow to the coherence and solidarity of evangelical communities. A series of

new antireligious laws and legislative policies was adopted in 1929, constituting a second blow. Historians of the Soviet period have called the myriad
policies, that were introduced or accelerated beginning in the late 1920s,
part of the "great break" (Rus. *velikii perelom*), a pivotal moment in the
process of inventing socialism. Numerous spheres of political, economic,
and social life were affected. A compendium of new initiatives adopted at
this time began to remake evangelical communities.[86]

A declaration of 25 January 1929 claimed that all religious and church
property was now the people's property. Church buildings and religious
objects of ritual value were turned over "by special resolution to local authorities or central governmental authorities for use free of charge to appropriate religious communities."[87] The law on religious cults passed on
8 April 1929 criminalized unregistered religious activity and prohibited all
forms of street evangelism. Only a group of twenty or more believers could
apply to register as a church. If their application was successful, they could
gather in an approved location. If registration was denied, any gathering
was considered illegal; such groups were automatically forced underground. Registration was frequently denied with no explanation and no
right to appeal. Even registered communities had to obtain additional permission to publish any religious literature, and they were forbidden from
engaging in all forms of religious education, charitable activities (even
among members), and mutual aid or cooperative societies. It was no longer
possible to organize any specialized activities for children, youth, or adults.
Registered religious communities withstood repeated attacks from state
officials and the voluntary organizations of the Militant Godless, which at
its second congress, also in April 1929, declared Baptists and Evangelical
Christians as belonging to an "international bourgeois military-spy organization." Contact with foreign religious organizations became strained, and
official exchanges and liaisons ended altogether in 1935. *Baptist Ukrainy*
ceased publication in 1928. One year later the activities of the Baptist Union
were severely curtailed; the Union was likewise definitively closed down in
1935.

To illustrate the radical change in religious life after the April 1929 law,
consider the following: From 1921 to 1925, 364 religious buildings in Ukraine
were closed. After the edict, in a three-month period, from November 1929
to January 1930, 202 religious buildings were closed.[88] In 1926 the All-
Ukrainian Baptist Union claimed to represent approximately a thousand
congregations with sixty thousand members; by 1931 fewer than ten
churches had retained official sanction.[89] The greatest number of church

closures that occurred during this period was in Odesa (63), followed by Kharkiv (53).[90]

Changes occurred not only in terms of the intensity and numbers of church buildings shut down but also in how it was done. Taxes and registration were effective bureaucratic means used to close down churches. Officials would reassess the value of a building, thereby rendering the taxes unaffordable. New registration procedures were complicated. A community had to furnish a petition signed by fifty official members and a receipt showing that the petition had been published in the newspaper.[91] A person could only be a member of one community; double membership was strictly forbidden.[92] A community was obliged to declare its history, date of founding, number of members, valuables, and relics, and a list of the religious literature contained in the church's library. Every church had to reveal each of its member's age, gender, social status, and nationality. Of course, surrendering such information facilitated state efforts to monitor members, activities, and communities.

In 1929 an Evangelical Christian community in the village of Novyi Merchyk near Kharkiv applied to open a school of literacy for children.[93] The community would pay the rent, the teacher's salary, and provide teaching materials. Yet they were flatly told, "The business of people's education is firmly in the hands of the state. No other organizations, and certainly not religious ones, have the right to open an educational establishment." The resolution, written almost a week after the request was made, ended by saying that if the Soviet's decision was not heeded, "repressive measures would be taken against the community."[94]

At first, church closures and seizures followed legally sanctioned procedures. But after 1929, the decision of a single person could shut down even major urban cathedrals. On 3 February 1930, the secretariat of the Kharkiv District Executive Committee (Rus. *Okrispolkom*) decided at a single meeting to close six Orthodox cathedrals, including Uspenskii Sobor, the main Orthodox cathedral in Kharkiv.[95] That same month, four prayer houses in Kharkiv were closed.[96] The evicted believers requested permission to meet at the German Lutheran church, which remained open.[97] When permission was denied, they petitioned to meet in private homes. Their applications included the specific dates when prayer would take place and an additional reason to meet in a home aside from no longer having a church, such as to accommodate people who were ill and unable to travel.[98] Such requests were usually denied. Devout believers resumed the pre-1905 practice of meeting clandestinely in members' homes, outdoors, or in half-built buildings.

## The Fate of Evangelical Leaders

Barely a year after the April 1929 legislation was passed, the number of registered evangelicals had dropped by four-fifths.[99] This was partly attributable to the fate of their leadership. Ivan Prokhanov, the English-educated president of the Union of Evangelical Christian Churches, was not allowed to return to the Soviet Union after he attended a congress of the Baptist World Alliance in 1928 in Toronto with twenty-eight other delegates from the USSR. He emigrated to Berlin, where he lived until his death in 1935.

Pentecostals were even more harshly repressed than the Baptists. I. E. Voronaev, the Pentecostal leader who returned from America to evangelize, was accused of subversive, anti-Soviet activities and charged with monetary irregularities in 1930 even though the union he had founded had declared its loyalty to the Soviet state. Soviet sources claim that he renounced his faith and left the ministry in 1930.[100] He actually spent two years in prison in Odesa and one year in exile in Karaganda before he was rearrested and sent to a Siberian labor camp in 1936, where he is believed to have died in 1937. His wife was sentenced to internal exile in Kazakhstan and given permission to return to the United States only in 1960. She died there in 1965.

By eliminating evangelical leaders and active members and closing prayer houses, Soviet authorities forced a radical decline in membership in the 1930s. Underground conversions continued to occur, but the penalties for "creating counter-revolutionary nests" had become far harsher. Soviet propaganda persisted in slandering evangelical leaders by claiming that they drove their followers insane, ordered them to fast to death, challenged them to throw their children in front of moving trains to test their faith, and other such depictions of fanatical devotion. Although many recognized these characterizations as caricatures, deep suspicions still remained about the psychological health of evangelicals.

It was always hard to state with confidence how many evangelicals there were, but after 1929 it becomes exceedingly difficult. At the beginning of the twentieth century, groups were loosely organized and believers had multiple affiliations that defied tight denominational classification, and in the 1920s membership growth was so rapid that it became difficult to keep accurate records. But by the 1930s evangelical authorities themselves were destroying records that might prove incriminating. Many groups, especially the Pentecostals, were resigned to an underground existence, by preference in the 1920s and by necessity in the 1930s. They defied mandates by gathering informally under the cover of birthdays, anniversaries, and visiting the sick. The strict antireligious policies led believers and clergy alike to prefer informal knowledge of membership, rituals, and organizational structures.

The very refusal of evangelicals to renounce communal religious life earned them the full wrath of Soviet authorities in 1929. They resisted the creation of differentiated spheres for the secular and the sacred, arguing instead for God's law, as articulated in biblical principles, to be the foundation for the state's laws. They asserted that it was the obligation of believers to realize the principles of the "blessed kingdom of God" in an earthly existence. This refusal to respect the relegation of religion to a private sphere by maintaining vibrant communities that promoted an alternative moral order provided the underpinnings in the first half of the twentieth century for the characterization of evangelicals as "dangerous." This defiance was couched in an ongoing acceptance of Soviet authority, which allowed evangelicals to violate Soviet laws in a nonconfrontational and undetectable way, thereby ensuring the continuation of their communal life.

### The Effects of Erasure

Especially after 1929, Soviet authorities vigorously pursued a three-fold secularization process to preclude a meaningful role for religious organizations in the moral and political life of Soviet citizens. They attempted to first, dismantle the authority of the Orthodox Church and other religious institutions; second, erase the presence of the religious in the public sphere; and third, propagate another belief system, socialist ideology, based on other forms of knowledge that similarly offered unifying traditions, answers to existential questions, and a sense of identity—albeit without the beauty that characterized Orthodox ritual.

Daniel Peris characterizes the result of Soviet antireligious policies in the 1930s as amounting to a "nationwide Potemkin village of atheism."[101] With the state in control of property, education, and other social services, in barely a half a dozen years the public sphere was purged of traces of "the religious" as a meaningful paradigm to understand social reality. I propose that these efforts essentially "reconstructed" belief in the supernatural but did not annihilate it.[102] One of the critical and unintended by-products of these policies was to relocate expressions of religiosity into an atomized and privatized sphere, which over time fostered ignorance of religious practice. This impeded communal and sometimes even familial socialization to a religious way of life. Ignorance, however, falls short of a secular worldview and is certainly a far cry from the "militant atheism" the Bolsheviks professed to want to make a broad cultural ideal.

In considering the ramifications of such repressive measures, I have taken inspiration from Danièle Hervieu-Léger, who suggests that religion at its essence is a particular mode of believing that serves as a chain of memory that links generations. Her studies of secularization are based on Western European societies where, she argues, religious communities have become "amnesiac," that is to say, they have become unable to maintain this chain-like function of transmitting meaningful traditions and have inadvertently fostered forgetting. This is the means by which European societies have become secularized.

Stalin's policies aided in the making of a New Soviet person by "breaking the chain," and secularizing Soviet society by making the religious unavailable. Urbanization, mobility, and advances in education also had a corrosive effect on traditional forms of religious life. Yet, in many respects, the promises of socialist modernity, liberty, material well-being, and self-fulfillment remained frustratingly elusive, leaving individuals searching for meaning. The traumatic events and massive social transformation of the early decades of Soviet rule provoked uncertainty and new existential questions, to which ideology could not always provide comforting responses. These quandaries left religious proclivities and dispositions largely intact even as possibilities for religious expression were foreclosed, which helps explain the vitality of folk customs and the cult of the "soul" in Slavic culture.[103]

The ability of Soviet ideology to function as a "chain of memory," linking generations in a sustained meaningful way also began to wane. As a result, ideology, like religion, was subject to the twin processes of loss and reconstruction. As the original revolutionary fervor and enthusiasm diminished over generations, people reconstructed traditions, identities, and quests for existential meaning in a private and personal way. Soviet state holidays provide an illustration of this phenomenon. Christopher Binns argues that because the official meaning of Soviet holidays and commemorations diminished over time, individuals infused these days with personalized rituals, ultimately restoring meaning, but not in the way that was intended. The Great October Revolution holiday may have been celebrated, but that did not mean that the Revolution or the system it spawned was.[104]

In sum, although religious institutions lost their influence, it would be a mistake to assume that belief was eradicated, as these are two distinct processes. Indeed, in response to a question on religious belief in the 1937 census, 57 percent of the population aged 16 and over declared themselves to be believers.[105] In other words, an irreconcilable paradox was created in the early decades of Soviet rule. The authority and meaning that religion had in people's lives was chiseled away by breaking the chain of memory of belief and tradition that links generations and groups. But with its failed promises, brutality, and violence, socialist modernity was itself becoming a source of bitter disappointment and keen disillusionment for many, which kept existential yearnings and spiritual searches alive.

# Chapter Two

# Enlightening the Faithful, 1941–1988

Two factors played a key role in sustaining evangelical communities until the Soviet system collapsed in 1991. First, wartime conditions prompted a policy shift away from a broad assault on organized religion to an attempt to coopt the power it held and the allegiance it could inspire by reinstitutionalizing the infrastructure supporting religious life in the Soviet Union. In an ironic twist of fate, then, after a decade of repression which saw a severe decline in overt religiosity in the 1930s, the German attack on the Soviet Union in 1941 in a sense actually saved Soviet evangelical communities by allowing them to reemerge. The second factor was Khrushchev's decision to release a number of political prisoners in the 1950s, many of whom were clergy. Their return infused these isolated evangelical communities with new vitality. These two factors triggered an unforeseen resurgence of religion that itself gave way to a renewed antireligious campaign in the early 1960s that focused this time on advocating atheism through the popularization of science.

## War and the Merger of Sacred and Secular Goals

As the entire population was mobilized for war, churches were reopened, and it became more possible to worship without fear of retaliation. Several factors contributed to the relaxation of antireligious policies manifest in the disbanding of the Union of Militant Atheists in 1942, the suspension of antireligious periodicals, and the reintroduction of religious publications. For one, clergy were among the most effective promoters of patriotic zeal. The Russian Orthodox Church's Metropolitan Sergii issued a pastoral letter on 22 June 1941 with a strident appeal to patriotism, calling for the defense of the motherland in the name of Orthodoxy. Leaders of the evangelical movement published a similar statement in *Bratskii Vestnik* (Brotherly Herald), their main publication, which read: "Dear Brothers and Sisters, The time has come to show, not with words but with deeds, our sincere feelings for our Motherland and for the events the country is experiencing. The time has come for believers in the Lord Jesus Christ to demonstrate our love for our dear Motherland. Many brothers will be called to the defense of our homeland. We call upon them to fulfill their duty to the end, not out of fear of punishment, but out of conscience."[1] So the ardent evangelical advocacy of nonviolence could be amended when violence meant defense of the "dear Motherland."[2]

When the Germans occupied Ukraine in 1941, they put up signs that read, "The time of Stalinist atheism is gone. The German authorities give you the opportunity to pray in freedom again."[3] Karel Berkhoff notes that Protestant groups under the Reichskommissariat in Ukraine were treated with "magnanimity" because of their pacifist beliefs. German officials overrode bans on evangelical religious activity put in place by local police, village elders, or district authorities and allowed Baptist and Evangelical Christian missionaries once again to publish religious literature, offer religious instruction, and travel about Ukraine preaching. The Reichskommissariat did not last long in Ukraine. By late 1943 the Red Army was at the Dnipro River, and by March 1944 the Germans had lost all of Ukraine. Yet it was during this period that Sunday and Easter were reinstituted as days of rest, structuring time, once again, according to a religious calendar. The patriarchal administration of the Russian Orthodox Church was officially reestablished in 1943. Metropolitan Sergii was elected Patriarch of Moscow and All Russia. In Ukraine this reopened the never-resolved issue as to why there was not a Ukrainian Orthodox Church and drew attention to the fate of the Ukrainian Autocephalous Orthodox Church, which had been outlawed in 1921.[4]

The westward shift of the Soviet border was a second factor contributing to the relaxation of religious prohibitions. The annexation of ethnically Ukrainian lands in 1939 added thousands of Orthodox Churches to the Soviet Union. By 1948 there were 14,329 active Orthodox churches in the

USSR, but only 3,217 of them were in Russia.[5] Western Ukraine and Lithuania also added vibrant Catholic communities. The Ukrainian Greek Catholics, resentful of occupation, saw their faith as an integral part of their nationality, and they saw their communities as a base of potential political resistance to Soviet authority. The Soviet reaction was to outlaw the Ukrainian Greek Catholic Church outright in 1946.[6] The Polish territories incorporated into Ukraine and Belarus were strongholds of Pentecostal activity and the annexation of Transcarpathia brought numerous Hungarian Reformed churches. The new territories added immeasurably to the religious mosaic in Soviet Ukraine and specifically added substantial numbers of Protestant communities.

Even areas of the Soviet Union like Kharkiv, where public religious life had been decimated during the 1930s, rebounded with stunning velocity during the war. After four years of intense fighting, during which the front lines cut through the city four times, Kharkiv oblast emerged from the war with ninety-eight evangelical communities and a combined total of 9,500 believers, a significant rise in membership after the assault the group sustained in the 1930s.[7]

The All-Union Council of Evangelical Christians and Baptists (AUCECB) was created as a governing body in 1944 under the jurisdiction of the Council for the Affairs of Religious Cults of the Ministry of Religion.[8] At the time, it was difficult to imagine the substantial impact this union would have, both in giving evangelical believers a presence abroad and in dividing them sharply at home. The union formalized the loose interdependencies that had emerged among Evangelical Christians, Baptists, and Pentecostals. Although there were clear differences in theology among the three groups, the union was trumpeted as an example of socialist ecumenism. The government justified the configuration by the fact that all three denominations practiced the same key rituals (baptism and communion) and subscribed to a theology of nonviolence, which facilitated state monitoring of conscientious objectors. After 1960, the union included Mennonites as well.

A series of tensions rapidly developed when the Pentecostals officially joined in August 1945 with the stipulation that they would cease practicing spiritual gifts (speaking in tongues, prophecy, and faith healing) in services and thereafter do it only in private.[9] This was clearly a very significant and highly controversial concession. But the approximately three hundred Pentecostal communities entered the union because it was the only way to legalize their communities.[10] Within a year, a majority of them had withdrawn their memberships, preferring an "underground" illegal existence to a circumscribed and compromised legal one.[11]

The union was designed to become a strong, centralized organization, a bureaucratic pyramid, which would exercise significant oversight over evangelical life. Routinization of religious life was supposed to dampen fervor, as it so often had in other parts of the world. The union leadership was appointed by state authorities and was thereafter self-elected, which effectively excluded the opinions of individual communities in terms of electing future leaders and prolonged state involvement in denominational affairs. Some resented this as unnecessary state interference and a fundamental violation of the principle of separation of church and state. Others objected in harsher terms, claiming that any state authority over aspects of congregational life constituted a form of "false teaching" and that anyone who upheld this authority—meaning the union leadership itself—should be excommunicated. Another point of contention was underrepresentation of Baptists and, to a lesser extent, Ukrainians. Although there were about three times as many Baptists as Evangelical Christians and most Baptists lived in Ukraine, the union had twenty-eight Evangelical Christian delegates and only nineteen Baptists. The predominance of ethnic Russians in union leadership became an issue because only they could approve the appointment of pastors and deacons. A number of groups located primarily in Ukraine, such as the Pure Baptists, Evangelical Free Christians, Evangelical Christians-Perfectionists, and Ukrainian ECB Community declined membership in a union with "Moscow-dominated Baptists."

The union developed its own eighty-page publication, *Bratskii Vestnik*, which was published two times a year right after the war and later increased to six times a year. It had an official circulation of 3,000, which was increased to 5,000 in 1966.[12] Although half of the union churches were in Ukraine, *Bratskii Vestnik* was printed only in Russian. In the early 1950s, one-fifth of all communities were still without clergy; given the highly limited opportunities for clerical training and the dearth of religious literature, this publication provided much-needed doctrinal instruction.[13] Its chief editor, the Reverend A. V. Karev, served as general secretary of the AUCECB for twenty-seven years, representing the union on thirty-nine journeys abroad.

All in all, the postwar period was pivotal, marking an attempt by the state to reckon with religion and the tacit acceptance of the futility of pursuing a steadfast policy of church destruction and imprisonment of clergy, as they had in the 1930s. Wartime reorganization of religious life irrevocably shifted the status of churches and prompted a new orientation to organized religion. The state offered limited toleration of organized activities in return for certain state services, which, in essence, was the policy that the

Orthodox Church had advocated since 1927. After the war, the state attempted to monitor the remaining religious organizations so as to discourage new conversions, especially of youth. Ironically, the state's strategy to
achieve these goals involved creating formal, hierarchical organizations
that indirectly helped these sects evolve into denominations by obliging
them to make formal, canonical, and institutional what had up until then
been largely diverse, orally transmitted practices upheld by informal, local
leaders.

### Khrushchev's Reforms and a Religious Offensive

Nikita Khrushchev was in power as first secretary of the Communist Party
from 1953 to 1964. Although Khrushchev is widely viewed as a reformer,
long celebrated for his advocacy of destalinizing Soviet society, he made the
realization of atheism one of the goals of his regime.[14] Along with banging
his shoe on the UN podium in 1960, he is known for his memorable proclamation, "We will see the last believer!" Khrushchev's strategy for hastening
the demise of religion differed significantly from that of Stalin, who made
far swifter use of execution and imprisonment to eliminate and intimidate
clergy and believers.[15] Yet, as we have seen, the severity of Stalin's religious
policies waxed and waned in tandem with national crises. In contrast,
Khrushchev's policies constituted a turn away from the use of raw coercion,
terror, and humiliation that characterized the 1930s, embracing instead
sustained antireligious propaganda that reached its apex from 1959 to
1964.[16]

During this campaign, a great number of religious communities were
simply shut down. The targets of closure were clear. Denominationally, the
Russian Orthodox Church was hit the hardest, losing 40 percent of its
churches during the five-year campaign; Baptists lost 22 percent of their
churches. Geographically speaking, Ukraine was the locus of the greatest
number of closures. In 1958, 54 percent of all registered religious communities in the USSR were in Ukraine; 43 percent of those, or 4,370, were closed
down.[17] Nonetheless, many of the campaign initiatives triggered unforeseen
consequences that served to widen the spectrum of views within the party,
in the bureaucracy, and especially among the populace as to the necessity to
eradicate religion and if so, which means were acceptable to use. Some initiatives undermined long-term prospects for stamping out religion by galvanizing vocal dissenters who challenged the regime on its own terms—and
proved to be formidable foes. Eliminating these staunch critics, authorities

came to understand, was much more costly than tolerating their religious communities.

Scholars have debated Khrushchev's role in the first, brief antireligious campaign of 1954, the so-called Hundred Days campaign.[18] Some suggest he was instigator; others assess his role as terminator. All agree, however, that he played a critical part in what has proved to be an important precursor to the multifaceted antireligious campaign of 1959–1964 in which the state proved itself flexible and willing to use a variety of disciplining techniques. The campaign was spurred by the recognition that religion, as a reactionary remnant from the past, would not disappear on its own. The wartime reprieve of religious restrictions was recast as a "departure from Leninist norms." The nature of propaganda shifted from antireligious tracts to an affirmation of a scientific basis for knowledge. The scholarly journal, *Nauka i Religiia* (Science and Religion), was founded in 1959 to promote an atheist worldview by linking religion to ignorance and by showing how explanations for various phenomena previously thought to be divinely bestowed or ordained, could actually be explained in verifiable scientific terms. The divine powers of mystics and the miracles they performed were mocked as sham practices, deceptions of innocent, ignorant people. Some of the greatest Soviet scholars of religion also began to publish monographs during this period. Although some of these monographs are colored by an ideological agenda and have entirely predictable findings, others are informative.[19]

The twin goals of divesting Soviet society of Stalinist excesses and religious belief involved shaping the direction of social change. The Communist Party began to take an active role in crafting certain moral values and practices to ensure that such change occurred as rapidly and as fully as possible. To this end, the Communist Party program of 1961 included a "moral code of the builder of communism."[20] It exalted twelve moral principles that reflect the ideals of Soviet society and that Soviet citizens were urged to use to guide individual behavior. This code lauded such principles as devotion to the communist cause, conscientious labor, collectivism and mutual assistance in the spirit of comradeship, honesty and truthfulness, moral purity, modesty and unpretentiousness in social and private life, and a reaffirmation of the merits of a strong family life. In addition to affirming these attributes, the moral code also urged an "uncompromising attitude" to such moral ills as injustice, parasitism, careerism, lust for money, and, of course, to "enemies of communism, peace, and freedom of nations." These renditions of virtue and evil would have had strong echoes among evangelicals whose own biblical interpretations encouraged them to follow a very similar moral code of conduct. Asceticism, mutual aid, industriousness, and the centrality of the family had long been values they championed and tried to foster.

An antireligious campaign that featured church closures and the propagation of communist morality and science were only part of Khrushchev's efforts to spur reform. In his Secret Speech of 1956, Khrushchev acknowledged "excesses" and "errors" committed by Stalin and the Communist Party and put to rest the myth of the infallibility of the Party. To signal a clean start, Khrushchev launched a destalinization campaign and authorized the release of many political prisoners from labor camps. Among their ranks, of course, were numerous religious dissidents. Evangelical communities were revitalized with the infusion of believers, many of whom were trained clergy and nearly all of whom had strengthened their faith in the camps. The vast network of camps and prisons served as a base from which new converts could be gained; the practice of exiling clergy simply dispersed these communities geographically.

Destalinization also included a selective relaxation of literary censorship and the publication of books that, because of the politicized nature of their content, previously would have been turned down. One of the beneficiaries of this new policy was Alexander Solzhenitsyn, whose book *One Day in the Life of Ivan Denisovich* was published in 1962 during the Antireligious Campaign and received an extremely wide readership, both in the USSR and abroad. The book is a searing portrayal of life in a Stalinist labor camp and an indictment of the Soviet state for its massive sponsorship of repression. It also indirectly presents a rare and rather sympathetic portrait of evangelical believers and illustrates the tactic of "defiant compliance" that I will argue was the essence of evangelical dissidence.

Solzhenitsyn, whose piety and devotion to Orthodoxy is well known, juxtaposes the worldviews of the protagonist, Shukov, a political prisoner who struggles mightily to survive the camps and fiercely resents the injustice that has befallen him, with that of another character, Alyosha the Baptist. Solzhenitsyn's fictional depiction of the encounters between the two men accurately reflect evangelical values and provide insight as to why evangelicals continued to transgress Soviet ideology even when doing so courted the possibility of imprisonment. At one point, Alyosha encourages Shukov to pray and explains how and why one should pray. Remarkably, this is one of the most straightforward renditions in Soviet literature of Baptist practice, a veritable how-to guide to prayer.

In contrast to the political prisoner, Alyosha the Baptist has large reservoirs of energy and good will, which he uses to assist other prisoners in the social Darwinian world of the camps. Alyosha sees himself as victorious in his daily battle with the authorities because he refuses to renounce God. Neither they nor the draconian conditions of the camp can get the better of him. By refusing to compromise his faith and by accepting suffering, Alyosha becomes a martyr for his faith and assures his salvation. His ability to transform suffering into joy provides witness to God's grace and deepens his own faith. His suffering therefore becomes a source of joy.

Shukov says to him, "You see, Alyosha, somehow it works out all right for you: Jesus Christ wanted you to sit in prison and so you are—sitting there for His sake. But for whose sake am *I* here? Because we weren't ready for war in '41? For that? But was that *my* fault?"[21]

In contrasting their respective responses to the vast injustices and physical suffering of camp life, Solzhenitsyn illustrates the symbolic resources different cultural traditions offer that affect the capacity of suffering to become a redemptive mechanism of agency and not just a critique of an oppressive ideology. Soviet dissidents challenged the political order in moral terms. They universalized their own individual grievances with state power, their own quests for social justice, into a broader political and philosophical critique of Soviet society. The mission of Soviet dissidents, and of the intelligentsia more broadly, was to offer a broad spectrum of solutions to social ills and ethical dilemmas and inspire others, especially those in power, to recover their moral conscience and recognize individual sovereignty and reason as a means to individual liberation.[22] Yet, it was an ambitious and amorphous project. The individual suffering dissidents endured was supposed to trigger benefits for others, often entire classes or categories of people, at some later date—but the fact of their incarceration radically compromised the potential effectiveness of their struggles. Thus, in a way they suffered senselessly.

Talal Asad writes of how secular politics use and interpret violence:

> In secular redemptive politics there is no place for the idea of a redeemer saving sinners through *his* submission to suffering. And there is no place for a theology of evil by which different kinds of suffering are identified. ("Evil" is simply the superlative form of what is bad and shocking.) Instead there is a readiness to cause pain to those who are to be saved by being humanized. It is not merely that the object of violence is different; it is that the secular myth uses the element of violence to connect an optimistic project of universal empowerment with a pessimistic account of human motivation in which inertia and incorrigibility figure prominently.[23]

For evangelicals, human motivation is secondary to the will of God. There is little inertia or incorrigibility in Alyosha's world, as Solzhenitsyn depicts it. This is because the body, as a site of agency, is a forum where believers can exhibit moral self-mastery over physical desires and pain and be rewarded with the knowledge that they remain moral. The meaning of pain and suffering is recast through mastery into a source of virtue. Believers understood the evil of the camps as the "unsaved" are serving the devil, not as ruthless government officials pursuing ill-advised policies. They saw themselves as the elect in a fallen world. Faith and the born-again experience had sealed their fate. They anticipated ongoing battles between good and evil forces, even an apocalypse, and these expectations were often reaffirmed by the dreadful camp conditions. For those believers in the camps, daily life offered unprecedented opportunities for evangelization and witness, which, in turn, strengthened the faith of those who suffered and added purpose and meaning to an otherwise unbearable existence.

My intention is not to minimize or somehow suggest that evangelicals did not really suffer in the camps. Rather, like Solzhenitsyn, I wish to show how faith can provide a means to interpret suffering in such a way that cognitively and emotionally, a believer can mobilize a sense of agency and power by redefining the meaning of pain into a means of self-actualization as a moral person.[24] Such frames of interpretation that harnessed feelings of mastery and empowerment were vital to survival in the camps, and were quite helpful to all believers coping with daily hardships. In many ways, then, *One Day in the Life of Ivan Denisovich,* as a microcosm of Soviet society, revealed how the innocent suffered and how believers coped with injustice. Indirectly, this amounted to a suggestive endorsement of faith and could even be read as an affirmation of the righteousness of a religious basis for morality, which is surely not what Khrushchev had in mind. At such moments, his twin goals of destalinization and the promotion of atheism were decidedly at cross purposes.

## Sowing the Seeds of Division

During the Antireligious Campaign, in an effort to curtail the recently reinvigorated activities of evangelical communities, "New Statutes" governing communities in the AUCECB were implemented in 1960 to replace the ones introduced in 1944. There was mounting concern not only over the growth of evangelical communities in the USSR but also in their position abroad. The creation of the AUCECB gave evangelicals a rightful place at the table of acknowledged religious organizations—indeed, one sanctioned by the state—and paved the way for Soviet evangelicals to participate in a meaningful capacity, once again, in international denominational and ecumenical organizations. In 1955, Iakov Zhidkov, a leader of the All-Union Council of Evangelical Christians-Baptists, became a vice president of the Baptist World Alliance. The AUCECB joined the World Council of Churches in 1962, one year after the Russian Orthodox Church did.

The growing presence of Soviet evangelicals in international religious organizations highlighted the "Sovietness" of evangelicalism in the USSR. The extreme persecution of believers in the 1930s coupled with the state's continued suspicion of minority faiths led to communities characterized by a closed system of membership, a deep suspicion of outsiders, hierarchical understandings of authority, a highly literal interpretation of the Bible, and an austere communal ethos. These attributes generally did not apply to most communities in the West that claimed to profess the same faith.

New state mandates would further distinguish the tenor of religious life in the USSR. In 1960 a "Letter of Instruction" sent to pastors of all registered churches stated that children under eighteen were no longer permitted to attend services and that baptizing anyone under thirty years of age was discouraged. In addition, the amount of time during services devoted to preaching was reduced, and all evangelical and proselytizing activities were ordered to cease. Along with these new restrictions, longstanding discriminatory practices were revived, such as restrictions on educational opportunities, discrimination in the military, job terminations, and random arrests and imprisonments.

Some clergy and believers were dismayed at the capitulation of the AUCECB to the wishes of a hostile state.[25] In response, in 1961 they formed the Action Group (Rus. *Initsiativnaia Grupa*) to protest these "New Statutes," which they understood to be unnecessarily restrictive state interferences in congregational life.[26] The group was led by A. F. Prokofiev, G. K. Kriuchkov, and G. P. Vins, and it quickly gained enough momentum to split the ranks of Baptists—a split that remains in place to this day. Preexisting tensions over the acceptable levels of compromise with the Soviet state and ongoing conflicts between Baptists and Pentecostals fed the protest. The *Initsiativniki* turned to member churches for support after they failed to convince the leaders of AUCECB to write new statutes.

As early as 1956, a breakaway group, mainly from the Donbas and eastern Ukraine, calling itself "Pure Baptists" voiced its opposition at an illegal congress in Kharkiv to the hierarchical aspects of the AUCECB and the incorporation of Pentecostals into the Union; the group even questioned the legitimacy of the AUCECB altogether. The Pure Baptists joined the *Initsia-tivniki,* together amounting to about 5 percent of the total membership of AUCECB, and split off in protest.[27] In June 1962 the *Initsiativniki* declared the twenty-seven leaders of the AUCECB excommunicated for propagating "false teaching" and declared their intention to set up a parallel organiza-tion, which they did in September 1965, the Council of Churches of Evan-gelical Christian-Baptists (CCECB). These events were chronicled and circulated in *samizdat* publications, which further courted the ire of Soviet authorities.

In 1963 the AUCECB held only the second congress of its long history (the first was its founding in 1944) to address the problem of schism and to propose compromise solutions. Ninety-four members of the dissident re-form group were known to be in prison at the time, including two of its leaders, G. P. Vins and A. F. Prokofiev. Vins was from a prominent Baptist family. His father, P. Ia. Vins, immigrated in 1911 to Canada with his family when he was thirteen years old. He studied for two years at a Bible school in ·Philadelphia, Pennsylvania, followed by three years of seminary training in Louisville, Kentucky. He worked as a pastor in Pittsburgh before returning to the Russian Far East in 1926. Vins's father was repressed during the purges of the 1930s and died in a camp in 1937.

His wife, Lydia Vins, founded a group called the Council of Prisoners' Relatives in early 1964 in response to her son's arrest and the arrest of oth-ers. Lydia Vins's initiative represents one of the very few moments when evangelical believers would openly and forthrightly defy Soviet authority. The group produced a bulletin about six times a year that listed all known prisoners, including details of arrests, trials, treatment in prison, and deaths. The Vins family gained an international reputation for actively protesting arrests and imprisonments and making the suffering of believers in the USSR a cause célèbre.[28] Her son, one of the leaders of the *Initsia-tivniki,* was released from prison in 1979 and was later deported with other dissidents in an exchange for Soviet spies held in the West. When he arrived in the United States, he was received by President Jimmy Carter, another Baptist, and began his work with the Slavic Gospel Association.

In the end, state attempts to regulate congregational religious practice yielded entirely counterproductive results. As an organized dissident movement, the *Initsiativniki* were able to generate attention in the West for the plight of believers in the USSR and even buttress an international cam-paign to highlight the abuse of human rights in the USSR. For the first time, global ecumenical leaders lodged an effective protest to Soviet religious poli-cies. The negative international attention contributed to revised legislation in 1975 and to a policy of mutual accommodation that stabilized church-state relations.

In sum, Khrushchev's efforts to redeem the system by reducing the number of political prisoners inadvertently revitalized evangelical communities, in turn prompting the state to tighten the regulation of local congregational life through registration. The response to these measures led to a serious rift among believers, dividing them into two groups. One preferred to tacitly accept the obligation to register and continued to quietly circumvent policies it deemed in conflict with their faith. The other group, the *Initsiativniki*, advocated civil disobedience, openly challenging the authorities by refusing to register. The following two ethnographic portraits illustrate the ramifications of belonging to a "registered" group that accepted, at least in word, the new statutes and what it meant to belong to an "unregistered" group that openly defied them.

### Defiant Compliance of Registered Believers

The Khrushchev-era emphasis on propaganda, enlightenment, and the promotion of science as an antidote to religion took many forms. Staging organized public debates to educate and enlighten the populace, a practice that had been used in the 1920s, was revived. The idea was to use science to prove the irrational, superstitious nature of belief in higher powers and to free people from the slavish, senseless practices that passed for devotion in favor of reliance on rational understanding. The goal was no less than redefining how one knew something to be true.[29] The debates were meant to showcase the merits of verifiable, cognitively acquired knowledge over superstitious corporeal sensations that the illiterate and uneducated misrecognized as knowledge and truth. With education, the "masses" (Ukr./Rus. *narod*) were meant to invest authority in knowledge and in scientific methods of argument over the clergy who implored them to follow dictum slavishly, on blind faith. This line of argumentation, as Nancy Ries has noted, trades on an understanding of the *narod* as "suffering masses" who are united by "soul" (Ukr./Rus. *dusha*), defined as the "ability to feel what is right and what is wrong and to repent somehow."[30] As such, the authorities thought the debates would reduce the suffering of the people by showing them the error of their superstitious ways and lead them to abandon the authority they had invested in the divine.

In the 1920s, these debates often produced unintended and counterproductive results, prompting the Antireligious Commission to issue warnings not to "conduct debates with sectarians if there is no challenger well versed in the Bible" and, later, to avoid debates with "priests or sectarian preachers," before formally forbidding such debates altogether in 1928.[31] When this tactic of antireligious propaganda was revived in the 1960s, the results were no more successful.[32]

Karl Jablonsky's experiences illustrate why such warnings were issued. These days he has a full mane of white hair, and he still vividly recalls his participation in these debates over forty years ago. Having emigrated, he now lives in Philadelphia, which is where I interviewed him.[33] He is an ethnic Pole from a Ukrainian-speaking area of Ukraine, but the language of religion for him is Russian. His wife is a Ukrainian-speaking Ukrainian from Kharkiv. His willingness to confront the authorities stemmed from well-honed abilities he developed as a child. His father, a Polish Catholic, converted and later allowed his home in Kamianets-Podilskyi to be used as a house church. In 1936 the family's house was confiscated, and his father was arrested and sentenced to twelve years of internal exile in Nizhne-Novosibirsk, a town in northeast Kazakhstan, to which place the family accompanied him.

Upon returning to Ukraine, Jablonsky reconfirmed his commitment to the faith by becoming christened in 1948 at age nineteen and by becoming an evangelist. His family's unsavory political biography complicated his efforts to study and find employment. He moved to Chernivtsi, another city in Western Ukraine, where his past did not haunt him as much. There he studied, became an economist with a specialty in statistics, and worked at the district executive committee (Rus. *Raiispolkom*). He became a pastor at a registered church there in 1957 after a laying-on-of-hands ceremony conducted by other pastors. The membership at his church grew at an annual rate of sixty to eighty new members. In keeping with the New Statutes of 1960, he was instructed to ask the usual 250 or so children present to leave the room before he preached, which he claims he steadfastly refused to do.

As part of the strategic shift to "persuasive propaganda" to discourage religious participation, Pastor Jablonsky became the centerpiece of a local antireligious campaign that played out in the media. "Soviet authorities crawl around inside the church with boots on," (Rus. *lezt' vnutr' tserkvi sapogami*) is the phrase he used to explain how the ground began to shift beneath his feet:

> They began to write articles about me in the newspapers trying to compromise me before the people. One article they wrote, entitled, "Whom do Baptists serve?" repeatedly referred to me by my first

and last name. They wrote that I work for Americans, that I receive money, dollars, from Rockefeller and from Ford. At that time [during the Cuban Missile Crisis] the relationship with America was very strained. Then they added that the Baptist faith is an American religion that embodies American politics. They launched this huge criticism in the newspapers, on the radio and on television. But this turned out to be not enough. It didn't help. People knew it was lies, that they were being deceived. And even more people came to church.

Media-based propaganda essentially traded on two tropes: attacks on religious practice were often personalized and focused on the demonization of a single individual, usually someone in a position of authority, or else they drew on established stereotypes of the Baptist faith as "foreign." During World War I, when the enemy was German, it was suspected of being a sinister means of turning Slavs into Germans. During the Cold War, and especially during the Bay of Pigs and the Cuban Missile Crisis of 1962, propaganda suggested that it was providing a means for Americans to penetrate the Soviet Union.

After the media campaign, local party officials organized a debate between members of the academic community, who represented a scientific viewpoint, and members of the clergy, who represented a "vestige of the past." The logic was that religious belief and spiritual proclivities thrived on ignorance of rational scientific explanations for natural phenomena. The scholars were to demonstrate that God does not exist, that Jesus Christ was not the son of God, and that humans evolved from primates. The clergy, on the other hand, were allowed to state their beliefs, to outline the biblical and historical justifications for their practices, and to explain the traditions that affirmed these beliefs. In essence, they were allowed an uncensored forum from which they could proselytize before thousands of spectators. The authorities assumed that the erudition of scholars would confirm that the biblical view of creation was nonsense, a realization that would lead to a general unraveling of faith, resulting in a reluctance to endorse organized religion. They further assumed that minimally educated, self-taught clergy would not have an effective response to the scientific proof of evolution and to the scientific critique of biblical accounts of history. They underestimated the ability of clergy to present a coherent, accessible depiction of the black-and-white "truths" as they understood them to have been depicted in a sacred text and totally discounted the degree to which such a presentation would resonate with the religious sensibilities of those in attendance.

Clergy were well rehearsed at presenting these truths and often demonstrated a unity of voice; scholars with different proclivities, abilities, and interests, of course, voiced a plethora of opinions that were often not as readily understandable.

In Jablonsky's case, two debates were advertised in the newspapers and over the radio, with equal time allocated to each side. Twenty-two scholars and two clergy, the head of the Baptist Union in Chernivtsi oblast and Jablonsky, as deputy head, debated the existence of God.

> Perhaps they thought that people would be afraid to say that they were for the Baptists. Yes, yes. They thought that victory would go to the side of science. But the scholars sank. Some said one thing, and others contradicted them. They embarrassed themselves in front of the crowd. The people saw this and the victory went to the Baptists. Everyone in the hall shouted, "Hooray! Victory to the Baptists!" and the room filled with applause. And on that note, the debate ended.

When I asked Jablonsky whether he had expected such an outcome, as is often the case with Baptists, he made a biblical reference to the story of David and Goliath, suggesting that the outcome could not have been other because the righteous will always triumph over more powerful foes.

Yet, the debates proved to be just the beginning of the attempt to discredit him, as the antireligious campaign moved to new heights:

> They prepared for half a year how to avenge the Baptists for their victory. They said that the entire city administration was shamed because of the incident. They found an actor and paid him to say that he was a Baptist. Six months after the debate, they announced one morning on the radio and in the newspapers that this so-called Baptist—his name was Zahoriuk—sacrificed a woman. They claimed that the two of them had committed adultery and that he came to me, as his pastor, asking for advice after having sinned. They said, I advised him that God would forgive the act of adultery if he sacrificed her, if he killed her. He supposedly did this. He supposedly killed her. They wrote in the newspapers and even announced on radio that he carved up her body, cooked her head, boiled one hand, and while he was throwing the other body parts into the river one night, the police caught him. And now he sits in prison and says that I forced him to do it. Do you understand that this is just a provocation? It's deceitful. The newspapers even showed photos of her body parts and of the

police catching him in the act of disposing of her body. They said the
Baptists did it under the leadership of their pastor, and they gave my
name. All of this was just nonsense. It wasn't true. It was just lies.

The grotesque detail of the offense was rather typical of antireligious
charges. Beginning in the late 1950s, the Soviet media featured highly personalized articles about clergy and the various criminal offenses with which
they were charged. From 1961 to 1964, at least 350 Baptists and over 260
Pentecostals were charged under Article 227, meaning the "infringement of
the rights of citizens under the guise of performing religious rituals"; such
people usually received a sentence of three to five years.[34] The charges, at
times reminiscent of tsarist anti-Semitism, often included child sacrifice,
mass suicides, and "swindler" clergy.[35] Indeed, many people who went to a
service for the first time during this period told me that they were haunted
by the thought, "What if the propaganda is true?" right up until they
walked through the door. They had these fears even though they were accompanied by a close friend, colleague, or neighbor, to whom they knew
such nonsensical caricatures of human sacrifice did not apply. Still, they
had to surmount their fears before attending. Even if readers dismissed
such articles in the press as crude propaganda, they nonetheless functioned
to keep alive the idea that Baptists were "dangerous."

After the accusations of murder and dismemberment, Karl Jablonsky
was arrested. He says he never knew the man who supposedly killed the
woman at his urging and certainly never advised him or anyone else to sacrifice another human being. He warned the police that just as the loss at the
debate worked to the advantage of believers, this spectacle would also serve
to strengthen Baptist communities. He was summoned to answer to the
charge of murder before a "show trial" (Rus. *pokaznoi sud*), which was
filled with students, members of the Komsomol Youth League, factory
workers, and others who received half-day tickets to observe. When Jablonsky saw Zahoriuk in the courtroom looking rather fit and healthy, he says,
he knew at once that this "actor" could never have spent the last few
months in prison.

The trial provided another public spectacle to paint a portrait of Baptists
as slavish, fanatical believers willing to subordinate reason and logic to the
whims of superstition. The trial lasted five days; by the end the people in the
courtroom were shouting, "Zahoriuk isn't guilty! Pastor Jablonsky is! Shoot
him!" Jablonsky recalled how on the last day people came with knives and
when the morning session ended, they shouted, "He'll be executed anyway!
What's the difference whether they shoot him or we make mincemeat out

of him!" When the decision was handed down that Zahoriuk was to be executed for the murder of the young woman, the crowd became even more agitated and called for Pastor Jablonsky's execution as well, threatening to stage another trial if justice was not rendered that day.

"But God saved me," Jablonsky calmly explained, "and none of that happened." Jablonsky was sentenced to five years of internal exile in Pavlodar, Kazakhstan, a small town with a community of believers who had been praying for six months that God would send them a pastor. After his first visit to one of their services, the members of this community elected him pastor. For Jablonsky, his family, and this community, it was all evidence of God's grace. They were able to read a divine purpose and a positive meaning into a ghastly worldly ordeal. The community needed a pastor, and God had sent them someone experienced, so they felt blessed. Pastor Jablonsky believed that his conviction and devotion were so strong that he was not only spared harm but was also rewarded by being sent to a place where he was able to continue serving God in a meaningful capacity. For other believers, his triumph over suffering at the hands of a "diabolical" government was interpreted as evidence of the protective power of faith and prayer, the goodness of God, and his benevolence toward the faithful. The Soviet state's attempt to erase the expression of religious belief at best simply displaced it. Another pastor took over in Chernivtsi and now a community in Kazakhstan had a pastor too.

When Jablonsky's five-year term was over, Ukrainian republican authorities informed the Baptist Union in Moscow that he was not welcome in Soviet Ukraine and denied him a Ukrainian residence permit. The Baptist Union responded by proposing that he live in Moldova, a republic neighboring Chernivtsi, his former home. In 1973, Jablonsky left for Chişinău, the capital, and was soon elected Bishop of Moldova at the All-Moldova Congress of Baptists, becoming a "people's hero" of another sort. He held this position for nineteen years, traveling around the world to twenty-five different countries, including many Western ones, a rare privilege for a Soviet citizen during that time. By the time he retired in 1992, two of his three children had already emigrated as refugees to America and in 1993, he did too. He now lives on the first floor of a duplex house in one of the so-called Russian neighborhoods of Philadelphia with his daughter and her family overhead. He is an active member of the Slavic Baptist church discussed in the next chapter and carries on there with his pastoral duties.

His son stayed behind and represents the next link in the chain of the family's intergenerational struggle with the state over faith. The biography of his son Ivan is no less harrowing. He served in the army in the Far East, but unlike his older brother, who served as an armed soldier and returned to Ukraine, Ivan was exempt from active duty on religious grounds and was part of a construction battalion (Rus. *stroitel'nyi batalon*). In the Soviet Union, conscientious objectors served alongside men with a criminal record or a history of mental illness. All share the army's assessment that they are physically fit for service but for various reasons unfit to carry weapons. According to his parents, Ivan was severely hazed and savagely beaten throughout his army service, an experience that is common. Those with a criminal background tend to be quite familiar with institutional life, often coming from either prisons or orphanages, and prey upon believers, who are not supposed to fight, curse, or engage in homosexual activity, and those with mental illnesses, who are often incapable of defending themselves. Several of the men I interviewed had hazing (Rus. *dedovshchina*) experiences in the army that were so traumatically violent that they were driven to contemplate suicide. No one ever said into my dictaphone that he was repeatedly raped by other men, but this is what I understood. Others attribute post-service problems with wife-beating to humiliations and violence incurred during military service.

After the army, Jablonsky's son married and settled in the Far East because he thought there was a need for believers there. This view was not shared by local authorities. One evening he and his wife arrived home and as they lit the stove, a bomb exploded. The house burned down and both he and his wife were hospitalized with severe burns over much of their bodies. At that time, Karl Jablonsky was already the bishop of Moldova, and he traveled to the Far East to meet with the local authorities. He explained to them that his son was a principled young man (Rus. *printsipial'nyi mal'chik*) and that nothing they could do would get him to leave or give up his faith. He reminded them that charges could be brought, but as believers, they would never do that. Rather, he was asking that his son be left alone. He simply wanted the harassment to stop. Later, another bomb exploded, but this time only the house was damaged; no one was injured.

Why would Karl Jablonsky and his son simply accept this injustice and not defend themselves or seek retribution in some way? Like most evangelicals, they believe that when Jesus ushers in the Kingdom of God, the wicked will be punished and the righteous redeemed, which is why they made such limited efforts to pursue justice in a worldly way. Their theology of evil says the wicked who serve Satan will be delegated to God for punishment. Their goal is to separate themselves from the damned in order to maintain their spiritual and moral purity. In direct contradiction to revolutionary ideology, they reject the possibility of creating social justice through political means. Efforts to realize justice and moral righteousness are best directed to personal social worlds, they reason, where they can truly bring about change, not to macro forces or institutions. One's ability to resist and overcome evil, as Karl Jablonsky, his father, and his son feel they have done, is understood as part of God's plan to separate the redeemed from the sinner, which is why, even after his house was bombed for a second time, his son never considered leaving. Demonstrating his faith and protesting injustice are accomplished by remaining in this village. It took an offer from an American missionary organization to start a church in Omsk, Siberia, to get him and his family to relocate. He lives there now and intends to remain in Siberia, he and his father having left Ukraine long behind. Ivan has no plans to join the rest of his family in Philadelphia, reasoning that there is a greater need for evangelizing in Russia than there is in America. Antireligious policies may have succeeded in deracinating him from Ukraine, but far from obliterating his faith, they rooted him in Russia all the more.

After describing the wrenching multigenerational tragedies that have befallen his family, the key point that Karl Jablonsky wanted to be sure that I grasped is that he, his father, and his son were all members of registered churches. He felt that there was propaganda of another kind here in the United States that led Americans to believe that unregistered churches in the Soviet Union were especially targeted for repressive measures and that their members were especially persecuted.[36] In contrast, he thinks it is impossible to make a clear judgment who suffered more because the tactics differed.

In large part, he is right. During the Antireligious Campaign, churches that grew in membership were the ones targeted for repressive measures, regardless of registration status. As far as the state was concerned, the essential difference between registered and unregistered churches was the various means used to repress them. Staged debates and show trials, like the ones Karl Jablonsky experienced, were used against registered churches to curb their growth by destroying the authority of their leaders and humiliating believers into sequestering belief in a privatized, censored sphere that was invisible and inaccessible to others. Arrests, imprisonment, and denial of parental rights tended to be used against unregistered church members to get them to cease meeting clandestinely.

In other words, the Soviet government was quite flexible in the methods and goals of persecution it employed, reflecting a knowledge of the communal life of registered and unregistered churches, and a willingness to adapt the strategy to the goal. Jablonsky understood the policy of registration as a purposeful—and successful—attempt on the part of the Soviet state to split the ranks of believers. Persecution was not simply targeted at unregistered churches over registered ones. Soviet authorities were ultimately more pragmatic. Rather, under Khrushchev's watch membership growth was the issue that concerned them. The policy shifted when the authorities acknowledged that not all believers could be dissuaded; the new goal became thwarting conversions. Much like the Truman Doctrine, they too adopted a policy of "containment" regarding religion. Evangelicals were proving difficult to eliminate, but perhaps they could contain them.

Still, it is worth noting the extraordinary reversal of fortune Karl Jablonsky experienced, from camp inmate to religious ambassador for the USSR. This came at a price. Travel abroad, especially to capitalist countries, was a privilege accorded to only a few. Karl Jablonsky stressed the extent to which Soviet clergy were "scripted" when abroad and also closely monitored when foreign clerical delegations came to the USSR. The constant affirmations of religious freedoms he and other state-sanctioned clergy provided explain in part why there was so little Western protest over infringements of religious liberties in the USSR and why Westerners thought it was only unregistered churches that were persecuted. Unregistered clergy, of course, had no possibility whatsoever of traveling abroad, whereas clergy such as Jablonsky were allowed to partake in international ecumenical organizations, with the price that they had to spread misleading information as they did it. The state used him and other clergy to improve its image and uphold its record on human rights abroad, while he, and others like him, used the state to maintain the communities under his jurisdiction and to give Soviet religious denominations a place in global ecumenical organizations.[37] Such was the limited toleration the state offered to sects and the services clergy offered to the state in return.

## The Underground Life of Unregistered Believers

Jesus' famous dictum, "Render unto Caesar the things that are Caesar's, and unto God the things that are God's" has been a guiding principle of a believer's obligations to authority. However, the issue of registration in the eyes of some meant that the laws of Caesar (the Soviet state) were in conflict with laws of God. They chose to privilege sacred obligations over secular ones and refused to allow the state to monitor and regulate communal worship. Given the diverse disciplinary tactics the state used, I wish to consider how an unregistered, illegal status affected communal life and how, when clerical and secular authorities are understood to be in a permanent state of confrontation, beliefs, practices, and religious sensibilities might be affected.

Mikhail Mikhailovich has spent all of his life as a member of unregistered house churches in Kharkiv, which means that he and his family know the camps, the fear of arrest, and an iron commitment to their faith and to other believers as well.[38] Now, in post-Soviet Ukraine, he is head of a group called the Independent Baptist Brotherhood, a unifying successor group for unregistered churches. He marvels at the freedoms believers have now, especially at how easily the stringent hardships have been forgotten. He condemns the changes that have beset the Baptist and Pentecostal congregations around him (see chapter 5) and maintains a steadfast allegiance to the old ways of religious practice.

Given the circumstances Mikhail Mikhailovich was raised under and those that exist now, he has managed to adapt quite successfully. After years of working in a factory, he became a pastor in 1988 and studied in Nyack, New York, at the Alliance Theological Seminary as part of a project entitled "Leadership Training" (Rus. *Obuchenie Rukovoditelei*), a program specifically designed for missionaries and clergy from the former Soviet Union who will serve there. The job he has now, which helps support his six children, is to create journals, magazines, and radio programs to promote the Baptist faith among youth in Ukraine. He also teaches at the Christian University in Donetsk.

Like Karl Jablonsky, he is another example of an intergenerational encounter between state and faith. He was born in northern Siberia, about five hundred kilometers north of Magadan, where his father was serving part of a twenty-three year prison sentence. He speaks with great admiration of his father, who is now over ninety years old, lives with him, and is still in reasonably good health. He attributes this to the fact that "God has compensated him for those years."

Initially, his father was sentenced to ten years of internal exile in 1934 for refusing to use a weapon when he was drafted into the army at age nineteen. His mother joined him in the north, where they married and had three children. His father was one of the few who had a wife. Prisoners would come to their house with sewing requests for his mother, shoe repair requests for his father, and for meals, which served as pretexts for believers of a variety of denominations to congregate at their house for singing and recitation of memorized passages from the Bible. The day before his father was to be released, he was rearrested on the grounds of "religious convictions" (Rus. *religioznye ubezhdeniia*), which implied propagating religion. His father was given another ten-year sentence, which eventually became a thirteen-year term; he was incarcerated in the prison across the street from their house. When the prisoners were taken out and loaded onto trucks and driven to work, Mikhail Mikhailovich recalls, he and his sisters ran down to the lane trying to catch a glimpse of their father. In time, this too became impossible when his father was transferred three hundred kilometers to the north to serve the final years of his sentence. He was released in 1957 as part of Khrushchev's general amnesty.

His father went to the camp a Baptist but returned a Pentecostal, believing in baptism of the Holy Spirit, speaking in tongues, and practicing other charismatic gifts. The familial denominational split remained; his father became a leader among Pentecostals as much as his son was among Baptists. Unregistered Baptists shared much in common with Pentecostals, the overwhelming majority of whom were unregistered. Back in their village near Kharkiv, the family would sometimes go to a home Pentecostal church and sometimes attend a registered Baptist church. Their Baptist church was closed down as part of the antireligious campaign in 1962, but the congregation rented space during off hours from the central Baptist Church, which remained open throughout the campaign. The central Baptist Church followed the Letter of Instruction issued in 1960, which said that children were no longer allowed at services lest the pastor be removed.[39] Two deacons—Mikhail Mikhailovich described them as "old grandfathers"—stood at the doors before each service and were charged with ensuring that no children entered. Once these deacons were distracted by conversation, Mikhail Mikhailovich claims that he and his friends would enter the church, hide in the balcony, and remain there for the entire service. Of course, other members knew children were there but refused to ask them to leave. Difficulties of this sort prompted his family to create a home church, the solution of many Pentecostals.

They divided their house into two parts. His family lived in one part, and the other side served as a half-way house. "Brothers," meaning fellow believers, lived there after they were released from prison and before they created their own families. Usually there were about six of them living in the house at any given time. They had services with about twenty people in attendance on the bachelor side every Sunday and holiday. Anyone who had been sentenced to prison had their belongings confiscated and their housing privileges revoked. Therefore, it was very common for newly released prisoners to have nowhere to go. Longstanding believers frequently told me that they took in believers released from the camps to live with them. The process of remaking the self after the trauma of the camps is essentially dependent on two components: first one must find the words to articulate the trauma, as difficult as this is, and then one must find someone who can listen and actually hear those words.[40] As Talal Asad has noted, the ability to recover, to continue to live sanely, after a traumatic experience is dependent on the response of others, especially their ability and willingness to listen and truly hear what another has endured.[41] Coming back to a community where the traumatic experience is prevalent, where full articulation is not needed for full comprehension, is extremely helpful in the healing process. In the context of these communities, where people are linked through faith-based moral obligations to assist each other to make everyday ends meet, dependencies become interdependencies, which also furthers healing. So, especially for returning prisoners, home churches also became homes.

Mikhail Mikhailovich explained the meaning these house churches had for youth:

> As we lived in a village, besides my family, several other believing families, and the brothers came. There were some young people who were older than us [Mikhail Mikhailovich and his sisters] and they said, "Let's learn to play musical instruments, domra, balalaika, guitar." And so we organized a small orchestra and then we organized a Bible study group. We did all of this at home.

The performative aspects of these services are especially relevant for young people, what with the prescription to avoid secular forms of entertainment and mass media and the preference of most parents that children not join the Pioneer and Komsomol organizations. Having eliminated the standard diversions for leisure, evangelical communities, including even home churches in small villages, countered with participatory musical performances, either in the form of choirs or small musical groups as well as regular face-to-face meetings for the purposes of Bible study. In this way, the home not only became a sacred place, but it also functioned as something of a total institution, the hub of social, leisure, often professional, and, of course, spiritual needs.

Their house was raided several times during services. Birthday parties served as the usual pretext for meetings. This was the most plausible explanation as to why a large group would be gathered. Such pretexts helped to avoid paying fines and to escape the charge of religious indoctrination. Fines were deducted directly from a person's paycheck, allowing no chance for challenge and automatically alerting employers to the "antisoviet tendencies" of their employee. If a person continued to allow believers to meet in the home after having been fined, the next step was arrest and imprisonment.

In the summer it was possible to organize large gatherings in the woods. A mixture of Pentecostal and Baptist believers gathered in the woods in mid-summer to celebrate *Troitsia,* Trinity Sunday, and again for *Zhatva,* a fall harvest festival, and usually at least one other time in the warmer months.[42] The goal of these outdoor gatherings was to give believers a chance to meet with others outside their group and to reaffirm their faith and the righteousness of the lifestyle they chose regardless of the perils it yielded. Larger meetings had additional import for young people searching for a spouse, for it was forbidden to marry a nonbeliever.[43]

Although warm weather offered such possibilities for assembly, winter presented entirely different logistical challenges. Mikhail Mikhailovich explained how a believer in a nearby village allowed winter services to occur at his house at least once a year from 1967 to 1980. These gatherings were semi-clandestine events, often fulfilling the function of cathartic release:

> One brother lived in Artemovsk and he practically consecrated his house to holding services. There was almost no furniture in the house. And when we came, whatever little furnishings there were, we carried outside so we could gather in the house. And people stood there, packed against one another, to such a degree, and this you will have difficulty imagining, that when the service was over, water trickled down the walls. That's how much perspiration there was in there. But for us it was a meeting of the best kind! We preached, prayed, sang, and talked. There just were no other possibilities.

The hostility of the outside world was proportional to the intense expression of fear and gratitude they experienced at these clandestine meetings. If they could trust few people "from the world," they could at least form strong bonds of solidarity between members and revel in the communitas they experienced during these sessions. Although Soviet accounts of Pentecostal prayer meetings emphasize the hysteria and pathology they induced in believers—the "shaking," as Soviet sources called it—others, like Mikhail Mikhailovich, referred to the overwhelming, all-encompassing feeling of joy and exuberance these meetings produced.[44]

Once the service began, usually no one was allowed to enter. The service unfolded in a prescribed fashion, even if it was unknown if anyone would repent or the number and types of prayer requests (which were often more like public confessions) that would be offered. For the first hour or so, the believers sang, followed by three or four "brothers" giving sermons that were often highly evangelistic, stressing salvation and the importance of moral behavior. Sermons were interspersed with prayer and speaking in tongues, when everyone prays out loud simultaneously, each person engulfed in his or her own pleading to God—but somehow as a collective, unified endeavor, beginning and ending in perfect concert, with chaotic sounds in between. This is meant to be an expressive evocation of passionate devotion, at once an individual, intimate dialogue with God, out loud and in public, and a collective, single gesture of glorification to God, that distinguishes Pentecostal services from the Soviet Baptist version. It is the sweat and steam running down the walls and the human exuberance of vivacious, expressive worship that forms the core of doctrinal debates between Soviet-era Pentecostals, who see this fervor as evidence of the presence of the Holy Spirit, and their Baptist brethren, who prefer a more formal, cognitive, and orderly form of worship. Yet the common terms in which these theological debates were conducted, as well as their shared perils in an earthly realm, kept Soviet Baptists and Pentecostals interconnected.

## Challenging the Moral Order

During the Soviet period, competitions called "socialist emulation" (Rus. *sotssorevnovanie*), were organized to motivate the workforce. As part of this, each collective was obliged to write a statement of the group's "socialist self-obligations" (Rus. *sotsobiazatel'stva*) detailing what it would do to fulfill the country's current economic goals. Sometimes, each member of the collective had to do this as well. Of course, there was the obligatory acknowledgment about respecting the ideals of socialism—which included an atheist worldview—and staunch believers, such as Mikhail Mikhailovich, found this objectionable. To write it meant to write something that was not true, which was strictly against his principles. Yet, to refuse to write it ushered in other problems.

At one point in the 1960s, Mikhail Mikhailovich refused to write his "socialist self-obligations" at the factory where he worked. At first his boss demanded, then he threatened, then he scolded; then his tone softened to a request and finished up with a plea for him to write it. Periodically, inspectors would verify that everyone had complied; if they were to discover that Mikhail Mikhailovich had refused and had not been obliged to comply, then his boss would have problems too. The longer the situation went on, the more anxious his boss became. Finally, after nervous imploring by his boss, Mikhail Mikhailovich decided to write what he would oblige himself to do to fulfill the government's plan for his factory: "I, Mikhail Mikhailovich, promise, *esli Bog dast' silu i zdorovie*—*if God grants me strength and health*—to. . . ." and he carried on writing what he was supposed to. Relieved that the formality was accomplished and thinking he knew what was written, his boss never read it and simply filed it. Later, however, an elderly inspector stumbled upon the reference to God and showed it to Mikhail Mikhailovich's boss. What to do? They both realized that to report it would have meant problems for all. They decided to simply refile it and pass it on, with the hope that the usual inertia would overcome subsequent inspectors.

Alexei Yurchak has argued that the willingness of Soviet citizens to engage in these endless ritualized forms of discourse contributed to the illusion of the timeless nature of the system.[45] He also notes that *how* the discourse was represented became more important than *what* it represented. The insertion of this small phrase, which some might have spoken but few would actually have written in this context, constituted a violation of established practice. In other words, most factory workers would have simply written their *sotsobiazatel'stva* in a "constative way," to use the framework Yurchak has adopted, reflecting a certain compliance that might not have risen to the level of active endorsement but was at least an acquiescence to the system and its rituals of affirmation. Mikhail Mikhailovich, however, wrote his in a "performative" way, as a defiant statement, to provoke a reaction. Clearly, he did not see this as an empty ritualized gesture devoid of meaning. His inserted phrase was such a sharp deviation from "authoritative discourse," from what one was expected to say, that it constituted a broad condemnation of the foundation upon which the system based its legitimacy. It surely would have been punished if it had been recognized for what it was.

Mikhail Mikhailovich's boss came to him, ashen, claiming that he felt as if he were sitting on the edge of a volcano. "It would have been better if you wrote nothing at all, than to have written that!" said the boss. He feared that the fleeting reference to God would destroy his career. Mikhail Mikhailovich, on the other hand, was quite pleased. He had fulfilled his workplace obligations by writing it and his own principles by writing it the way he did. This is one of the many ways in which believers were defiantly compliant in their confrontations with the state, a strategy that served them quite well as a group, because it frequently left the state with little punitive recourse.

## Defiant Compliance of Unregistered Believers

The need for evangelicals to reconcile conflicting moral mandates to respect the law of God and the law of the land yielded a strategic response I characterize as "defiant compliance." Matthew Guttman uses a similar term, "compliant defiance," in his study of politics in a poor working class neighborhood in Mexico City.[46] He uses the term to invoke the resentment and simmering hostility Mexicans feel over obligations to accept injustice and limits on autonomy. In contrast, I wish to place an accent on "compliance" to authority, always an overriding commitment for evangelicals, which obliged them to articulate their defiance to state mandates compliantly.

Both religion and politics are concerned with the nature and practice of power and authority and with regulating moral conduct. Submission to authority, be it divine, civil, or clerical, is a doctrinally enshrined belief and a widespread cultural practice among evangelicals in Ukraine and elsewhere.[47] Compliance with divine guidance combines with state and economic exigencies and forms another set of moral mandates regulating individual behavior. The theology and moral views of evangelicals aim to make believers peaceful, law-abiding, and governable citizens. The emphasis is always on compliance as the ideal to be realized, even when compliance had to be done in a defiant spirit. Even when uncompromising defiance was understood as the only possible response, this defiance was often couched in other forms of compliant, conforming behavior, which not by design but by effect, made the defiance harder to detect.

Mikhail Mikhailovich explains how the attitudes in Kharkiv toward confrontation with the state began to change over time:

> At that time [1960s], we often got summonses to come to the KGB for talks. I know that they called me down not just one time and demanded to know when and where we would have an outdoor service. I always responded the same—even if I knew that it was still not decided, or if we would have one at all—I never said yes and I never said no. I simply declared, "There will always be one!" Let them think that. There will always be one! Somewhere! I would say, "No matter how you ask the question, the answer will always be the same. The service will always happen because people must live!" Of course, in different regions there were different reactions to such a response.

Mikhail Mikhailovich referred to different regions because these outdoor services frequently included believers from different oblasts who traveled to Kharkiv by train to participate. So even though the Kharkiv community would organize large revival-like meetings three times a year or so, this was a fraction of the total number of outdoor services that he and other members of his underground house church attended each year. He noted that it was not difficult for the authorities to learn of these gatherings. All they had to do, he contended, was to follow "modestly dressed women" and "men who refused to curse," readily identifiable as believers, one marked by dress, the other by habit. If authorities had gained information about a group's departure for a service in another town or city, sometimes believers were arrested as they disembarked from the train.

> What to do? Khrushchev promised to show us the last believer, and here we have so many young people coming, and they all claim to believe. We gathered by the thousands for those meetings in the woods. In essence, the principle was as follows: In the beginning when we gathered in the woods, the authorities would come, either the police or the procurator, they would surround us and shout into their megaphones, "You all need to leave. Don't break any laws." Of course, believers were not trying to break any laws. When a person is deprived of the right to live, what should he do? He's only left to die! But still, he'll live.
>
> They [the believers] shouted back, "We're not breaking any laws. You should change the laws. You've closed all the prayer houses. This means that our possibilities are limited."

The police would round up the organizers, the preachers, and the choir and usually hold them for fifteen days and dock their pay accordingly. I asked Mikhail Mikhailovich whether he suspected that there might have been informers among the members or visitors who could have told the authorities of their outdoor services. He noted that although unknown people never showed up spontaneously to a home church, the purpose of these larger outdoor services was specifically to evangelize, to attract new converts. As a result, no one was turned away. This was their response to contradictory mandates: their religion urged evangelization and their state forbade it. Even as antireligious policies began to soften under Brezhnev, which allowed religious communities to serve existing believers, the state never relaxed prescriptions against evangelizing and other activities designed to attract new followers, such as these outdoor services.

Soviet evangelicals were propelled to continue evangelizing because they subscribe to a doctrine of dispensational premillennialism, which means that they believe that the Second Coming of Jesus is imminent and that all who are saved will be raptured and allowed into the Kingdom of Heaven.[48] Those who are not, who remain in a state of nonbelief, will perish in the Battle of Armageddon and suffer eternal damnation. Fear of this moment, called the Great Tribulation, keenly motivated them to witness about their faith and to evangelize among the unsaved. But obviously, it was often difficult to distinguish between a genuine religious seeker and a person who was asking questions to gain information that could be used against the community. When I asked Mikhail Mikhailovich how he and others navigated such contradictory mandates and the potential penalties, his answer surprised me:

> You know, Christians never had such suspiciousness [of visitors being informers]. In essence, we never had such fears that someone would appear and suddenly hand us over. These services were absolutely open to all people. If you want, please, come. We understand it like this: We don't hurt anyone; we don't do anything that hurts our state. If, for example, some people became believers, then they worked conscientiously. They took care of their families. But, of course, when we came to the factory after having been at a Christian service and after having received fifteen days for it, the entire collective would meet and would judge me by all asking "Aren't you ashamed? You, young man, go there and believe all that gibberish?" And let's say a believer responds, "What's the problem? I conscientiously fulfill my responsibilities. I don't curse. I never steal from the factory." And sometimes they reacted by saying, "If only you would steal! If only you would drink! Just don't go there!" There were lots of moments like that. Do you understand?

The evangelical ethos demands strict obedience to God, respect for authority, and moral self-mastery, all of which were rigidly and unwaveringly advocated in communal life. Hence, Mikhail Mikhailovich refused to steal, drink, or engage in the lax workplace discipline, characterized by the legendary patterns of "slacking and storming."[49] By renouncing these common cultural practices that flout the authority of the state and refute the legitimacy of its socialist ideology, he and other evangelicals indirectly endorsed state authorities and validated socialist morality. Mikhail Mikhailovich's refusal to steal and cheat his employer questioned the morality (or lack thereof ) of those accepted practices and raised doubts as to what constituted resistance and collaboration, which is why it was so

disconcerting to his colleagues that he was simultaneously arrested repeatedly and a reliable "Stakhanovite" factory superworker. The real Stakhanov
was an idealized (and often cynically viewed) labor hero, whereas Mikhail
Mikhailovich's enthusiasm and dedication were genuine. He was fastidious
in his compliance with workplace discipline, fulfilling many of the principles of the moral code of the builder of communism, and yet unwavering in
his defiance of all state mandates he understood to be in violation of biblical teachings.

This is why, regardless of arrests and fines, he and other members of his
house church continued to evangelize. Along with large outdoor gatherings that involved numerous underground communities, young people
traveled to villages to proselytize. Usually once a month during the warmer
seasons, they would walk to a village where someone had a relative or
friend, and once in that village, the group began to sing hymns, preach,
read passages from the Bible, and discuss the merits of a religious lifestyle.
But a particular outing to evangelize in a small village outside Kharkiv in
1964 would be pivotal. After an encounter with state authorities there, the
youth group decided to change how they reacted to confrontations with
the police:

> We were maybe about 20 people. We walked for about two hours,
> about 10 kilometers. And when we arrived there, people in that village
> gathered around. We sang and preached and told them about God. Of
> course, people listened with great interest. They wanted to listen. But
> suddenly a car appeared. The police [Rus. *militsia*] were bringing
> some representative from the local authorities. Whoever was reading
> from the Bible didn't hide. He just stood there. The police called out,
> "Him! Him! Get Him!" But the girls didn't want him to be taken
> away, and they began to protect him. When the police grabbed him,
> one group pulled him one way and the other pulled him in the oppo-
> site way, almost tearing him to pieces.
>
> They shouted, "We have a right to be here! The Constitution guar-
> antees it!"
>
> "We'll show you the Constitution!" they responded.
>
> And then the head of the police, or maybe a lieutenant colonel,
> maybe a major, I don't remember—he had a lot of stars on his
> shoulder-strap—tried to take control of the situation. During the
> fight, they ripped his sleeve.
>
> When they brought us to the police station, he said to us, "The
> only charge I'm making against you is for the sleeve. I'm not giving

you a sentence [Rus. *srok*] for singing, but only for ripping my sleeve. You have damaged my property.

Because of his reaction [which they understood to be quite mild], we came to a new conclusion and began to talk about it. "Wait a minute," we said, "it's in fact written in the Bible that when the apostles were called, they went without protest. That means that no force was used. State authorities invited them, and they went." And after that we called all our young people together and said, "Friends! We shouldn't act that way. If they want to take us away, let them take us away." When we leave for a meeting, each of us should be prepared for that. We should say, "Mom, maybe I will return home and maybe I won't. Maybe I'll get fifteen days or maybe they'll give me some other kind of sentence. OK?"

After that, we came to the conclusion that, as Christians, we should never defend ourselves. If they pull us into a car, we'll go. If they try to take us away by saying, "Everybody out!"—we'll leave. After we started to react like that, then the authorities changed their tactics too. They would come to a service, let's say one at our house, and they would enter and say, "End the service!" and we would respond, "Yes, we'll all pray and then we will leave." We prayed. We left. Quietly. And then each of them sitting in the car would take us to the police station, and file charges saying that we resisted arrest, broke this, smashed that, and so on. Yet we left quietly and peacefully. They just wrote lies to put us in a bad light.

The arrested youth were impeccably compliant in their defiance. Their actions constituted a public rejection of Soviet ideology, authority, and power and a quiet submission to the state's disciplining response. Evangelicals proclaimed God to be a higher authority than the state and its laws, and this became the justification for Mikhail Mikhailovich and others to violate unrepentantly selected laws and cultural practices in pursuit of fulfilling their moral obligations as they understood them. At the same time, conscientiously complying with the repercussions was understood as another form of witnessing, of actualizing their faith.

Christel Lane speaks of how religious communities "accommodated" Soviet restrictions by molding their practices to fit within them.[50] Such a conceptualization, however, misses two key dimensions of the evangelical strategy. This approach overlooks that the process of adjustment was mutual. Accommodation was forced on the state as well. Second, believers attempted to demonstrate the sacred qualities of labor, collectivism, and allegiance by becoming model citizens and exemplary members of socialist society. These forms of public proselytizing were often packaged in acceptable rhetoric of submission and ritualized actions of obedience, even though they were fundamentally an act of defiance.

James Scott's analysis of "weapons of the weak," of passive-aggressive forms of protest by victimized peoples to oppressive forces, also does not apply.[51] Believers did not see themselves as weak, given their divine alliance. The term "weapons" implies intent to harm or engage in battle, which I do not believe they would recognize, given their belief in the necessity to "Render unto Caesar" and their lack of commitment to pursuing worldly forms of justice. Other analysts use a language of "struggle," "protest," or "passive resistance" to describe the variety of reactions certain faith groups had to Soviet state restrictions. Those terms, however, do not capture the far more subtle, pervasive, and nonconfrontational challenges that believers incessantly issued, vacillating between hypercompliance and brazen defiance, which I am calling "defiant compliance."

Whether we speak of Karl Jablonsky's son responding to violent state harassment by refusing to leave and remaining a target or Mikhail Mikhailovich irking his coworkers with his refusal to steal and cheat the factory, we must recognize that believers obliged others to reckon with their religious lives. It is the delicate balance of confrontation through submission, of couching acts of total defiance in apparent acts of compliance, that distinguishes the evangelical response to state mandates they found objectionable. In many respects, these responses mirror a theological tenet that encourages believers to submit to the will of God and surrender autonomy so as to be empowered and liberated. The patterned response of defiant compliance, of challenging from within, on the terms of the state but based on entirely subversive values—this is what gave the resistance they offered its force and often left the state with little punitive recourse. In this way, evangelicals challenged, circumvented, and even subverted Soviet secularism. By insisting that religion be less marginal, less sequestered in an invisible sphere, and, therefore, less of a private individual affair, they attempted to reenchant the public sphere by elevating the authority of God's law over secular law.

## Coming Out from Underground

Following the ouster of Nikita Khrushchev in 1964, policies concerning religion were reassessed. Brezhnev lacked Khrushchev's antireligious ideological conviction. The Central Committee of the Communist Party released a declaration in November 1964 entitled, "On Errors Committed in the Conduct of Atheist Propaganda." Along with the familiar acknowledgments of "excesses" committed in the name of enthusiasm, there was a growing and undeniable awareness that antireligious campaigns drove religious groups underground, which ultimately was highly counterproductive. Underground groups were far more difficult to control or even influence.[52] The views of evangelicals changed too. As communities grew, unregistered groups saw multiple advantages to registration. Although believers managed to congregate regularly in both large and small gatherings, the problem of staging rituals to confer status within the community was far harder to solve.

Ivan Iakovlevich has been a lifelong Pentecostal believer. In 2001 he became a pastor thanks to a correspondence course he completed at an evangelical seminary in Kyiv that was built with financing from the United States, mostly from the Southern Baptist Convention.[53] His father converted to Pentecostalism when he was imprisoned as a juvenile. His mother was raised Baptist but converted to Pentecostalism when she was seventeen years old, after her mother did. When Ivan Iakovlevich was a child in Kharkiv, there was not a single registered Pentecostal community. He and his family gathered two or three times a week for services in small, fractured groups in constantly changing locations. The incessant rotation of location mandated a vast informal communicative network simply to convene. As the membership grew, the problem of the lack of fixed location grew more and more insurmountable.

Evangelical baptism is preceded by a lengthy period of study as an adult candidate, which includes consultations with the pastor and with the members of the Fraternal Council, the governing body of the community, before an individual is allowed to undergo full-body immersion baptism and become a member of the church. The ceremonies themselves were secretly orchestrated clandestine rituals conducted after dark in a forest river or lake. In 1981 there were 350 political prisoners in the USSR, some of whom were charged with distributing or printing religious literature and others with "organization of or active participation in group actions which disrupt public order."[54] This was a reference to conducting rituals, usually baptisms. Until the mid-1980s, Pentecostal believers in Kharkiv staged baptisms by using informal networks to pass along the date, the time of the train leaving the city, and the zone for which to buy a ticket. Each zone contained a half-dozen or so stations. No one knew at which station they would disembark until an appointed person gave a signal at a particular station, which was then communicated domino-style to other members of the group, after which all would disembark. Sometimes they would arrive at the river to find a police barricade awaiting them because an informer had betrayed them. The police would fine or arrest the men and force the women and children to disperse. Usually, the group tried to reconvene at another place along the riverbank. Often enough, their alternative plans met with success, and the baptism, despite the considerable interruption, would proceed apace.

In the midst of this ongoing confrontation, one that was increasingly tiresome for the Soviet state to wage, especially in view of their limited success, Soviet Ukrainian authorities agreed to allow the first legal Pentecostal church to be built in Kharkiv oblast. In 1981 four members of this community purchased a private residence that they were officially allowed to convert into a prayer house. Mikhail Mikhailovich's father was one of the earliest sponsors of this endeavor. The house is located next to a pond at the very end of a long dirt road, quite a distance from any form of public transportation, in a district of small private homes. The remote, inaccessible location of the church is itself an emphatic statement about the Pentecostal belief in separation from the world. Chapter 5 describes how this community has fared in post-Soviet society.

Ivan Iakovlevich's parents were among the earliest members of this church. The original community numbered some seventy adult members, all of whom contributed money to buy the house and the time and effort to transform it. Expecting each day that Soviet authorities would send bulldozers to destroy it, they continued the renovation and expansion of the house, adding a large meeting hall to the front of the structure. For this community, a legal existence in a registered church building that the members had designed and built themselves did not only allow them to tame the improvisational and sporadic nature of their activities, it also fostered a greater sense of belonging to the city and to this community.

The Word of Life Pentecostal community, like all other Protestant communities in 1981, still faced enormous challenges: there were few ordained clergy, not enough Bibles, and almost no hymnals, and members were still harassed by supervisors, neighbors, and authorities. Yet during Brezhnev's rule and especially afterward, as the millennial commemoration of Christianity in 1988 loomed, the authorities assumed a stance toward religion of reluctant and tacit acceptance. Coercion was used much less frequently. There was a continued reliance on propaganda, which was increasingly ignored. Even when the socio-political conditions in Soviet society relaxed in the 1980s, the tenor of these communities was already established as significantly more conservative, legalistic, and literal in doctrinal interpretation, especially when compared with their coreligionists in the West. The insularity of the Soviet evangelical movement from religious trends occurring elsewhere in the world perpetuated and even normalized the austere, legalistic, and ascetic qualities of Soviet religious communities. The charismatic movement, for example, which celebrated the "gifts of the spirit" in an expressive, exuberant form of worship, made enormous inroads in evangelical, especially Pentecostal, congregations around the world in the 1960s. Pentecostal congregations in the Soviet Union, in sharp contrast, were removed from this and remained among the most conservative of all evangelical groups.

## The Soviet Christian Emigration Movement

The general apocalyptic orientation of evangelicals, led to a tacit acceptance of the conditions of their worldly experience and focused attention away from this world to preparation for the afterlife. Soviet evangelical communities, confident of their impending salvation, had little desire to pursue civil liberties and social justice as sacred causes, sharply distinguishing them from dissidents and human rights activists. Although their views constituted a critique of the Soviet status quo, they did not overtly seek to challenge it, except for when they felt morally obliged to do so, as in the instance of military service. Rather, most preferred to participate in their own parallel communities, schools and organizations founded on an alternative moral code and to live "*vnye*" (Rus. beside) socialist society to a far greater extent and far more elaborately than other underground groups, such as literary clubs and cafés.[55]

Any sense of activism, of directed attempts at transformation, were addressed toward changing individual moral worlds and not the macro forces shaping social institutions and political life. They encouraged empowerment on the micro level through individual moral asceticism. This orientation translated into an emphasis on improving marital relations, strengthening the family unit, building relationships with other church members, and on developing networks of self-help to improve the lot of the poor and disenfranchised.[56]

Recognizing that family socialization was the prime means of perpetuating evangelical communities, authorities sought to block the involvement of children in church activities as a means of breaking the "chain of memory" of religious knowledge and practice. They understood that religion links generations to each other and to far larger communities through a common mode of believing distinguished by an appeal to a legitimizing authority of tradition learned largely in the home. If this chain could be broken, as it already had been for many families in the USSR who had become, as it were, religiously illiterate and could neither practice nor share them with their children, then the general secularization of Soviet society would deepen and ultimately become irreversible.

Heightened concern with the exposure of children to religious doctrine prompted authorities to revive a policy, initially aimed at Orthodox underground groups and then applied more widely to sects, of forcibly removing children from their parents and placing them in state-run boarding schools to prevent religious indoctrination. For some, this form of harassment prompted a more determined withdrawal from society and an even more strident reliance on God for protection. For others, as one of the last and most unbearable forms of coercion used by Soviet state authorities, it prompted a worldly solution: emigration.

In 1963 a Pentecostal congregation in Chernogorsk, Siberia, issued an appeal to "Christians of the Entire World" for assistance to emigrate out of the USSR. This incident, as startling as it was, was only part of a broader effort on the part of certain religious groups to emigrate from the Soviet Union. The Dukhobors and Molokans had emigrated for reasons of conscience around the turn of the century. And Soviet authorities had allowed the repatriation of some German Mennonites and Lutherans beginning in the 1920s. Pentecostals hoped these privileges would be extended to them.

In 1963, thirty-two members of this Siberian congregation, many of whom had had their children forcibly abducted and placed in state orphanages, decided that they faced a choice: a life of continual harassment by state authorities or emigration. They formed a delegation, led by Khariton Vashchenko, entered the U.S. embassy, and asked to emigrate out of the USSR. The U.S. ambassador explained that an embassy cannot grant asylum, so they were released to Soviet authorities with assurances that no harm would come to them. Yet Khariton Vashchenko was imprisoned three months later, and the rest of the community noted only a temporary easing of restrictions.

In 1966, Premier of the Soviet Union Alexei Kosygin, the nominal head of government from 1964 to 1980 who held office for almost the entire period that Leonid Brezhnev was general secretary of the Soviet Communist Party, declared that for purposes of family reunification, the Soviet Union would allow limited emigration. The Brezhnev era, commonly referred to as the "period of stagnation" or "real socialism" and characterized by tight travel restrictions and highly circumscribed contact between Soviet and

Western citizens, provided the backdrop for the third wave of emigration from the USSR. Soviet Jews became the main beneficiaries of this new policy. Religious conviction and a desire to live in a Jewish state initially motivated Jews to emigrate. Those who were denied permission became known as *refuseniks*. Mounting international protest over their plight prompted a relaxation of Soviet policy at the same time that the Hebrew Immigrant Aid Society (HIAS) decided to offer the controversial option in 1976 of settling in the United States and not only in Israel.[57] By 1989, 97 percent of the refugees requested asylum in the United States.

After the Soviet Union signed the Helsinki Accords of 1975, agreeing to allow emigration and to respect freedom of conscience, fifty-two Pentecostals claiming to represent twenty thousand others made a direct appeal to the Pope for Christian unity and support for persecuted religious minorities in the USSR. In 1976 they appealed to the World Council of Churches in a forty-eight–page letter that listed the names of ninety-seven Pentecostals seeking to emigrate. Although these actions yielded no tangible results for Pentecostals, evangelicals were further encouraged by the election of Jimmy Carter, a Baptist, to the presidency in 1976.

Khariton Vashchenko's brother, Petr, was in prison in 1963 when the first group of Pentecostals tried to emigrate via the U.S. embassy in Moscow. Undaunted by their failure, Petr, his wife Augustina, and three of their children (two of whom had been forcibly removed from the family and were living in boarding schools at the time of the 1963 attempt) along with another mother and her sixteen-year-old son made another attempt to emigrate using the same means on 27 June 1978. The Vashchenko's seventeen-year-old son charged past the Soviet guards and was apprehended and beaten; while this was going on, the rest of the group dashed past the Soviet guards and into the U.S. embassy compound.

Little did they know that they had just begun a five-year residency in the U.S. embassy and that their actions would trigger an international campaign that dubbed them the "Siberian Seven." They forced U.S. embassy officials to reckon with the plight of evangelical communities in the land of the "militantly godless" by refusing to leave the embassy except on a plane bound for the United States.

Interestingly, during this ordeal, the Twelfth World Pentecostal Conference took place in Vancouver, Canada, in September 1979. Formal ties between the registered Pentecostals with the AUCECB and the American Assemblies of God were established in 1967, after which the Americans always held that the Pentecostal congregations should indeed register with state authorities, as they themselves did. Soviet delegations from AUCECB

routinely attended various international Pentecostal conferences from the
1970s on. At the Vancouver Congress, however, eight hundred Soviet Pentecostals sent an appeal on behalf of the forty Pentecostals who were in
camps in 1979 and on behalf of a growing movement of Pentecostals,
which they claimed numbered thirty thousand, seeking to emigrate as religious refugees. The Siberian Seven, who had been living in the U.S. embassy for over a year by this time, also sent an appeal. Yet the conference
planning committee declined to put the issue of Soviet Pentecostals on the
program.

There are several factors explaining the lack of Western evangelical response. First, the believers who were the most severely persecuted
belonged to unregistered groups. Therefore, Soviet attempts to paint them
as violators of the law had some credibility, especially when the overwhelming majority of Western Pentecostal leaders had registered their
churches with their respective state authorities. Delegations from the Soviet Union, like the ones Karl Jablonsky participated in, included members of registered communities who reported a lack of state interference in
religious observance. Western ecumenical leaders quite simply did not appreciate the potential implications of registration with Soviet authorities
and therefore were hesitant to back clergy who seemed to violate the law.[58]
In some instances, they displayed a lack of basic knowledge about evangelical life in the USSR, such as when Jimmy Swaggart, the founder of the
Pentecostal Praise The Lord Ministry, after a trip to the Soviet Union in
1986, said:

> I doubt seriously there is an underground church in the Soviet
> Union, at least as we think of it here in America. I know we hear sto-
> ries of Christians meeting out in the woods and things of this nature;
> however, when one starts to think about it, this would be very diffi-
> cult.
>
> *First of all*, there are very few telephones (at least that Christians
> have) in the Soviet Union. Secondly, the weather is almost always bad.
> Thirdly, it would be very difficult to get the news to any appreciable
> number of people to meet anywhere—and really, it is not necessary.
> The churches are open and the people can go.[59]

Swaggart's assurances notwithstanding, it was precisely these practices
as we have seen, that were quite common in Soviet evangelical communities. Although AUCECB leaders were allowed to travel to international

ecumenical conferences, they were quite guarded in the details they divulged, which led to the affirmations of the misperceptions articulated by Jimmy Swaggart. In essence, Western ecumenical leaders were constantly receiving diametrically opposed portraits of a believer's life in the USSR, and most endorsed the opinions of (Soviet state-approved) clerical leaders and therefore refrained from any kind of concerted protest. Those that understood the difficulties that unregistered communities faced were often concerned that efforts to defend them might jeopardize the relationships they had with registered clerical leaders and might result in their being denied entry to the USSR. Unlike the other Western counterparts to religious minorities (Jews, Mennonites, Lutherans, and so on), Western evangelical leaders never encouraged or facilitated emigration out of the Soviet Union.

As for the Siberian Seven, with each passing year of residence in the embassy basement, American officials grew increasingly embarrassed and strained by the Pentecostal protest in their midst. In 1983 the INS finally granted them refugee status and allowed thirty members of the two families to emigrate to the United States, where they still live to this day. More important, their protest laid the groundwork for later legislation that made evangelicals the last wave of Soviet refugees to the United States.

The fear of state reprisals had begun to ebb considerably by the 1980s. Active believers were no longer sentenced to the camps in the same sweeping way as they once had been although it still happened. Fines, rather than imprisonment, were now the main means of punishing transgressors of atheist ideology. Propaganda that celebrated science and "communist morality" was preferred to coercion as the means of thwarting interest in religion. By 1980, just as Ronald Reagan assumed the U.S. presidency and became a powerful spokesperson for the interests of conservative Christians, Boris Perchatkin amassed thirty thousand members under the "Christian Emigration Movement in the USSR," most of whom were Pentecostals striving to practice their religion elsewhere.[60] In a symbolic gesture of protest, they staged a five-day hunger strike to coincide with the first week of the Helsinki Review Conference in Madrid in 1981.

This Soviet Christian Emigration Movement vitally depended on affirmation from Western authorities, which was not forthcoming. In 1980 Perchatkin was rearrested after escaping from prison the previous year, and received a new two-year sentence.[61] From 1979 to 1981 thirty Pentecostals were arrested, some for refusing to serve in the Red Army, but most for involvement in the Christian Emigration Movement.[62] Vasilii Shiliuk, a Pentecostal preacher and emigration activist, was sentenced in 1983 to three years in prison for unauthorized activities. With the leaders of the Emigration Movement in prison, appeals to emigrate were silenced. In the end, even though the "Siberian Seven" were finally allowed to emigrate in 1983 through rather exceptional means, the overall campaign for emigration failed. Although it was impossible to foresee at the time, the failure was only temporary.

*Part Two*

# MISSIONIZING AND MOVEMENT

## Chapter Three

# The Rewards of Suffering

### *The Last Soviet Refugees*

As the Soviet Union prepared for the millennial commemoration of Christianity in Kyivan Rus', Mikhail Gorbachev in 1987 took the bold step of announcing that all victims of religious persecution could apply to emigrate as part of his greater campaign of *glasnost*. Soon thereafter, the U.S. Congress passed the Lautenberg Amendment in 1989, which made religion the cornerstone of Soviet refugee policy and extended the benefits Soviet Jews had already received to Evangelical Christian, Ukrainian Catholic, and Ukrainian Orthodox believers. Those people affiliated with any of these denominations who could demonstrate "well established histories of persecution" under the Soviet regime became eligible to emigrate to the United States as refugees if they had family ties or some other form of sponsorship in the United States. Notably, they were not required to prove fear of *future* persecution; *past* membership in a persecuted religious group would suffice. That U.S. emigration policy recognized persecution in the USSR of a mainly religious nature speaks volumes about the priorities of governance here.

Cold War tensions partially explain the preferential treatment Soviet citizens received along with the fact that they are Caucasian, of Judeo-Christian background, and are usually educated or skilled. Approximately five hundred thousand Soviet evangelicals have immigrated to the United

States, some as refugees, others through family reunification. The strong geopolitical implications of Soviet refugee resettlement remove it from the traditional academic rubric that frequently considers refugees and migration in tandem with issues of development. From 1945 to 1991, U.S. policies toward Soviet refugees were clearly a function of foreign policy interests that played out against the backdrop of the Cold War. For Americans, defections from the socialist Soviet Union to the capitalist United States were a reaffirmation of the righteousness of the West's economic and political systems in spite of its social ills and shortcomings. For Soviet citizens, emigration had other, equally significant politicized meanings. It was an emphatic rejection of the Soviet system, one of the few possible forms of overt political protest that evangelicals in the Soviet Union ever engaged in. In other words, the adversarial relationship that certain groups had to Soviet authorities ensured that the U.S. government would view them favorably. Given the vibrancy of religious life in this country compared to other Western democracies, it is perhaps not surprising that groups from the Soviet Union who sought to emigrate in the name of religious freedom were preferentially selected for refugee status by U.S. lawmakers.

Refugees from the former Soviet Union provide a particularly dramatic example of what a state must do to curtail outmigration and of the degree to which a receiving society, in this case the United States, has shaped the geography of migration by selectively accelerating the inflow of refugees from certain areas of the world and grinding others to a halt. By extension, emigration from the Soviet Union illustrates the compromised agency of individual refugees in determining equal treatment from state bureaucracies. Foreign policy priorities created the political possibility to emigrate and social institutions, in this case religious institutions, eased the settlement process for refugees.

For Soviet believers, 1989 proved to be a historic juncture: remarkably, the Soviet Union was willing to let evangelical believers go, and the United States was willing to let them in. The political liberalizations that occurred in the USSR in the late 1980s, while welcome, had a sharp negative impact on all sectors of the economy. Nearly all Soviet citizens saw their standard of living plummet, which led to "instability emigration," a desire to escape the economic chaos of the so-called transition to capitalism. In addition to economic decline, other linkages with the United States were occurring at this time, and they stimulated a desire to emigrate. A barrage of American missionaries promising salvation arrived in Ukraine, right alongside American media and popular culture displaying images of glamour and wealth and American multinational corporations offering a plethora of longed-for consumer goods. They served as magnets, as cultural bridges, transporting Soviet citizens from the "proletarian paradise" to the perceived land of milk and honey. These bridges fostered the illusion of familiarity and fed the desire to emigrate.

The approximately five hundred thousand Soviet evangelicals who relocated to the United States became members of transnational, linguistically based religious communities committed to missionizing in the former Soviet Union and beyond.[1] These communities illustrate several dynamics that are relevant for evangelical life in Ukraine as well as for global Christianity more generally. First, the rapid and massive exodus of longstanding evangelical believers that began in 1989 occurred at a critical juncture of religious revival in Ukraine. Just as it was becoming possible to create religious communities legally, to "harvest" new converts from among the many religious seekers, the majority of clergy and established believers emigrated. This was additional motivation for foreign missionaries to travel to the former Soviet Union to "plant" churches and to respond to the quests of the "unsaved" by imparting *their* understandings of evangelical practice.

Second, it became inherently difficult to maintain the inward-looking, highly conservative, ascetic religious practices that developed in part as a specific reaction to Soviet rule after longstanding believers left in droves and massive political and economic changes altered the contours of religious life. It was not any easier for believers to maintain these practices after they relocated to the United States and confronted consumerism, the pressure to make money, and a vibrant religious marketplace that mandated that churches compete to retain membership, a dynamic fully unknown in the Soviet Union. Marketplace dynamics exerted considerable pressure to compromise with youth, who suddenly had the ever-present option of joining an American evangelical church that does not mandate such strict moral asceticism. The ease and rapidity with which Ukrainian evangelicals can potentially adapt to American mainstream culture bespeaks the degree to which difference is racialized in the United States. As white Europeans and members of religious denominations that are considered indigenous, Ukrainians face few barriers to assimilation. Each successive generation always has the choice between continued membership in an ethnic congregation or new membership in an American one. Membership in an ethnic religious organization can both facilitate ethnic identity retention and serve as a bridge to assimilation in mainstream American society.

Third, religious-based networks placed Soviet evangelicals in a transnational field of believers, which shaped the attachments that developed to Ukraine and to the former Soviet Union more generally. These communities are actively involved in missionizing in the former Soviet Union and are committed to providing charitable assistance to Ukraine. Indeed, this is one of the distinguishing features that separate them from American evangelical churches. Scholars have explored how "long-distance nationalism" ties immigrants to vibrant networks and political projects in their homeland.[2] Little research has been done, however, on how immigrant congregations connect believers to transnational communities that are active on a global scale.[3]

## Instability Emigration

Prior to the closing of the Soviet borders in 1926, the first wave of emigration sent Jews; Mennonites; believers from various offshoots of Orthodoxy, such as the Dukhobors and Molokans; and political dissidents to North America and beyond to escape poverty, discrimination, and political repression. The 1940s saw another wave of emigration when the approximately 7.2 million refugees from the Soviet Union were displaced by World War II. People from regions not part of the USSR as of 1939, but later annexed, automatically qualified as displaced persons. Ukrainians from eastern Ukraine were confronted with a policy that categorized them as "Soviet" and mandated forced repatriation to their "homeland," the Soviet Union. These refugees fought to gain recognition as a persecuted Ukrainian minority subject to cultural Russification via eradication of their language, ideological Sovietization, and official state policies of atheism that were particularly punishing to practitioners of Ukrainian churches because of their supposed nationalist agendas and subversive political activity. Of the four hundred thousand people admitted to the United States under the Displaced Persons Act between 1947 and 1955, about eighty thousand were Ukrainian, and most were Ukrainian-speaking Catholics.[4] The Protestant DPs among them joined established communities of Slavic Protestants created during earlier waves of immigration. By 1967 there were some fifty thousand Ukrainian Protestants in the United States, united in two specifically Ukrainian associations, the Ukrainian Evangelical Baptist Convention and the Ukrainian Evangelical Alliance, or in one of several Slavic evangelical unions.

Another wave of immigration came just as the Soviet Union was collapsing. The Russian-speaking population in the United States surged to over four million, with residential concentrations in northeast urban centers, including Philadelphia. After Vietnamese and Chinese, Ukrainians are the next largest immigrant group in Philadelphia. The combined total of Ukrainians and Russians, which tops fifty thousand, represents the single largest foreign-born population in the city.[5]

Ukraine's former statelessness and its position as a "borderland," a buffer zone wedged between larger states and empires, have dramatically affected the process of emigration and resettlement. In the first half of the twentieth century, immigration officials sometimes misidentified Ukrainians as Russians, Austrians, or Poles, and Ukrainians themselves tended to self-identify in religious or regional terms to compensate for the disjuncture between their perceived and their assigned identities.[6] Ukrainians were often—and to this day sometimes still are—labeled "Russians," reflecting the widespread misconception among Americans that the multinational Soviet Union was a monolithically Russian state.

Much like the blanket designations "Hispanic" or "Asian," "Russian" becomes a projection of general regional origin and linguistic ability that creates the illusion of perceived cultural commonality among Soviet refugees where perhaps little existed prior to migration. Émigrés might have come from a non-Russian republic and Russian might not have even been their first language, but the imperial identity and its related cultural attributes become highlighted when one moves abroad. The waves of refugees from Soviet Ukraine, therefore, embody the wounds of colonialism after decades of non-assimilation to a Russified Soviet ideal and illustrate the ramifications of having been a stateless people for so long.

National and ethnic designations are the least meaningful to evangelicals. Aside from religion, they self-define by language and geographic origin. They consciously form religious communities that present themselves as "Ukrainian-speaking," "Russian-speaking" or "Slavic," this last a homogenizing label that encompasses the various geographic origins and multilingual abilities of members. When congregations privilege use of the Russian language, they can incorporate other immigrants from the former Soviet Union—often the first targets of proselytizing. Language reinforces the "ethnic" nature of congregational life and becomes the basis upon which refugee churches forge ties with each other.[7] Where there is a higher density of evangelical refugees from Ukraine, such as in Sacramento, congregations adopt informal names to reflect the specific city or region of origin of their members, such as "Lvivska." There were fewer evangelicals in Kharkiv than in many other Soviet cities and they have not settled in such a geographically concentrated way to have created a "Kharkivska" community in Philadelphia or elsewhere.

In contrast to all previous waves of emigration, the last Soviet refugees were the first who could entertain the prospect of returning home, temporarily or permanently, and of maintaining contacts with family and friends. Yet, virtually no one practices "flexible citizenship," as Aihwa Ong documents the Chinese capitalizing on twofold economic and residential opportunities.[8] Nearly all aspired to become American, to bring their entire multigenerational family to live permanently in America. Paradoxically, the new possibilities for retaining ties to Ukraine, combined with heightened consumer expectations, played a key role in stimulating outmigration in all its forms.[9]

## A Moveable Feast: Distinguishing Features of the Last Wave

Across America in the 1990s, communities of Soviet evangelicals sprang up in residentially compact clusters of families and believers united around churches. This last wave of refugees from Soviet Ukraine, compared to the three waves that preceded them and other immigrant groups more generally, has lost extraordinarily little in the process of relocating, prompting a Jewish émigré to claim enviously that evangelicals have a "moveable feast."[10] Highly favorable emigration policies have allowed nearly the entire membership of many Soviet congregations to relocate rapidly to the Pacific Northwest, to traditional Ukrainian immigrant communities in Pennsylvania, and to mid-sized American cities not formerly noted for their receptivity to immigrants.[11] Their tight webs of family, residential, and communal networks, formed in response to the hostile conditions of life in the USSR, offer a continuum of meaningful social relationships, even after emigration.

The earliest evangelical refugees had no relatives in the United States, making it necessary for organizations, such as American Baptist Church, the Southern Baptist Convention, or Lutheran Social Services to sponsor these "free cases." These religious organizations, in conjunction with individual congregations, assumed responsibility for the resettlement of refugee families. These intermediary organizations play a critical role in organizing assistance to newly arrived families and therefore direct immigrants to a particular area and divert them from others. The pivotal position of these denominational organizations also reveals why evangelical believers have become concentrated in several cities, such as Sacramento, Portland, and Seattle, as well as in several states, such as Pennsylvania. In each instance, these communities would never have grown had it not been for such sponsoring church organizations. After 1992, immigration regulations changed, and emigrants were obliged to have some family connection in the United States. Congregations became clusters of residential and familial networks as local churches helped families who were in the United States to sponsor their relatives under the Family Reunification Act.

Given the low incomes and large families evangelicals usually have, they qualify for extensive state assistance, as they did in the Soviet Union. Clergy and informed networks of family and friends quickly help recent arrivals learn of government programs to help the working poor. Acquainting new non-evangelical immigrants with such services becomes a point of contact with secular immigrants, a means of exposing them to the congregation, demonstrating the usefulness of church affiliation, and creating debt obligations. Indeed, the Southern Baptist Convention sponsors a Ukrainian pastor in the Philadelphia area, whose specific job is to develop ethnic congregations. He helps immigrants from Ukraine who have no religious affiliation resettle by providing services, counsel, and other assistance they need. In this way, American religious-based social services and ethnic evangelical congregations make religion and congregational life a fundamental part of the arrival and resettlement experience.

Theologically, evangelicals from the former Soviet Union have much in common with conservative American evangelicals. Essentially, it is the interpretation of evangelical worship that has its roots in Soviet culture as well as the historical experience of being a believer in a hostile society that sets them apart.[12] The single most distinctive factor of Soviet evangelical practice is "legalism," or the extensive restrictions on gendered behavior that are surveyed and sanctioned by a hierarchical chain of authority in the name of faith and justified by biblical citations. These restrictions are primarily oriented toward maintaining tight group solidarity and firmly demarcating the group from the world. The more traditional Soviet evangelicals disavow political participation of any kind in the United States, including community organizations, school organizations, or neighborhood associations.[13]

Virtually no one I interviewed regrets the decision to emigrate. Simply put, their biggest problem is language. In addition to complicating the process of finding work, it is no longer possible to missionize. As one pastor flatly said, "We understand that the central aim of our church is evangelization." The old practices of going to prisons and orphanages, visiting the elderly, and traveling from village to village singing psalms and spreading the Gospel have come to an end. It is a bitter irony for them that language has created a barrier against proselytizing far more insurmountable than any the Soviet state could erect. Limited English-language ability among the first generation fuels a mission orientation to the homeland and helps maintain the "ethnic" nature of the community.

The arrival of Soviet evangelicals reintroduces the working-class nature of Soviet emigration. Most early twentieth-century immigrants were relatively uneducated and worked in manual-labor jobs in the United States. Refugees who arrived after World War II were often from agrarian regions and had few other skills. The robust nature of the U.S. economy allowed most of them to attain middle-class status. Jewish émigrés who arrived beginning in the late 1970s were motivated by greater educational and professional opportunities.[14] Given their educational backgrounds and professional skills, once they were out of the Soviet Union, they rapidly became part of the transnational professional class, staffing universities, laboratories, and offices around the world. In contrast, evangelicals knew that their prospects of pursuing higher education or of holding a job with significant responsibility in the USSR were limited. The ideological components of education served as disincentives for evangelicals to encourage their children to pursue specialized study. As a result, successive generations internalized modest educational and employment aspirations. Arriving in a new country without language and other skills does little to raise those aspirations.

Today, many evangelical men begin working in construction brigades for companies that were started by a handful of Russian-speaking evangelical entrepreneurs and sometimes work for other entrepreneurs from the former USSR.[15] Especially in the beginning, women tend to be employed in minimum-wage jobs as chambermaids in hotels, kitchen staff in restaurants, or housecleaners or babysitters in private homes, although many hope these jobs will be a stepping stone to better ones. The minimal commitment of women to a fixed work schedule leaves them free to fulfill their church obligations, which include attending at least one of the three services offered each week, each of which lasts for two hours or more. Children are usually involved in a roster of church-related activities: youth choirs, youth groups, youth group exchanges with other émigré congregations, and missionary and other charitable work.

Religion, class, education, and the embrace of different political agendas for Ukraine (or perhaps none at all) distance evangelical refugees from previous waves. This alienation develops even though the majority of refugees from each wave have been from Ukraine and speak or at least understand common languages. The commonality of their shared experiences of Soviet socialism are overridden by the importance of religious affiliation. This, in turn, informs the rapport they maintain with family and coreligionists in

Ukraine and lays the groundwork for the types of the communities they create after emigration.

Two communities in Philadelphia, both established by immigrants and refugees who settled prior to 1989, and a rural community illustrate this fragmentation and show the diverse transnational fields of which religious communities have become a fundamental part. Each of the three congregations profiled below is ethnically and linguistically mixed, although a significant proportion of each membership comes from Ukraine. They have labeled themselves differently: Russian, Slavic, and Ukrainian to signal their different orientations to Ukraine and to other believers from the former Soviet Union.

## Russian Baptists: The Amish as a Model

In 1988, a Soviet evangelical congregation took root in a rural area in the foothills of the Appalachian Mountains in central Pennsylvania. Nearly two thousand Baptists from the former Soviet Union have settled among a population of about forty thousand over a decade, radically altering the delivery of social, medical, and educational services in the county. The origin of the community is striking for its whimsical character. One man, a multigenerational Baptist with the biblical name of Ruvim, had a vision in 1986 that the Soviet Union would fall apart and that all of its believers would leave. Understanding this exodus to be imminent, he decided to leave as "one of the first, rather than as one of the last."

His parents had Baptist friends who had emigrated to the United States in 1929, a year of sharp repressions against all religious denominations in the Soviet Union. The daughter of this couple visited Moscow twice in the 1970s and Kazakhstan once as well. Ruvim never met her, but she left her address with mutual acquaintances. By the 1980s, Ruvim was a disabled worker in Kazakhstan who was preaching full-time with five married children. After his vision, as he traveled about evangelizing, he mailed two letters from fifteen different cities to the daughter of his parents' friends. She received one of the thirty letters, and thus the emigration process began. In 1988 Soviet authorities granted permission for Ruvim and his wife and the families of three of their children to leave. They traveled from Almaty via Moscow, Vienna, and Rome, eventually landing in Pennsylvania, where this woman lived and where Ruvim and his relatives have remained ever since.

Once settled, Ruvim began preparing papers for his remaining children and their families to emigrate. Those who married into the initial families that emigrated also began the process of helping their relatives emigrate,

Figure 3.1: Baptismal ceremony in rural Pennsylvania. Photo by the author.

who then sponsored other relatives, and so on in a chain of emigration. From a single friendship formed in the 1920s and one man's vision, the central Pennsylvanian foothills of the Appalachians became an area of Soviet Baptist settlement.[16]

This community is made up of various nationalities, although most members are from Kazakhstan and Ukraine. Few are actually from Russia, but members of the surrounding community refer to them as Russians and they refer to their church as a "Russian Baptist" congregation. Much as Soviet leaders intended, the lingua franca is indeed Russian, even though a linguistic swirl of English, Russian, Ukrainian and *surzhyk,* a creole mixture of Russian and Ukrainian, can be heard.[17] The only languages that are formally used are Russian and, on a limited basis, English. The importance of nationality has receded in favor of a religious identity. They relate openly to Baptist immigrants from other parts of the former Soviet Union and easily incorporate new arrivals into their community. Family ties and generation are important factors that shape with whom one will interact and to whom one can turn for help. The pull of family ties and the necessity to pool resources along family lines means that there is an informal breakdown in immigrant congregations along republic of origin. Soviet residence restrictions led to limited mobility and to large extended families usually living in close proximity to one another. However, there is little attempt to unite Ukrainians with other Ukrainians or to form a bloc of members from a particular republic or city.

When I first began studying this community in 1998, very few of the parents, and almost none of the grandparents, spoke any English. They were educationally ill-equipped to learn a foreign language and had access to almost no ESL services. The parental generation struggled mightily to learn enough English to be gainfully employed, whereas the older generation aspired to learn enough English to pass the citizenship exam. The older generation had no plans to work or to socialize with anyone other than fellow Russian-speaking believers.

One older man, a Ukrainian who lived for many years in Kazakhstan and now considers himself Russian, claimed that the Amish, many of whom live in close proximity to Soviet Baptists, are a model for his community to emulate. The ability of the Amish to preserve a distinct religious and cultural identity while surrounded by mainstream society is, he felt, exemplary. Indeed, many Baptists frequent Amish businesses and farms for produce and other goods. He explains his choice of model as follows:

> This is not the first wave of Russian immigration. And where are those Russians? Why have the Amish been able to keep their culture? We are not trying to assimilate to American society. No, to the contrary, we want to keep our language, traditions, habits, and culture. We do a lot to maintain them. We teach our children, we hire teachers, both Baptist and non-Baptist, to help them with Russian and to teach them our history. You're interested in how we could maintain our faith during Soviet times. But you won't understand. We survived with the help of God. My mother always said, "Only by looking at the children and serving God could I survive. Otherwise it would have been easier to just sit down and fold my arms."[18]

In other words, the familiar cultural practices of isolationism and suspicion of people "from the world" so long honed in the Soviet Union should now be harnessed to insulate themselves from the secularism and non-Russianness surrounding them. The old reaction of retreat, he reasons, will once again allow them to survive. And he is not alone, especially in his generation. Although this was the dominant sentiment in this community when I began this research, it had waned considerably when I finished in 2005; indeed, it was considered outright ridiculous by younger people. Several factors that do not affect the Amish served to soften the advocacy of isolationism and led to doubts as to whether the Amish were really a viable model after all.

First, a key difference between the lives of evangelicals in the USSR and in the United States is that it is possible to openly evangelize here; this is the primary argument made by younger members of the community against this engrained ethos of disengagement from the world and in favor of English-language outreach. The Amish, of course, simply rely on high birth rates to grow their communities, a strategy that has been successful to date. There are few in this community who continue the Soviet evangelical tradition of having "as many children as God gives"; not many families have more than three children.

Second, the impediments to pursuing higher education and job opportunities in the United States seem less insurmountable than in the USSR. Whereas the Amish have their children in special schools and are not obliged to pursue education beyond the eighth grade, nearly all parents in this community express a clear commitment to having their children receive a university education. Lack of financing, early marriages followed by children and other factors do not always make this feasible. Nonetheless, that education is endorsed as a goal—and one that clearly mandates knowledge of English—integrates first- and especially second-generation immigrants squarely into mainstream American society.

Third, the lure of shopping and the acquisition of "status symbol" material goods are further incentives to assimilate, and the Russian Baptists have far more exposure to American consumerism than the Amish do. By 2005, most members of the parental generation were speaking some English. Their progress was inversely related to the Russian-language ability of adolescent or young adults. A wide linguistic gulf was already forming between monolingual Slavic grandparents and their Americanized monolingual grandchildren.

## Signs of Strain

There are at least four former pastors among the members of this community, and the issue perennially arose as to whether the church should split into a second community, even a third, to accommodate preferences for

Soviet-era traditions. Some advocated division as a means to prioritize missionizing in the former USSR, financed by simply renting space from American congregations and forgoing the construction of their own church building. Renting involved compromise, such as tolerating the drum set the other group used during their services, which was totally anathema to a Soviet understanding of sacred music. Those opposed to division countered that for children, it is far better to have a single large community with its own church building that can offer a spectrum of activities, friends, and potential mates, even if it means reducing the amount of assistance they can send back to the former USSR.

The issue was resolved when three members of the community agreed to sign the bill of sale for a parcel of land. After several years of collecting fifteen hundred dollars from each member of the church toward the construction of a new facility, they broke ground in 2003. With the members themselves building the church during their free time, they completed a vast starlike structure in 2005 that seated one thousand. In this way, they indirectly reaffirmed their commitment to a future in the United States by subordinating evangelizing and missionizing in the former Soviet Union to solidifying their community in the United States.

Other issues chiseled away at Soviet-era values. Strains were visible each time they were obliged to reevaluate accepted practices in light of the new circumstances they confronted in the United States. For example, a woman was excommunicated when she left her husband and five children to be with an American man "of the world." Her former husband remarried another member of the church whose husband had died. They are now expecting their eighth child in their new family. Virtually no one recognized divorce, and many frowned on remarriage. So some objected to their continued attendance, and especially membership, in the church. They feared that such laxity would compromise the totalizing, eternal commitment they understood marriage to be.

In another instance, a woman left her husband because he had been beating her. In spite of their belief in nonviolence, adulterous betrayal is the only recognized grounds for dissolving a marriage. No other reasons are permissible. In the Soviet Union, domestic violence was a private affair, something a woman had to grapple with alone, if she could. But once in America, this woman involved the police. She sought counsel and shelter at a women's center that also arranged for free legal services. Her teenage children, influenced by American values and an Americanized sense of entitlement, encouraged her to leave their father in spite of the pastor's repeated efforts to keep the family together. His actions are against civic law, and her actions are against church law. Another kind of judgment day will present itself when the community votes on who will be allowed to retain church membership and who will be excommunicated.

Evangelicals in Soviet Ukraine were mostly pacifists and usually fulfilled mandatory military service by serving in special brigades that did not carry weapons. In America, several young men from this community voluntarily joined the armed forces as a means of receiving a higher education. When I asked one of their parents whether their son serves with weapons, they sheepishly said, "We don't know." I suspect that they do know. Reversing a commitment to pacifism and turning to the army as an *enabling* institution to obtain higher education is a controversial idea within the community.

## Missionizing in Ukraine

Even as the ethos of the community Americanizes by relaxing the long list of behavioral prescriptions, a mission orientation to the "homeland," broadly understood as the former Soviet Union, helps maintain the "Russianness" of the community and hold at bay the permissiveness of Americans, even of American Baptists. Extensive indirect missionizing occurs as the church sponsors two missionaries and annual youth mission trips to the former Soviet Union, usually to Ukraine or Belarus, and provides humanitarian aid to the needy in Ukraine. Two women with ties to Zaporizhzhia, an eastern Ukrainian city, organize bimonthly shipments of two or three tons of clothing, toys, food products, and other items to orphanages, boarding schools, and congregations. Gathering donated goods, organizing them, packing them, documenting everything for customs, and arranging for the goods to be trucked to Philadelphia, placed in a container, loaded onto a ship, sent to Ukraine, and distributed throughout villages in twelve oblasts is a colossal undertaking. On the Ukrainian side the job is no less monumental. A small group of women in Zaporizhzhia provide close supervision of the distribution to the intended recipients to avoid seeing the goods end up for sale at some sidewalk bazaar. Relying on informal, local assessments of which families and institutions are in need, a small group of women on both sides of the ocean manage to deliver literally tons of aid directly to the needy, independent of their religious affiliation.[19] These shipments go exclusively to Ukraine for two reasons: they graft onto preexisting informal networks that are highly efficient, and the Ukrainian government is one of the few in Eurasia that allows Protestant denominations to deliver humanitarian aid directly. These immigrants have simply reoriented their evangelical efforts to the former USSR with the same zeal.

Now that they have their own building, the members of this community have become more rooted in America. As they have become more financially secure, they have indeed attained the material comforts they had originally sought in emigrating. Even if they were rapidly dissuaded from their original embrace of the Amish as a model for the future of their ethno-religious community, I see no signs of abatement in their attachments to the former Soviet Union, which take the forms of missionizing, charitable, and other outreach activities. The emerging religious marketplace in Ukraine, with its comparatively few legal restrictions, plus the personal networks of these members suggests that the era of closed, isolated communities has indeed come to an end. In its place has emerged an active transnational social field of believers that is connected to both a country of origin and an adopted country via religious commitments to evangelize.

## The Slavic Baptist Church: Assimilating to Stay Ethnic

The modest white sign in the front yard of the brick Methodist church in suburban northeast Philadelphia does little to suggest that the gathering of hundreds of citizens from the former Soviet Union is only the latest incarnation of a Slavic Baptist church of long standing. The Russian Baptist Church of Philadelphia was founded in 1912 by immigrants from the Russian Empire who worked in the burgeoning industries and ports of Philadelphia as both countries underwent enormous transformation. Some of its earliest members were converts from Orthodoxy.

Immigrants created the first Russian Baptist Church, but the second generation had some difficulty sustaining it. Its cyclical developments and continued dependence on immigrants for its existence is a fine example of the dynamics of assimilation at work in American society and the role that religion plays in them. The pressures of assimilation and job mobility gradually drained the concentration of Russian-speaking Baptist believers in the Philadelphia area. The tragedy of World War II nonetheless revived this congregation by providing a second wave of immigration. The quorum of believers that arrived after World War II not only reinvigorated ethnic churches but was also broad enough to accommodate even minority evangelical faiths and to cater to different language preferences with the advent of communities that billed themselves as Ukrainian-speaking, or this one, which was always Russian-speaking.

The Wilson Doctrine of national self-determination had validated the creation of new eastern European states on the basis of recognized nationality; the "affirmative action empire" that the Soviet Union had become had instilled a national consciousness in many of the refugees. The First Russian Baptist Church was obliged to redefine itself after World War II as a Russian-Ukrainian Baptist church in recognition of the multinational, multilingual nature of its membership. The church was located on Roosevelt Avenue and Seventh Street; thanks to the post-1945 wave of refugees, it had over 150 members. A highly active Russian-speaking pastor served the congregation for thirty years until 1974.

They had considerable difficulty finding a replacement, eventually finding a retired pastor who led the church until he was eighty-three. He was the son of Russian immigrants but had always worked in an American Baptist church. He led services in English for the dwindling number of second-generation members of the First Russian-Ukrainian Baptist Church.

Nelly was a member of this church at that time. She was born into a Ukrainian family in Cheliabinsk, Russia, and lived in Germany in a Displaced Persons camp for three years after World War II before emigrating to Brazil. After four years in Brazil, a member of this church sponsored her family to come to the United States in 1958. She recalled that they did away with the male choir because the membership had so declined. With fewer and fewer children, eventually there was no need for Sunday school. Then the general choir disbanded too. There were many issues discouraging continued membership and allegiance to this church. First, the ethnic character of the neighborhood had become Hispanic. The remaining members lived elsewhere and were obliged to travel. Social mobility, the search for professional opportunities, and the overall white flight to the suburbs prompted residential relocation. The members of the second generation spoke English, married non-Slavs, and always had the option of joining an American church. Her own family illustrates the dilemmas of accommodating the needs of a multigenerational family. Nelly speaks Russian with her parents, Ukrainian with her husband, and English with her children. English has become the language of prayer for her, reflecting the degree to which she now thinks in English. As her children grew older, they switched to American churches.

The church was down to twenty-six official members, with only fifteen attending regularly. Most spoke only English; many were elderly. In 1990 they sold their church building and the English-speaking First Russian-Ukrainian Baptist Church became a Hispanic Pentecostal congregation.

When the last wave of Soviet refugees began to arrive in the United States, there was no longer a single Russian-language evangelical church in Philadelphia.

That same year, two young brothers arrived from Moldova; one of them enrolled in a Baptist seminary in the United States and trained to be a pastor. Thanks to his bicultural education, bilingual abilities, and awareness of the history of this church, Sasha, as most people call him, has remained acutely aware of the perils of depending on new waves of immigrants to keep the congregation alive, and that has affected the direction in which he leads this community. He explains his vision for the future:

> When the members of the church asked me to be the leader, of course, a very serious question was before us: what should we do next? We understood that in reality if we don't do anything, the Russian church will close. There will no longer be a Slavic church. With prayers, we asked God to give us a vision as to what we should do.[20]

One of Sasha's first steps was to relocate the church to one of the many "Russian" neighborhoods of northeast Philadelphia, where large numbers of immigrants from the former Soviet Union live. About twenty people joined him at the new location. At the same time that he reinforced the ethnic nature of the church community by relocating it, Sasha also took the bold step of embracing "Americanizing tendencies" and maintained the partial use of English during the Sunday morning services (Russian is used exclusively in the Sunday evening services). To this day, several of the oldest members of the English-speaking Slavic congregation follow the service through headphones in simultaneous translation. Other members, such as Nelly, who were fluent in both Russian and English, began to teach English as part of the Sunday school curriculum to children. The pastor explains how these decisions relate to his solution to assimilation, the single biggest threat to Slavic churches:

> Most of the kids that grow up in this church have an American worldview. But Russian churches have the tendency to limit themselves by insisting on Russian culture. To a degree, this pushes our children away because the Russians want, [correcting himself] the Slavs want to be with other Slavs. On the other hand, this discourages our children, who are already becoming American. For them, English is the mother tongue and American culture is their native culture. For older people, who will never be American, this pushes them away.

Accommodating the needs and desires for the communal and spiritual life of multigenerational families in a single institution can be challenging. This is the only post-Soviet immigrant church I have seen that consciously introduces aspects of American culture in English alongside modified Soviet-era Baptist traditions. When asked if this strategy has been successful, Sasha responds, "God began to bless our work, and God began to reveal himself in many peoples' lives, and many Russian speakers came to God." This is now the largest Russian-speaking church in Philadelphia, and immigrants are the main source of membership growth. Many members are from Moldova, as Sasha is, and others are from Ukraine. He explains how he recruited new members to his church from among the arriving refugees:

> There was only one place where they [refugees] could be and that was church, and in this place people understood them. It is a colossal job . . . finding free furniture, there's no money; you have to register the children for school, find doctors, sometimes pregnant women arrive or older people who are sick, you have to get them registered for medical help, fill out the papers for all the subsidies, find money to pay for an apartment and on and on. It's a huge amount of work, but we do it to help these families. We preach the Gospel and help the families that come here. And that's how the church grew. In the first four years, we had eighty members.

> But there were many people—a lot of them—who simply used us. They just thought, "Aha! You are believers. You must help. It's your duty." They used us and then they left or went away, but we just don't see them. A lot of other people tried to use our church as a means to emigrate. It used to be possible to file for political asylum from the U.S. Some people came to me, proposed money, because they were clearly not believers but wanted to get political refugee status. They tried to find out how to do this, what papers are needed from the church, or they "became" some kind of believer to become a refugee. It's a colossal job, and I can tell you that working with immigrants is entirely different than working among believers in a Baptist church in Russia or Ukraine.

The strategy of assisting and courting new immigrants has worked. There are now approximately 240 official members of the church, not counting children. The church holds 450 and they always have to bring in extra seats. With no church office or paid staff, organizing the various programs to serve the needs of members, old and new, is particularly challenging. Still, they manage to work around the schedule of the Methodists, from whom they rent space, to organize a Sunday school, youth groups, choirs, Bible study groups, and the missionizing and outreach activities of an evangelization council. They are also attempting to organize their own borrowing library with books, films, and music. Sasha details how he envisions new undertakings:

> What kind of future does our church have? I think the future of the church lies in the fact that we must find the means to serve different groups of people. First, we must continue to do what we are doing— serving the Russian people. The future of our church, on a spiritual level, is to find a way to serve the youth of the second generation of immigrants. If we don't do that, then our church will be in the same situation that it was two times before. That's why we have to find options, forms of assimilation. Otherwise there will not be a future for this church. Unfortunately, only a few Russian churches understand this. Lots of churches that are being organized now, who haven't lived through what we have, don't understand this. They have entirely different priorities, but in thirty years they will have to face it. You've been to our church and to many others. You've seen the differences in services, in the style, in the sermons. We are much more Americanized even though we have a lot of Russians and use Russian language. . . . We do it so that people will come. We don't want to be one of those, you know, build a fence around ourselves and say, "We're Russians. We're this, this, and this." By making these changes, we're already addressing the problems of the future.

Notice that Sasha continually refers to "Russians" and "the Russian people" even though only a small percentage of the membership is actually from Russia. The majority are from Moldova or Ukraine. Yet this pastor has adopted the American projection that immigrants from the Soviet Union are "Russian" because they use the Russian language to unify the otherwise multilingual abilities of the membership.

As perhaps might be expected of a church founded in 1912, this church is more oriented toward missionary work in their neighborhood among the fifty thousand Russian-speakers in the Philadelphia area, only 5 percent of whom are Baptists or Pentecostals. They rely heavily on personal invitations from friends and neighbors to attend services and other church activities, which is the primary strategy for garnering converts used by evangelicals in Ukraine today.[21] For some, an invitation to church might be accompanied by a separate invitation to tea or dinner, where a small group of members of the church will speak to the potential convert about God, faith, and congregational life. Most people who convert after they have emigrated do so because they know someone who introduced them to a particular church community of which they wanted to be a part. The appeal of a certain theology, ritual, or some other denominational specificity is usually secondary. So far, the pastor concedes, the arrival of already converted immigrants from the former Soviet Union is a far more meaningful source of membership than missionary efforts in the United States among non-affiliated Russian-speakers. Only two people from nominally Orthodox backgrounds have converted and joined this church after having immigrated to the United States.

Of the seven Ukrainian- or Russian-speaking Baptist churches in the Philadelphia area, this is the only one associated with the American Baptist Church. Four of the others are connected with the Southern Baptist Convention, and the remaining ones do not have any union affiliation. All six Pentecostal Russian- or Ukrainian-language churches in Philadelphia are independent. Sasha prefers to attend conferences organized by American religious organizations, rather than one of the several Slavic Baptist unions.

Evidence of "Americanizing tendencies" in this community is manifest in the conscious decision to relax the legalism engendered in Soviet evangelical communities, or the "order" (Ukr./Rus. *poriadok*), as believers call it. Women are not obliged to cover their heads, although about half of the (mostly older) women do it anyway. Members are not forbidden to wear jewelry and makeup and, in general, people are more casually dressed. This pastor, like most American-trained clergy, consider the long list of rules governing behavior a "barrier," whereas most Soviet believers consider them an actualization of their faith, part of the witness as to how their faith has affected and improved their lives and made them moral people.

The relaxation of behavioral prescriptions is accompanied by a different hierarchical structure and delegation of authority. In a significant break with inherited tradition, this church has a "pastor service" (Rus. *pastorskoe sluzhenie*), meaning that the head pastor plays a much more prominent role in the service than he did in the USSR, where the pastor was usually one of three or four men who would preach during any given service. Ironically, pastors at more traditional churches have a much smaller role during services, but overall wield more authority than their counterparts at "Americanized" churches, where services are led by a single pastor.

Soviet-era evangelical congregations made decisions concerning congregational life, finances, and cases of excommunication after an open discussion and vote by the entire membership, either during or following a service. Although the open forum had the advantage of presenting a seemingly democratic, egalitarian attitude toward all members, it often stretched a two-hour service into four hours. Smaller, older congregations in Ukraine today and the more traditional immigrant congregations maintain this tradition. This "Americanizing" church, however, delegates all organizational, financial, and logistical matters to a church council (Rus. *tserkovnyi sovet*). The entire membership is consulted only in extraordinary circumstances.

Any member can be elected to the church council and play an advisory role in congregational life. In more traditional churches, only pastors, deacons, or other male church leaders can assume positions of authority in a fraternal council.

To keep the interest of the younger members of the community, this church has broken with the norm of using only an organ and choirs. They have introduced more contemporary music, using electric guitars and other instruments to alter the tone and ambiance of the service. To underline the unity of the congregation, at communion this church follows the common American Protestant custom by asking all members to receive communion at the same time, not individually, one after the other, as they do in Ukraine.

## Uneasy Accommodation

For some, this church's Americanizing tendencies give it too little "order." For others, it is not American enough. Whereas the Russian Baptist church attempted to isolate its members from the greater American society while maintaining many vibrant connections to Ukraine, the dynamic at play at this Slavic Church for the new arrivals is exactly the opposite. Liuba is forty-seven years old and emigrated to the United States in 1990 with her husband and two children. Her biography illustrates the complications of navigating worldly as well as cultural divides. She is a Ukrainian who speaks Russian with her children and Ukrainian with her parents. She was born in Ukraine, was partially raised in Kazakhstan, and lived in Kishinev, the capital of Moldova, for the last fourteen years before emigrating. In Moldova she attended a church that shared space with Pentecostals and had a multinational, multilingual membership, although Russian was used during services.

Her family had no relatives in the United States, so the Ukrainian Baptist church in Philadelphia sponsored them. They met her family and two other families, thirteen people in total, at Kennedy Airport and arranged housing for them all. Liuba and her family were members of the Ukrainian Baptist church for eight years. They switched to the Russian-language Slavic church when her daughter married a Russian-speaking Ukrainian who wanted to continue attending his church. When her daughter switched her membership to accommodate her husband, Liuba switched to accommodate her daughter, and her parents switched to accommodate her. She explains that the change was not difficult to make:

> You know, it's a purely Ukrainian church and, how can I tell you, in Ukraine, they looked at us a little strangely. As I told you, we have long noses and curly hair [that is, they look Jewish]. In Kazakhstan, they considered us Ukrainians because no one around us spoke Ukrainian. We came to Kishinev, Moldova, and we were Ukrainians among Moldovans. Here we went to the Ukrainian church, and they called us Moldovans. We're not Moldovans. . . . I consider myself a Ukrainian, although I've lived almost my whole life in other places.[22]

The mobility of Soviet society and the Russification of many regions of the USSR diluted her Ukrainianness in the eyes of other Ukrainians living abroad, albeit not in her own. It was her Ukrainian identity and residence in Moldova, however, that helped her adapt and feel at home in this Russian-speaking community.

Soon after her daughter had a child, this four-generation family was forced to make another decision. Her daughter objected to attending the Slavic Baptist Church because it lacked childcare facilities during the service, which most American churches have. Liuba's daughter graduated from an Ivy League university and is perfectly bilingual and bicultural. Liuba's daughter and her husband decided to switch to an American church, presenting a dilemma for Liuba. Her elderly parents, longtime Baptists, speak only Ukrainian and Russian and were not pleased with the Slavic Baptist Church. Her son does not speak Russian well, as he has been educated entirely in the United States. She would like to find a church that the entire four-generation family could attend, but finding a single institution that can accommodate her parents' ideas about the "order" one should find in church life, her children's ideas about convenience and choice, and her own need to belong to a group that will help her maintain connections to her Soviet past and American present, is a formidable challenge. She is not

entirely happy with the Americanized version of the church life she knew
in the Soviet Union that is available to her in Philadelphia:

> I don't want to say anything bad, only good. It's just that this
> church is different. This church is built around pastoral leadership
> and growth. We grew up in a church where everyone is a little part of
> the church, like an organism. We are used to feeling like a single or-
> ganism and to participating in all of the decisions of the church. At
> this church, there is a pastor and there are those who come [Rus.
> *prikhozhane*], to listen to what the pastor says. . . . We want to go
> somewhere where we will feel comfortable. For now we are still com-
> ing here once or twice a week. A problem for us is that we want to
> find a church where the whole family can go. We grew up in one
> church, and everyone in my family wants to find a church that we
> all can attend. We don't really want to go to an American church be-
> cause my parents don't know English. But there are American
> churches with older people, and they do a synchronic translation for
> them. That's a possibility. I don't know. We'll see.

She and her parents have begun to explore other options. She is now visiting a newly opened Russian-language church in Philadelphia that was
started with the sponsorship of a Ukrainian-language church in the suburbs and the Southern Baptist Convention, which is closer to home and
more old-world in style. Her bilingual, bicultural children have chosen
membership in an American church. Her parents clearly feel most comfortable in a traditional community that tries to maintain the practices they
were accustomed to in the USSR. So her generation, the one that took the
initiative to emigrate, becomes the pivotal one. She has the most difficulty
deciding where she belongs or where she would like to belong. Nearly all of
her friends are fellow believers. Splitting her time among work, family, and
church obligations, she finds that there is little time left for cultivating
other relationships, which means that there is a great deal at stake in the
choice of religious community. Returning to Moldova in 2002 did little to
clarify her thinking as to who she is and who she is becoming. After an absence of twelve years, she describes how she felt when she returned home:

> We understood how much we had changed over the years.
> Maybe people there changed too. But we understood that although
> we call ourselves "Russians" in America—everyone here is a Russian

whether they speak Russian or Ukrainian—there we understood that we are not as Russian as we think we are. We are already becoming assimilated [Rus. *slivaemsia*]. There's integration [using the English word]. This is nonetheless America. That means a melting pot [Rus. *plavil'nyi kotel*]. Whether you want it or not, slowly you will be . . . remade.

Ironically, after her trip to Moldova, she realized that it would be possible to join an American church. Re-immersing herself in her former life, even if only briefly, for the most part served to illustrate just how Americanized she had become. I have seen this happen many times to immigrants. Even though they surround themselves with people, communities, foods, media, and so on from the former Soviet Union, the processes of change and adaptation steadily progress. Although things seem to have stayed the same, often it takes a trip "home" to prove just how distant they have become from their former selves and just how many of the cultural norms not only have been forgotten but also have become impossible to relearn.

## The Ukrainian Baptist Church: Diasporic Dimensions of a Religious Community

The classical concept of diaspora has generally been linked with Jewish, and later Greek and Armenian, traditions and is used to evoke a group that has been subjected to some catastrophe resulting in forcible dispersion. In spite of the catastrophe, or perhaps because of it, the group maintains strong ties among ethnic kin and to the homeland, which is manifest, in William Safran's words, in a "political obligation, or the moral burden, of reconstituting a lost homeland or maintaining an endangered culture."[23] In his highly influential article, he argues that groups that were forcibly expelled not surprisingly tend to feel this moral burden to protect a threatened people, state, and culture more acutely than other diasporic groups. Indeed, the traumatic nature of displacement is a key distinguishing factor that sets the World War II wave of refugees apart from other refugees from Soviet Ukraine and contributes to their identification as a diaspora. This group, much more than most, has been reluctant to shed their "ethnic" identity in America.

Among the numerous displaced persons that arrived from Ukraine after World War II were Ukrainian Baptists from western Ukraine. They initially joined the Russian-language Slavic Baptist Church discussed earlier. The large number of Ukrainian speakers among this wave prompted seven Ukrainians to organize their own breakaway Ukrainian-language church. Although this church has diasporic roots, recent arrivals at the Ukrainian-language Baptist Church now constitute over half of the current 263 members of this church, and more than half of the seventy-five children and forty youth. The growth of its membership comes from two sources: children of members who become members and new immigrants. For the past five years, the church has steadily christened and added fifteen or so new members annually. I never went to this church without the main hall being so packed that parishioners spilled out into the standing-room places on the staircase leading up to the entrance. Over five hundred attend the service every Sunday morning.

The current pastor of this church emigrated to the United States in 1992 when the congregation had only about fifty members and became pastor in 1999. Like 45 percent of his membership, he is from L'viv in western Ukraine. Even though this congregation has been Ukrainian-speaking since its inception, the membership is nonetheless made up of Ukrainians, Russians, Belarussians, and Poles. As a general congregational rule, they resist translating Ukrainian sermons into English, but they will translate from English into Ukrainian when necessary. Already on Sunday mornings they feel compelled to introduce some English into the services to ensure that they remain meaningful to young people. One of the three or four preachers will preach in English with simultaneous Ukrainian translation provided.

On my initial visit to this church, the first preacher spoke in Russian, much to my amazement. I later learned that he is from Omsk, Russia, but is married to a Ukrainian-speaking Ukrainian from Poltava who wanted this to be the family church. Deacons who speak Russian as a first language and visiting preachers are allowed to preach in Russian. Sometimes poems are read or hymns are sung in Russian. The dicey linguistic politics of a nascent nation-state trying to shake its colonial past, even an ocean away, still remain. In the United States, any militancy on issues of language or politics more generally is frequently overridden by the ever-present priority to expand membership. Because of the "minority status" of Ukrainian, the pastor explains the church's position on language as follows:

> As Christians, we don't establish differences based on language. For us, it's not important. But nonetheless, we want to maintain our identity, our language, and our culture. We want to keep this alive on American soil. But when we have people who want to be members of

a Ukrainian church and they are preachers, we don't prohibit them. They speak in whichever language is their native one, in whichever language they can. Of course, we don't allow Ukrainians to preach in Russian, but Russians and Belarussians preach in their language.

In other words, the church is unquestionably national, without being nationalist. It is pro-Ukrainian without being anti-Russian. Language is the central feature that distinguishes it from other Baptist churches, and language forms the basis upon which they organize exchanges with other immigrant congregations and the basis upon which they structure missionary activity. They are less concerned about Russian-language encroachment because the most potent threat to the lifeblood of their communal identity comes from assimilatory tendencies to an Americanized English-speaking lifestyle rather than from preferences or pressure to Russify.

Beyond introducing limited preaching in English and Russian, the content of sermons is also changing in tandem with the ethos of communal life more generally. The pastor explains:

> The sermons are different in America from how they were in Ukraine. I don't know how they are now [in Ukraine], but I can say how they were before. Earlier when the pastors preached, we wanted to save believers from the influence of atheism, from the influence of that foreign ideology, so we taught them differently. Well, in America we don't have that. We preach more about the glorification of God and of Jesus Christ, about salvation, about bringing people to Christ. That's how our church is different from the churches in Ukraine. . . . In Ukraine we had more songs written in minor keys, whereas in America more are in major keys. As I said, when they persecuted us, when our parents, brothers, and sisters were in prisons, were thrown out of work, schools, and institutes, of course, our spirits were, well, like those of all the Ukrainian people. Ukrainians don't have many songs in major keys. With all that happened—the Ukrainian people were under such an authority—of course, the songs were like that and this influenced church culture. In America, songs are more light and joyful. They infuse hope and allow faith to lift a person up in ways that are different from those in Ukraine.

The familiar emphases on separating from a corrupted and corrupting world, on enduring suffering and apocalyptic visions of impending punishment for the unjust—these themes have softened in the United States.

There are, however, new "demons." More traditional evangelical churches, such as this one, are concerned about the growth of the charismatic movement in Ukraine, which is discussed in chapter 6, as well as among Slavic immigrants in the United States. Sometimes preachers point out the "doctrinal errors" of charismatic Christians to reaffirm the righteousness of their more ascetic style. Some of the newfound objections to a worldly life in America include sexual permissiveness and especially homosexuality. As voters, evangelicals from Ukraine are socially conservative, even single-issue voters when the topic is abortion or the definition of marriage. Yet their endorsement of pacifism and a positive role for government in alleviating social suffering, buttressed by their own occasional dependence on social service programs, leads them to reject many of the economic aspects of conservative agendas. They embody the influences of both Jerry Falwell's Moral Majority and Jim Wallis's Sojourners, making it difficult to characterize their politics categorically.

Especially in the minds of older believers, here, as elsewhere, there is a relaxation of the legalism, of the plethora of behavioral prohibitions and mandates, that so characterized membership and devotion in Soviet Ukraine. Members mention that this community, like nearly all others in the United States, offers a variety of structured children's programs, whereas very few congregations in Ukraine even have a formal education program because of financial restrictions. Dress still remains quite formal and modest, for men and women alike. Yet there is far less pressure for women to cover their heads, and as a result fewer do so. More disturbing to this pastor is the encroaching tendencies of women to wear makeup and jewelry. Under the influence of American consumerism, he fears, the withering away of modesty may be the first step toward abandoning the moral values of asceticism and self-control. In the same breath, he concedes the need to bend to certain American cultural practices concerning language, dress, and gender roles in order to grow their church membership and retain the second generation, which translates into a willingness to compromise.

## Outreach and Retention: Twin Challenges

Efforts to missionize in the United States are multifaceted and curtailed by many factors. Northeastern Philadelphia, the neighborhood where most immigrants from the Soviet Union have settled, is very suburban, even though it is technically part of the city. Public transportation is sporadic and often unreliable. Many women believers do not drive, which lead to constant problems of transportation. This problem is compounded by work demands that severely curtail the time available for church activities. As one member of this church said, "We have a lot of financial obligations. We have to work more at lower-paid jobs in order to earn enough to pay for the houses we buy, cars, education. We can't give as much attention as we should to our spiritual lives. But we came with suitcases, and as we stand on our own feet, we must begin to take care of others and to think about our neighbors. That's our Christian obligation, to help our neighbors." This man calls attention to a significant diversion for believers in the United States that was largely absent in the Soviet Union: consumerism. Once in the United States, buying things, traveling, acquiring big-ticket items like cars and appliances comes within reach, and most immigrants are eager to work to acquire them all.

This is why the pastor finds believers in the United States more "closed" than they were in Ukraine. The need to work to satisfy consumer appetites has a significant impact on the ability and will of believers to proselytize. The pastor considers the outreach activities of his church in the United States to be very important:

> We have a lot of problems, but mostly the problem of trying to save people, to save the people who come, to embrace them so that they will come to our church. It's not that we need some specific number. But it's necessary for the members of our church, as believers, we believe in God, and we feel the blessings of God, and through the prayers of our church we want blessings to influence others, to touch their souls, as it does the heart of the church. When a person is outside of the church, he feels the influence of the world, and it is not always good. It is negative, especially because he doesn't know the language, doesn't know other things, and he falls under the influence of bad people. But when a person is part of the church and even if he falls into a bad situation, there will always be someone to pray for him, someone to be happy for him, someone to go to with problems, and that person feels cared for and protected, from God and from other people. When Jews or Russians need an operation or in some way are in a dangerous situation, they ask the church to pray for them. . . . Different people come with different problems, and we want the church to save them, to provide pastoral care [Ukr. *dusheopikunstvo*] for believers first of all, but also to give the same help to unbelievers.

We want the church to continue to progress, to grow both in number and, especially in the spiritual sense, meaning that people live honestly. We teach people to live honestly. We preach that people should not go against their conscience, that they shouldn't break the law in America, that they should earn money honestly, that they have compassion for others, that they help their neighbors, their families, and their fellow believers in Ukraine. Of course, we want to save our youth, our children. We want them to become Ukrainians, to remember where they come from, and to keep their identity. That's our goal.

They use a multitiered strategy to attract new believers to the community and to retain the Ukrainianness of older converts. The state of Pennsylvania gave a $25,000 annual grant to support a full-time social worker from the community to help resettle new immigrants from the former Soviet Union who have no family in the United States. The immigrants helped by this program are not necessarily believers; indeed, they are not even always Ukrainians. With public financing, this community social worker tries to make arrival in the United States a theologizing experience, attaching religion from the start to settlement in the United States, much like the Ukrainian pastor hired by the Southern Baptist Convention. The community complements the social worker's efforts by supplying new families with food, furniture, and other basic necessities. If the immigrants have relatives who are members of the church community, in addition to the services described above, they also receive a $100 payment from the church to help with settlement expenses.

Retaining the Ukrainianness of believers is far more challenging. For over forty years, this church had a Ukrainian-language radio show once a week, which financial constraints forced them to sell in 2001. The Ukraine Cultural Center in suburban Philadelphia is an important locus of activity for Ukrainians from a variety of faiths. The church's choirs perform there periodically, and some of the members send their children to the center's Saturday school, where Ukrainian language, history, and culture are taught. One of the main purposes of the Slavic Baptist unions is to provide opportunities for congregational exchanges, which are particularly important to young people and to their parents who would like to see them marry believers from the same ethnic and linguistic background.

The demands on clergy to maintain an active congregational life are intense. The norm is to have (and attend) three services a week, one in the middle of the week and two on Sundays. Clergy are as a rule bi-vocational and work a day job in addition to running the congregation, which is unpaid. This is the reason that several "brothers," or male members of the church, preach during services, lessening the focus on a single individual and encouraging broader lay participation.

In terms of missionary activity, the pastor of this church says quite forthrightly that "the first priority of our church, as we come from Ukraine, is to remember our country, our homeland, and of course to help people living in Ukraine." For first-generation immigrants, the missionary impulse gets turned toward the country of origin, largely out of recognition for what the pastor calls the "language barrier, culture barrier, and even social barriers." Commitment to the homeland becomes the rationale for an extensive roster of missionary activities in Ukraine. At the time of our interview, the church was sponsoring eight full-time Ukrainian-speaking missionaries in Ukraine, all but two in western Ukraine.[24] By missionaries I mean that the church simply pays Ukrainian believers to live in places where there is no established Baptist community to preach and to offer services such as Bible study groups. Such missionaries are supported by monthly payments from the congregation of fifty to seventy dollars. This is a novel means of missionizing that requires little institutional support. In many statistical counts of missionary activity in Ukraine, this form of "church planting" would not likely be acknowledged. It requires only modest resources, which Ukrainian believers are able to accumulate in the United States, and a language barrier that decisively redirects the moral imperative to missionize to their country of origin.

The congregation also sends periodic parcels to families in need in Ukraine as part of a collection they take up once a month for the poor. Knowing that I have done the majority of my fieldwork for this project in Kharkiv, the pastor used an example from that city to illustrate this practice. A friend of a member of the church unexpectedly became the sole caretaker for his five grandchildren when his daughter died. Members of the church raised $400 and also shipped a container of clothes, food, and other necessary items to the elderly man, which cost an additional $500. In another instance, the church sent $1500 to a young man with cancer in Kyiv oblast to pay for surgery and postoperative treatments. A twenty-three-year-old girl in Volyn needing an operation on her foot received $1250. In 2003 alone, the church sent over twenty-five thousand dollars to Ukraine in response to such specific requests for assistance. That same year another five thousand dollars was sent as a contribution to building a new church.

The extent of economic dislocation the collapse of communism unleashed in Ukraine is perhaps most vividly demonstrated by this immigrant congregation's support of a missionary pastor in Buenos Aires, Argentina. The pastor is originally from Ternopil, and his job is to proselytize in Buenos Aires among immigrants from the former Soviet Union who arrive in Argentina with hopes of finding a job. What they usually encounter, however, is unemployment, disorientation, and lack of access to any form of government or charitable assistance. The Argentinean embassy in Moscow reportedly makes available the addresses of "Slavic and Ukrainian churches" as it gives out visas. The pastor in Buenos Aires tries to help "our people" (Ukr. *nashy liudy*) find work and housing. In addition to supporting the pastor from Ternopil as a missionary in Argentina, the community sends at least a thousand dollars a year to Buenos Aires to assist an orphanage run by a Ukrainian Baptist church and more sporadic sums to "our people" working in Ukrainian Baptist churches in Paraguay and Uruguay.

## Religion, Missionizing, and Movement

If religion is the factor that made it possible to choose to emigrate, interestingly, it is also the factor that is almost always evoked to explain the choice *not* to emigrate. Those who refuse to emigrate often claim that the need for evangelization and proselytizing in Ukraine is more pressing because of the wounds inflicted by socialism. This overrides any desire for increased material comfort or fears of renewed religious persecution. For those who do leave, however, the obligation to evangelize remains. Migration situates this basic activity in a transnational social field, the essence of which is found in personal relationships that cross national borders. Georges Fouron and Nina Glick Schiller write, "Underlying the use of this concept is the hypothesis that ongoing transnational social relations foster different forms of social and political identification than connections made simply through transborder forms of communication."[25]

As we have seen, the members of these congregations send missionaries and themselves become missionaries to Ukraine, delivering money, medicine, information, and other forms of charitable aid. Given their transnational familial networks, missionizing projects, youth group exchanges, and other connections with the former Soviet Union, at virtually every church service, here and in Ukraine, there are a half-dozen people who stand and offer greetings or report back on a recent trip to another congregation abroad. Soviet evangelicals blend aspects of their culture and a religious lifestyle in a setting of increased material comfort in the United States while retaining strong links and building social relationships with coreligionists elsewhere in the world. Many refugee networks are so embedded in religious communities that they are rendered inseparable. Religious institutions function as the nodes in interlinked networks that unite migrants spread across continents.

Religious institutions are effective institutional bases from which to reproduce an ethnic religious identity by maintaining a sense of continuity, identity, and belonging in spite of the disruption to daily life brought on by migration. Belonging in a transnational religious community that frequently meets face to face strengthens the allegiance of members to each other. Soviet evangelicals share several characteristics with other cultural diasporas: they have become dispersed due to negative circumstances, they retain collective historical and cultural memories, and they exhibit ongoing interest in and support for their homeland. The last wave of refugees from the Soviet Union rapidly relocated entire congregations and the multigenerational families that constituted their membership. They are committed to maintaining some kind of an "ethnic" church in the United States, be it Russian, Slavic, or Ukrainian, and providing charitable and missionary assistance to fellow religious communities in Ukraine. They have no desire to return to their homeland permanently, but they do evince a strong commitment to return frequently in order to missionize.

Even though there is a growing tendency among scholars to refer to all dispersed peoples as constituting a diaspora because of mounting possibilities to maintain connections with a homeland, we still need a typology or further refinement of the concept. One cannot assume that migrants from a particular country, region, or faith will form a single diaspora. Interethnic and interconfessional relations in the country of origin are likely to form the bedrock upon which future interaction among migrants evolves after resettlement. Particularly if the circumstances of displacement involve violence toward a broad cross-section of the population, as it did in the case of post–World War II Ukrainian refugees, this sharply influences assimilation trajectories and political commitments to the homeland.

Most immigration research focuses on the experience of acculturation, on being an ethnic "other" as it precedes—for white migrants—assimilation to American culture. This focus places enormous emphasis on the racialization of difference. Yet globalizing forces of communication and transportation have alerted us to new means of crafting difference and the complex levels of identity and community allegiance it creates. Diasporic attachments are a critical element determining the vitality of refugee groups and the extent of their simultaneous activity in the United States and in their homeland. This is a particularly subtle issue for Soviet refugees given their origins in the USSR, a federated, multinational empire that has since collapsed.[26] Relocation is increasingly mediated by global voluntary organizations, such as religious organizations or religio-ethnic institutions, which ultimately are quite resilient, flexible, and effective in shaping resettlement and ethnic group formation.[27] Supranational religious denominations, such as Judaism and evangelicalism, have brought Americans and American culture into the life of refugees much in the same way that the Ukrainian Orthodox Church or Ukrainian Greek Catholic Church have linked their members more firmly to Ukraine by merging a commitment to God and country. The importance of religion and its transnational linkages in the latter half of the twentieth century as a force shaping the dynamics of migration and resettlement, diasporic or otherwise, was considerable. The magnetism of religious communities lies in the fact that they operate at multiple levels, forging intersections between the ethnic and the religious, the local and the transnational, the political and the cultural. They have the flexibility to maintain an ethos of inclusion alongside firm boundaries of exclusion.

Some members of the second generation of this wave of refugees might fulfill the stated wishes of their parents and grandparents and remain part of these hybrid transnational religious communities, harboring aspects of Ukrainian or "Slavic" culture and maintaining links to their country of origin through religious communities. In doing so, they also—unwittingly, as it were—increase Protestant diversity in America. All evidence suggests, however, that successive generations will not fulfill these wishes. The Soviet-era anti–social mobility, anti-consumerist, and ascetic components of their religious practice and communal ethos are inevitably found to be untenable in American society. The desire to retain members, especially successive generations, is a strong factor prompting compromise and relaxation of moral prescriptions. In the fifteen short years since the collapse of the USSR, transnational religious movements collided with Soviet socialism to create mediated cultures and global religious communities based on transnational institutional linkages that have shaped new practices, identities, and understandings of community and morality, both in the former Soviet Union and in the United States.

# CHAPTER FOUR

# MISSIONIZING, CONVERTING, AND REMAKING THE MORAL SELF

At exactly the same time that U.S. immigration policies changed to allow the recognition of persecuted evangelical believers as refugees, prompting the mass exodus of longstanding believers and their relatives, very significant changes concerning religious policy also occurred in the Soviet Union. The millennium commemorations in 1988 of the thousand-year anniversary of Christianity in Kyivan Rus' and the vast popular interest it generated in religion prompted a sea change in religious policy.[1] In October 1990 one of the primary goals of Soviet ideology, to establish a scientific atheistic worldview, was abandoned when the Supreme Soviet adopted legislation that guaranteed freedom of conscience and accorded legal status to religious institutions. In essence, the Soviet state pledged to cease impeding the establishment of places of worship and persecuting individuals who chose to practice their religion openly, regardless of affiliation.

In the late 1980s, increasingly vocal claims to a nation's right to self-determination became a viable strategy for political and cultural elites to challenge Soviet hegemony. This meant that national and religious resurgences occurred simultaneously and were often mutually reinforcing. With less fear of state retribution, some clergy and religious institutions used their moral authority to support nationalist movements as oppositional forces to Soviet rule, which increased the popularity of these groups. Much has been written about the role of religion in enhancing claims to national distinctiveness and about the importance of "religious nationalisms" in bringing an end to seventy-four years of Soviet rule. Protestants and other religious groups that are supraethnic and "non-traditional," rarely lent active support to nationalist political agendas.

Many individuals in the former Soviet Union have argued that the ideological vacuum left in the wake of the collapse of communist ideology as a viable worldview and a source of individual and collective meaning was simply replaced with a religious-based orientation to self and society. The disorientation prompted by convulsive social change as the Soviet system began to fall apart and fifteen nation-states, each with one or more "national religions" quickly emerging to take its place, certainly did cause some to embrace religion as an anti-Soviet alternative, a new moral compass to guide their ideas and behavior amid social confusion and economic collapse. Yet this is only part of the story.

The sharp rise in conversions to evangelicalism in a formerly socialist society undergoing rapid and sweeping change shaped transformations on multiple levels: for individuals, for communities, and for the social order more broadly. Foreign missionaries have played an evolving role in this process. They began with "fire and brimstone" preaching in stadiums and on the streets to gain converts. These efforts were more visible than they were fruitful. In Ukraine, the strategy shifted quickly into substantial—and largely successful—efforts to build an evangelical infrastructure. Foreign religious organizations sought to establish Ukraine as a Eurasian base for evangelical missionary and clerical training. Within fifteen years of the collapse of the USSR, Ukraine not only was the recipient of substantial numbers of missionaries, it also began to supply them.

## Changes in the Religious Landscape

The success of any religious resurgence is predicated on favorable political and legal conditions. The religious landscape after 1989 developed very differently in Ukraine than it did in Russia, largely because of the different trajectories Orthodoxy took. The institutional structure of Orthodox national churches mirrors the ideal of a nation-state, with each people ideally constituting a single ethno-religious community. In Ukraine, the political struggles after independence to create a single Ukrainian Orthodox Church, canonically recognized as independent from the Russian Orthodox Church and capable of buttressing the legitimacy of an independent Ukrainian state, compromised the role of clergy as moral leaders as they battled among themselves for property and power.[2] The sustained efforts of intellectuals, dissidents, politicians, and diaspora leaders failed to unite the three Orthodox churches in Ukraine: the Ukrainian Orthodox Church-Kyiv Patriarchate, the Ukrainian Autocephalous Orthodox Church, and the Ukrainian Orthodox Church-Moscow Patriarchate. These seemingly intractable problems, combined with the Orthodox Church's history of complicity with the Soviet state, tarnished the reputation of Orthodoxy in general and brought an end to the state-backed monopoly status of the Orthodox faith in Ukraine.

This political bickering indirectly contributed to making Ukraine a model of religious pluralism among formerly socialist societies. When a single church cannot dominate and influence religious policy, as it can in Russia, Belarus, and other countries with a strong majority adhering to a single denomination, there is a greater degree of de facto religious freedom. This religious pluralism, combined with a nominal commitment to Orthodoxy among large sectors of the population, has made Ukraine one of the most active and competitive "religious marketplaces" in Eurasia. Indeed, José Casanova claims that "of all European societies, Ukraine is the one most likely to approximate the American model," which he characterizes as "a free, and highly pluralistic indeed almost boundless religious market."[3]

The different statuses of the Orthodox churches in Ukraine and Russia is compounded by a second factor, namely, that Ukraine is a country with particularly deep religious traditions and where religious participation in a variety of faiths has always been exceptionally high. During the Soviet period, two-thirds of the Orthodox churches were located in Ukraine, even though the population of Ukraine is one-third that of Russia. Should the three Orthodox churches in Ukraine ever unite, the Ukrainian Orthodox Church would overnight become the largest Orthodox church in the world.[4] There are also more Protestant, Roman Catholic, Jewish, and "New Religious Movements" in Ukraine than in Russia. Only the number of Islamic and Buddhist communities in Russia exceeds those in Ukraine.[5]

Vasyl Markus has written, "Ukraine must be viewed as a modern secular state, in whose formation the religious factor historically played a significant role and where even now, in the postcommunist environment, religion cannot be underestimated."[6] The inherited cultural tradition of religiosity and religious affiliation as a marker among Ukrainians and between Ukrainians and others, was never entirely extinguished by the Soviet regime in spite of the impressive efforts to do so. Rather, it provides the cultural groundwork that has allowed missionaries from many denominations and national backgrounds to help recreate robust religious-based communities after 1991. The secularism of the present is challenged by the importance of religion in the past and by an embrace of cultural traditions rooted in religion as a signifier of group and individual identity. As an ever-widening spectrum of denominations openly competes for members, religious life in Ukraine resumes its vitality. Over a thousand new religious communities currently register annually in Ukraine.[7]

The difference in the degree to which religious authorities are located abroad is the third factor that distinguishes the religious landscape in Ukraine from Russia. Ukrainian government and clerical leaders have to reckon with the fact that not only the nontraditional religions, such as Baptists, Pentecostals, Jehovah's Witnesses, and so on, have transnational connections, so do the so-called national ones. The Russian Orthodox Church in 2005 still controlled 9,049 of the 12,845 Orthodox communities in Ukraine, and the Vatican is the spiritual authority for the over five million Ukrainian Greek Catholics, who have 3,317 parishes.[8]

The Soviet regime sought to eradicate religious practice with antireligious campaigns in order to erase religious identities, especially those that aligned with national identities. It is critical to note that this failed effort was even less successful in Ukraine, where not only did religion become a source of solace, it became a politicized form of resistance as well. When Ukrainian and Russian government leaders make religious policy now, they have to reckon with these historical legacies by adapting to them, which explains in part the different positions the Russian and Ukrainian states have taken toward foreign missionaries.

Numerous studies of freedom of conscience and religious tolerance in the former Soviet Union have come to the same conclusion: with the exception of the Baltics, Ukraine consistently ranks highest among the former Soviet republics, significantly above Russia and Belarus.[9] Since the fall of the Soviet Union, policies regulating local religious organizations, the flow of missionaries, and the myriad forms of financial, material, and logistical support they offer have evolved very differently in Russia, Belarus, and Ukraine. Legally, the Ukrainian government insists on fewer restrictions for nontraditional religious communities and foreign religious organizations, which has in turn generated greater religious diversity in Ukraine. In essence, Ukraine followed the patterns set in 1905 and 1917.

In contrast, in a 1997 vote of 358 to 6, Russia's Parliament passed a bill establishing two categories of religious institutions, traditional and nontraditional, in contradiction to the Russian Constitution, which states that all religions are equal under the law.[10] Traditional religious communities, legally referred to as "religious organizations," are defined as those with an established presence in Russia of fifteen or more years and include Ortho-doxy, Judaism, Islam, and Buddhism. This special status allows religious organizations and their individual centers to legally act as a corporate body, to own property and commercial enterprises, to run radio and television stations, to distribute religious literature, to conduct services in alternative locations (such as hospitals and prisons), and to receive tax exemptions.

Although Catholic, Protestant, and breakaway Russian Orthodox de-nominations have been in Russia longer than fifteen years, they were denied this status and classified as "religious groups." They are denied these privi-leges and are subject to cumbersome, annual registration procedures. Regis-tration, as an erratic and time-consuming bureaucratic exercise, becomes a means to systematically disempower targeted denominations.[11] The aim of the law was to restrict "totalitarian sects" and "dangerous religious cults." In practice, however, the law discriminates against less established religious groups, especially Protestant and parachristian denominations, such as Je-hovah's Witnesses and Mormons, by making it difficult for them to establish institutional bases. Infringements on religious liberty are compounded by the fact that almost half of the regional authorities have passed legislation that is even harsher toward "foreign sects."

In November 2002 Belarus passed even more restrictive legislation.[12] It obliges all religious organizations to re-register by 2004 and criminalizes unregistered religious activity. Any group without the status of "religious association" cannot shield its religious literature from state censorship, is not allowed to invite foreigners or have them lead religious organizations, and, most harsh of all, is not allowed to engage in any publishing or edu-cational activities. In order to attain the status of "religious association," a group must fulfill three requirements: it must have at least ten registered communities; each community must have at least twenty adult members; and one of the ten communities must have been registered as early as 1982. In 2002 there were 2,830 registered religious organizations in Belarus, of which 895 are evangelical Protestant.[13] All minority faiths, including Pente-costals, the second most numerous denomination in terms of number of communities, denounced this bill as repressive.[14] Of course, electronic me-dia and the Internet allow missionaries to exert influence in places where they are not welcome. State institutions in Russia and Belarus that seek to limit evangelical proselytizing will increasingly be forced to monitor multi-ple spheres—to less effect.

There is no equivalent legislation in Ukraine restricting the activities of certain denominations. In 2002 there were no reports of nonnative religious organizations having difficulties obtaining visas for foreign religious workers or registering with state authorities.[15] Writing from a missionary perspective, Howard Biddulph asserts, "The Kuchma presidency has followed a fairly consistent policy of egalitarian treatment of the four traditional churches [the three Orthodox Churches and the Greek Catholic Church] since 1995, seeking to reduce or resolve conflicts and to promote mutual tolerance. It has also taken a full toleration position toward the overwhelming majority of nontraditional faiths, including NRMs [New Religious Movements]. Officials of the State Committee for Religious Affairs, who administer religious policy and most of the judiciary, are the most visible supporters of that relatively full-toleration perspective."[16]

I do not mean to suggest that there are not violations of freedom of conscience in Ukraine. Yet the difficulties of ensuring religious tolerance in Ukraine stem from two sources: interference of local authorities in the workings of local religious institutions and inconsistent implementation of the national law guaranteeing religious freedom. In Russia and Belarus the problem is the law itself: it allows the state to selectively restrict certain religious organizations. This is a critical difference.

Ukrainian government and cultural leaders remain concerned over two issues of religious life in Ukraine. First, the splintering of the Orthodox Church into various denominations impedes national unity and complicates the recognition of the Ukrainian Orthodox Church by the Constantinople-based universal Orthodox Patriarch.[17] The second issue is the growth of nontraditional religious groups and the growing presence of foreign missionaries in Ukraine buttressing these new religious institutions.[18] In 1999 alone, over 2,600 foreign representatives from a wide spectrum of religious denominations visited Ukraine.[19] In 2001, 463 long-term evangelical missionaries were working in Ukraine. Nearly 350 of them were American.[20] Notably, some 900 Ukrainians served as missionaries in 2001, over a third of them in Russia. The flourishing of these religious groups strains the ideal of Ukrainians as a unified ethno-religious people and creates local communities with transnational ties that effectively bypass the significance of the nation-state as a source of identity and allegiance. Additionally, the nascent Ukrainian state is denied the possibility of a partnership with the church to generate legitimacy and loyalty amid economic difficulties and charges of political corruption.

Given the new possibilities for exploring religion and individual spirituality that emerged after 1990, we must explain why evangelicals in Ukraine have been the beneficiaries to such a significant extent of this religious renaissance. The hordes of evangelical missionaries who began to arrive in

Ukraine in the late 1980s introduced their imaginings of higher powers, the sacred, and morality to Ukrainians. Once the religious imagination was awakened, they presented their faith not against Orthodoxy but against Soviet socialism, with its condemnation of religion. For this message, there was a ready audience. A secondary project for evangelical missionaries was to explain the superiority of conservative Christianity over the other faiths now on offer in an awakening religious marketplace.

All of the Orthodox Churches in Ukraine consider Orthodoxy an attribute of Ukrainian nationality. That is to say, a Ukrainian is by definition Orthodox. A significant exception is made for Ukrainian Greek Catholics, who for historical reasons belong to a different, albeit related, national denomination. Orthodox identity is geographically defined and automatically inherited. Therefore, in the eyes of Orthodox clergy, there is no need for foreigners to missionize in Ukraine because all Ukrainians have a religious identity, whether or not they choose to act on it. The Orthodox understanding of religiosity as an inherited ethno-religious identity is dramatically different from the "born again" conscious experience of adult conversion upon which an evangelical identity is predicated. For evangelicals, anyone who has not been "saved" through repentance and conversion inspires proselytizing. Evangelicals realize their faith by acting on the moral obligation to save the unsaved, to church the unchurched, and to witness to others by recounting their own experience of conversion. One group claims "every believer is a missionary" and encourages proselytizing to anyone outside the faith group, and the other group recognizes citizenship almost as a stand in for religiosity.

Well-financed missionizing activities by foreigners and by nontraditional religious groups have prompted a profound desire to reign in proselytism that is palpable among government leaders, clergy, and the population at large. Evangelical missionaries inspire disdain because proselytizing trades on the arrogant assumption that Ukrainians are in need of saving and that somehow their faiths are inadequate. Foreign religious organizations are seen as chiseling away at the status of the national churches. These resentments are reflected in the continued reference to evangelical communities as "totalitarian sects." Yet precisely because the atheist component of Marxist-Leninist ideology has been so vigorously and widely rejected, evangelicals have achieved measured growth. The associations of evangelicalism with the West and opposition to Soviet power rendered it not just attractive but, for some, even fashionable. Most Ukrainians were nominally Christian to begin with, and they were among the fiercest critics of Soviet ideological pronouncements on religion and moralities. Many were eager to reject the past and to begin acting on religious sensibilities and beliefs they already held.[21] Converting did not oblige them to see themselves as "sinners" or to negotiate two different belief systems, as has been documented in so many other mission fields.[22]

Evangelical denominations represented an alternative to Orthodoxy, and joining a community with a history of opposition and noncooperation with Soviet authorities simultaneously became a means of desovietizing and joining a new global Christian community. The worldview of Ukrainian evangelicals is something of a countertext to both the revolutionary modernist vision of Soviet society and the newly established post-Soviet notions of national identity and national history that attempt to reverse the inherited colonial narrative of historical development. This challenge to the past and the present, combined with the perceived "democratic" workings of Protestant denominations, partially accounts for the success of evangelicals and distinguishes these communities from more traditional and hierarchical denominations, such as Orthodoxy and Catholicism.

Further, Orthodoxy does not depend on a rational appeal to the intellect, as Protestantism does. Evangelical faiths are centered on each believer reading the Bible individually, and communities provide small study groups to *explain* the doctrine, its symbolism, and its application to everyday life. This forum for introducing and explaining religious belief and practice was highly valued by those who sought to *understand* religion in addition to experiencing it. Orthodox theology is centered on mystery, on the wonder of the Incarnation, and on reverence for the divinity. Several scholars who have studied conversion narratives of converts to Orthodoxy have found that the beauty and allure of Orthodox art forms, such as sacred choral music and icon painting, are sparks for igniting spiritual sensations that lead to conversion.[23] Orthodox converts understand religious art to be divinely inspired. Experiencing the beauty of these art forms becomes something of a spiritual encounter leading to conversion. In contrast, evangelicals studiously avoid "idol worship," as they call reverence for icons.

Converts to evangelicalism consistently responded to open-ended questions concerning self-identification by saying that they are either "believers" or "Christians." Other attributes, such as denominational affiliation, much less nationality, residence, profession, gender, or social roles (mother, elderly, and so on), were cited after they noted they lived a religious life. Ukrainians use the term "believer" according to its original meaning, to indicate quite simply conviction, a faith that rests on a trust in God.[24] Reference to a particular denomination or a specific body of doctrine, as we would expect belief to be defined in most Western societies, is largely absent. After decades of an official state policy of atheism, the dimensions of a religious identity ultimately collapse into two categories of people: believers and non-believers.

## Western Missionaries

A reduction in legal restrictions on foreign religious organizations in Ukraine has led to a flourishing of religious activity. To illustrate the growth of evangelicalism, consider that just prior to the USSR's official dissolution, in the fall of 1991 twenty to fifty Evangelical Christian or Baptist churches were being established and registered per month in Ukraine.[25] By the mid-1990s, 3,600 Protestant churches were formally registered in Ukraine; by 2000 there were over 5,000.[26] By 2001, the Institute of Religion and Society (Ukr. *Instytut Relihii ta Suspil'stva*) in L'viv, western Ukraine, estimated that a quarter of all religious communities in Ukraine were Protestant.[27] Baptists claimed to have had over five hundred thousand adult registered members in 2005.[28] There are even more Pentecostals if one includes charismatics among them. This growth occurred as the overwhelming majority of long-standing evangelical believers were emigrating to the West. Therefore, nearly all of the evangelicals filling these churches are recent converts.

In the early years following the collapse of the Soviet Union, mission funding and overall financial support from the United States were critical to the rapid growth of "church planting."[29] This new circulation of missionaries undid the isolation imposed by the Iron Curtain, leading to interconnections that international agencies, transnational religious communities, and individual foreign missionaries offered at a pivotal moment to religious communities forming in Ukraine. It is difficult to state with any certainty how many missionaries traveled to Ukraine. Operation World reported that there were 1,681 long-term foreign missionaries supported by seventy-seven different missionary organizations from twenty-two different countries working in Ukraine in 2001.[30] About five times that many short-term missionaries visit Ukraine annually, some as preachers and others to do charitable work. The overwhelming majority of them were American. Yet these numbers are an approximation at best. To cite only one of the problems, consider that the Assemblies of God, one of the largest Pentecostal denominations in the world and sponsor of a Pentecostal seminary in Kyiv, does not release any statistics on the location or number of its missionaries. Many missionaries are self-sponsored or sponsored by a single congregation and, during the period when visas were required, entered on tourist or student visas, so they do not figure into any statistical accounts of the foreign missionary presence in Ukraine.

Foreign missionaries come to Ukraine to conduct evangelization, which they understand to be the delivery of the Christian message of salvation through faith in Jesus Christ to the unsaved. The intended outcome of evangelization is conversion of the listener and a deepening of the faith of the proselytizer. While virtually all mainline Protestant churches (Presbyterian, Methodist, Episcopalian, and so on) have long-term missionaries in Ukraine, they are primarily involved in relief work and are not particularly visible to those who are not directly affected by their services. Evangelical Christian organizations, in contrast, use myriad forms of public evangelization to prompt conversion and attract new members to their congregations.

Over fifty missionary organizations are quite active in Ukraine, including the International Mission Board of the Southern Baptist Convention, the largest denominational organization, as well as interdenominational missions organizations such as Youth with a Mission, which has over a hundred long-term missionaries in Ukraine at any given time; CrossWorld and Mission to the World. Besides the Southern Baptist Convention, the other denominational organizations especially active in Ukraine are the Assemblies of God and the networks of the Churches of Christ. In addition to these U.S.-based agencies, missionary organizations from Canada, South Africa, and Germany each support between ten and twenty long-term missionaries in Ukraine as well.

In the early 1990s, foreign missionary organizations pioneered a two-pronged approach to providing assistance. On the one hand, they sent clergy and lay leaders to garner converts by renting halls and even stadiums for collective prayer and provided leadership for emerging communities. At the same time, they also provided vital financial assistance at a critical moment to establish the necessary infrastructure to maintain growing evangelical communities by building prayer houses, printing Bibles and religious literature, and offering humanitarian services. There are now three evangelical seminaries in Kyiv alone, a Christian university in Donetsk, and a theological center in Odesa, which is also home to the largest Christian publishing house in Ukraine and the sponsor of a major initiative to present archival documents of the evangelical experience under Soviet rule on CD-ROM. Of course, the process of creating an evangelical infrastructure reveals significant power differentials, with money from the West coming to cash-strapped communities in Ukraine. Therefore, these interconnections are built against a background of stark inequality. This is not to suggest that Ukrainians are powerless or passive in this collaboration. Each of these institutions relies to some degree on foreigners to staff them but nonetheless have Ukrainians at the helm.

The assistance of international agencies is largely infrastructural to avoid the cultural barriers that often prevent proselytizing from leading to conversion. No one is more aware of the perils of culture clash than the Western missionaries themselves. Western assistance flows indirectly in the form of material support precisely because most misunderstandings among believers or among missionaries and potential converts are about mutually offensive cultural practices, not theology.

To overcome this, the missionary organization SEND's strategy is "simply to help the Ukrainian Church with the tools and people to reach their own country for Jesus Christ, and to launch a missionary movement from Ukraine into the former Soviet nations. Whenever SEND enters a country where there is a small church presence, we seek to partner with the local church."[31] In other words, this and other missionary organizations, in word and often in practice, recognize the importance of linguistic and cultural competence for effective missionizing.[32] Therefore, their priorities are to establish local leaders who can more effectively evangelize other locals. This strategy was tremendously successful in Latin America.[33] Initially, North Americans evangelized there with little success. After World War II, missionary efforts shifted to locals evangelizing other locals. Throughout the region, especially in Guatemala and Brazil, the result of this shift has been dramatic. In these two countries, evangelicalism is slated to overturn the historic dominance of Catholicism.

Throughout the 1990s, however, the means of missionizing took many forms. Two examples of long-term American missionaries involved in what they call "leadership development" should help illustrate the breadth of activities evangelicals have undertaken to garner converts and spread the faith. The first missionary is engaged in activities that concern all of Ukraine, and the second one works in Kharkiv.

### Books and the Word

Tom Allen is a forty-year-old father of four girls from Michigan who has lived in Ukraine since 1997 as a long-term missionary. His first assignment was to teach and be an administrator at a Baptist seminary that opened in Kyiv in 1995. He put his training in library sciences to use at the seminary by starting a digital library collection that is considered a vital part of the seminary's distance education programs. The majority of students are nonresidential, some traveling as far as seven time zones, from Siberia to Kyiv, to study. On the growing importance of the Internet and e-mail for education and missions, Tom says, "If we are going to meet the needs of the Russian-speaking world, we must leverage this technology for the Kingdom. . . . Our primary goal over the next four to five years is to develop educational resources which will help Russian and Ukrainian ministries by using the very best technology and methodology to address these unique needs."[34]

The unique needs he refers to are, in his view, first and foremost a historical legacy of evangelical believers in the Soviet Union being cut off from educational opportunities in a society that values education highly. This has had the detrimental effect of lowering the status of Christian education and, indirectly, of believers and evangelical churches. The comparative lack of educational credentials among believers in a society that values book learning is compounded by a dearth of Christian literature and a general lack of resources to build traditional libraries. To remedy this, Tom has trained church librarians in partnership with READ Ministries and aims to create a resource network and an association of church librarians.[35] So as evangelical churches are being created, he is busy helping them develop digital and traditional libraries that will be run by someone who can officially be called a trained church librarian, thereby professionalizing what has been a lay volunteer position. READ Ministries also sponsors an experimental form of ministry that they call "bookmobile evangelism." Roving evangelists bring bookmobiles stocked with Christian literature to rural areas and to otherwise isolated believers. Tom trains people who can manage these mobile libraries. By professionalizing the volunteer lay activities of believers, he gives them skills at no charge as they bring books, a diversion, and evangelicalism to isolated villagers. In essence, his missionizing activities create libraries and train librarians to create other libraries so as to spread the Word through the word. After nine years in Ukraine, Tom plans to return to the United States to pursue a doctorate in information science. Additional training, he believes, will help him develop distance education software, build digital libraries, and create websites and web portals for Christian resources based in Ukraine but destined to be used throughout Eurasia.

## Christian Business

This highly applied approach to missionizing is replicated by Steve Johnson, who left a career in sales to become a full-time missionary in Kharkiv in 1995.[36] He owns an apartment there and has no plans to leave. With funding from three congregations in Minnesota and one in Arizona, he created the Center for Leadership Development to teach and support "Christian practices" in business. His goal is to increase the success rate of Christian-run businesses by providing assistance on issues like decision-making, financing, and marketing. Open to believers and nonbelievers alike, the Center for Leadership Development offers business seminars, English-language classes, and an international mentoring program that relies on the missionary impulse of American businessmen to volunteer their time and advice to budding Ukrainian entrepreneurs. Visiting businessmen finance their own short-term missionary trips to Ukraine and, once in Kharkiv, offer supplementary guest lectures, seminars, and individual mentoring. The center rents a classroom at the Kharkiv National University, which puts it in close proximity to its target group, young, educated future professionals.

The curriculum revolves around developing what Steve calls the "Four C's": calling, character, competence, and community. The goal is to link business goals with life goals. A considerable amount of attention is devoted to identifying a vocation, or "calling." This idea of a calling represents a Weberian blending of professional and religious pursuits to achieve the kind of worldly gain that will have positive spiritual and moral meaning and lead to salvation. Developing one's calling involves identifying the gifts bestowed by God and using them to perform good works. Weber noted that the idea of the "calling" was one of the highest expressions of Christian morality among Protestants. Success in fulfilling one's calling connotes a blessing, or being in God's good favor. In other words, the accumulation of wealth can be seen as a virtue because wealth can be used as an instrument of piety. By making work, industriousness, and diligence in an earthly calling a religious imperative, by extension there is a divine injunction to maximize profit. In essence, this is what Weber was referring to when he noted that a "Protestant ethic" was one of the cultural elements, along with numerous structural factors, that helped to bring about modern Western capitalism, replete with industrialization and the wealth it delivered.[37] Like Weber, Steve also suggests that the moral principles of ascetic Protestantism are conducive to good business practices and generating wealth.

The fulfillment of one's calling demands "character," or virtuous traits, an essential element in leadership. Certain world leaders are selected and studied for their exemplary character traits and moral courage. First on the list, of course, is Jesus Christ, along with other biblical figures, such as Moses and Daniel. Several political leaders, Abraham Lincoln and Winston Churchill to name two, are chosen for consideration of their "character" and how they used it to make decisions and lead others. Individual profiles illustrate the virtues of industriousness, delayed gratification, and discipline and how they can lead to worldly success, a reliable indicator that one is among the select who can expect salvation after death. Here Steve stresses the need to be honest and punctual and the importance of keeping one's word. Stressing the importance of not cheating also is an issue. Anyone caught cheating has their exam crumpled up in front of everyone and is asked to leave the program.

Calling and character need excellence—"competence"—in order to make a difference. The purpose of bringing in mentors from America is to introduce students to businessmen who have "reached a high degree of competence in their respective fields" and to present them as role models and mentors. A steady stream of American businessmen arrive on short-term missionary trips and offer seminars and meetings with students on all facets of running a business. In this way, business acumen is equated with sacred knowledge, business ethics with personal morality, financial success with salvation, and capitalism with Christianity. These types of skill-driven short-term missionary trips often do indeed deliver tangible benefits to Ukrainians, whereas the benefits of purely evangelizing trips are often more negligible.

The last component of the program, "community," refers to the importance of "consistent interaction" in order to engage the "vital work of relationship building," deemed so essential to business success. This last element suggests that professional and religious communities can be the same. One can strengthen moral "character" at the same "community" at which one can strengthen business "competence." The success of all three projects hinges on building relationships, the foundational one, of course, is with God. The capitalist business practice of building networks, which is seen as legitimate, helpful, and even essential, is highlighted, whereas the socialist-era practices of *blat*—connections and "canals" that link an individual to a circle of people providing access to knowledge, services, and money—are not addressed. Communal membership helps maintain and strengthen commitments to developing the four C's.

Steve was inspired to create the center after his participation in the CoMission, a consortium of evangelical Christian groups that, on the heels of Campus Crusade for Christ's *Jesus* film project, embarked on a collaborative endeavor to introduce a course on Christian morals and ethnics in the Russian school system.[38] The project ended amid charges of proselytism and "sheep stealing" from the Orthodox. During his travels, Steve noticed interactions with government bureaucrats, school administrators, and individual teachers were consistently easier in Ukraine because of reduced government interference and less hostility among the population.

In 1995 he made the decision to relocate to Kharkiv. He lined up four congregations in the United States to be his sponsors, founded the center, bought an apartment, and began to lay down roots in Kharkiv. One hears numerous laments in Ukraine about the need to cheat, lie, or steal just to earn a meager living, about rampant corruption among government officials who have abandoned any commitment to pursuing the collective good in favor of self-enrichment, and about the ruthlessness and omnipresence of organized crime. Competing, often contradictory, moralities govern business practices, which creates unpredictability.[39] Steve feels his own calling is to develop a sense of business ethics and biblically based morality among young entrepreneurs, one by one, in an effort to affect change on the overall methods of doing business in Ukraine.

Oleg's experiences as an environmental inspector in Kharkiv illustrate some of the more frequent dynamics in the workplace against which Steve and the center struggle. Oleg recounted how all inspectors, environmental or otherwise, as representatives of the state with the power to discipline and punish, hold vast latitude to abuse their positions by using them for informal income supplementation.[40] Oleg's colleagues were constantly on the take, but he asserted that as a newly converted Christian, he could not accept bribes or "presents" (the English word is used), which made him persona non grata at his workplace. The dominant pattern among his colleagues was to inspect an installation, find some sort of fault (whether it actually existed or not), threaten to report it, accept a bribe, and then not report anything. Oleg's refusal to do this was condemned by his coworkers because, in their minds, it threatened their livelihoods. Finally, his boss forced him to resign from a job he had enjoyed. "That is what God wanted," he explained. "I understand that I myself would not have left. But it's good that it happened. I am thankful to God. I am trying to pay more attention to what God has given than to what he has not." Living by these "Christian values" can make one an unwanted outcast in the workplace. Steve has designed his program to help believers marshal a certain moral justification in going against cultural norms, forge a commitment to following this path and then, whatever the consequences, use the benevolence of God and his shepherding of believers through life according to his plan as a frame to cope with the ensuing hardship.

In trying to provide justification and motivation for individual believers to challenge what they feel are the morally abhorrent cultural practices that hold sway in the region, a group of Baptists, with Steve as a peripheral participator, opened a Christian café in Kharkiv with financing from several small religious organizations in the United States. The designation

"Christian" was intended to signal that smoking and alcoholic beverages would not be allowed and that "easy listening" music would be featured instead of rock music. The intention was to provide a meeting place for young believers that would validate their values and lifestyle choices. The other stated goal of the café was to illustrate, against popular conventional wisdom, that it *was* possible to operate a business honestly and legally in Ukraine—it was this aspect that sparked Steve's interest. The café owners vowed not to pay bribes to government officials, to pay salaries on time, and to try to fulfill all legal obligations, which included paying taxes fully.

After only two years, alas, the café ended up proving the opposite point: apparently it is not possible to be in business in Kharkiv right now if one does not "play the game without rules."[41] In the end, the sanitation inspectors did them in. The straw that broke the camel's back was when the inspectors claimed, after a string of other violations, that there was insufficient refrigeration capacity. Instead of paying a bribe to get rid of this and other violations, the cooperative group that managed the café tried to respond within the confines of the law. So they frequently incurred additional expense, and sometimes for nonsensical reasons, as when they purchased and used an additional refrigerator they did not need. At a certain point, it was no longer financially possible to respond to the inspectors. After two years, the Christian café filed for bankruptcy and closed its doors.

For Steve this is a lamentable situation, and it motivates him to chisel away at the business practices that prevail, practices that are enabled by the breakdown of political order and the subordination of the law and weak state institutions to predatory economic pursuits. Such a volatile business environment demands above all an accurate knowledge of laws, rules, and regulations, so that they can be effectively subverted. Steve contends that Ukrainian converts need business seminars that teach entrepreneurial techniques based on biblical principles as a counter means to "subvert" and remake the very economic practices he finds so immoral.

American evangelical missionaries in Ukraine share with colonial-era evangelical missionaries a "vision of reconstruction" for the societies they encountered.[42] In discussing the ways in which evangelical missionaries in colonial South Africa were "cultural agents" of capitalism, Jean Comaroff and John Comaroff note how these missionaries set out to convert non-believers to their theological orientation *and* to reconstruct the tenor of their everyday lives. In a way that would certainly please Max Weber, evangelical missionaries in South Africa in the nineteenth century and evangelical missionaries in twenty-first-century Ukraine share a belief in industry and order that prompts them to "reconstruct" the societies they encounter by teaching their fused understandings of moral order and economic exchange as part of an overall program to promote capitalist ideology among the peoples they attempt to save. Comaroff and Comaroff refer to this as a "moral economy of choice that echoes, on the spiritual plane, the material economies of the free market."[43] Both projects, conversion to faith and to capitalist practices, include convincing non-believers of the advantages of pursuing salvation as a laudable goal that is achievable through the adoption of certain disciplining practices that yield wealth and a higher moral standing.

In 2005, Steve decided to turn over the leadership of the center he created to someone else while he focused his efforts on opening an English-language church in Kharkiv with an American pastor in the Vineyard evangelical tradition. The Vineyard movement, of which he was a part before he came to Ukraine, began in the 1970s in California. Although Vineyard churches embrace charismatic teachings, such as healing and the transformative powers of the Holy Spirit, they do not call themselves "charismatic." Rather, they prefer the term "empowered evangelicals." This new church will have a symbiotic relationship to the Christian Leadership Center. A contributing factor in Steve's decision to leave the center was that although he claims to have discouraged his students from using the center as a means to get to the United States, many did just that. With evangelical credentials in hand, a half-dozen students have gone on to pursue undergraduate degrees at Jerry Falwell's Liberty University in Virginia, and Steve wonders whether, once their calling, character, competence and community have been shaped by life in America, they will return to Kharkiv. He now chooses to work with less entrepreneurial believers who he hopes will stay in Ukraine.

## Ukrainian Evangelism

Even as foreign missionary assistance serves to connect Ukraine to the West and to global Christian communities, it also serves to tie it to the former USSR. Within the former Soviet Union, other power differentials help make Ukraine a base for theological training for the entire former Soviet Bloc. Nearly all Ukrainians have at least passive fluency in Russian, and about a third of the 47 million Ukrainians are native Russian-speakers. With a population that possesses imperial "cultural capital," Ukraine is an ideal location to train missionaries and clergy destined to serve in other parts of the former Soviet Union. So as evangelical initiatives tie Ukraine into a global community of believers, those same initiatives also reinforce

Ukraine's ties to its Soviet past. The shortage of clergy of the early 1990s is already coming to a halt.[44] As of January 2005, there were 173 theological institutions in Ukraine, with 9,494 full-time students and an additional ten thousand studying by correspondence.[45] Ukraine is on its way to becoming an exporter of pastors and a training ground for clergy who will serve in the former Soviet Union.

The emphasis I have placed thus far on foreign missionaries in terms of institution-building and "leadership development" should not obscure an even more important development. Namely, Ukraine itself has become an important source of missionaries. An indication of the depth of religious sentiment in a particular region is the number of communities needed to support a single full-time missionary. This reveals how robust local communities are and how committed their membership is to evangelization. In the case of Ukraine, in spite of its less than enviable economic situation, it takes 6.4 communities to support a single missionary. This contrasts sharply with the levels of support exhibited in surrounding countries: 16.9 for Russia; 92 for Belarus; 24.5 for Hungary, 57.4 for Slovakia, and 62.6 for Romania. Only Poland, which requires 9.7 communities to support a missionary, is even close to the level of commitment to outreach exhibited by Ukrainians.[46]

There is not only a willingness among Ukrainians to support missionaries, there is also a willingness to serve as one. As early as 2001, almost four hundred Ukrainians were serving abroad as full-time missionaries, nearly all of them in Russia, and over five hundred more were working "cross-culturally" within Ukraine. Although the population of Russia is three times that of Ukraine, the 914 Ukrainian evangelical missionaries vastly outnumbered the 396 Russian missionaries.[47] None of the countries mentioned above comes close to supplying as many missionaries as Ukraine does.

Although foreign financial assistance arrived at a critical moment to create infrastructure, it is mainly the efforts of Ukrainian evangelicals that have made these communities grow. By relying on the mobilization of personal social networks, these communities have developed active memberships that are engaged in a variety of intracongregational activities, charitable initiatives within their cities, and outreach programs that extend beyond Ukrainian borders. These public activities give them a significance and visibility that often exceeds what membership numbers alone would suggest.

Historical and anthropological studies of the spread of world religions have generally chronicled how they have overwhelmed local cultures and local religious traditions and sought to explain why. Religion is often evoked as a catalyst of the Weberian modernist shift from a traditionalist and mystical understanding of social order to one based on rationality. Alternatively, others have picked up on Geertz's insight that each cosmology has its own logic—when conversions occur, it is largely attributable to the logic of that world religion echoing in some meaningful way the logic of the indigenous cultural tradition. In other words, since it makes sense to convert, people do.[48] Thanks to the work of John and Jean Comaroff and Peter van der Veer, we have refined our understanding of how cultures undergo change when confronted with prolonged missionizing.[49] These scholars have prompted us to abandon the idea that those visited by missionaries are passive agents in a transformative historical process that dismantles local cultures only to reconfigure them into the likeness of Western capitalist values and practices. Rather, they have convincingly argued that missionizing is a mutually transformative process, affecting both the missionizer and the convert, albeit in different ways.

Peter van der Veer, writing of other colonial contexts and religious encounters, stresses the importance of not seeing the processes of encounter as one in which one group unilaterally modernizes the other, whose role is then limited to reaction. He writes, "The immense creativity in colonial encounters, both on the part of the colonizers and the colonized, is often done little justice in accounts that rather stress failure than innovative practice. The colonial era makes new imaginations of community possible, and it is especially in the religious domain that these new imaginations take shape. In that sense, conversion to another faith is part of a set of much larger transformations affecting both converts, nonconverts, and the missionaries themselves."[50] The legal and political conditions that emerged in Ukraine allowed foreign missionaries, such as Tom and Steve, to settle and work in Ukraine. The experience has transformed them as individuals as well as the Ukrainians who avail themselves of "bookmobile evangelism" and "leadership training." My point here is not to glorify, endorse, or condemn the arrival of foreign missionaries in Ukraine. Rather, I want to explore how these "new imaginations of community" take shape, to illustrate the agency of Ukrainians in reacting to this encounter, which facilitates not just the imaginings of, but also actual membership in, a global community of believers. The desired consequence of these "creative" encounters, conversion, is the first step in forming these new communities.

## What Is Conversion?

Although there is widespread agreement among scholars that conversion involves "radical change" and introduces a "new universe of discourse," there is little consensus about the level on which this change occurs and the specific themes of this discourse.[51] I use the term conversion to refer to a self-transforming experience imbued with spiritual meaning that leads to an ongoing religious mode of experience. Conversion is a process, not a single event, that leads to self transformation and occurs in a dynamic field of people, ideologies, and communities. The essence of the "radical change" brought about by conversion is the new intellectual and social tools that the convert acquires. I pay particular attention to the moral dimensions of these tools and analyze how they enable the convert to parlay a particular experience into knowledge and into an ongoing mode of experiencing that alters established meanings of self and social relationships and the moral obligations that link them. For this reason, I will focus on what conversion narratives reveal about remaking core elements of the self as well as about reconstituting a meaningful sense of identity and belonging.

I take inspiration from Clifford Staples and Armand Mauss, who have written that conversion as a process of self-transformation leads to "the creation of a new vision of who we really believe we are when all our social roles and self-presentations are stripped away."[52] This approach to conversion echoes the numerous conversion narratives told to me by Ukrainian believers. The interaction of good and bad spiritual forces is the primary animating force in the evangelical religious imagination and mystical conception of the world. Converts reformulate their understandings of existence to focus on the dueling supernatural forces of good and evil, as represented by God and Satan, as they vie for control over the fate of individuals. Following the Pauline paradigm of sudden and dramatic change, most believers spoke of an encounter with a spiritual force, which they understood to be God, that constituted for them a life-changing moment, after which previous beliefs and allegiances were no longer tenable and easily renounced. They consistently positioned God during this revelatory moment in an assertive role as the creator of the experience, with the believer an almost passive recipient of God's grace. Conversion, as a pivotal experience that includes a profound epiphany, makes possible the dual processes of self-transformation and commitment to a religious community with its accompanying lifestyle and belief system. The reward for being "born again" and leading a moral existence is salvation, a blissful, eternal afterlife.

Most studies of conversion have been written by psychologists and have attempted to identify patterns as to who converts and why. Such studies have mainly focused on individual agency, sometimes extending to the family, in analyzing how a new faith is chosen. The main contribution of these studies has been to dispense with the idea that conversion is induced by passivity, social pressure to conform, or brainwashing.[53] In other words, the role of missionaries in prompting conversion is secondary to individual seeking. These studies have concluded that converts are more likely than nonconverts to have reported a stressful childhood, a negative opinion of their parents, and a high incidence of paternal absence, all factors that came up again and again in the life histories and conversion narratives that I have heard over the years.[54]

The general critique I have of psychological studies of conversion is that even if they can identify predisposing personality traits, social influences, or stress factors that indicate who is susceptible to conversion, they do not indicate cause. Causal factors are not found consistently among all converts. And such theories do not account for individuals who embody the same traits and are exposed to the same stresses but do not turn to religion. For this reason, I consider the process of converting as inextricably embedded in the cultural fabric of relationships, ideologies, and moralities. By examining the contextual matrix of conversion, one can gain insight as to how an individual can become predisposed to conversion, regardless of the details of their biography. By taking a long view of evangelical practice over time in Ukraine, we can see the dynamics of conversion at this particular historical juncture and how they have influenced who converts and the types of communities that are forming.

The diachronic view becomes important, because as we saw in chapters 1 and 2, even individual communities change their goals and engagement with the social and political order and this, of course, influences what type of person would be motivated to convert and why. At times during the Soviet period, conversion was so tightly monitored that it embodied dissident-like defiance. In a post-Soviet world, conversion provides a platform from which to rupture and discard inherited moralities, memories, and relationships, with justification for doing so on higher moral grounds. It serves as a means to reconstitute lives and soften the dislocation individuals inevitably felt after the fall of the Soviet system. The important point is that each convert is the motor of his or her own self-transformation.

## Misha: The Importance of Dialogue

Misha's path to faith illustrates a number of dynamics that are representative of the numerous conversion narratives I have heard over the years. His experience marks a number of the perils of post-Soviet economic life and shows how conversion can serve as a means of self-transformation by

Figure 4.1: Misha. Photo by the author.

redeeming past mistakes and by remaking them into a source of inspiration
for others. More than most, he illustrated to me the emergence of a religious consciousness and certain religious sensibilities after conversion as a
result of embracing a "universe of discourse," or tropes of talk and patterns
of reasoning. He is originally from a village outside of Yakutsk, the capital
of the Sakha Republic in Siberia, but I met him in 2003 in Kyiv, where he
was studying to become a Pentecostal pastor. Although his family practices
shamanism, he converted to the Baptist faith. After five years as a Baptist,
he found the power of the Holy Spirit undeniable and switched to a Pentecostal Charismatic Church. By the time I met him, I was no longer surprised by the practice in certain evangelical circles whereby members call
each other almost immediately by diminutive forms of first names and not
by the full first name, as one would expect. I responded in kind by suggesting that he call me "Katia." I first formally interviewed him after he and six
other women performed a healing ceremony at a homeless shelter where he
was volunteering nearly every day. Misha's year of pastoral study was financed by one of his spiritual mentors, an American Pentecostal missionary whom he had met in Yakutsk. His American mentor had returned to

California with his family the year before but continued to send money every month to support Misha and his missionary work in Kyiv.

Perhaps because Misha is studying to become a pastor, which entails learning the rhetorical techniques of constructing one's own conversion experience as an inspiration to others or perhaps because he spends a great deal of time witnessing and offering testimony to the greatness of God, Misha had an established narrative of how he found God that he effortlessly recited to anyone willing and curious enough to listen. More than any other individual I interviewed, Misha exemplified the tight relationship that can develop between communally recited narratives of religious experience and the formation of the self as a fundamentally religious person replete with sensibilities that yield experiences of a transcendental nature and heightened spiritual consciousness. Indeed, each time he repeated his conversion narrative, it seemed to become a more real, meaningful, and defining experience. Barely five feet tall with a soft stuttering voice, he is a deeply shy man. Yet he relishes the attention he receives when he proselytizes. The evangelical practice of testifying to the presence of God and to the vital presence of the Holy Spirit in one's life reaffirms not only belief but also the power of faith to redeem sin and instigate sweeping changes in a person's character and life. Reciting one's conversion narrative, especially to the unsaved, affirms one's fundamental being as a believer and the power of God to reverse a descent into sin and provide rebirth through conversion to a moral life as a Christian.

Misha was the sixth of ten children born into a Yakut family. When he was born, his mother lost a great deal of blood and almost died. Weakened and overwhelmed with caring for so many other children, Misha was given to his aunt and uncle, who had no other children, to be raised as their child. Sadly, his aunt died when he was five years old, and he was returned to his parents. The adjustment was difficult for all concerned. He was sent to an *internat,* a Soviet boarding school, over the long winter months and only returned home in summer, an arrangement that he fiercely resented. Feeling abandoned and alienated from his family, he did not do well in school and frequently fought with his parents. Eventually, his mother threw him out, and he vowed never to return. He says flatly, "I never knew any love from my mother."

He landed in Moscow and began to work with his brother. He describes their business as providing "interbank financial services," but I would characterize it as loan sharking. He and his brother procured money from various sources and lent it to individual businessmen who could not otherwise acquire bank credit.

We lived a worldly existence. We didn't know God. We were real sinners. We went everyday to restaurants, to the *bania* to get massages [from prostitutes]. We had that kind of disreputable [Rus. *raspushchennaia*] life . . . Once I earned money, I thought I could live like that and that I wouldn't suffer. But it was all a deception [Rus. *obman*]. Because of money, I began to really suffer. . . . Through me, a man received a large sum of money, nearly $100,000, but they deceived me. They promised me 12 percent interest on the total and a two-room apartment, a car, plus the money back because I was able to get credit for them. Out of avarice and greed, I decided that I would get the money back myself. Because of that, I suffered. I told him that he had a month and a half to get the money back to me. He didn't react. Then I gave him a week more. Then I told him I would take care of him. . . .

At first, I wanted to kidnap his children. He had a little daughter, and for a month I observed the family, watched when they left the house, noticed what time they went to work, when they went to day care [Rus. *sadik*] and with whom, when they returned, and so on. But then a voice appeared and said, "You can't do that. Children should not suffer because of this." I listened to that voice, and that's why I searched for another way. I warned him one more time, telling him that he had a week to give the money back or he would die, and I hung up. I watched him constantly. One day, when he came home, his driver dropped him off, and he came into the building alone. He began to come up the stairs—his apartment was on the seventh floor—and I had turned out the lights so that it would be dark. I waited in the shadows.[55]

Misha knew how to box, how to throw a punch of lethal force. In the darkness of the corridor, Misha jumped him, knocked him to the concrete floor, and beat him. The neighbors heard the ruckus and called the police. Before the police arrived, Misha had beaten him so thoroughly that he had broken several of his bones; he would require weeks of hospitalization. He interpreted his own behavior in the following way:

I thought I had acted justly. I thought, an eye for an eye and a tooth for a tooth. I thought that was justice. But now I understand everything differently. That's not justice. We must love our enemies. But then I didn't know that. Then I thought that if someone offended you, you had to give it back.

When the police arrived, Misha was arrested. He explained that the man had violated a contract. But soon he learned that the contract itself was an *ob-man*. Although the contract was notarized, the notary had been a fake, an un-registered, nonexistent bureau. The Ministry of Internal Affairs summarily declared the contract null and void, nothing more than a worthless scrap of paper, which invalidated the possibility of civil proceedings. Prosecutorial ef-forts began to focus exclusively on charges against Misha for assault. When I asked if it had made a difference that he was a Yakut, he said, "Of course, it played a big role. I'm not Russian. They would have treated me differently if I had been a Russian. It's always been like that, especially in the center."

In 1994 he landed in a Murmansk prison, diagnosed with tuberculosis. For two years his health deteriorated steadily, and with only two months to go in his sentence, he became terribly ill. Conversion is frequently a re-sponse to crisis, a coping strategy that enables an individual to overcome difficulties by reordering or opening a relationship to higher, more powerful forces and by creating potentially supportive relationships within a new community. For Misha, during this period of acute illness, when he weighed only eighty-two pounds and was fed intravenously for two months, a mis-sionary from Finland and a missionary from Norway came to him.

The two Europeans explained to him that God loves him, that Jesus loves him, that every person is a sinner before God. They told him that if he repented, God would heal him. Most memorably, they told him that sin leads to death. It was this last phrase especially that stuck with him. *Posled-stvo grekha est' smert' i bolezn'* (Rus. The consequences of sin are death and illness). He says that he can still remember hearing them say it.

> They repeated this phrase several times. They spoke Russian very badly, but they said very clearly, "Misha, Jesus loves you." They said that they would return in three days and that I should think about re-penting and that they would pray for me so that God would heal me. They left me the Bible. There was a chapter, "If you are sick," and "If you are alone," "God has redeemed you," and I began to read these chapters of the psalms. I realized that I am a sinner before God. I asked this higher power, if there is a God who created this world and created me, I said I was a sinner and please forgive me. Then I couldn't really pray. I didn't know how. I acknowledged all my debts and forgave my enemies. I didn't want to die. I really wanted to live. Before that, I always called up all my gods, those of my ancestors, the god of the sun, the spirit of water. But they didn't come to me, and they never gave an answer. But when I repented, I really felt lighter

inside. I felt as if something was happening inside me. It was the Holy Spirit, but I didn't know it. I was in such a state. When they returned, they said, "Misha, we want you to repent," but I told hem that I already did. They prayed for me. We all started saying "Hallelujah!" I felt real joy. They said that God would heal me. They left, and I was lying there. In the night, the air that I was breathing became hot, really hot. I could feel real heat inside of me. I threw up, and there was part of my lungs, lots of blood, 120 grams of blood, and I began to cry. At first I thought that God didn't forgive me and that I was dying. For the next three days, I continued to vomit blood, but less and less.[56] I began to understand that it was the Holy Spirit that was in me, that hot, powerful force. I understood later that the Holy Spirit healed me. I didn't know it at the time. On the fourth day, I wanted to eat, for the first time in two months. On the fifth day, I was outright hungry. When I said I wanted to eat, the nurse cried. She couldn't believe it. And since that time, I've been telling everyone, if you repent, God will heal you. A week later, the doctors couldn't believe it. After two weeks, they considered me cured of tuberculosis, and I was transferred out of the medical unit.

I have heard Misha retell this experience, obviously so meaningful to him, to a doctor who is not a believer. Not surprisingly, the doctor suggested that instead of the Holy Spirit miraculously curing him of active tuberculosis, perhaps the original diagnosis was incorrect and he simply recovered from some other illness. But Misha would not have any of that. He now believes that divine power is the causal force for all events in our lives. It has become his "master attribution scheme" that explains all. He was convinced that he was dying, that he had been about to slip away, and that the heat of the Holy Spirit restored his life by chasing out the evil that had overtaken his life.

After being released from the medical unit, Misha was returned to a regular jail cell where twelve men were housed together. Among the prisoners, he began to speak of his healing experience, of the value of repenting. One day, one of the other eleven men with whom he was sharing a cell became so fed up with his preaching that he threatened to throw a table on his head if he wouldn't shut up about "his God." Out of pride, Misha explains, he refused to back down and challenged him to a fight. For the skirmish, he received thirty days in solitary confinement in a small, cold, poorly lit cell. The dim light could not hide the abhorrent sanitary conditions. The worst thing, Misha said, was the ever-present pungent smell of bleach that permeated the air, making it impossible to breath normally.

At first I did some exercises to warm up. But then I heard a loud voice say, "Son, what were you punished for?" I didn't understand—there was no one. Only four walls. Who spoke? But then again I carried on with my gymnastics, and again, that loud voice said, "Son, what were you punished for?" I stood up and knocked on the door. I asked the guard if he had heard a voice. He said, "No, maybe you're going crazy." Maybe I was, I thought, because it was a loud voice. How could he not have heard it? Again, I did exercises and lay down on the bed. The third time the voice spoke, I stood up and a light, a cloud, appeared. A white, cloud-like figure. Right away I went down on my knees and began to repent. I began to cry, and God began to show me all my sins that I had done throughout my life. The first thing I understood was that I needed to forgive my mother. I needed to love my enemies, and my mother had become my enemy.

The voice of Satan told me that I shouldn't forgive them because they threw me out, my mother abandoned me, and I suffered so many years because of that. God spoke to me, but Satan did too. I couldn't understand this. But God said, "Repent, repent." I did repent, and I felt the love of God very strongly. I can't explain it with words. [He begins to cry and can not speak for a while.]

God started to speak to me. He hasn't left me since. On that day I began to see my life unfold before me. I started to see where I will study, where I will preach. He showed me my calling. Through me God speaks.

Although he mentioned that after he was released from prison he continued to hear the voice of Satan trying to coax him back to his old life, I asked whether he even now hears the voice of Satan. He said, "No, of course, not now. I've accepted God now. The voice of God is stronger. I have power from the moment God spoke with me, and from the moment when I repented fully. Those who have God don't suffer, and I don't suffer."

When he was released from a three-year sentence in February 1997, he went straight to the Good Samaritan Baptist Church in Murmansk. They fed him and prayed with him, but they wouldn't let him spend the night in the church. Offended, Misha went to the police and asked them to lock him up for the night so that he would have a warm bed to sleep in. That's how his freedom landed him back in jail the very first night. He eventually obtained money from state authorities to purchase a ticket to Moscow, where he petitioned other state authorities, who eventually gave him a ticket to Yakutsk.

In Moscow, he made it a point to visit the man he had beaten to ask for his forgiveness. The man didn't understand the gesture, Misha claims, because he is proud and lives another life. But Misha asserted that he had begun to live his life for God, and this meant demonstrating love for his enemies, first for the man who deceived him, then for his mother who abandoned him.

## A New Universe of Discourse

Misha's conversion experience is reminiscent of George Herbert Mead's early insight that a new "universe of discourse" becomes available to the convert to recast selfhood and to find new meaning in social life.[57] Conversion is given meaning through narrativization, through linguistic representations.[58] Narrativization is the key to understanding an *experience* that comes to be understood as a *religious* experience, provoking the dual processes of self-transformation and commitment to a religious group. The meaning imparted to an experience becomes the vehicle of parlaying it into a mode of continued experiencing. Templates of narrativization are readily available to individuals—like Misha—who have heard frequent "testimonies" of transcendent conversion experiences during services, on television, and in Christian literature that predispose converts to understand sensations and sensibilities in certain culturally inscribed ways. It is in the retelling of the "conversion experience" that the experience itself is reconstituted and made meaningful.

The retelling of the experience serves to sustain an ongoing sense of transcendental reality in the narrator's life, a continuing recognition of divine presence, which has been ushered into the convert's life. By acknowledging a relationship linking the narrative, the original encounter, and ongoing spiritual experiences, one must also reckon with the fact that conversion narratives evolve over time in tandem with available templates, life circumstances, and the social and cultural context in which the narrator lives. These stories must adapt and evolve in their constant retelling in order to remain meaningful.

In her study of American Baptist fundamentalists, Susan Harding argues that becoming a believer in its most basic essence brings about a shift in speech by introducing a narrative tradition of witnessing between the believer and God and between the saved believer and the unsaved listener.[59] By actively listening, one experiences belief vicariously, and this becomes the first step to converting. Recall that Misha heard the missionaries' words "the consequences of sin are sickness and death," and this ultimately initiated the conversion process. By speaking or witnessing, Harding claims, the believer uses a particular narrative tradition that celebrates submitting to God's will, placing it as "the centering principle of your identity, your personal and public life, your view of human nature and history, and joining a particular narrative tradition to which you willingly submit your past, present and future as a speaker."[60] Indeed, even in his weakened and vulnerable state, Misha nevertheless "heard" the basic message of redemption and transcendence delivered by these European missionaries in their broken Russian.

Witnessing, and the rhetorical devices it involves, including reciting how one converted, becomes a means of reaffirming belief and of reaffirming one's willingness to submit to the will of God as one hears it; ultimately it is a means of inspiring others to believe, which explains why Misha felt compelled to speak incessantly about his spiritual encounter. Harding's study makes the significant contribution of drawing our attention to the importance of narrating the conversion experience and the ensuing dialogue with God in terms of sustaining and strengthening *generative* belief for the narrator. I am particularly interested in how believers speak about the past in conversion narratives and how it specifically relates to transcending the past. If "speaking is believing," as Harding argues, conversion narratives offer insight into how converts fashion new dispositions that predispose them to embrace an identity as a "believer" as evidenced by the observance of a new moral code advocated by religious communities.

Other studies have considered how individual discourses about the past might be used to understand and decipher the present. Serguei Oushakine has found that the first post-Soviet generation, when asked to self-identify, exhibits "aphasia," that is, the loss of a metalanguage in which the self and subjectivity can be articulated.[61] He writes:

> this fundamental lack of mediating structures that makes it hard for the individual to assume a certain subject position *vis-à-vis* social changes brings with it the problem of subjectivity, the problem of one's self-localisation and self-description in regard to the processes that have yet to be loaded with graspable meaning. To put it differently, the lack of mediating structures coincides with the lack of "tools" with which to understand the transformation. Without such tools, neither the changes themselves nor one's relation to them can become meaningful.[62]

Conversion becomes a way to meaningfully complete the "transition" of self-transformation by forming a bridge from one's former Soviet self to a new form of subjectivity deemed more moral and more in keeping with the new cultural context. Religious organizations are highly developed mediating structures that deliver via the dual processes of conversion and becoming "saved" the social, moral, and, perhaps most of all, rhetorical tools for reconstituting the self. Conversion puts an end to aphasia by introducing an autobiographical template and a framework for repositioning oneself in the world, in a particular community, and in a relationship with the divine. In doing so, a narrative of self, identity, and belonging is reconstituted.

Misha, as well as many other believers, alluded to a fear of losing this dialogue with God. Believers express gratitude for this presence that vastly reduces loneliness and provides a measure of assurance that one is protected and living a righteous life. These sentiments were echoed by Oleg, who became a Baptist in 2000 at the age of thirty-four. He explains how listening to God has transformed his patterns of daily living and how the importance he places on maintaining this dialogue with God sustains these changes:

> I didn't become, rather I am becoming a different person. The process is moving along. I would say that earlier I ran after sin—I used to like to drink, to be with girls, to look for adventure. All of that interested me—now sin inspires in me the fear of God. I'm not interested in it anymore. I'm afraid of losing contact with God, of becoming lost. God not only helps you, but he will find the best solution for you. There's contact with God, and there's a certainty that God will always help you. And there's a wish not to lose this contact, a fear that it might break down.[63]

What Misha and Oleg interpret as an animated, vibrant dialogue with God, others might dismiss as "conscience," "intuition," or "sensations." But it is really something more. For them, this dialogue offers assurances of an omniscient, omnipotent, ever-present partner who will indicate the proper life course to take, if only one will be open to hearing or seeing the signs. This explains in part the serene inner peace believers claim to find after conversion. As a result of this "dialogue," believers can rest assured that they have a protector. This "conversation with God," the "inner voice" to which believers can appeal, has enormous significance for generating and strengthening belief, especially if an individual is repeatedly confronted by situations that are difficult to decipher and moral quandaries that resist resolution. Of this dialogue between God and convert, Harding writes:

> Among fundamentalist Baptists, the Holy Spirit brings you under conviction by speaking to your heart. Once you are saved, the Holy

Spirit assumes your voice, speaks through you, and begins to rephrase your life. Listening to the gospel enables you to experience belief, as it were vicariously. But generative belief, belief that indisputably trans-figures you and your reality, belief that becomes you, comes only through speech: speaking is believing.[64]

We saw how Misha's conversion narrative highlighted the importance of speech: the Holy Spirit spoke only to *him* while he was in solitary confine-ment. The guard heard nothing. And now, with his new lease on life, Misha sees his calling as preaching, endlessly repeating for inspirational purposes, for himself as much as for others, how the Holy Spirit brought him under conviction by clearing his body of illness and of refining his spiritual self through continued dialogue. His sees his calling as allowing God to speak to him and through him. He in turn will serve God by listening faithfully to his voice, by following the paths God opens in visions. This sense of calling also involves telling the unsaved how they too can initiate such a dialogue, end aphasia, ease loneliness and uncertainty in this world, and look for-ward to salvation as one of the "saved" in the next.

## Sergei: Empowerment through Submission

This dialogue with God, which converts cite as one of the key benefits of becoming religious, has very significant ramifications for how one sees one's place in the world. The new obligation as a believer to attempt to ful-fill the will of God faithfully also mandates that the convert reformulate a sense of individual agency and autonomy. For most believers, individual agency is recast within the parameters of listening to God's voice and over-coming temptation from the devil. Everything, from the progression of history to the decisions individuals make in the course of a day, is under-stood to be the result of higher powers setting destiny. There is no chance, no happenstance, no luck, only the dueling forces of benevolence and evil that decide our fate. "Blessings," however a believer might identify them, are understood to have been bestowed because the believer correctly fol-lowed the directives of God over those of Satan.

For the first several months into this research, I was puzzled by this. I took it to be an abdication of responsibility for one's life course. If every-thing was controlled by God and was simply unfolding according to a pre-fixed plan devised for each and every one of us, how was it that believers could claim to feel empowered? Why would they ever go out of their way to try to accomplish anything if the outcome was preordained anyway? I mistakenly understood the universal explanation for all occurrences linked to God's omnipotence to mean an erasure of all sense of agency. Rather, part of the "radical change" that ensues after the process of conversion is a redefinition of agency, submission, and empowerment. Once an individual begins an ongoing dialogue with God, in which the convert recognizes God as the voice giving direction, the task of the convert becomes listening to that voice and faithfully following its lead. Although an active shepherd-like role is projected on to God and a reactive, sheep-like role to the believer, there is still a certain measure of initiative that plays directly into feelings of empowerment. If a believer listens well, hears God's voice, and fulfills his wishes, the believer can be assured that many "blessings" will flow. In other words, by submitting to the will of God—and there are various points where one must choose to do so—one can harness the power of God for oneself and thereby become empowered to achieve. By surrendering all notions of personal autonomy, one is actually better able to fulfill one's wishes because one has come under the protective wing of God. If a convert's relationship with God is revealed to be strong through the convert's own observance of morality, piety, and holiness, the convert will be rewarded with eschatological hope and the promise of salvation. What appears to be a paradox, empowering oneself via surrendering autonomy and relegating oneself to the role of sign reader, can also be understood as a means of navigating both the secular and sacred worlds, much like the paradoxical strategy of defiant compliance discussed earlier. Much of this reasoning is predicated on a fundamental change in how one understands good and evil. An individual who listens to and seeks to fulfill the will of God, as it is revealed in words, visions, and other symbolic forms of communication, will be rewarded by being on the triumphant side of the battle between evil and benevolent forces. Individuals can justify virtually any decision by asserting that it was the will of God.

The experiences of Sergei illustrate how a reformulation of good and evil, virtue and vice, right and wrong can be symbolically reformulated in religious experience and used to shift how an individual enacts moral principles. Sergei situates his conversion within a particularly stark and prolonged battle between spiritual forces for human souls. Born and raised in Kharkiv, he is the only son of factory workers. When I interviewed him, he was thirty years old and already the father of three. He had recently become a Pentecostal pastor at the Word of Life Church described in chapter 5. He recounts how years ago, a destructive and suffocating force repeatedly came to him in the night over a five-year period, which he came to understand was the devil. By this time, his wife had converted to Methodism, but Sergei remained a nominal Orthodox believer, which means that he claims to have believed in God but was otherwise entirely nonpracticing. What he did practice, however, was a variety of martial arts and meditation. As he explains:

> Then I experienced some kind of a spiritual world, I don't know what I should call it, but the devil came to me and choked me. I couldn't do anything about it. In the morning, I would start to live normally again. I was happy, I worked, I trained—at that time I really devoted my life to kung fu. But in the night I would go into contact with the other world, with the devil. That's how I understood it. The devil would come to me in the night and choke me, and this lasted for about five years. I was already married, but he would choke me. I didn't know, was this a dream? It was horrible! I couldn't sleep. In the course of the night, he would choke me five or six times. I knew that if I went to any doctors, they would just put me in a psych ward and that would be it. But you know, I was a normal person. I understood everything. I served in the army, and everything was OK. I did more and more martial arts and began to meditate more seriously. But this just brought me to a spiritual death. That is to say, I was really agitated. I had a lot of worries. I didn't know what to do. I brought holy water home and sprinkled it around and took out knives just to go to sleep. I began to baptize everything. That's the way it was. But still he would come and laugh at me and choke me. I saw him. Sometimes I would turn on the light and still I would see him.[65]

With the urging of his wife, he began to attend her Methodist church. The first time he visited a service, he repented, which is highly unusual, and he eventually became a deacon. His nightly visits from the devil began to change. One night, as he was being choked, he yelled out, "In the name of Jesus Christ, away with you!" And at that moment, the devil vanished—only to return again.

> I kept on repeating the same phrase, and eventually he left and I fell asleep. But I understood that it was God who did it. For me this was confirmation that God had saved me, not the holy water, not baptizing everything, not the "Our Father" prayers. But the blood of Jesus Christ. I understood that there was a God and that he sees me. I left everything that I did before. I confessed and renounced all of that.

Throughout the course of many years, the devil came to me, but then Jesus expelled him from the house. The devil came back about a month later, then a year or so later, then in two years, but he couldn't hold his ground. Now I'm already a believer, and I will drive him away. I repeat that phrase in my sleep.

Although many things could explain feelings of panic-induced shortness of breath or gasping for air in the middle of the night, Sergei attributed it to the devil, and he interpreted his triumph over it as evidence of the power of God. Perhaps he himself was struggling with some form of stress induced by conflicting sexual impulses. Note that he says, "I was already married, but he would choke me" as if the fact of marriage should establish his sexuality and its propriety. He also made the point of stressing how happy he and his wife are together with their three children. This is a familiar rhetorical technique. Many converts enumerate the "blessings" that have been bestowed upon them since converting, as further evidence of the righteousness of the path they have chosen.

Sergei understands his coming to faith as the result of a victorious battle of God over the devil. Nothing he did with his worldly powers was of any use. The devil still plagued him. Later, through informal contact with Pentecostals, Sergei learned of the Holy Spirit. Intrigued by the doctrine, he switched his membership from the Methodist Church to a traditional Pentecostal congregation. In 2001 he was ordained in a "laying on of hands" ceremony as pastor and now serves a congregation of about six hundred.

## Conversion and New Moralities

Eileen Barker argues that many converts to the Unification Church are idealists who joined the church to express their idealism through action, especially those who had perceived idealism and altruism as discounted by society at large in favor of materialism and self-advancement. She writes:

> The Unification Church offers the potential recruit the chance to be part of a Family of like-minded people who care about the state of the world, who accept and live by high moral standards, who are dedicated to restoring God's Kingdom of Heaven on earth. It offers him the opportunity to *belong*; it offers him the opportunity to *do* something that is of value and thus the opportunity *to be* of value.[66]

She goes on to characterize converts to the Unification Church as individuals who have a strong sense of service, duty, and responsibility and are also achievers grappling with an unfulfilled yearning to contribute to the greater good of humanity. These converts, she argues, find a means to realize their idealism as members of the Unification Church.

There is a similar dynamic driving conversion here. In these circles, by witnessing, missionaries and converts are perceived as *doing* something of value and by extension they are licensed to see themselves as *being* of value, a sentiment that often eludes them in the wider society. Thanks to newly awakened religious sensibilities, they see themselves as having become better, more moral people; as having developed deeper, more committed relationships; and this leads to improved perceptions of self-esteem. Perhaps most important, narratives reveal a self-image as a reliable, respectable, person (Ukr. *poriadna liudyna*, Rus. *poriadochnyi chelovek*). In many instances, this change was part of adapting to the ethos of the congregation they had joined, which they perceived to be markedly "kinder" than the greater society.

Lena, a student in Kharkiv, explains how she became interested in exploring the Baptist faith when she was sixteen years old and living with her family in Luhansk. Her parents were not believers but her grandmother was. Her grandmother took Lena to church and Sunday school as a small child. When she was sixteen, one of Lena's friends celebrated his birthday by throwing a party and inviting his friends. For nonbelievers, religious and state holidays have traditionally held little meaning, although this is changing. Birthdays remain, however, the single most important and joyful day of the year. In spite of this, only Lena and her brother came to the party. It was extremely cold that day, and the other guests simply stayed at home. Lena was indignant:

> That really bothered me, and I thought, what is that kind of friendship worth? I began to compare the relationships among young people in this group with the relationships among young people in the Sunday school I used to attend and came to the conclusion that the latter were far more favorable. They were calmer, not aggressive, and they had a sense of purpose in life. I was drawn to them again. The first Sunday after that party, I called my grandmother and asked her to take me to church, and we went together.[67]

A failed birthday party ushered forth a renewed interest in pursuing a religious lifestyle. The very day she returned to church, she repented and claimed that she felt, as she described it, "a huge sense of relief, as if I had been given a long, white robe and my task now was not to soil it." I interviewed her five years later, when she had already become a member of a Baptist church, and she claimed that her childhood impressions had only been confirmed many times over. "People here are not like those in the world," she said. "They are much better. Much kinder." The perception that believers relate to one another differently than nonbelievers do, that there is genuinely more solidarity and mutual support in the community, which serves to foster an atmosphere of kindness, is a key point of attraction. I have heard converts claim on many occasions that they are better able to reject manipulative patterns of interaction, the "functional friendship" that characterizes mainstream society, and to relax the defenses needed to guard against being deceived.[68]

Lena looks around her community and sees people at peace with themselves, engaged in genuinely caring relationships. This is very likely an idealized view. But that she perceives such an atmosphere in her church community and adapts herself to it, both consciously and subconsciously, becomes relevant because she uses it to conclude that she has embarked on a path that is making her into a better, kinder person. Neither Lena nor anyone else I ever interviewed recognized this sense of becoming a "better" person as an arrogant judgment of superiority over other people because they understood such impulses to be God-given, as a reward for faith.

Besides the feeling of a kindness-induced greater connection to other people, other respondents alluded to various other benefits associated with becoming a believer. Some scholars have argued that faith communities that demand significant sacrifice or sweeping changes in behavior from their members generally have congregations with more highly committed members, and it is this that makes them attractive in spite of the high costs involved in joining. In other words, "strict" congregations are able to offer a plethora of activities because they have active and committed members giving their time, money, and participation.[69] So even though one is required to give a lot, one is entitled to receive much as well.

Shura, a fifty-five-year-old accountant from Kharkiv who became a practicing Baptist in 1993, explains how conversion has changed how she relates to others:

> Now as I'm no longer part of the church choir, I have more time. I visit the sick—believers and nonbelievers. I visit the elderly parents of one of my friends. I help them take care of themselves. If I wasn't a believer, I would help, let's say, only my close friends. Now for me

> there are no longer strangers. . . . For a worldly person, it is, of course,
> strange. We're not relatives. But at the same time, we're much
> more—we're brothers and sisters in faith.[70]

Shifts in attitudes toward those outside one's circle and by extension the obligation to help them, what I am calling a new moral code, can be difficult for the nonbeliever to understand and accept because they represent such a break with accepted cultural practices. Turning to religion to encourage mutual assistance and interdependence as a new norm is in sharp distinction to the mercantile, instrumental, and tactical appeals to religion for personal material benefit that Melissa Caldwell and Galina Lindquist report among Russians and that many non-evangelical Ukrainians project onto Protestant converts.[71] For Lena and Shura, the motivation to convert or to encourage others to convert stems from a desire to change certain patterns of behavior, specifically those that relate to commitments to provide mutual assistance to others. They advocate an alternative way of situating oneself in society in which a rapport of responsiveness is ideally extended to all.

Encouraging a change in behavior can also work in the opposite direction, however. When a member of a faith community violates its communal norms, however they are understood, a rigorous sense of order mandates that that person be excommunicated (Ukr. *vidluchaty,* Rus. *iskliuchit'*). Usually the offender is given a trial period during which the person is allowed to try to amend the errant behavior. If insufficient modifications are made, the entire congregation usually participates in an open vote to determine if the person should be excommunicated or not. In Soviet-era congregations, mothers were even asked to "testify" against children, wives against husbands, to ascertain if the rules of communal morality had been violated. Frequent contact among members allows for close scrutiny of behavior. The possibility of quickly identifying transgressions leads to greater accountability to the group and makes it easier to uphold the norms of morality and behavior that define the group. In short, members subscribe to a new moral code and tolerate the restrictions on their behavior that set them apart from the society at large not only because their spiritual and emotional needs are met, but also because membership often yields specific social and material rewards. As growing numbers of people gather in congregations regularly across the country, they reaffirm these moralities, practices, and identities, starting with changing the individual as an initial and strategic step to transforming the social.

## Realizing a New Moral Order

Conversion recasts notions of authority. Patricia Ewick and Susan Silbey have found that some conversion narratives reveal "subversive stories" that undermine established authority structures, whereas others constitute "hegemonic tales" that serve to uphold the status quo.[72] In my experience, conversion narratives have elements of both and regardless of which direction they lean, moral principles are used to justify the "subversive" and "hegemonic" dimensions. For example, evangelicals are at once supportive of established authority, be it the state, the law, the clergy, and so on, even as they try to redefine what those authorities can and should punish as transgressions, muddying the boundaries between the subversive and the hegemonic. Several studies that consider morality in isolation from religion acknowledge only that social change prompts a redefinition of commitments that affects moral understandings.[73] In transition societies, a fractured social order yields competing moral orders and contradictory moral judgments of the behavior of other people, especially when contrasted against one's own actions. By divorcing morality from religion, such studies can only identify the fluid and diverse socioeconomic circumstances that individuals or groups encounter and how they interpret them morally. Evangelical religious groups merit our attention because they attempt to articulate and impart a single shared moral order. Indeed, it is this very act of imposing a unified total view of personal and social morality that inspires disdain among nonevangelicals. I am suggesting that there is growing receptivity to this project in Ukraine. Conversion serves as a means to cut through the thicket of moral quandaries one encounters in post-Soviet society by providing a comprehensive—and rigid—moral vision and reaffirming the righteousness of that vision by participating in a community that attempts to realize and uphold that moral vision. In other words, conversion in its most basic form brings forth moral change by establishing new forms of authority and commitments to submit to those authorities.

Diane Austin-Broos describes conversion as a "cultural passage," with a definite direction and shape that lead to reidentifying, reordering, relearning, and reorienting.[74] The idea of a passage is useful in that it suggests an open-ended journey, with the conversion as a point of departure rather than an attained destination. Although this passage often begins with experimentation and is frequently characterized by starts and stops, in many respects it never ends.

Many of my respondents claimed the immediate catalyst to explore religion was a combination of psychological and social stress brought on by serious illness, seemingly intractable family problems, persistent unemployment, and other such troubles, which led to feelings of acute powerlessness and helplessness. Many converts reported sustained interaction during these stressful periods with converted kin, friends, or trusted mentors. This is reminiscent of John Lofland and Rodney Stark's early contribution that "attachment" is at the heart of conversion.[75] As Chana Ullman has written, "conversion pivots around a sudden attachment, an infatuation with a real or imagined figure which occurs on a background of great emotional turmoil. The typical convert was transformed not by a religion, but by a person. The discovery of a new truth was indistinguishable from a discovery of a new relationship, which relieved, at least temporarily, the upheaval of the previous life."[76] A convert rewrites autobiography into pre- and post-conversion periods, retrospectively seeing signs of the impending conversion in one's deep past as an affirmation of the righteousness of the Christian life one has adopted and as a means of bridging the two periods, the lost and the saved. Misha has used his conversion to divide his life into the "bad," "sinful," "misguided" phase and the new period of redeemed hope as a result of being "saved." In this way, conversion provides a symbolic transformation of the crisis experience that leads to redemption and salvation.

### Religious Encounters and the Converted Self

Conversion opens a dialogue with God in which the convert gains a conversation partner who is understood to give directives from an omniscient, omnipotent position. The dialogue erases former understandings of luck, chance, intuition, and randomness. The mystical indicators that a person experiences are now understood to be the very voice of God. The job of the convert is to respond to divine instruction so as to be victorious in the daily battle between good and evil forces. A believer's life is now allied with God and dedicated to God, which means that there are certain disciplinary practices rooted in moral values that one must accept. One engages in these practices and espouses these values as witness to the positive life changes that conversion has brought. New practices and values are the public side of this transformation and mark communal membership.

All of these changes remake a person's sense of self on a very fundamental level. Converting to evangelicalism in post-Soviet Ukrainian society entails redefining fundamental cultural categories, such as agency and power, familiar and foreign, space and time, and gender and class, leading to revised notions of selfhood based on certain emotions and disciplinary practices. With being saved comes the obligation to evangelize, to tell others of the redeeming power of faith as revealed in the Gospel. When foreign missionaries began to arrive in the late 1980s to evangelize Ukrainians, they did not engage Orthodoxy as an indigenous faith per se. Rather, western missionaries cast their faith as a source of "truth," "goodness," and "moral empowerment." They contrasted the superiority of their belief system with the "atheism" they projected onto the Soviet socialist social order and its collapse. Therefore, efforts to convert others were aimed at moving individuals from a position of nonbelief in a "dead" communist society lacking in morals to a "born again" experience of moral renewal leading to membership in a global community in this life and salvation in the afterlife.

The majority of evangelicals in Ukraine today were nonpracticing and nonreligious prior to their conversions. This is an important distinction that separates the narratives I present here from other studies of conversion. "Conversion" is most often used to describe an individual who has simply transferred membership from one religious community to another, usually within the same tradition, but not always.

Individuals choose a particular faith in part because it resonates with some aspect of an individual's historical experience. This connection with the past in post-Soviet Ukraine usually centered on a pronounced desire to change or even reject an individual's past private and social life. I have argued elsewhere that evangelical faiths derive a good bit of their appeal from propagating a "new beginning as a different (and morally superior) person."[77] Whether this sense of moral superiority is justified is another question entirely. The point is that people come to think of themselves as having become more moral. The new collective identity and group membership that conversion delivers is marked by subsequent individual behavior modifications as public manifestations of inner spiritual change. Being "born again" plays a pivotal role in assimilating, mediating, and subsuming other social forms of identity and committing one's life goals and everyday practices to be in keeping with religious doctrine and a particular moral code. Foreign missionaries sometimes helped spark the dual processes of conversion and self-transformation. But it is communal membership that helps sustain these changes so that over time they evolve into dispositions and naturalized proclivities.

## Part Three

---

# A WORLD WITHOUT END

CHAPTER FIVE

# GOD IS LOVE

*New Bonds, New Communities*

There is a wide spectrum of potential religious communities to join in Ukraine today, and it continues to expand. Here I illustrate aspects of that spectrum by profiling two pairs of partnered congregations, two Baptist and two Pentecostal. All are located in Kharkiv. In both cases, the Soviet-era central Baptist and Pentecostal congregations experienced such rapid growth that both spun off "daughter congregations." (Such gendered language is commonly used.) Both "daughters" are slated to replace the "mother" as the new central church for each denomination in Kharkiv. In both instances, Western missionaries played a prominent role in "planting" the new church by securing funds for a new building, training clergy, or shaping the atmosphere in the new daughter congregation.

I have a two goals in contrasting these two pairs of churches and comparing the dynamics driving intra-congregational change. First, I wish to show that the legalistic, formalized, and fundamentalist atmosphere that was created during the Soviet era in Pentecostal and Baptist communities is not only difficult to sustain after immigration, as we saw in chapter 3, it is increasingly impossible to sustain in Ukraine too. Much of the formality and moral asceticism in post-Soviet society is withering in favor of more charismatic forms of worship. By considering these two pairs of congregations, we can see the ways in which internal developments, collaborative interaction among Ukrainian communities, and engagement with people and forces outside the group have altered the ideological and behavioral patterns within Soviet-era congregations. The fundamentalist attributes of Soviet-era communities are vanishing primarily because they are abandoning their "separatist" stance against the world and opting for a more accommodationist and integrationist ethos that places increasing emphasis on evangelization, witnessing, and outreach to "save" the unsaved from moral ambivalence, false teaching, and a denial of salvation.

This new emphasis on outreach involves extending the commitments a believer should have to other coreligionists to include anyone in need, regardless of whether or not they are a believer. This new readiness to orchestrate a collective response to need also begins to institutionalize volunteer charitable responses to social ills, which, in turn, slowly reshapes attitudes and commitments to the state. Although all four congregations still prioritize moral reform in intimate zones of life over projects to reform the political or economic order, mounting efforts to project "God's law" onto the secular laws of the country increasingly place these congregations in a worldly domain and further erode separationist tendencies.

My second aim is to show that the dichotomy between the choices of a national or foreign faith is increasingly a false one, if it ever had any validity. As Terence Ranger writes of Africa, "we should see mission churches as much less alien and independent churches as much less African."[1] The same could be said of religious life in Ukraine. As I have noted, the national Ukrainian churches have links to institutions and hierarchies located abroad, be it the Vatican or the Moscow Patriarchate. In spite of government and popular fears of the encroachment of a new form of imperial domination brought on by Western missionaries, it seems to me that a different dynamic has been unleashed.

By exploring attitudes toward Western missionaries and visiting foreign preachers, we see a highly discerning selection of certain attributes and practices—and a rejection of others. Rather than suggesting that missionaries and the forms of global Christianity they represent amount to another hegemonic ideology "converting" Ukrainians to its worldview, I wish to argue that a blending of cultural influences is occurring, albeit against a background of inequality, that alters notions of morality and religious practice in novel ways. Ukrainian believers selectively appropriate, modify, and sometimes reject the practices missionaries offer in spite of the clear power differentials that exist between international missionary organizations and local Ukrainian congregations. The process of local adaptation in Ukraine and elsewhere places these global models of religious institutional organization in a permanent state of evolution because the models are constantly transformed as they are applied. Conversion to an evangelical faith exerts appeal because it opens up access to new zones of contact. In this way, all religious organizations are obliged to respond to the local context in which they function as well as to articulate the links they offer to individuals, communities, and institutions beyond Ukrainian borders. The visiting preachers, missionaries, and dignitaries from abroad underline the global dimensions of religion today, even as they simultaneously serve to locate Ukraine within it.

In short, the watershed arrival of global Christianity to the formerly sequestered communities of evangelical believers in Ukraine has created a point of intersection where different cultural traditions blend. Local faith-based communities in Ukraine have become sites of cultural innovation as members take cultural values born of another historical experience and add them, often in a modified form, to their own cultural repertoire. These emerging new communities are at once highly local and transnational in orientation. They are also increasingly politically aware and engaged. As we will see, for these four congregations in Kharkiv, the impetus for change and cultural fusion came as much from interaction with each other as it did from outside influences.

## God Is Love: Two Baptist Communities in Kharkiv

"God is Love" is painted over the arched opening to the nave of the central Baptist church in the city of Kharkiv, evoking the Augustinian idea that the love of God inevitably involves other relationships. This saying implies that the power of love must flow through the entire social body, touching all who inhabit it, regardless of their status, and that this love cannot not simply be contemplative but rather performative, as in deeds of mercy.[2] "God is Love" is advanced as the central orienting principle of communal life at this church.

The rest of the interior feels distinctly Slavic, with pale blue walls, reminiscent of the imperial buildings in St. Petersburg. Biblical citations painted on the walls and potted plants are the only other decorations, reflecting an austerity that characterizes Protestant congregations and sharply distinguishes them from the sumptuousness of Orthodox churches. This is the oldest surviving Baptist community in the city. Founded in 1892, it has been located in its current building on a quiet residential street, safely surrounded by fences, since the 1940s. The church is part of a small complex that includes a large meeting room, a kitchen, offices, and music

Figure 5.1: Original Central
Baptist Church. Photo by the
author.

rooms, all of which were built by members of the community. Individual
believers have for decades now taken turns renovating and maintaining the
buildings as well as providing all secretarial and administrative duties.

Like all religious institutions in the region, its history was shaped by
policies that vacillated between strong repression of religious organizations
and resigned toleration of their existence. Nonetheless, during the Soviet
period it remained the heart of the Baptist community in Kharkiv. Currently, five pastors and twenty-two deacons serve the nearly 1,250 members
of this church, its four daughter churches in the city of Kharkiv, and two
additional ones in the suburbs. The six additional churches were opened
between 1987 and 2002, and each began with a handful of believers from the
central church. There were two reasons for the expansions: the central
church could no longer accommodate all of the potential congregants, and
there was a shift in thinking on outreach. Rather than the church acting as
a privileged enclave, always available to anyone who sought it out, there

was a growing sense of obligation, even commitment, that believers should bring the church to the people.

By virtue of being the oldest Baptist church in Kharkiv, this community is one of the more traditional. Like most longstanding communities, there has been a sharp decline in the Soviet-era membership thanks to emigration. The traditional ethos and formality, along with the older membership to whom that appeals, distinguishes this congregation from others in the city. Dress remains rather formal. Women wear only skirts and cover their heads. Men wear dress shirts buttoned all the way up. The music played during services includes only vocal ensembles, organ, and some orchestral instruments, certainly no electric instruments.

I hasten to add, however, that in the five years that I spoke with members of this church and attended its events, I saw much of this tradition and formality change before my very eyes. When I began this research, there was much suspicion over who I was and a great deal of caution in dealing with "a worldly foreigner" without authorization from the pastor. That I did not cover my head sharply marked me as an interloper and explained why many believers were initially hesitant to speak with me beyond the level of pleasantries. I saw this attitude soften considerably over the years as suspicion turned into curiosity. Granted, this is in part attributable to the fact that I persisted in showing up over several years. Yet other factors, such as ongoing contact with foreign visitors and preachers, receipt of humanitarian aid from the West, and the practice of sharing "greetings" from members who had visited other congregations or countries, which happens at least five times during the average service, also steadily softened the guarded attitude toward Westerners as embodying corrupting forces.

The reaction to foreigners parallels the reaction to American popular culture. When the Soviet Union was collapsing and new ideas and influences were pouring in, the familiar pattern of retreating from the world was the response of most believers to the movies, music, and clothes that were flooding the airwaves. American mass culture was deemed godless. Many relied on their communities to provide a refuge, a fortress, from which to protect their children from the sin and worldly forms of entertainment that they had always refused, which were now so omnipresent. Over time, however, believers simply stopped being shocked by American films, soap operas, and music videos. Even if they still regarded it with the same disdain, the fear and hostility toward Western influences had steadily subsided.

By 2005 I was already hearing complaints about women not covering their heads consistently and nostalgic laments about the relaxation of "order" that had characterized the devotion, conviction, and righteousness of their services in years past. Many young members now balance church and communal obligations against those of the workplace, whereas before it was understood that church membership came first. Many longstanding believers regretted these changes, which they understood to be the first step on an irreversible slide from a state of piety.

Although multiple factors contributed to the erosion of order, allowing foreigners into the community was at least one that they could regulate. By 2000, foreign visiting preachers were coming to this church only three or four times a year. Several active members of this congregation disapproved of American missionaries, such as a pastor serving in one of the village congregations:

> We approach missionaries with caution. They live in an entirely different way, with different habits, relationships and norms. That's why not everything that they preach agrees with us and is accepted. For example, they think that believers should be rich, that they shouldn't be sick. But Jesus Christ didn't live in luxury. He took all illnesses on himself and other things like that. That means that if I am poor and sick, I won't go to hell. But that's not the only thing. Foreign missionaries say that our faith is steadier. They are in a very difficult spiritual situation. There [in the West] false doctrine, Satanism, even cults that practice human sacrifice [a common trope of Soviet antireligious propaganda] is very developed. As the Bible says, "In the last days false prophets will appear." In this respect, things are better here, and they can learn from us. But we have to be careful that certain tendencies from the West don't penetrate our communities. . . . Americans really welcome the arrival of our believers there, and I already explained why, it is because our believers improve the spiritual climate in America.[3]

He is very critical of the negative and antireligious influences that he sees as pervasive in American popular culture and holds them responsible for the relaxation of moral asceticism, which is what allows him to think that the faith of Ukrainians is stronger. They are willing to commit to sacrifice more. The use of sharply defined standards of morally appropriate behavior not only allows this pastor to claim that Ukrainian believers are closer to God than the unsaved, but such standards can also be used as a measure of who is a better evangelical. In this competition, Americans always come up short. In spite of economic and other disparities, Ukrainian believers see their conviction as deeper than other coreligionists because of their unwavering practice of biblically ordained moral principles.

Yet alongside this suspicion of corrupting, spiritually weakening tendencies in the West, the pastor nonetheless recognizes that in terms of two aspects of religious life that were thwarted by Soviet politics, congregational organization and international affiliation, the Ukrainian communities have a lot of catching up to do. At the time of this interview, a delegation from the church community was in Holland. Although Ukrainian piety may be exemplary, in terms of their methods of preaching, staging events, and organizing other outreach activities, Ukrainians stand to learn from their Western counterparts. Whereas believers tried to elude detection from the state and outsiders in general before, they now recognize that they must engage the unchurched, and this requires outreach skills and strategies that the clerical and lay leadership have yet to develop fully.

Whereas this pastor notes the positive effects that the arrival of Soviet evangelical refugees has had on improving the spiritual climate in America, Olga, a thirty-five-year-old wife of a pastor and a mother of three, emphasizes the positive effects for American missionaries when they come to Ukraine. Of course, the *intended* recipient of missionary efforts is unconverted Ukrainians. Committed Ukrainian believers are meant to experience an expansion and deepening of their faith as a result of the missionary encounter. However, she sees the dynamic unfolding in the opposite way:

> I see them as brothers and sisters in faith, which is why I relate to them well. It's another thing that they are people from a different culture and from different circumstances. That's why sometimes I think some of the examples they give when they are preaching are funny and why I'm amused during certain moments of the sermon. They don't always understand everything. But I like them. They have a certain joie de vivre, a certain openness. Our people are more beaten down by life. And that's even taking into consideration that our believers have a much more optimistic view of life than nonbelievers.
>
> Their trips here are good for them. It's a feat of faith. For them to come here is like a spiritual shock. They have it too good, and they have started to fall asleep. Once a foreigner said to me, "I thought that I would teach you something, but it turned out that I have learned from you. We have a lot of what they no longer have. For example, kids here play and run around together. There they more and more talk through the computer."[4]

She articulates a common sentiment, that for all of the harshness of Soviet society, it left in its wake a certain pious purity that translates into richer relationships, be they with God, with fellow believers, or among children. It is a depth of commitment and a willingness to sacrifice that she sees as missing in the wealthier and more comfortable West, where a higher value is placed on money and "idols," such as the computers that have already captivated the minds of so many children. Olga and her husband could have applied to emigrate but chose not to. She explains her decision, as many do, by claiming that much spiritual work remains to be done in Ukraine, a society that offers a sea of unsaved souls and yet has communities of deeply committed believers. Although she harbored no ill feelings toward those who emigrated, reasoning that "God called them to go," clearly she was unconvinced that America delivered on the promise that immigrants project onto life there. Skeptical of anything material—and even more so of spiritual benefits that America offers—she has no plans to emigrate.

The enthusiasm for the United States is more palpable at the central church's main daughter congregation, where the presence of Americans continues unabated. At any given time, usually a half a dozen American missionaries are there in some capacity. This congregation was started by thirty members from the central church on Orthodox Christmas, 7 January 1993. Initially, they rented meeting space, but by 1997 they had purchased land and began to build a church in a bedroom community (Rus. *spal'nyi raion*) with a half a million residents and easy access to the metro. Indeed, there is no need to give directions to this church beyond stating the metro station. When passengers emerge from the metro, the church's cross towers above the urban landscape, visible to all. The church was built with the express purpose of making it a church-planting center. In other words, this church, its activities, its clergy, and its parishioners are meant to be a magnet, drawing in new members and then spinning off other daughter congregations.

The new church building is spacious, and the main hall easily accommodates its current congregation of three hundred. Upstairs there is a meeting room used for youth services and an English-language church with about ninety members, most of whom are African and trying to find a bit of respite from the abundant racism they encounter.[5] There is also a library, Sunday school classrooms, and rooms for music rehearsals. The entire church, with the exception of the roof, was built with financing from a group of Southern Baptist Convention churches in Georgia and Alabama. A church in Ohio paid for the roof. There have been about six Southern

Figure 5.2: New Central Baptist
Church. Photo by the author.

Baptist long-term missionaries from the United States working with the community since its inception. Depending on their skills, these American missionaries offer free English language classes, sometimes medical care, and often biblical instruction to members or potential members of the church.

The church's senior pastor was Ivan Stepanovich, a lifelong believer who retired in 2004 at the age of seventy-seven. He was very forthright about how he struggled to maintain the "order" that so characterized Soviet-era evangelical communities, meaning the strict personal code of moral behavior that focused largely on delineating appropriate or inappropriate gender-based forms of dress and behavior. He contrasted the differences in worship between Ukrainians and Americans as follows:

> Our church is much more spiritual. They [the Americans] have given in more to the flesh. Our church is more traditional, whereas theirs has been too reformed. Whenever our believers go abroad, whether it is to America or to Europe, if they have allowed prima

donnas to emerge, already there is not the same kind of spirituality as you find here. How many pastors they have who are divorced! Can you tell me that this is normal? They can drink a glass of beer, and nothing will happen. But here, if I drank a glass of beer today, tomorrow I would no longer be a pastor. They bring us a lot of good but a lot of bad also. As long as we are still building our church, we will be patient, but after that, it's good-bye. I tell them, "If you want to help us, thank you, but don't bring us your Western customs."[6]

He and other conservative believers use these culturally infused moral perspectives to judge the depth of conviction—and moral worth—of others. Anyone who does not exhibit the same self-sacrificing, disciplining measures will inevitably be deemed to have inadequate faith. Difference yields disadvantage. Conformity—even hyperconformity—translates into status and respect.

It becomes challenging for pastors such as Ivan Stepanovich to accept material assistance, which they so desperately need, while keeping out the influences and habits of those who bring that assistance. One of the Western customs that arouses the most ire is clothing and styles of dress. In Ukraine, it is standard for women in Baptist and older Pentecostal communities to cover their heads, to wear only long skirts, and to abstain from makeup, jewelry, or bodily ornamentation of any kind. Even very devout and well-intentioned Western missionary women often show up in jeans wearing lipstick. It becomes difficult for the leadership of these Ukrainian congregations to justify and maintain the biblical reasons for these restrictions on dress and behavior when Westerners, who are supposedly there to assist in the spiritual development of the country, flagrantly defy the norms of behavior that are so vigorously espoused by Ukrainian believers and upheld by local evangelical communities.

One woman from the central Baptist congregation housed three visiting American missionaries during their trip to Kharkiv. They asked her to call her pastor to see if they could preach during the Sunday morning service. Over the telephone, the first question the pastor asked her was, "How are they dressed?" She glanced over at three Americans in sweatpants, T-shirts, and flip-flops. "As if they are going to the beach," she responded. "Well, then let them go to the beach," he retorted. The dress of these American missionaries during a casual encounter was enough to preclude the possibility of preaching in front of a Ukrainian congregation. For Ukrainians, purity of belief and depth of conviction are esteemed attributes that are expressed in modest and respectful clothing. When norms of dress are violated, it challenges commonly accepted notions of piety, which has a chilling effect on relationships between believers of the same faith from different cultural traditions.

In addition to attire, preaching style, including differences in both content and delivery, is another arena where cultural differences are abundantly apparent among the Southern Baptists and the Ukrainian Baptists they are ostensibly trying to assist. Not all Ukrainian Baptists criticized the American style of preaching—some even advocated it as a model, and many newer congregations have outright adopted it—but nearly all noticed clear differences. Ukrainian respondents commented how American preachers often begin sermons with a joke, smile throughout, and generally make far greater appeals to emotion. Sermons by American preachers are more readily understandable because they use personal information and stories about family life to explain passages in the Bible and personal anecdotes to illustrate how they became believers and strengthened their faith. This contrasts sharply with the characterization of Ukrainian sermons as "lectures." One young woman claimed that the delivery style of Ukrainian pastors was so wooden that if you put an apple on the pastor's head at the beginning of the sermon, it would still be there at the end. The formality of sermons, much like the formality of dress, is taken as an indicator of conviction and devotion.

The contrast between the casual approach of American preachers and the earnestness of Ukrainian pastors masks the fact that it is the American preachers who often are able to devote hours to the preparation of their sermons. They often have the benefit of prolonged, specialized training and are not obliged to work a day job to meet the family's expenses. Almost all Ukrainian Baptist clergy are bivocational, which American missionaries consider a significant problem. Ukrainians continue to see preaching as a "calling," which leads them to divorce it from such worldly matters as remuneration. Decoupling money from pastoral service automatically eliminates the opportunists who might choose this profession simply because it provides a reliable source of income. An additional complicating factor is that Ukraine has no tradition of tithing, or making regular financial contributions of support. At both of these Baptist churches, and even more generally in Ukraine, most in attendance contributed one hryvnia when the basket was passed, or about seventeen cents. Very few congregations are financially capable of supporting even a single pastor and his (usually) large family. Yet, holding a full-time job to provision a family is, of course, an immense compromise on any pastor's time.

As a result of the bivocationality of clergy and, until recently, the absence of any formal training, usually three or four "brothers" preach at every service, each elaborating on a theme that the first preacher has presented. Such a format enhances the improvisational nature of sermons and lay participation. Paradoxically, the formal Ukrainian style often overlays tremendous stream-of-consciousness preaching, whereas American preachers plan and consciously insert spontaneity and humor into their sermons.

## Provisioning Members and the Charitable Impulse

In the USSR, the workplace, especially collective farms and factories, often functioned as something of a "total institution," supplying not just employment but other needed services (medical care, child care, recreation, and so on) and access to material goods, such as housing. In many ways, evangelical communities are an extension of this Soviet-era phenomenon. Under one roof, individual believers can find a sense of belonging, identity, and a measure of economic security. Sometimes informal workshops are set up right on church grounds that offer a wide variety of services (for example, carpentry) to potential clients and job opportunities to members. The male members of both of these Baptist congregations form construction brigades that are highly sought after by outside employers because of the assumption that, as believers, they will not drink or steal. The pastor provides an additional (free) layer of managerial and disciplinary oversight, should any conflicts arise.

Church members also patronize each other's businesses and barter services. During an interview with a member of the daughter Baptist church, another member rang to inquire where she could get some shoes repaired. The respondent told her the name and address of a fellow believer who mended the shoes of other believers for free. She later explained how the hairdressers, plumbers, seamstresses, and other skilled members of the congregation regularly provide services to fellow church members for no charge.

These orchestrated economic activities of exchange provide a much-needed safety net for members, especially women, at a time when the state's ability to provide employment and assistance to the poor has withered. Although converts often experience the loss even of longstanding friendships because they have embraced a faith that remains culturally stigmatized, they nonetheless gain membership in a vibrant and highly active community that provides for their spiritual, social, and even material needs.

Conversion is frequently a response to crisis, a coping strategy that enables an individual to overcome difficulties by reordering a relationship to higher, more powerful forces, and by creating relationships within a new community. Sometimes the plight of a single person or family becomes a cause célèbre and the entire congregation mounts an effort to help out. Two examples, one from the original Baptist church and one from the newer one, illustrate the types of problems that individuals confront and the way in which community members in Kharkiv can and do respond to each other's needs. Participating as either a recipient or a provider in these acts of mutual assistance strengthens feelings of belonging and allegiance to the faith group and to the local community.

Svetlana is an Armenian refugee who fled her home in Baku, Azerbaijan, in 1988 as a result of ethnic strife and political instability. She first settled in Yerevan, where she became a Baptist, and in 1998 relocated to Kharkiv after her daughter did. She joined the central Baptist church. She claims, "I am a person without a homeland. My heart doesn't lie anywhere. If I had the possibility, I would emigrate again. I'm not proud of that, but if there was such a possibility, why not?"[7] At this point, her sense of belonging is not in any way tied to place or to a particular national way of life. As a deracinated Armenian who has been obliged to relocate several times, church membership was an effective way to reestablish a sense of stability, belonging, and community.

Birgit Meyer claims that the success of evangelical communities in Africa can be attributed to their dual recognition of being marginalized and of being forgotten, all the while situating believers in a meaningful way within "the wider world." Conversion delivers membership in a local community of "brothers and sisters" and assures believers a place in a transnational organization. Meyer writes, "The mass appeal of PCCs [Pentecostal charismatic churches] can be explained, at least in part, against this backdrop. Adopting a strategy of extraversion, which deliberately develops external links and promises connection with the world, PCCs nevertheless have to address a politics of identity and belonging, in which fixed markers govern processes of inclusion and exclusion, both in Africa and in the diaspora."[8] Not only for Africans but also for other diasporic peoples, such as Armenians and Ukrainians, membership in a community that is at once local and global is appealing. Most likely, wherever Svetlana moves, she will find other believers and be accepted into their community regardless of where she is from and where she might move to next.

In a similar vein, writing of the spectacular rise of Pentecostal communities in Latin America, where many members are rural migrants who have relocated to the cities in search of work, David Martin claims that religious communities cater to the "mobile self" by enhancing the portability of identity.[9] Participation in church communities can provide a sense of continuity in the face of radical disruption through the repetition of rituals, prayers, and other daily activities. For believers such as Svetlana, the portability of her religious identity has played a crucial role in softening the negative effects of relocation, and hence it has become more meaningful.

Starting over again in Kharkiv has not been easy. "I believe in God," she explains, "and I have given over to him all my struggles, and I know that he will never leave me. He will always help. . . . I never complain, and I never ask people for help. I only ask God knowing that he will help me through other people." She gave an example of how she believes her faith and prayer have helped her resettle: "When we arrived here, we had to pay to get a place to live. We didn't have any money. I asked one of the sisters [a female member of the church] to lend me some money. She also didn't have much money, but she evidently spoke to the members of the church because the next time I came to church, the pastor received me and gave me the money as an interest-free loan. To this day, I give back a little each month, about ten hryvnia [about two dollars]. But I never asked for it, and I will never ask for money." In the face of a crumbling state social service sector, church communities provide members with a safety net of sorts. In this effort, they are often assisted by coreligionists abroad, who send shipments of humanitarian aid to Ukraine and rely on particular congregations to distribute it. Svetlana and her family, for example, get their clothes this way.

Particularly for the displaced, religiosity provides a continuity of daily practices, a portable identity and mobile membership in a community founded on providing mutual assistance. Although Svetlana has been deracinated, her nationality rendered a burden, and her homeland inaccessible, she has found community membership in Kharkiv, which confers an identity as a moral person, provides an ongoing sense of belonging, and assures that she will not suffer alone. In an era of increased and often unwanted mobility, the stability and adaptability of a religious identity based on this kind of omni-sited community membership exerts mounting appeal. Although the embrace of a national identity can mean living in exile or in the diaspora, there are no believers in exile. Individual believers mediate the negative effects of social change and the disruption of mobility by recasting their identity through conversion to reorient daily life to a local community and simultaneously reach beyond state or territorial borders by connecting to a global community of believers.

Tanya, a young Baptist convert and member of the new Baptist church, experienced difficulties of another kind. Her experiences of communal assistance provided one of the more dramatic examples of a community's ability to care for one of its members. She and her child left her first husband after he and a friend beat her one New Year's Eve to the point that she required prolonged hospitalization. Several years later, she married a man who gave up his job as a pastor with the Salvation Army. Together they converted and joined the new Baptist church.

He was employed in one of the church brigades and received his salary directly from the pastor. Tensions arose when she inadvertently learned that he was stealing on the job. Given the tight connection between his job and their membership, if this were to become known, the ramifications would be felt on multiple levels. Marital tensions increased when she became pregnant. Her husband, mother, and sister all wanted her to have an abortion. When Tanya refused, her husband deserted her.

Tanya was facing substantial medical bills and no means to pay for them as well as the prospect of single motherhood with two small children and nowhere to live. Tanya explains the reaction of her fellow members: "My friends said to me, 'Do you believe in God? If your faith is strong, than God will not leave you. If you don't commit sins, then God will bless you and your child. Put your trust in God.' I remembered Andrei [a fellow believer] and his fifteen children and thought, if they can somehow live, than I can make it too."[10] She went to her pastor for advice and he rallied the members of the church to her cause.

Not only did they collect enough money to pay her medical bills and to support her after the birth, but on the day of her caesarean section the entire congregation also fasted and prayed for her and her newborn. Every day someone from the church came to the hospital to take care of her. When her milk supply proved inadequate, another mother from the church even shared her breast milk. At the time of the interview, her son was six months old, and Tanya was still being entirely supported by the congregation, an act of generosity that would probably be beyond the capacity of even the most dedicated of friends. She was richly rewarded by the community for following the moral dictates of her faith over the worldly opinions of others.

Because of the sweeping and foundational effect of religion on a person's way of thinking and behaving, old friends often become alienated by a convert's new commitments and activities. Ruth Marshall-Fratani has written, "Friends, family and neighbors become 'dangerous strangers,' and strangers, new friends. The social grounds for creating bonds—blood, common pasts, neighborhood ties, language—are foresworn for the new bond of the brother or sister in Christ."[11] Usually only the very oldest, very best nonbelieving friends remain with the convert and become the first to whom the convert witnesses. New attitudes and obligations toward others outside one's circle can be difficult for the nonbeliever to accept because they represent a break with cultural norms that say that moral obligations to provide assistance extend to kin and kin-like friends, certainly not to strangers. Here we have a reconfiguration of relationships and an elimination of the concept of "strangers" among members. Tanya's actions upheld the moral beliefs of her community, and she was rewarded for it. It was irrelevant whether Svetlana was from Baku or Kharkiv—her membership was evidence of a moral commonality, and this translated automatically into communal assistance.

## Responding to Social Needs

The essence of outreach programs is to extend the impulse to assist fellow believers in need, as revealed in Svetlana and Tanya's experiences, to nonbelievers as well. This represents a break with older evangelical communal practices of observing sharp membership demarcations to foster a rich inner-looking congregational life by separating from the world. Western missionaries place a premium on reaching the unsaved and therefore have played a role in reorienting services and assistance to the unchurched. Some, such as Olena Petrivna, a middle-aged woman who was christened in 1979 and is a member of the newer Baptist church, find the "religious shoppers" who respond to such outreach efforts an intrusion, even a dilution of congregational life:

> A lot of Christians adopted the American idea that we should help the world. But the world then comes into church. They think it is possible to move beyond traditional values and canons as long as it's in the spirit of attracting the unsaved. This doesn't mean that I'm against nonbelievers coming to church. I myself came to church for the first time as a nonbeliever. But we have to surround them with love and teach them, and not build everything around them. For example, on the third floor they built a café [really, just a gathering space]. But why do they allow smoking there? So that it will be lively? So that young people can meet there? One shouldn't go to church to be entertained! All the reverence is lost.[12]

She disagrees with the emphasis on outreach to nonbelievers, maintaining that "Christianity is truly a narrow and prickly path, and not everyone can live by the Word of God." She thinks, as many did during the Soviet period, that believers and nonbelievers must find a middle ground, that it is futile to try to cultivate a sense of spirituality, a desire to dialogue with God, among nonbelievers. Nonbelievers must be searching for a way to express their faith and be inclined to dedicate their lives to pursuing that faith. She and others accuse American missionaries of making compromises with respect to the demands of membership and the rigors of moral asceticism to bring more nonbelievers into the fold. Echoing Soviet-era priorities, she stresses the obligations believers have to their community over the obligations believers have to serve the world.

In spite of such objections to relaxing the stringent moral code to accommodate and attract more people, social service outreach is a domain where institutionally there is widespread endorsement and implementation of American models. All Baptist and Pentecostal communities offer, or aim to offer, a wide spectrum of free educational, musical, and social programs. Now allowed to expand the social support services that the state is no longer willing or able to provide, basic church activities now include providing material and other forms of support to orphanages, boarding schools, and other state-run institutions.[13] To members and potential members they offer summer camps, after-school activities, clothing redistribution, job referrals, and elderly visitation, to name the most common outreach activities. Sunday school, adult Bible study, small prayer groups, and a multitude of vocal and musical ensembles round out their offerings. As religious organizations assume more and more functions of the state by expanding the assistance they offer to members to include the unchurched, they are obliged to consider the dynamics driving poverty, disenfranchisement, and social suffering. As a result, their expectations of the state begin to shift and, potentially, their engagement in politics as well.

## Commitments to the State

Ukrainian and American evangelicals in general share minimal expectations from the state in terms of assistance to the poor, and Ukrainian evangelicals are increasingly willing to shore up the shortcomings of state services themselves. However, it is easier to remake the obligations one expects *from* the state than it is the obligations one feels *to* the state. For Ukrainians, the morally compromised, corrupting attributes of the world include the state and doing its bidding. The strong patriotism of American evangelicals is often bewildering to Ukrainian believers and to Ukrainians more generally, so long accustomed to maintaining a cynical, defiant stance toward state authorities. The state is almost universally seen as an adversarial force that must be resisted on moral grounds.

Reflecting the Anabaptist origins of Protestant religious doctrine in the former Soviet Union, evangelical communities both before and after 1991 have advocated nonviolent resolution of conflict and refuse to take up arms. Ukrainian Baptists are always stunned to learn that American believers serve in the armed forces. A Baptist of long standing, surprised by a group of young American cadets visiting the new Baptist congregation, commented, "How deep can their faith be? . . . How can a believing Christian study in a military academy? They could give him an order and he would have to shoot! That means that for him, the interests of his government are higher than the interests of God!"[14] In the same spirit of nonviolence, some Ukrainian believers criticize the American attacks on Afghanistan and the war on Iraq as unfitting of Christians, who, they argue, should categorically oppose the use of violence. Some understand violence and suffering as evidence of a greater drama, the struggle between the divine and the satanic, and not as a human response to specific social and political circumstances. Witness how an older woman who became a Baptist during World War II understands the September 11 attacks:

> When Americans come here, we don't like their behavior. They sit in church, leg to leg. How is such a thing possible? Liberties with clothes, cosmetics, and other such things—everything comes from America. They have moved away from God. And now, look at America! They live without God, and He sent them a punishment. September 11th is a sign, the finger of God showing the whole world to be careful. God allowed that so that they would repent! If they will not repent, He will destroy them! And in time, we will be punished too. Where can you see this? Vodka is sold day and night! Where are we heading? Do you think we will escape punishment for this?[15]

Much like Jerry Falwell and other American fundamentalists, this woman understands the violence inflicted on Americans on September 11 as a punishment from God for moral laxity. Jerry Falwell, speaking on *The 700 Club* with Pat Robertson, said, "I really believe that the pagans, and the abortionists, and the feminists, and the gays and lesbians who are actively trying to make that an alternative lifestyle, the ACLU, People for the American Way—all of them who have tried to secularize America—I point the finger in their face and say, 'You helped this happen.' " To this statement, Pat

Robertson, a Pentecostal pastor and former presidential contender, replied, "Well, I totally concur, and the problem is we have adopted their agenda at the highest levels of government." Later Falwell was forced to issue an apology for his comments and for using this tragedy to advance his particular moral vision and political agenda for American public life.[16]

Susan Harding has written about how evangelical apocalyptic language reveals the extent to which believers see events like 9/11 as a sign of impending "End Times," as biblically grounded indications that the world is approaching the end of human history.[17] Explaining why the innocent suffer poses a quandary for evangelicals. If God is omnipotent and has a plan for each of us, as they maintain, then nothing happens outside his will. If God is benevolent, then he should not harm innocent people. If tragedy befalls someone who seems pious, the most obvious way to understand this is to reckon that perhaps the person was not so virtuous after all. Believers attempt to read tragic events as signs, as part of a dialogue with God. What is he trying to tell us? The invocation of evil, as in the older woman's explanation above, is part of a premillennialist narrative that states that the Great Tribulation, or the end of time, will soon be upon us and will resolve into suffering for nonbelievers at the Battle of Armageddon and into glory for believers. This reckoning will precede rapture, or the Second Coming of Jesus Christ. In other words, events in history, especially tragic ones on a grand scale like 9/11, are all merely part of God's plan to separate the redeemed from the sinner. Evocation of this narrative often further strengthens the resolve and urgency with which individual believers attempt to save the unsaved through evangelism and proselytizing.

A younger woman who is also a member of the new church says of September 11, "I think more and more often that the church in America is dying, spiritually dying. And the proof for me is the events of September 11. Nothing is done without the will of God, and if God allowed those events—in the birthplace of Baptism [*sic*], that means that it was a punishment for spiritual lapses and a warning against future spiritual degradation."[18]

These interpretations of the events of September 11, beyond reinforcing the disdain and distance at which American believers are held, also reveal a particular conception of and relationship to God. God for Ukrainian Baptists is often a powerful, benevolent overseeing force that punishes transgressions, much like a strict father. The "fraternal" [Ukr. *braters'kyi*] relationship to God that they see Americans advocate in their discussions with potential converts, almost like a life partner, smacks of a lack of respect. Fear of God is a principle that is instilled in childhood and continues to guide and shape behavior in adulthood. The fear of God and his ability to punish inappropriate behavior evolves for many into a fear of offending God and the fellow members of one's congregation. Because the Americans they encounter do not exhibit the same fear-induced respect, discipline, and self-sacrifice in the name of faith as Ukrainian Baptists think they themselves do, they attribute to Americans a lukewarm commitment to living according to the Bible. The willingness of Americans to endorse their state's policies and trust their leaders without serious reflection is seen as further moral capitulation to worldly forms of authority, when one should serve the divine. In other words, the biblical dictum of "rendering unto Caesar what is Caesar's" is applied with far more discrimination in Ukraine, reflecting a continuing suspicion and distrust of the state on moral grounds.

### Changes at the Helm

In the spring of 2004, at the age of seventy-seven, Ivan Stepanovich, the senior pastor of the new Baptist church retired. The struggle to maintain order largely went with him. His fatherly pastoral care to his aging and mostly female parishioners was handed over to a new "senior pastor." An indication of the many changes to come, Andrei, the new senior pastor, was only twenty-four years old and had been ordained just three years earlier. His appointment represented a clear break with cultural traditions that equate authority with age. His main credential for the job, like the pastor before him, was that he was raised in a multigenerational evangelical family, a "Baptist dynasty," as the young man called it, that had longstanding membership at the central Baptist church. In spite of his youth, this allowed older members of the congregation to recognize him as one of their own (Ukr. *svii*). Although he became a pastor after studying at a local bible college, his real school of faith is his own family's biography. Andrei preaches in the main hall downstairs on Sunday morning, Sunday evening, and Thursday evening, the three main services that members are expected to attend.

There can be no doubt that he sees himself as a member of a new generation. Within five minutes of meeting me, he told me that there are twelve thousand Orthodox churches in Ukraine and twelve thousand Protestant churches—so he no longer thinks it's fair to call Ukraine an Orthodox country anymore. Clearly those that backed his candidacy were counting on his youth, energy, and innovation to appeal to the next generation and help grow the membership and his Soviet-era credentials to make him a legitimate leader in the eyes of the older members of the congregation.

Andrei was not the only contender for the job. The pastor of the "upstairs" English-language church, affectionately known as "Pastor V." to his English-speaking flock, himself only thirty years old, was also considered for the job. As a recent convert who speaks excellent English, his understanding of faith and worship have been far more influenced by Americans than most of the downstairs congregants. Pastor V. explains in English how he came to his faith while studying law:

> I was first ignited to preach the Gospel by an American Southern Baptist pastor who came and preached, as they say, hellfire and brimstone. I really loved this style. I was just searching for a church at this point. That's how I ended up in a Baptist church. . . . I wanted to know the Bible. I wanted to know what it was all about. I wanted someone to explain it to me. There was no person in the Orthodox Church, or in the Catholic Church, no such person anywhere else. That's why I came to the Baptists. They were preaching there. Baptists do have liturgy but it's a worship service. It's a liturgy service because it's all regulated and everything. But it's not out there [meaning, shrouded in mystery as Orthodox liturgies are]. Do you know what I'm talking about? From my personal experience, I love preaching. I love the thoughtful explanation of the Word of God. I could take it and I could go with it.

Pastor V. highlights a point that very frequently arises in interviews with recent converts of all persuasions. The Soviet-era suppression of overt religious practice, far from stifling or eradicating religious beliefs, simply stifled discussion, which over time meant that knowledge was forgotten, with ignorance taking its place. Many Protestant denominations, but especially evangelicals, have a prominent instructional element to their services and congregational activities where the Bible and religious doctrine is explained. For some religious seekers looking to shed their inherited ignorance of religious practice, small Bible study groups and "spiritual mentors" are perceived as some of the advantages that evangelicalism offers.

Pastor V.'s religious sensibilities have been heightened over the years thanks to sustained mentoring since 1999 by a Southern Baptist pastor who worked in Kharkiv as a long-term missionary and now mentors him by e-mail. Although he has no formal seminary training, he became a pastor in 2005. He is very welcoming of the American influence in Ukrainian evangelical religious life, seeing it on balance as having had overwhelmingly positive effects. He says quite matter-of-factly, "If you see any church recently built in all of Kharkiv oblast, it was built with American money."

The English-language services that Pastor V. offers in the upstairs church started in a very serendipitous way. Three students from Africa studying in Kharkiv came to the church and asked to speak about God. After their first conversation with him, they began to attend services. Then they began to bring their friends. This growing group of "dark-skinned" believers, as the Ukrainians called them, sat with the foreign missionaries for whom Pastor V. translated during services. In 2003 Pastor V. led English-language services on Christmas and Easter, and seventy people attended. This became the impetus to hold monthly—eventually weekly—English-language services for the now about ninety who attend on a regular basis. They meet upstairs, in a segregated space on the third floor, on Sunday afternoons.

Essentially, three types of people attend these services: Africans; a handful of Western missionaries living in Kharkiv, including Steve Johnson, the founder of the Leadership Training Center mentioned in chapter 4; and religiously inclined English-speaking Ukrainians whose faith has been shaped by American influences. Besides being an unusual collection of believers who represent "unwanted" elements in the eyes of most Ukrainians, he claims what makes his congregation distinct is "authentic fellowship" and "spirit-led worship."

He has very definite views on how the Baptist faith was practiced during the Soviet era and how that legacy continues to impinge on communal life today. For him, this legacy provides a foil against which he reacts. He understands the "order" of older Baptist communities to be a "means of self-defense." The defensive stance toward the world and the extensive prescriptions on behavior provided an efficient means for believers to delineate who was a member and who was not. Even after 1991, he reasons, the flooding of socialist societies with consumerism and Western mass media only accelerated the allure of a secular lifestyle and initially reinforced the impetus to withdraw from the world. Baptists had battled Soviet ideological influences, now they had to battle Western consumerism. This is why, in his view, changes were slow to come to local churches in terms of their style of worship, dressing, and behavior. The main catalyst for change was youth and the desire not to lose another generation to secularism.

There are indeed sharp generational splits in nearly all the congregations I have visited, regardless of denomination. Older people have always had a significant presence. They have time and inclination as they confront ailments and their own mortality, so they become reflective. There are also a significant number of people in their twenties, who came of age when religious affiliation was no longer stigmatized. Moreover, their youth was characterized by processes of desovietization, in which religion and Western pop culture both played a role. Therefore, early on, many churches, including this new Baptist one, had a quorum of young people. The middle generation of Soviet-educated adults is conspicuously absent.

The desire to continue to encourage young people to come, even to accommodate "youth culture," as Pastor V. terms it, has become a priority for him and a justification to "relax the tension." For example, in the downstairs church, under Ivan Stepanovich, the older pastor, it was mandated that women cover their heads. As of 2005, under his youthful senior successor, it was no longer a stated rule but rather an "expectation" and "a custom." But in Pastor V.'s church, women are not required to cover their heads or abstain from wearing makeup and jewelry. He even takes it a step further:

> Right now, if a young girl in a short skirt and a see-through blouse walks into the church, we're not going to bother her. We're not going to come to her and bang on her head saying, "You should leave the congregation! Don't come again!" We figure that we will see a change in the way she dresses and in the way she uses her makeup. That is, if the change will be as it is meant to be. The change will come as a consequence of her transformation of mind and heart. Through the work of Jesus Christ.

In a break with tradition, he is not obliging the curious to exhibit modesty and piety *before* he welcomes them in. Potential converts do not need to meet him halfway. He is willing to take them "as they come." He stops short of halting all pronouncements on dress and asks the "worship team" and others who stand before the congregation to dress "appropriately," but he never specifies exactly what this means.

Deemphasizing the rigorous enforcement of dress codes, and the judgment that inevitably follows should they be violated, is part of his goal to establish "authentic fellowship." What he means by this, in essence, is the cultivation of a feeling of belonging and peace that arises when one comes to a place surrounded by accepting friends who are united in common purpose. He understands this common purpose as "spirit-led worship." I see the common purpose as a collective effort to uphold a reformulated moral order, which is sustained through the collective effervescence achieved in "spirit-led worship."

He characterizes his services as "joyful," full of song and clapping, and notes that this joy is ushered in by numerous participants: a worship leader, a worship team, choirs, and extensive lay leadership in the service. This "spirit-led, spirit-inspired worship" is most evident in the music. Nearly all

Baptist and older Pentecostal churches in Ukraine feature only organs and vocal ensembles, some rejecting even the inclusion of an acoustic guitar. The English-language church follows the practice of many American Baptist churches and allows electric guitars, basses, keyboards, among other instruments. "We just don't have drums," he explains and then quickly adds, "So far. Drums would be a rather radical step. We can't go that far yet." But one senses, especially given the high levels of African membership in his congregation, that it is only a matter of time before they add drums, even if some members of the downstairs church will see it as the ultimate capitulation to the profane in a sacred space. While cognizant of the disapproval older members express toward his church, he remains convinced that the goal is growth, the personal transformative growth of individual believers in their faith and the growth of this and other Baptist communities in Ukraine. With this in mind, he confidently introduces change after change and adds, "I think we will see more younger churches in Ukraine taking this particular avenue."

I, too, see his church, with its shedding of fundamentalist, morally ascetic prescriptions on behavior and its advocacy of the charismatization of religious experience, as having a domino effect on the emerging evangelical life in Ukraine. The upstairs church will influence the downstairs church, and the new central church will influence the old one. In fifteen short years, these trends have taken root and placed the religious life of the formerly sequestered Soviet evangelicals within worldwide trends of charismatic global Christianity.

## From Austerity to Ecstasy: Two Pentecostal Communities in Kharkiv

Pentecostal communities in Ukraine today exhibit a more intense version of virtually all of the dynamics of change we saw in the Baptist communities. Historically, as I noted in chapters 1 and 2, Pentecostals were more conservative and were seen as more "sect-like" than Baptists. A greater proportion of Pentecostal believers met clandestinely in underground communities. As a result, vast numbers of Pentecostals qualified to emigrate as political refugees, and most did. Although Soviet-era Pentecostal communities were far more conservative than Baptist ones, in post-Soviet society the roles have been reversed.

Pentecostals exhibit little of the critical reaction Baptists so freely espouse toward Western cultural values and the introduction of charismatic

Figure 5.3: First Pentecostal Church in Kharkiv oblast, exterior. Photo by the author.

traditions. Fewer longstanding Pentecostal believers remain in Ukraine, which means that there is far less concern over watering down or even eliminating Soviet-era practices. Conservative Pentecostals who chose not to emigrate and who insist on maintaining the full spectrum of Soviet-era understandings of belief, ritual, and piety have been obliged to shift back to home churches, as they did in the Soviet era, where they can legislate any form of behavior they deem appropriate. The only difference is that now they are unlikely to get arrested for it. A second factor is that there are far fewer large-scale, well-funded American organizations directing and shaping post-Soviet Pentecostal life. There is no denominational equivalent to the International Mission Board of the Southern Baptist Convention for the more decentralized Pentecostals. As a result, change has occurred in a more grassroots way among Pentecostals, and it was been implemented far more swiftly.

The first legal Pentecostal prayer house in the oblast, the Word of Life Church, opened in 1981. Four members, including Mikhail Mikhailovich's father, whom we met in chapter 2, were given permission to purchase a brick house at the end of a dirt lane, right next to a pond, in a district of the city with many small private houses surrounded by fences, chicken coops,

Figure 5.4: First Pentecostal Church in Kharkiv oblast, interior. Photo by the author.

and gardens. All members participated in renovating the house into a large, open meeting space with two small offices off to one side. One of the members of the church painted a large mural in the main hall of Jesus leading shepherds through a field with the biblical citation, "I am the bread of life." Rarely do Protestant churches have large painted images personifying Jesus Christ. When I asked the head pastor about it, he made it clear that he had never really considered how unusual it was to have a large painting at the forefront of the church. One of the members could paint, so, quite simply, just as the electricians and bricklayers did what they could to build the church, she painted the mural. The ceiling is pale blue and decorated with imperial, baroque-like ornamentation.

Previously, the isolation of being tucked away among private homes in one of the few truly rural areas of the city was seen as an enormous advantage. Now, of course, the head pastor deeply regrets the location. Among the numerous changes that have beset this community, is the fact that Barabashova, the sprawling market that Kharkovites proudly proclaim is the single largest outdoor bazaar in the world, sprang up between the metro and the church. After one emerges from the metro, one is obliged to snake through throngs of crowds in innumerable tight corridors of small booths pulsating with postsocialist bargain hunters in an outdoor consumer paradise. After exiting the market, the aspiring worshiper must still traverse a series of dirt roads that leads to the pond and the church. Even with this chaotic market, a worldly incursion if there ever was one, the location remains isolated and inaccessible.

The other very significant change is that, of the original six hundred members, only twenty or so remain, most of whom were too old and frail to emigrate. Nearly all the other members emigrated to the United States in the 1990s. Many return to visit, and some of them finance the church's charitable initiatives. Other than members' regular contributions, the main source of outside financial support is from émigré members. During services, time is allotted for visitors from other congregations or those who have made visits to other congregations to individually stand and offer greetings. Anthony Giddens refers to the overall phenomenon of bringing people from disparate places together as the creation of "distanciated relations."[19] Although this church is located in a remote and inaccessible part of the city, it is nonetheless a prominent domain where not only frequent face-to-face contact among local members occurs but also disparate people and places encounter one another. Occurrences abroad or in other regions are increasingly experienced by the membership through personal announcements of participation made during services.

Giddens understands the globalizing reorganization of time and space as largely hinging on the stretching of social life to span great distances. The charitable impulses of believers who have emigrated abroad remain oriented toward their home country, as we saw in chapter 3, which connects members of this small, physically isolated community to fellow believers on multiple continents. As Giddens writes, "larger and larger numbers of people live in circumstances in which disembedded institutions, linking local practices with globalized social relations, organize major aspects of day-to-day life."[20] Religious communities are indeed laden with social relations that span great distances and are increasingly the sites where the local and the global interlock in powerful ways to shape the consciousness, everyday practices, and identities of individual believers.

Because the Word of Life is the single oldest Pentecostal community in the oblast, it retains a more traditional service and ethos, even though its membership consists largely of recent converts. In contrast to the Baptist partnership depicted above, where the ongoing presence of American missionaries and formidable levels of Western financial support have served as catalysts for change at the newer congregation, here the main catalyst is the daughter congregation, which has since become a megachurch. As in the case of the Baptists, the daughter congregation was also slated to become the main Pentecostal Church in the city, replacing the original community. The Good News Church started in 1994 with seven members from the original community. It is referred to as a "neo-Pentecostal" or "charismatic" church to reflect the vast differences in orientation, atmosphere, and sensibility from Soviet-era Pentecostal congregations. The Word of Life Church draws doctrinally on what is often called "classical Pentecostalism," or the form of Pentecostalism that was founded in the early twentieth century in the United States. Pentecostal congregations in the USSR, as we saw, had little contact with their Western brethren but much contact with Soviet Baptists, with whom they shared some common attitudes toward the sacred and toward worship.

Most notably, Soviet Pentecostal congregations were insulated from the charismatic renewal movement that entered national debates in America in the 1960s when the rector of an Episcopal Church in Van Nuys, California, received spirit baptism, began speaking in tongues, and introduced an ecstatic and experiential aura to religious practice. The charismatic movement received a further boost in the late 1960s when Catholic students at Duquesne University, Notre Dame, and the University of Michigan began to speak in tongues, igniting the Catholic Charismatic Renewal.

In religious life throughout Eurasia, "Pentecostal" (meaning Soviet-era) congregations are delineated from the more recently created "charismatic" ones, even though elsewhere, including in the United States, charismatic churches are usually considered a form of worship within Pentecostalism.[21] Underlining the temporal, rather than the doctrinal, distinction the term *charismatic* makes in Ukraine is that both types of churches practice glossolalia, prophecy, faith healings, and other gifts of the Spirit.[22] For both Pentecostal and charismatic churches, "Baptism in the Holy Spirit" is an essential rite and a fundamental part of the born again experience.

Seven members from the Word of Life Church, all recent converts, with the help of a Pentecostal church planter from California who lived in Kharkiv for three years, grew the Good News Church into a charismatic megachurch that within eight years of its founding already had twenty-five hundred members. Volodya, a young and dynamic man, eventually became the head pastor at Good News. In the beginning, the American missionary helped Volodya by preaching at services through an interpreter and advising on outreach issues. As church membership soared, to mark the success of Good News, Volodya was appointed to the prestigious post of head of the Pentecostal union for Kharkiv oblast, a position he held until 2004. During this time Volodya presided over the fastest-growing church in the fastest-growing denomination in Ukraine.

Word of Life has been partnered with Good News since its creation and, especially among the youth, there is a great deal of exchange and mutual assistance between the two. Until 2004, the head pastor of the mother church could frequently be seen at the daughter congregation as the dynamics began to change with swelling memberships at Good News and aging ones at Word of Life. Even more rapidly than in the Baptist case, the new church was becoming the central church and planting many more churches than the original congregation had. By 2002, while the Word of Life was holding steady with six hundred members and three pastors, the Good News church had fifteen pastors and four times the membership.

## Bringing the World In

In addition to the charismatic approach to worship, three factors sharply distinguish the Good News Church from the Word of Life: openness to outsiders, gender roles in religious practice, and theological location on the liberal/conservative spectrum. In terms of openness, it is important to note that although Word of Life sees itself as an evangelizing church that engages in missionary work for the purposes of recruiting new members, many of the members still retain great suspicion of the world and of worldly people. I have seen pastors and deacons whisper to each other while leading a service to discuss unknown and unannounced arrivals, such as myself. I realized the extent to which interlopers were unwelcome on the day that I came to the service not knowing that it was for members only. Once a month congregational business is discussed in an open forum before the entire membership. This is a common practice, and I had seen it done elsewhere—one service stretched out to four and a half hours. This particular night about two hundred people showed up. When the pastor began to speak of congregational business, one of the deacons got up and interrupted his speech by whispering something to him. The pastor continued by saying that anyone present who was not a member should leave at this time. I, alone, with my head uncovered, stood up and walked out.

In sharp contrast, the Good News Church has adopted the American habit of having greeters at the door at every service. Everyone is welcome. Young people hand out announcements with the service program, notes about upcoming events, and various biblical quotations with commentary. They introduce themselves by first name to newcomers, smile, and try very hard to create a jubilant aura that magnetically draws the curious in. Once

Figure 5.5: Neo-Pentecostal church in the Metalworker House of Culture. Photo by the author.

inside, pastries, dumplings, tea, and other beverages are for sale to the left. To the right, books, videos, cassettes, posters, and other religious paraphernalia is for sale. The Metalworker House of Culture, which Good News rents, was built as a theater, and its stage is spacious and its red velvet seating is comfortable, especially compared to the wooden benches at the Word of Life. Below the socialist realist mosaics celebrating the labor of metalworkers, are lists of all the members who have birthdays that month and an announcement board with congregational activities.

The two churches coordinate their evangelizing and outreach efforts. Groups from the Word of Life regularly visit the women's prison and an orphanage, and groups from the Good News Church visit the men's prison and a juvenile detention facility. Both offer a full array of children's programs, including Sunday school, music programs, and summer camps.

Historically, Pentecostal churches have stressed faith healing as a key doctrinal component.[23] Based on "prayer and fellowship," Good News also offers a full roster of self-help groups for recovering alcoholics, the terminally ill, singles, couples grappling with infertility, parents struggling to raise "difficult children," and so on. In this way, megachurches such as Good News assume a leading role in applying religious principles to solve tangible problems by providing a variety of accessible counseling services, healing-oriented services, and material assistance in the name of reaching the unsaved and strengthening their faith.

## Women in the Pulpit

At Word of Life, attitudes toward women's behavior and self-presentation remain a particularly poignant indicator of Soviet-era gender-based restrictions. Women and men used to sit segregated on opposite sides of the church.[24] Men did not wear ties, claiming that a tie points to the devil and to hell and, I would add, to the phallus. Women wore only long skirts and covered their head at all times. In contrast, today a challenge to the obligation of female members of the church to cover their heads is already under way. Some young women at Word of Life, as at other Soviet-era evangelical congregations and at immigrant evangelical churches in the United States, have begun to place a scarf over their head—but not to tie it. In doing so, these women acknowledge the symbolic practice marking submission and their God-given roles as wife and mother. Yet, by refusing to tie the scarf, they have begun its unmaking and thrown into public question their commitment to traditional understandings of submission. At new Pentecostal churches, such as the Word of Life's partner church, there is no obligation for women to cover their heads, so few do. Many of the younger women at Good News dress casually and no longer feel obliged to wear a skirt, as they still do at the Word of Life.

The most significant change of all is in female leadership. More than a decade after the fall of the Soviet Union, the Word of Life Church took what was for them the dramatic step of allowing a woman to be the choir director. Prior to this, women only participated in the choir as singers and taught Sunday school to children. Members of Word of Life evoke various biblical passages to show the righteousness of men to serve as leaders and be in positions of authority over women. They especially object to women in any way teaching or instructing men. In sharp contrast, the Good News Church allows women to become pastors. Far from equal, female pastors remain barred from performing any rituals (communion, baptisms, and so on) but that they even exist is remarkable. Women clergy are complemented by numerous female deaconesses and lay female leaders, who participate in services in highly visible roles. Indeed, most of the services at Good News are directed by women who, like a master of ceremonies, are responsible for setting the mood, either revving up the crowd for joyous, effervescent expressions of exaltation or lulling them back into a meditative state to hear a sermon.

Valentyna repented in 1993 in the Word of Life church but had second thoughts when she learned that she was now subject to a list of prohibitions. The two most objectionable restrictions for her were that secular sources of information, including television, were now forbidden and that she could no longer have an abortion. Barely able to make ends meet with two children, she refused to have another child, were she to become pregnant. She also refused to turn off the television. These two decisions made her continued membership at Word of Life problematic. She switched to Good News, which presents "guidelines" for behavior as opposed to prohibitions. For example, pastors advise parishioners not to make an "idol" of the television, but they do not forbid them to watch it. They acknowledge that it is acceptable to drink alcohol in moderation—to commemorate a special occasion, for example—but it is not acceptable to drink regularly or to become drunk. They do not yield on the abortion issue, but the tone of their condemnation is less absolute.

In 1997 Valentyna was baptized, and she eventually became one of fifteen pastors to the more than twenty-five hundred members. She describes becoming the first woman to preach during a service in August 2002, at the height of the summer growing season:

> It all happened by accident. Quite simply, there weren't enough brothers to preach that day, and it wasn't possible to postpone the service. The pastor proposed that I go up on stage. I was really nervous. I heard unfriendly heckling from the crowd. When I began to speak, everyone in the room froze, and then they talked about it for a month. Women go up on stage constantly but usually for only two reasons: to bring offerings or to read announcements. But now they are starting to preach. Just last Wednesday, one of the sisters preached.[25]

Not just the gender of the preacher but also the tone of the sermon is radically different in newer congregations. No longer "wooden lectures," newer Pentecostal pastors make ample use of the "call and response" technique to create drama and dialogue between preacher and congregation. Pastors ask provocative questions that elicit responses such as exclamations of affirmation or applause. Charismatic churches take the "infotainment" participatory aspects one step further and introduce theatrical interludes, puppet shows, and other performative genres to present stories from the Bible. Images link the human and divine realms in an economy of ritualized exchange, which is particularly accessible to the spiritually curious and to recent converts.[26] These newer, more expressive communities enact—indeed, viscerally experience—lessons from the Bible. They visually and viscerally inscribe the lessons in memory as opposed to instructing them cognitively. As a result, the whole tenor and atmosphere of the services is quite different.

Music plays a key role in either reinforcing the solemn, sacred, and restrained aspects of services or heightening the expressive, ecstatic mood. All evangelical congregations allocate a very prominent role to music to enhance spirituality and strengthen faith.[27] More traditional Pentecostal congregations, such as Word of Life, use only organ, piano, and acoustic instruments. Newer Pentecostal charismatic churches offer nothing short of a rock concert. Electric guitars, synthesizers, and a variety of percussion instruments at high volume accompany groups of animated singers and sometimes even dancers on stage. Worshipers in the audience dance, sway, embrace, and basically do whatever they feel like doing in cathartic release. Although Pentecostals technically frown on (or even forbid) dancing, that is precisely what takes place at these services. In sharp contrast, at Word of Life one stands quietly during song. The differences in atmosphere and style should not be reduced to a generational split among believers. I am constantly amazed at the number of elderly that attend these tremendously youthful and charismatic services that boom out Christian rock at volumes that I can barely tolerate. Similarly, Word of Life and other older congregations offer a full spectrum of youth programs and can generally count on numerous young volunteers to staff its many activities.

Although the community may have an American missionary to thank for introducing the alternative modes of worship at Good News, the spread of expressive and casual practices is mainly attributable to Ukrainians influencing each other through a multitude of exchanges among choral, musical, and youth groups and coordinated evangelizing efforts. The genuine appeal of these new practices, so cannily adapted to post-Soviet socioeconomic circumstances, is also undeniable.

## More Changes at the Helm

If the Baptist believers were shocked by the appointment of a twenty-four-year-old senior pastor, this did not compare to the reaction to the February 2004 revelations that beloved Pastor Volodya, the senior pastor at Good News, although married with two children, had had sexual relationships with men for years. He was summarily excommunicated from the denomination and overnight became persona non grata in the Christians of Evangelical Faith Pentecostal religious establishment, where he was serving as bishop.

His own congregants reacted somewhat more charitably. Many clergy and parishioners chose to remain within the church, privileging their allegiance to the person over the denomination's moral dictates and biblical interpretations. As a result, Volodya declared his church an independent Pentecostal charismatic church and carried on offering five services a week. Official membership fell from 2,500 to 1,700, but only five hundred or so were in attendance regularly.

In the summer of 2005 the mood, atmosphere, and "collective effervescence" at Good News remained a bit moribund compared to their earlier levels. Efforts at damage control were still ongoing. For example, during services preachers would stress that Pastor Volodya continued to receive a salary of only 300 hryvnia, about 60 dollars a month, or the equivalent of a monthly pension, and a woefully inadequate sum on which to support a family of four. They also staged skits to illustrate the falsity and harm of gossip. One sketch featured someone who is ill and tells a friend about his malady. As in a game of telephone, the malady is reported to be more and more serious as the people pass on the news, until the version has the person on the brink of death. Confronted by the distortion, the sick person's sorrow is evident. This skit was meant to illustrate that one should not believe everything one hears because it might be quite far from the truth and hurtful to the person about whom the comments are made. These skits were neither subtle nor effective.

Charismatic communities that can showcase magnetic personalities, such as Volodya's, offer distinct advantages and disadvantages. Should death or some other tragedy befall a much beloved and respected leader, the community can die with him, as former members try to recreate what they had elsewhere. Communities that thrive on the power of personality pose direct challenges to religious establishments. Volodya was meted out the harshest punishment available, excommunication, yet a large majority of his church's membership cast aside the judgments of the denomination's religious authorities. This is all the more remarkable given that of all the moral injunctions on acceptable and unacceptable behavior, the most arch opposition to any form of compromise, or even gesture toward compromise, is over the issue of homosexuality. There is little open discussion of homosexuality in the media or even among informal groups of friends. This is in part a reflection of the Soviet era during which homosexual activity, even among consenting adults, was a criminal offense. There was no legislation regarding lesbianism, because, like prostitution, it allegedly did not exist so it was not necessary to legislate against it.

The partnership between the mother and daughter congregations ended in 2004, as did all cosponsored activities and other exchanges. But the harsh and absolutist condemnations of homosexuality could not end the congregation itself. Some members consciously adopted a benevolent attitude of tolerance and allegiance toward Pastor Volodya. I had the distinct impression that others simply compartmentalized the unwanted information and refused to reckon with it. They steadfastly refused to speak with an outsider, such as myself, about the reasons for his fall from grace. The result of their refusing to leave this community, however, set a precedent. There is now a bisexual evangelical pastor at work in a megachurch in Kharkiv oblast.

## Fusing Beliefs and Sensibilities

In spite of the criticisms leveled against foreign missionaries and global Christianity as yet another hegemonic ideology "converting" Ukrainians to its worldview, I have argued that something more interesting is happening: cultural influences have blended across fields of inequality, and they have altered notions of morality and religious practice in unexpected ways. Religions, specifically the "world religions," have long been a force for cultural interconnectedness. The growing globalizing tendencies of religious affiliation, however, mean that religion creates identities and allegiances that are increasingly deterritorialized. That process of deterritorialization is driven by intensifying cultural interconnectedness, which allows believers to participate in and feel connected to multiple gathering points at once. American missionaries and financing have brought about changes in religious practice in Ukraine. By the same token, the presence of Soviet evangelicals adds to the diversity of religious life in the United States. The two phenomena are not in proportion, a clear illustration of the stark field of inequality in which these exchanges take place. As we saw in chapter 3, this inequality is a key factor motivating Ukrainian émigrés to use their newfound resources to return to Ukraine to affect religious life there.

Even as I stress the very transnational nature of these communities, religious practice is always grounded in a particular place, even as it transcends it. As a result of state policies that have fostered religious pluralism, Ukraine has emerged as a key recipient *and* supplier of evangelical missionaries, a place from which evangelicals emigrate and to which evangelicals return.

As identities and understandings of community and morality continue to evolve after the collapse of the Soviet state and the brutality of the post-Soviet aftermath I suspect that evangelical communities will remain visible and continue to expand their outreach programs. The are many reasons for this. Roger Lancaster asserts that the power of evangelicalism lies in the fact that "a religion of renunciation and despair opens up a space of order in the midst of disorder, morality in an immoral world, and a defined hope in a prevailing social terrain of hopelessness."[28] Evangelical communities in other regions of the world, especially in Africa and Latin America, have demonstrated an affinity for thriving in modern societies undergoing dramatic change. For individuals experiencing isolation, disenfranchisement, and disempowerment, they provide a sense of community and belonging, often sorely lacking in modern urban centers. Postsocialist life is long on choices and challenges but short on clear guidelines for behavior, beliefs, and methods of creating a clear sense of purpose. In such a context, the promise of a shared, meaningful life with a supportive group of like-minded people has profound appeal.

Much has been written about the role of the West in introducing democracy, capitalism, and market economies in Eurasia. An element that has received far less attention is the arrival of global Christianity and the creation of tight local and broadly transnational evangelical communities. Along with other aspects of Western culture and ideology that are indigenously adapted to local cultural values and practices, evangelical communities weave the supernatural into the social and political fabric of everyday life in Ukraine. As these four portraits have shown, these localized and transnational communities challenge traditional ties that link a particular religion to a certain ethnic group, social hierarchy, territory, and state. In return, they provide new social capital that links individuals to communities in another way by creating a sense of shared morality that translates into shared social bonds of mutual assistance. This collectivism moves to another level with the prominent emphasis that evangelicals place on outreach and evangelization. Evangelical communities are committed to creating voluntary organizations that can provide social services to the needy. As such, they articulate alternative understandings of the bonds of obligation that citizens should feel toward one another—especially the moral obligations that the haves should feel toward the have-nots.

# CHAPTER SIX

# AMBASSADORS OF GOD

The largest evangelical church in Europe today started in Kyiv. In many ways it illustrates a number of growing trends in global Christianity and emerging religious sensibilities in post-Soviet society. Known as the Embassy of the Blessed Kingdom of God for all Nations, or "Embassy of God" to its nearly twenty-five thousand members, the church was created quite recently, in 1994. It draws on a Pentecostal-charismatic tradition of expressive worship. As of 2006, the Embassy of God had opened over three hundred daughter congregations, most of them in major Ukrainian cities, such as Kharkiv. At least thirty of them are located abroad, including six in the United States. Missionaries from the Embassy of God compete with Soviet evangelical refugees for the souls of unchurched Slavic immigrants in Philadelphia, Sacramento, New York, and elsewhere.[1]

The founder and senior pastor of this church, Sunday Adelaja, came to Soviet Belarussia from Nigeria to study journalism in 1986. After the collapse of the USSR, he founded the Word of Faith Church in Belarus in 1989. It wasn't long before he encountered severe difficulties with the authorities there even though in his first four years he was not able to convert a single Soviet citizen, only other foreign students. Belarussian President Alexander Lukashenka had declared himself an "Orthodox communist" and presided over a regime that welcomed neither foreigners nor Pentecostal pastors.

Adelaja's possibilities for evangelizing were highly restricted in Belarus, so he decided to head south.

In 1993 he relocated to Kyiv, where he started up a Bible study group with seven people and began preaching in the open air throughout Kyiv. Indeed, in winter 1994 I remember seeing an African preaching to the swelling crowds that clogged the corridors of the Zoloti Vorota, a metro station in downtown Kyiv, when the weather had forced him indoors. I now understand this to have been Adelaja building the beginnings of his church. Later that same year, he reopened his Word of Faith Church with fifty members. His goal was to convert one hundred people a month and make them members of his church. After one year, the church had over one thousand members, and membership has continued to soar ever since. In 2002, he gave the church its current name to signal the church's new mission: to establish a public role for religion and to bring the faith to "all nations" through extensive missionizing.

In time, Sunday Adelaja also incurred the wrath of Ukrainian authorities. Unlike in Belarus, however, efforts to deport him from Ukraine were definitively blocked in 2004 by thirty-one members of the Ukrainian Supreme Soviet, including former Ukrainian president Leonid Kravchuk and former Prime Minister Yevhen. Zviahil'skyi. On three occasions they petitioned the State Committee for Religious Affairs in opposition to the treatment the Ministry of Interior Affairs had meted out to Adelaja, which included twenty-two lawsuits for various offenses and three years of close surveillance by the SBU, the Ukrainian successor to the Soviet KGB. Meanwhile, Adelaja's growing and increasingly vocal following took to the streets to protest threats of deportation, efforts to keep him from preaching, and the extensive bureaucratic difficulties and delays by city administration officials that effectively blocked Adelaja's church from purchasing land and obtaining a building permit to construct its own building.

In 2004 the popular protests and high-level government interventions yielded the intended result: Sunday Adelaja was granted permanent resident status in Ukraine and the Embassy of God was allowed to pursue its plans to purchase a large parcel of land in downtown Kyiv with the intention of building a hypermodern Ukrainian Spiritual Cultural Center, a religious "stadium" slated to seat fifty thousand people. As of 2005, the Embassy of God held thirty-eight services every Sunday in thirty different locations throughout Kyiv, and a central church building was meant to streamline and simplify the process of congregating.

It is not just the enormous size, the rapid growth, and the leadership of this church that makes it distinctive. This church represents a compelling example of innovative missionary dynamics and conversion practices at the dawn of the twenty-first century that have thus far met with spectacular success. Of all the vibrant evangelical communities taking root in Ukraine, the Embassy of God is perhaps the most vivid illustration of how evangelizing is integrating Ukraine and Ukrainians in the world in novel ways. As the activities of this church demonstrate, the interconnections among believers embedded in religious institutions are multidirectional and are often quite vibrant in regions of the world that otherwise have had little previous historical interaction and little current political collaboration. When a self-taught Nigerian pastor opens a church in Ukraine that sends Ukrainian believers to the United States, Germany, India, and the United Arab Emirates, among other countries, to save the unsaved and church the unchurched, it is no longer a case of the core exerting influence on the periphery. Rather, the interconnections and the cultural flow of ideas, objects, and people are also significant among non-Western regions as well as from the so-called Third World to the West. With cultural and linguistic fluency, the colonized missionizes the colonizer, as hundreds of Ukrainians have been doing in Russia for over a decade now. The Embassy of God is a highly innovative example of a religious community going global, and yet its heart and roots are very much in Ukraine.

Second, the strategy that Pastor Sunday has employed to bring nonbelievers under conviction and to yield such impressive and rapid growth trades on spiritually rooted understandings of illness and cure. The original and core membership of the church is made up of recovering addicts and their grateful family members, who see the addict's cure and transformation as a "miracle," testimony to "God's grace." With echoes of the debates over faith-based social service initiatives in the United States, the leadership of the Embassy of God argues that religious institutions are infinitely better equipped to deal with social ills than secular government programs. They understand the roots of social crises to be fundamentally spiritual and therefore, they argue, churches, with their spiritual resources, are uniquely positioned to take on the role of addressing social ills. To do so, the church advocates new forms of church-state partnership to address issues of healing, and social service provision more generally, by incorporating in such programs a significant component dedicated to morality and faith in an effort to "restore and rehabilitate the individual," as the mission statement of the church proclaims.[2] The leadership of the Embassy of God is striving to bring about broad-based political, economic, social, and above all spiritual reform of Ukrainian society by simultaneously imparting a sense of shared morality to individuals and by creating

Figure 6.1: Services at the Embassy of God. Photo by the author.

a host of social institutions that will be founded on biblical principles in an overall effort to reenchant society.

## A Church for People of all Nations

Peter Berger asserted in his landmark study *The Sacred Canopy* that religion simultaneously commands a "world-maintaining" and "world-shaking" power.[3] It is this "double function" of religion for individuals, social groups, and even for the political order that I would like to focus on because this, I believe, holds the key to the broad reemergence of religion across socioeconomic and ethnic groups in postsocialist societies and in particular the key to the spectacular success of the Embassy of God. This duality gives religion its unique power: it can be effective on the individual and communal levels by forging ardent dispositions and motivations and on the national and global levels as it engages the dynamics of political economy with clear ramifications for perceptions of political legitimacy.

In January 2005, Adelaja was invited to the King Center in Atlanta to participate in commemorative ceremonies to honor Martin Luther King Jr. I asked him if he took inspiration from Martin Luther King, another pastor who had set out to realize extensive political change. His answer surprised me. Rather than Martin Luther King, it is Martin Luther who inspires him. In fluent English, Pastor Sunday described the vision he has for his church and in particular how this vision has sharpened since 2002, when the church changed its name and orientation:

> From 2002 our church became more a church that will strive to bring the realities of heaven and the principles of God to every sphere of life. We're not just going to plant churches everywhere, but we're going to bring God to the ways of living of the people, to every stratum of the society, in the sense that we bring God to politics, to business. The church should now begin to view themselves as ambassadors of God. Wherever they are, they are not just there to make money or to do business but to really reflect God, His principles, His holiness, and to really bring them to the structure where they are working. We are now taking responsibility to improve the world and reform the Earth through the principles of the Kingdom, the real principles. Transformations. So it's like saying that we became a reformation church. A church that has set out to reform the whole society, to bring total change, like Martin Luther did. Just transforming the whole culture, actually.[4]

If early evangelical communities sought to establish a firm separation from the world because of its corrupting elements and later churches strove to be *in* the world but not *of* the world, the Embassy of God aims to remake the world in its own image, radically altering, once again, evangelical sensibilities and responses to worldly, profane matters. Let us consider the means and strategies by which this church is attempting to bring total change to Ukrainian society by transforming the culture through religion. The symbol of the Embassy of God is a globe with Africa forthrightly positioned in the center. The globe is capped by a golden crown with a cross. Just below the crown is a light emanating from Ukraine, which remains otherwise unmarked. The light from Ukraine shines throughout Europe and the Middle East. Africa figures prominently, but the light and energy of this church emanate from Ukraine around the world.

The word *embassy* in the name of the church connotes politics and state structures and suggests a symbiotic relationship between church and state in a region of the world with just such a tradition of "state churches." And yet, inherent in its very name, "Embassy of the Blessed Kingdom of God for all Nations," is an indication that the church seeks to reach beyond the limits imposed by state borders. The idea of the church as an "embassy" likens believers to ambassadors. When Pastor Sunday reminds his flock that "I am the church!" (Rus. *Ia eto tserkov*), he is encouraging them to see themselves in church, in Kyiv, in Ukraine, and in the world as ambassadors for Jesus from the Embassy of God. Theologically, the Pentecostal doctrinal emphasis on "a priesthood of believers" predisposes individual believers to active missionizing by offering an unmediated individual relationship to God, to the church community, and to the unsaved. The Embassy of God has simply enshrined this principle as a responsibility of individual believers in its very name.

The multilayered neighborhood-national-global orientation of the Embassy of God is one of the keys to this church's magnetic appeal. It has mastered the art of using small neighborhood- or profession-based prayer groups to foster a feeling of belonging, allegiance, and spiritual growth. Right above the preaching platform hangs a sign that reads "The Group of Twelve is a Place of Results and Harvest" (Rus. *Gruppa 12—Eto Mesto dlia Rezul'tativnosti i Zhatvy*). Services and special anniversary events reinforce feelings of patriotism and pride toward Ukraine by integrating national flags, traditional clothing, and appeals to commit to the nation and state. Yet the services are primarily in Russian—Adelaja does not speak Ukrainian—although some pastors and parishioners address the congregation in Ukrainian. The languages, sermons, symbols, and activities of the church communicate its global nature, as does the unending parade of foreign preachers and missionary delegations who are given the microphone at nearly every service. Members are integrated as individuals and as Ukrainians into a global community of believers pursuing a higher, moral order of existence. In this way, as David Martin wrote about Pentecostals in Latin America, the world becomes their parish.[5]

This church in particular skillfully crafts a multidimensional sense of nationality that is simultaneously nativist and cosmopolitan, that celebrates the bounded national community and moves beyond it. The Soviet-era aesthetic of national culture is apparent in the frequent appearance of folk dancers in folk costumes at most large-scale church events. They dance and perform along with pop musicians and Christian rock performers from around the world. Some people attend church services wearing traditional Ukrainian embroidered blouses and shirts (Ukr. *vyshyvky*).

Having a foreigner at the helm, and moreover a man of color, certainly does signal that this community is particularly open to newcomers and a likely destination of visiting foreign preachers, nearly all of whom are white Americans. They come at their own expense as part of their own missionizing efforts. These Western delegations are important for religious seekers who might view Protestant churches as a window or a bridge to the West. Indeed, among the Embassy of God's daughter congregations is an English-language church run by the pastor's Nigerian wife, Bossie. About two hundred people—Africans, foreigners living in Kyiv, visiting missionaries, and Ukrainians striving to improve their English-language skills—gather on Sunday morning in a rented meeting room at an Intourist Hotel.

There is nothing particularly Nigerian, or even African, about the services the Embassy of God offers, although the doctrine espoused by its leader draws on trends in theology that are well developed in Nigeria, such as an emphasis on faith healing, prosperity theology, and the evangelization of Muslims. The African tradition of independent churches is replicated in the Embassy of God network that marks the main Kyiv church as a hub but otherwise resists the creation of a denomination or a standard of theological unity.[6] Pastor Sunday has managed to make his Africanness seem like a signifier of spiritual enlightenment, a magnetic draw, a sunshine warmth that masks the pronounced racism in this society. Many Ukrainians remember the resentment they experienced over the foreign currency privileges African students enjoyed over the Soviet citizens who financed them. This combines with a basic lack of exposure to Africans and their cultures—there are fewer than two thousand Africans living among 47 million Ukrainians—to produce a distanced, fear-based racism that is quite openly expressed even by the most educated. Likewise, there is nothing particularly American or Western about this church either. Pastor Sunday himself never visited the United States until 2001, although he has since received numerous invitations, and his preaching is now regularly broadcast on TBN, the largest Christian cable network in the United States.

The main church is actually a rented sports arena, the only location that can accommodate the large crowds Pastor Sunday draws. Indeed, a gym and other sporting facilities continue to operate in part of the complex. Even during services, freshly showered men in black leather can be seen walking through the "church" as they leave the gym. The first time that I went to the Embassy of God, as I entered the main hall, instead of going left, I turned to my right and quickly found myself surrounded by sweaty boxers pummeling little black bags. Another wrong turn put me in the locker room. Eventually, I found my way to a cluster of desks in a three-room office suite off the balcony on the second floor overlooking the main arena. The door was marked with a gold plate announcing the offices of "People's Deputy L. M. Chernovet'skyi," who at that time was a member of the Verhovna Rada, Ukraine's parliament. There was no mention of the church. One of the two young American missionary women who worked for the church full-time explained to me that all members of parliament have a right to an office in town, outside of the parliamentary building. As a measure of protection for Pastor Sunday and the church, Chernovet'skyi chose this sports hall to locate his office. Although efforts to evict, deport, or otherwise silence Adelaja were ongoing, it was clear that city administration officials could not evict a People's Deputy from his own state-sponsored office. This was one of the many unusual forms of church-state collaboration that the Embassy of God has embarked upon, first to secure its position in Ukrainian society and now to strengthen it.

The first time I interviewed Pastor Sophia, one of two deputy pastors to Pastor Sunday who runs the Ester Women's Ministry, the small administrative offices were teeming with so many people that we took two chairs and sat outside the suite on the balcony overlooking the arena where services take place. She immediately apologized for the wartime conditions (Rus. *usloviia kak na fronte*)—in which we were about to conduct the interview. Looking over the balcony, we saw two tired men, cigarettes dangling from their lips, collecting the flotsam and jetsam strewn over the main arena in preparation for services. So far they had made a ten-foot-high pyramid of rubbish as they smoothed out the earthen floor to lay down pieces of tarpaulin over which they would place thousands of chairs for the imminent arrival of the worshipers and a multitude of tables selling a wide range of Christian wares (books, cassettes, calendars, DVDs, magnets, and other trinkets).

These men transform the sports hall in the evenings and on weekends into a church by adding a grand stage and preaching platform up front in the main arena. Dozens of state flags flank the stage on both sides, as is common practice in Pentecostal charismatic churches in Africa, the United States, and elsewhere. The first hour or so of each service is devoted to music and movement. When the music begins, parishioners take the flags from their stands and move about the crowd, creating a colorful, animated effect. The Ukrainian flag is *always* the first national flag chosen. After the Ukrainian flag, usually the American, Israeli, or German flag comes next, followed by the Russian flag, revealing the pro-Ukrainian and highly patriotic political orientation of the church. During my first visit to the Embassy of God, as this part of the service started, a member with whom I had spoken earlier rushed up to the front and picked up the American flag as a private sign

Figure 6.2: Christian goods for sale at the Embassy of God. Photo by the author.

of welcome to me. During subsequent visits I noticed a similar gesture of welcome was extended to Dutch, Swedish, and South African visitors. Within minutes, the large area to each side of the preaching platform and the wide aisles on the side are filled with national flags swirling in the arms of enthusiastic worshipers. In this way, national differences and state borders are recognized and celebrated even as their importance is diminished in a church for people of all nations.

## In the Beginning

The beginnings of this church were actually quite modest and strained. Adelaja began by preaching in a rented a room at the Polytechnical Institute in 1994, hoping to attract the more religiously curious students. In doing so, he was following a vision he had had in Belarus, where he saw himself ministering to a large crowd of white people who were being transformed by the Gospel. During this encounter with God, as he characterizes this moment, he understood that God was calling him to minister to Slavic people. This sense of a God-given calling is why he steadfastly resisted every effort to deport him from Ukraine. Belief in this kind of divinely ordained plan is what gave Adelaja the stamina to endure the arduous task of acquiring a following as a young African man in a highly racist society preaching evangelical doctrine in a historically Orthodox land. Adelaja reflects on what he now understands to have been a pivotal moment in the church's development and illustrates how he uses "dialogue with God" to guide the growth of the church.

One day when I got to the group, to the auditorium at the Poly-technical Institute, and after the lecture that I gave, one lady came to me and said, "My name is Natasha. Natasha Alcoholic"—here you say, "Natasha" and your surname—I asked, "Is that your family name?" She said, "No, that is *who* I am." I was so broken, I said, "Well, you will never be known as Natasha Alcoholic again." I felt like God was making me tell her that. "You will be a strong woman of God. God is going to use you. You will not be known as Natasha Alcoholic. You will be known as Natasha, a minister of God." But when I came home, I was very disappointed. I said that to her, but I didn't believe it myself. And I was crying because I couldn't sleep until three o'clock in the morning. I was praying and I thought, God, you were going to make something happen, and nobody is coming. And those who are coming are not even students from the school or market women. Just let ordinary people come! Normal people! Only alcoholics are coming. I never drink. I have never drank in my life. I've never had anything to do with alcoholics. Then, as I was praying like that, I said, God help me, you said I should do this work. Show me the way to do it. Then God spoke to my heart. I opened my bible to the Book of Mark, chapter 12, verse 37. I didn't see anything, but towards the end of it, I was really amplified. The last sentence said the poor people, the outcast, the unloved all felt welcome with Jesus. They felt loved by Jesus. I started meditating about that. . . . I felt that God was talking to me very clearly. If I could trust you with down and out people, with the poor and the outcast and, like with Jesus, if you could make them feel welcomed and to feel loved, then in time, I will be able to trust you with all people from this society. With the strong, with elites, the powerful and the politicians. That became a revelation. That became my policy. That was the key I was looking for. I was expecting normal people to come, but normal people will never come because they are looking at a black man. The racial thing would never allow them to come. The mentality here is that there is no way a black man will ever teach me. There is no way. I am not that limited to allow a black man to teach me. Then God gave me the key. Don't expect normal people to come to your church. Go and look for the down and out. They are already out. They are already down, already outcasts. The drug addicts, the bums, the alcoholics, they are blind to color. They just want somebody to love them. That's what became the key for this church. The church was known for the first few years as a church of alcoholics and drug addicts. I took Natasha and we went into the streets, to hospitals where they keep drug addicts and alcoholics, and we started to preach.

Fusing from the start cure and conversion, the church began to grow from the efforts of a black man with a vision and a white woman with an addiction.


## Love Rehab

The core of the church's outreach efforts initially consisted of curing addiction through faith healing. In addition to weekly services devoted to healing and periodic all-night vigils, the ongoing centerpiece of the church's faith healing program became the Love Rehabilitation Center, where the church claims to have "freed" over three thousand people from drug and alcohol dependencies. Pastor Natalya—the old "Natasha Alcoholic"—was the center's creator and formal director.

Based on her own experience as an alcoholic for thirty years, Pastor Natalya pioneered a multi-step program for healing that draws heavily on the famous twelve-step program used by Alcoholics Anonymous. Although she and the center's staff maintain that there are distinct differences between the two programs, I see tremendous overlap. Like the Embassy of God, AA's highly acclaimed twelve-step recovery program flatly states that alcoholism is "an illness which only a spiritual experience will conquer."[7] Rather than the "personal recovery" program AA advocates, Pastor Natalya's program situates the problem of addiction and dependence within the family. Given the tight housing situation in Ukraine, at once a legacy of the low priority the Soviet regime placed on providing non-industrial, nonmilitary services and the current skyrocketing real estate prices in most cities, few people, much less young people with addiction problems, live alone. Furthermore,

Figure 6.3: Embassy of God
healing services at a homeless
shelter. Photo by the author.

family relationships tend to be closer in postsocialist Ukraine than they are in most Western societies, and families are smaller. When even one person is rendered a burden thanks to addiction, the setback to the family is that much greater.

Pastor Natalya's program is outlined in a book published both in English and Russian entitled *The Way to Freedom for your Family* (Rus. *Put' k svobode tvoei sem'i*), which is specifically written for women who are relatives of an addict.[8] Perhaps the single greatest difference between the Embassy of God's program and AA's program is the positioning of the healing process itself. Alcoholics Anonymous, which is unabashedly "spiritual" with its highly religious vocabulary, is nonetheless nondenominational, nonprofit, and independent. Pastor Natalya's program draws on the Pentecostal theological tradition of her church and is buttressed by numerous biblical citations. She states that because of Jesus' suffering, humankind has the power to be freed from suffering and disease. If we have faith and live a spiritual, God-centered life, rather than one aimed at worldly pleasures, we are healed. She draws on her own biography as evidence.

Pastor Natalya became a believer in 1996, after a thirty-year battle with alcoholism during which her relatives constantly warned her that she would die like a homeless beggar. In her published account, she attributes the miracle of her cure to an encounter with God that resulted in an ongoing dialogue.

> Once after a period of heavy drinking, I started praying to the Lord even though I did not believe in Him. I had heard about Him from others who also wanted to quit their addictions. And I told Him that I did not want to live the way I was living. I also told the Lord that, if He really existed, He should take me out of the pit I was in. These simple words changed my life, and I felt peace in my heart that had never been there before. At that moment, I understood that God had heard me and answered me. From that time on, I never touched a glass of alcohol. God miraculously healed me of my addiction.[9]

The fifty-two-year-old pastor uses her own experience as testimony to God's healing powers. After thirty years of severe alcoholism, she was near death. She found God in a pivotal moment in 1996 that reordered her life and tamed her addictive tendencies. One year later she created the Love Rehabilitation Center in her home, and it now has ambulatory and residential units in Kyiv and two sister centers located in Minsk, Belarus and Vladimir, Russia. Then she became the pastor to a congregation numbering twenty-five hundred, one of the largest in Europe led by a woman. In 2005 she relocated to Berlin to open an Embassy of God church there. She credits her spectacular and rapid transformation from the depths of despair to the heights of accomplishment to the miraculous and wondrous powers of belief and prayer. This simple explanation and solution to addiction, hinging on a miraculous encounter with God, holds out the possibility that a cure is within everyone's reach.

One could argue—indeed, many psychologists have—that addicts who find God merely transfer dependencies and shift addictions. Pastor Natalya herself provides evidence of this when she dedicates the book outlining her prescription for recovery to "Jesus Christ, my beloved Husband and the Lord of my life" and to the founder of the Embassy of God "Sunday Adelaja, my spiritual father, precious pastor, teacher and apostle." As a twice-divorced single mother, she now champions Jesus and Pastor Sunday as the main men in her life. The Embassy of God pastor responsible for training new pastors, himself a former heroin addict twice sentenced to prison, estimated that half of the Embassy of God's pastors were former addicts. Other pastors and many members of the church are relatives of former addicts. Yet it would be an oversimplification to say that the Love Rehab Center merely shifts the epicenter of an addict's life from drugs to religion, although this is indeed a factor in recovery. Membership in this religious community, where addiction is not stigmatized and where the histories of personal triumph over evil and suffering assume redeeming meaning and usefully inspire others, clearly contributes to the healing process in a unique and totalizing way, at a minimum by removing the isolation and solitary suffering of living with a fallen past. This is much like overcoming the experience of being in the camps as described in chapter 2.

One of the cornerstones of the Alcoholics Anonymous program is the centrality they give to "fellowship" in the recovery process. AA claims that an alcoholic who has conquered dependence has gained a unique ability, the "power of the wounded healer," to inspire others to strive for recovery by sharing stories of dependence and struggles for recovery.[10] Testimonies of miraculous strength, of the resolve to turn away from drugs and alcohol and to embrace an all-knowing, all-forgiving God are also a common tactic in the healing process at the Love Rehab Center. Every day at the center and during every church service, individuals are given the opportunity to share their experiences of miraculous healing as evidence of God's grace and power.

The Embassy of God has packaged these testimonies in a flashy promotional book entitled *Look What God Has Done* (Rus. *Smotri chto sdelal Gospod'*). In a two-page spread, each pastor or lay leader, all of whose names are presented in a Westernized form without patronymic, recount the process of adopting a God-centered life after a pivotal flash of insight and the powerful experience of God's presence. Thereafter, numerous blessings flowed, including forgoing addictions, creating happy family lives, and becoming successful, productive, and respected citizens of Ukraine. Although the clergy of the Embassy of God recognize that the process of conversion is not swift for all, they choose to present it as a pivotal "transformational key encounter with God"—a life-changing experience, the cure from illness, and the key to success. Similarly, they stress the number of individuals freed from addiction, not those who dropped out of the program; the numbers joining the church, not those who leave.[11]

The AA program also relies heavily on individuals recognizing a higher power "as each person understands Him" and thereby also links conversion with recovery. Yet the AA program guidelines warn against expectations of a "God-consciousness" moment, cautioning that many have erroneously understood the recognition of a higher power to be a sudden, pivotal awakening—precisely what many members, including Pastor Sunday, claim it to have been for them. In contrast, the AA program stresses that the process of coming to God can often be slow, arduous, and frustrating. To this effect, the AA book includes a chapter entitled "We Agnostics," which aims to assist people to have a spiritual experience and to recognize a power that cannot be scientifically proven or experienced as present in their lives.[12]

The Embassy of God privileges the healing power of prayer and fellowship and the surrender of power over one's life to an omniscient and omnipotent God as a more effective means than medical intervention to conquer and overcome dependence. They are not opposed to medical intervention in principle, although private medical treatment is unaffordable and hence unavailable to most addicts and their families. Religion and fellowship, on the other hand, are offered free of charge and are positioned as the *best* therapeutic weapons against addiction.[13] So a "cure" is within reach of anyone who seeks it.

Talal Asad critiques a "secular understanding of pain" as a private and inscrutable experience and advocates instead that we recognize the "agentive" qualities of pain. He argues that "as a social relationship pain is more than experience. It is part of what creates the conditions of action and experience."[14] In reflecting on this insight in combination with my interviews with former addicts, who experienced extreme physical pain, and their parents, spouses and other loved ones, who experienced unrelentingly painful anguish and desperation, I have concluded that some forms of pain do indeed carry agentive properties. Pain can be so intense that it compels those who experience it to create new worlds in order to endure it. Pain forces its recipients to cast aside familiar modes of thinking and to embrace new modes of believing, experiencing, and reasoning. In this way, pain, even debilitating physical and emotional pain, can function as an agent of change.

Much of the healing process at Love Rehab centers on adopting religious frames of meaning to understand the suffering the addict has experienced and is experiencing. By evoking "Jesus as the answer," which they do incessantly, they equate Jesus' resurrection from death with the near-death experience of addiction and the resurrection-like experience of feeling healed. Ultimately, the introduction of evangelical faith to the healing process goes to the heart of the concepts of will and intentionality. The addict becomes "a sick person held captive by the devil." The devil, not the addicted individual, is to blame. He is the cause of all sin, the root of evil and suffering.[15] To expel the devil and his hold over the addict is to begin the healing process and the embrace of God. In other words, pain can facilitate a religious experience for the addict and those who suffer with the addict by providing religiously imbued frames of meaning, vocabularies, and sensations through which and by which to experience pain.

A new sense of power and direction is acquired, paradoxically, by admitting powerlessness and by surrendering the course of one's life to the will of God. In the therapeutic process, the healers at the Love Rehab Center from the very beginning ask family and friends to change their behavior and ways of seeing themselves in the world by acknowledging their powerlessness. Faith healing hinges on coming to see oneself as no longer autonomous but as part of a cosmic union with God in communion with fellow believers, and this, they claim, delivers the strength, power, and force to heal. As the individual acknowledges powerlessness, all agency, all control over behavior is transferred to God. For parents who have tried mightily to reverse a child's downward slide into addiction, this surrender is often a welcome relief and becomes the first of many changes in modes of thinking and believing.

George Saunders's study of faith healing in Italy uses De Martino's concept of a "crisis of presence," an acknowledged risk of not being there, to explain why and how individuals converted and embraced faith healing. Saunders argues that after conversion, those with afflictions begin to make decisions for themselves. They feel as if they are no longer passively manipulated by others, even as they transfer acknowledgement of power to God. He writes, "They have acquired a protector, a community, and a set of responsibilities all at the same time. They are liberated from their passivity. They have recreated their own histories and, in the process, have regained a presence in history itself."[16] Much the same dynamic is at work at the Love Rehab Center. The recovering addicts renounce all claims to agency and as such allow the agentive powers of pain to help them regain control.

No one can "commit" a friend or relative to Love Rehab. Once an addict asks to enroll, the new charge goes into quarantine for ten days. There are no more than ten people in quarantine at any one time. At the end of the quarantine period, the patient is switched either to the Love Rehab Center's residential program located in Irpen′, a suburb of Kyiv, or to an outpatient clinic in Kyiv called "New Beginning." The residence accommodates twenty-eight patients who live there for three to four months. The outpatient program is designed for up to thirty recovering addicts, who come each day for therapy, work, and, of course, prayer and spiritual counseling. Volunteer recovering addicts or their family members staff the Center.[17] The multidimensional program (Rus. *kompleksnaia programma*) they offer is aimed at healing the family and friends of the addict as well and incorporates them into many of its programs.

Indeed, some of the most enthusiastic and devoted members of the Embassy of God are the parents of drug addicts. One father who is a deacon and hugely active in church affairs told me how his son left Kyiv to work at a construction job near Irkutsk, Siberia, where they sold heroin on the streets "like ice cream." After two years in Siberia, he returned to Kyiv as a twenty-one-year-old addict. For four years, he and his wife struggled with their son's bewildering addiction and the rampage it led on their lives. "He carried everything out of the apartment and sold it to buy drugs. When we literally had no furniture and no possessions left, he took the food out of the refrigerator and sold that too," the father explained.[18] Numerous appeals to state agencies for help failed to produce any tangible results. Their own efforts and those of friends could not curb their son's appetite for drugs or cut off his access to them. At a loss over what to do with their only child, they approached the Embassy of God's Rehab Center, where he ultimately overcame his addiction.

The father's expressions of wide-eyed horror as he described this period of torment melted into proud proclamations of how his son has been clean for three years now and is even married and has a small child. The descent into this family's hell was triggered by their son's loss of bodily control. He no longer had a will, and they no longer had any power over his or even their own lives. And yet the pain of this period of living hell has been transformed into a privileged source of authority when witnessing about miracles. The simultaneous occurrence of conversion and cure meant that not only the addict, but his family members as well, acquired a protector (a new mode of seeing) and a supportive community (a new mode of being) that ultimately redeemed and made meaningful this prolonged period of suffering. After his son was cured, all three became members of the church. The gratitude for the cessation of the chaos that had ruled their lives during their son's addition and the evidence of the power of (pain-induced) faith to transform remains alive through their constant retellings of their conversions and of the "miracle cure" their son experienced.

### New Beginning

The New Beginning Center is located in a rented section of an old "House of Culture" (Rus. *Dom Kultury*), which also serves as one of the Embassy of God churches. During the liminal—and critically important—one- or two-year period after breaking dependence, many of the clients remain connected to the center as volunteer workers, as they attempt to "find what God has given them," as the director says. Because the center only occupies part of the building, recovering addicts interact with the other tenants, including a dance school with its many small ballerinas, a dozen or so small businesses, and the skeletal remains of the House of Culture and its cinemagraphic offerings. Thus, recovering addicts have daily exposure to ongoing "normal" life as they gradually reintegrate themselves into society by circulating together with non-addicts in the confines of the House of Culture.

In both centers, the residential and the ambulatory, the addicts are divided for treatment according to type of addiction and age. At any given time, they have thirty or so recovering alcoholics in treatment, who tend to be between the ages of thirty-five and forty. Approximately 60 percent of all clients are drug addicts, most are under twenty-five years of age, and at least two-thirds are male. The most common drug used is heroin, an injected drug, which means that the staff and volunteers of the Rehab Center are obliged to deal with HIV/AIDS as well. Ukraine has the highest level of HIV infection in all of Europe and the former Soviet Union. Although the HIV/AIDS epidemic is still considered nascent, as of 2005 1.4 percent of the population was infected with the disease. High levels of drug addiction are one of the main factors propelling the disease.

In addition to heroin, psychotropic drugs are increasingly common precisely because they are so inexpensive and easily accessible. About 10 percent of the clients are addicted to them. Young people make these drugs from legal drugs, such as antidepressants, that are readily available. These drugs are particularly debilitating and create what the director calls "thought invalids" because they impair reasoning.

In addition to the director, the outpatient center has one doctor on staff. She explained to me that after working in state-run rehab programs for nearly thirty years, she was forced to conclude that her efforts could only be described as "hopeless and senseless" (Rus. *bezyskhodnyi i bez smysla*). Much to her chagrin, she realized that she was only treating addiction in a cyclical fashion. Once her patients were released from the clinic, they reengaged in addictive behaviors with stunning regularity. She saw few addicts become cured and abandon drugs or alcohol completely. Initially, she sought an alternative at a Christian Rehab Center run by a Baptist church before switching to the Love Rehab Center several years ago. Although she is beyond retirement age, she remains committed to the center and its program of placing spiritual healing above medical intervention and of treating the family, not just the addict.

## Church and State Collaboration

"Everyone who works here is a former something," said Ludmilla Antonovna, the director of the New Beginning Center. She turned to the Embassy of God when her own son became an addict, a period she described as a "little hell on earth."[19] Many of her relatives emigrated to the United States, but she chose to stay in Ukraine. She found herself isolated and alone when her relatives blamed her son's addiction on her reluctance to leave Ukraine. Once her son enrolled at the Center, she began to volunteer as well, as is common practice although not a requirement. A capable and competent professional, Ludmilla gradually took on more and more responsibility as a volunteer until she was offered one of the few paid positions as a staff member.

Like so many other entrepreneurs in cash-strapped Ukraine, she dreams of tapping into the administrative resources (Rus. *admin resursy*) of the state to form what she calls a "partnership" to expand the programs the Love Rehab Center could offer. Speaking before the Orange Revolution, when the general opinion of the government was abysmal, she explains why she advocates a close association with state administrations and state-run social programs:

> Alone neither we nor the government will reach the results we want. First, we would like our church and the state to have a common understanding of these problems. Second, we would like to participate in joint projects and programs. We want to work together with the government to fulfill these projects, to fight these problems. We don't just want money. We've written government structures saying, "We are here. Please use us. We want to struggle with you against drug addiction, AIDS, against alcoholism, poverty and illiteracy."

Ludmilla is striving to fuse the church's unique ability to heal based on a therapeutic process founded on spiritual development and the state's administrative resources to do so on a large scale. Given her theological understandings of the causes of addiction, in her view the church is in a unique position to carry out the mission work of saving society's discarded souls. The state is the sole entity in a position to finance such a mission on the scale that those at the Love Rehab want.

Aside from the director and doctor, a sociologist and a psychologist are also on staff in a paid consultative role. The psychologist, who had worked as a school counselor, quickly came to appreciate the center's emphasis on healing the whole family. The sociologist was hired to help the center and the Embassy of God expand their programs by preparing proposals to win government contracts and grants from international funding agencies. Even though they understand and treat addiction in religious terms, they want their spiritual solution to be accepted in a secular realm by government officials. This eagerness to work with government officials and within government programs is a distinguishing feature of the Embassy of God's healing programs. Many religious communities in the United States, for example, remain reluctant to collaborate or coordinate with government or other secular social service providers.[20]

## Returning to the Streets

Pastor Sunday and Pastor Natalya began preaching in the streets to addicts, and that is where they have returned to showcase their accomplishments. The Love Rehab Center sponsored an annual March of Life parade through downtown Kyiv on the Day of AIDS Remembrance to raise awareness of the spiritual nature of addiction problems and the spiritual possibilities for cure the Embassy of God offers. Those who have been "saved" from drugs, sin, and eternal damnation march through the center of Kyiv with their children wearing vests proclaiming that they have been "Freed from Alcoholism" or "Freed from Drug Addition." Wearing colorful choir robes, members from each of the daughter congregations carry banners crying out "God is Love!" "Jesus is the Way!" and "Ukraine Chooses Jesus!" The endless columns of jubilant believers chanting, singing, and dancing along the city's main boulevards hammer home the growth of evangelicalism in Ukraine and the Embassy of God's position at the forefront of its revival. The highly emotive, open-air preaching in the heart of the city culminates in the foreign-born Pastor Sunday falling to his knees to bless Ukrainian soil.

The march also offers a public forum to promote the Embassy of God's view that the separation of church and state is a misguided principle. While they do not invoke the Orthodox-Imperial collaboration as a model, in effect what they advocate is a symbiotic relationship between the church and the state to resolve social problems. They see clear links between society and morality, between social disorder and individual moral transgressions. Pastor Sunday and his two deputy pastors, both of whom are women, preach to the crowds at the conclusion of the march by unleashing a tsunami of passionate emotion, imploring politicians not to take bribes, citizens to love Ukraine, and Christians to be civically engaged (Rus. *zanimat'*

Figure 6.4: March of Life, 2003. Photo courtesy of Nikolai Bylichev.

*grazhdanskuiu pozitsiui)*. Pastor Sunday is increasingly insistent on this last point, and he uses the march as a forum to stress the obligation of believers to become Christian activists for social change.

Ram Cnaan has studied the links among organized religion, social responsibility, and volunteerism in the United States. He argues that the provision of social and community services is not a product of a congregation's membership or size. Rather, it stems from the development of *congregational norms* of social and community involvement. In the United States, these congregational norms have become broader cultural norms of volunteerism forging a strong connection between organized religion and social responsibility that is actualized through volunteerism.[21] The link between volunteerism and local religious organizations has, up until now, been considered a uniquely American phenomenon. Other countries with high levels of religious participation, such as Ireland and Poland, do not have a developed tradition of churches providing social services.

Yet it is precisely this scenario that Pastor Sunday seeks to put in place: churches should lead the way in caring for the poor and the disenfranchised and along the way educate others to do the same, most of all the

Figure 6.5: March of Life, 2003.
Photo courtesy of Nikolai
Bylichev.

government. In a break with evangelical tradition in Soviet Ukraine, this church extols the believer's moral obligation to become engaged in political and social issues to resolve what they perceive to be social ills: addiction, HIV/AIDS, the decline of the family, abortion, homosexuality, and poverty. The March of Life is a means of acculturating other religious institutions and state officials to norms of charitable outreach in the name of creating and strengthening new religiously infused forms of social activism. Volunteering to address the spiritual and physical afflictions of drug addicts and alcoholics has already become a congregational norm at Europe's largest evangelical missionary church. The March of Life is a massive demonstration of evangelical values and social and political initiatives, a means for believers to act on this civic engagement with an ardent zeal to realize social change.

## A New Moral Majority?

Part of exercising faith, Pastor Sunday explains, is breaking down the barriers that lock religion into a privatized domain. This march was meant to be a catalyst to spur individuals into a politicized, activist mode and to signal to politicians that responding to the priorities of believers will surely benefit them on election day. Adelaja argues that religion should fully permeate the public sphere, and this march is but one means to advance this cause.

In 2005 the March of Life took on a new dimension. Designed to unify as many religious organizations as possible in a broad ecumenical effort to bring about social change, it was renamed the March for Jesus. This unifying gesture took on a decisively sectarian cast when the idea of marching for "life" was replaced with "Jesus." While bringing the weight and authority of other religious institutions to bear, the new name signaled that evangelicals were in the forefront. During the 2004–2005 Orange Revolution, religious institutions showed remarkable unity in pursuing concerted, coordinated action to overturn falsified election results and usher Viktor Yushchenko into office. With the notable exception of the Ukrainian Orthodox Church-Moscow Patriarchate, virtually all religious institutions lent their support to the "orange" opposition camp. The Embassy of God strove to maintain this momentum of unity and political engagement with the March for Jesus to spur additional ecumenical support for social reform.

The Orange Revolution was in fact the second time that a wide spectrum of religious organizations successfully banded together to steer government policy along "biblical principles." Since 2003 attempts to stage a gay pride parade in Kyiv have been thwarted by vocal opposition from religious organizations that otherwise have radically different political visions for Ukraine. Homophobia remains an issue capable of galvanizing highly disparate religious organizations and political parties to take coordinated action.[22]

In many respects, Pastor Sunday's stress on civic engagement harks back to the efforts of Jerry Falwell, Pat Robertson, Randall Terry, and Tim La-Haye to create and empower the Moral Majority. At that time, American evangelicals reasoned that believers should act to better American society immediately, since they understood it to be necessary to avoid the comprehensive damage at the Second Coming of Christ that could even adversely affect the saved. This, together with a charismatic interpretation of scriptural justification, was the rationale used to enter the political arena in the late 1970s. In many ways, Pastor Sunday's motivations are similar. He, too, believes that it is imperative to prepare the Kingdom of God on earth to the greatest extent possible by becoming politically engaged and reforming the society along biblical principles in advance of the Second Coming of Christ.

He and the members of his church were active participants in the Orange Revolution in 2004. Approximately four thousand members of the Embassy of God gathered on the main city square in Kyiv (Ukr. *maidan*) every day to protest the falsified election results by fasting, praying, and evangelizing on the square. They understood the public outpouring of moral outrage as evidence of the reawakening that was overtaking Ukrainian society. On the heels of the Orange Revolution, when there was still considerable optimism about the prospects for real change, Pastor Sunday said:

> We shouldn't be indifferent any longer to the life in the country we live in. We should no longer be Christians who just pray in the churches and who don't interfere, just make a living, go to work, get a salary and go to church. It has been like that for a while—Christians have been isolated from the everyday running of the country. We are now saying that the church is supposed to be the place where you are taught the total principles of God so that you might go from there to live those principles, not just in your daily life, but to enforce it everywhere you go so that you participate actively in making sure that nobody is hungry in the city or country you live in and in making sure that if you see evils, like alcoholism or drug addiction, that you are responsible to minister and to bring God to those people and to make sure that that is totally changing the old society. If the homosexuals want to march in the streets of Kyiv, we go out and say "No!" Righteousness will rein. We will stand for righteousness and uprightness. In politics, we will no longer just go out and vote. We will put godly people there.

Indeed, in 2006, one of the most prominent members of the church and a steady participant in these marches, L. M. Chernovet'skyi, was elected mayor of Kyiv, defeating two formidable opponents, the incumbent mayor and Vitaly Klitchko, a world-class heavyweight boxing champion and national hero. At the church's twelfth anniversary celebration right after the parliamentary elections, Pastor Sunday made an announcement about Yulia Timoshenko, the oligarchic former "Gas Princess," the populist force behind the Orange Revolution and, at that time, still a fierce contender to retake her old job as prime minister. He stated that although she was still an Orthodox believer, Yulia, as she is affectionately known, had been born again and baptized in the Holy Spirit.[23] She has made no public statements indicating that "she has given herself to the Lord at the Embassy of God," as Pastor Sunday asserts. Whether or not this proclamation is true, it signals the political leanings of this church and the level of government contacts it either has or aims to have.

The values advocated by the Embassy of God are not easily classified in terms that have currency in the United States, where evangelicals have a significant measure of political power. Clearly, in some respects they reflect the most dogmatic and unrelenting forms of conservative Christianity, as in their ardent opposition to homosexuality. Yet, their advocacy of government-funded programs for the poor and the disenfranchised echoes aspects of liberal, progressive politics. Their charismatic style is clearly contemporary, but the issues this church holds sacred, namely caring for the poor, echoes the original views of early Pentecostalism. Across a broad spectrum of liberal and conservative issues, the Embassy of God sees itself as taking the lead, of working with the state to steer social change to be in keeping with biblical principles of morality as they understand them. This is the latest incarnation of defiant compliance.

## Prosperity Theology

In the second half of the twentieth century, and especially since the mid-1970s, evangelicals worldwide began to come out from behind their fortress-like separation from the world, much as we have seen Soviet Pentecostal and Baptist communities do after the fall of the Soviet Union, and advocate a different form of engagement with the world, and specifically with money. The shared condemnation and antipathy toward the broader culture, so characteristic of earlier evangelical communities, wherever they may have been located, has given way to selective acceptance of mainstream cultural values. One strong statement of the embrace of capitalism and the values it has bred is the proliferation of evangelical churches that espouse "prosperity theology." These teachings advocate understanding wealth and privilege as "blessings" from God, as testimony to the beholder's faith and faithful living. Prosperity theology also indirectly endorses consumerism and materialism by melding the accumulation of money, goods, and privilege as evidence of "His Grace."

Earlier Pentecostal churches stressed a doctrine of holiness, antimaterialism, withdrawal from the world, and a guarded attitude toward the state. As a result, they appealed primarily to the poor and the disenfranchised, who could then interpret their poverty, oppositional stance, and marginalization as a source of moral richness. More recently, churches, such as Embassy of God, in sharp contrast, have recast the meaning of power, wealth, and material pleasures. Rather than espousing an antagonistic view of money as a corrupting force, they see personal wealth and professional success as evidence of a blessing from God, and they advocate instead a "morally controlled materialism" and a patriotic spirit.

The encouragement to pursue and accumulate wealth that prosperity theology prompts also recasts the meaning of education. No longer held at bay as a corrupting, polluting, and secularizing force, education becomes a means to fulfill one's calling and to serve God, country, and family by becoming successful and rich. Wealth is in reach of all who believe, which reignites the hope not only that change and victory over adversity are possible but that faith provides a means to realize this possibility.

Critics of prosperity theology claim that its cheap instrumental call to faith—God will make you rich!—subverts interest, concern, and responsibility for the poor. The lack of attention to the structural factors that predispose certain people and nations to a life of inequality—which has the effect of making the struggle for financial security seem downright futile—means that failure or disappointments must be explained as individual shortcomings, just as personal wealth is a sign of personal virtue. Prosperity theology asserts that only those whose faith is strong enough are worthy of prosperity, so only they experience it. In other words, the impoverished believer is morally indicted for not being a deep, sincere, or diligent enough Christian, and this is used to explain ongoing economic dissatisfactions and the suffering brought about by poverty.

I have heard many in Ukraine connect prosperity theology with what they perceive to be the "cult-like" aspects of evangelicalism. Critics see prosperity theology as a psychological trap that forces people, through duplicitous psychological pressure, to give money in the hopes of receiving even more, much like the deceitful pyramid schemes that circulated widely in the early 1990s. There is some truth to this. I have heard people testify to the glories that ensued when they contributed a healthy tithe. One of the more dubious inspirational stories I ever heard came from a man who explained that, in spite of business debts totaling over a hundred thousand dollars and constant violent threats from money lenders, at one point he gave a "significant" contribution to the Embassy of God. Magically, two months later, with no identifiable explanation, his debts were paid off and his business bounced back. The point of his story is that if you give, you will receive much more. He had little income, but still gave over 10 percent, and all his debts were forgiven. In spite of the stories of vanishing debts and magically appearing fabulous wealth that were recounted during witnessing at the services, the tremendous embrace of prosperity theology in Latin America, Africa, and now, I suggest, in Ukraine as well, means that for some, the "invisible hand" of market capitalism has been recast into the work of benevolent and evil forces, bestowing either blessings or suffering.

The Embassy of God's most famous member is Leonid Chernovet'skyi, a former member of the Supreme Soviet (Ukr. Verkhovna Rada), current mayor of Kyiv, and, together with his wife, owner of Pravex Bank, one of the largest banks in Ukraine with assets of over 400 million dollars. Commanding enormous wealth and power, Chernovet'skyi is effectively one of the ruling oligarchs of Ukraine. He is the Embassy of God's iconic representation of the "health and wealth" prosperity theology that Pastor Sunday preaches.

Most Ukrainians assume that oligarchs have stolen or in some other way immorally procured the startup capital needed to build their financial empires and large-scale business ventures. Chernovet'skyi retells his biography in such a way that he highlights the wealth of his wife's father, a Georgian, as an explanation as to how he procured startup capital to begin his businesses. Numerous press reports attribute that wealth to early entrepreneurial buying and selling of apartments and other valuables from Jews who were emigrating from the USSR in the late 1980s. Among the powerful protectors that Adelaja has secured, Chernovet'skyi remains his most significant and visible supporter. Chernovet'skyi explains how and why he converted:

> I was around 46 when I came to the Word of Faith Church, and now I'm 53. Before, I searched for God for many years, went to Orthodox churches, prayed to different icons while I was imagining God, lit candles. But, to speak honestly, I never had the feeling of communicating with God. I wanted to hear the Word of God, but no one there said anything about this in any of those churches.

> My actual turning to God is connected with my political ambitions, when in 1995 or 1996, I already don't remember exactly, in a really exhausting campaign, I tried to become a deputy of the Supreme Soviet. It wasn't working because, according to the election law of the time, at least 51 percent of the population had to vote. But in the Darnitsa district, where one of the largest radio electronic factories in all of Ukraine had shut down, no one wanted to vote. Twice I tried with

different PR campaigns to get people to vote, but they didn't believe in anything. They only spoke to me about sausage and other daily problems and they weren't at all interested in politics. And, I have to say, I was very far from thinking about how to protect people. That's why, through one of my former partners, I met Pastor Sunday who, in the presence of a huge number of people, prayed for me. I stipulated that my joining the church was dependent on a large number of people coming out to campaign for me—and I was really afraid of this because I didn't trust churches. And a miracle! Around one thousand of my future voters prayed for me and I saw in their eyes the fire of faith and happiness.[24]

Unashamed of the raw exchange of membership for votes he admits to here, Chernovet'skyi also joins the growing ranks of politicians the world over who have recognized that religion is politics by other means. Churches offer a highly efficient vehicle to spread a political message and build a popular base of support. They have an established infrastructure providing a platform for the moral authority of clergy to deliver and endorse a particular political agenda and the candidate who advocates it.

Addressing the instrumental value of conversion and church membership, Chernovet'skyi notes the many other "surprising events" that occurred in his life after he came to God. Although previously the "devil had attacked our family with terrible problems," he said he experienced a great deal more joy and peace in his family life. He does not ever publicly elaborate on the specific nature of these family problems, only noting that he gained strength, patience, and hope thanks to his newfound faith. The problems have to do with drug addiction. He sent his son and daughter to boarding school in Switzerland, and they returned home heroin addicts. His son, especially, developed a serious addiction problem that the Embassy of God's healers helped cure. This is perhaps part of his motivation to support Pastor Sunday and the activities of his church.

Chernovet'skyi fully funds a homeless shelter that has paid staff, including paid medical professionals, and numerous volunteers from the church. The center feeds about a thousand people a day and offers medical treatment, clothing, various hygienic services, and a park for children. Public recognition of his philanthropic efforts is one of the reasons put forward to explain his unexpected victory in the 2006 Kyiv mayoral election in spite of his controversial religious affiliation. Such charitable initiatives, especially directed at the homeless, remain rare among New Ukrainians.

Chernovet'skyi argues that churches create a "free space" and a "cultural logic" that has strong, albeit latent, potential for democratization, awaiting political conditions that will allow it to emerge. David Martin has echoed such sentiments after studying Pentecostalism in Latin America. Martin writes, "The framework of moral controls set by the strict rules of the believing congregation and the need to render individual accounts to God and to the brethren together enable the believer to internalize a self-control which can survive the buffeting of the corrupt world in which he or she has to earn a living, often outside corporate structures altogether."[25] This condemnation of corruption and monetary greed also explains the strong support among Embassy of God members for the popular goals of moral and legal reform espoused during the Orange Revolution and more specifically for the political agenda of Viktor Yushchenko.

Chernovet'skyi explained how his conversion contributed to a new sense of morality and how this influenced his politics and the legislation he proposed as a parliamentarian:

> In my opinion, the basis for the current crisis in Ukraine is the destruction of the spiritual core of the nation, the destruction of the markers of morality and justice in society. As a politician and believer, I am deeply convinced that the choice of a democratic government and the choice of a market-based economy is directly connected with Christian ideology, which is conducive to simple people living comfortably and politicians acting morally. Not long ago I began to think seriously about creating a new political party for Ukraine—a Christian liberal party based on Christian values, the principles of economic liberalism and Western European democracy. The ideas and programmatic goals of this party will support people with moral values, independent of whatever faith they practice. . . . I am certain that God wants all people to be free and materially provided for—but the most important thing is MORAL provision. I would build on this model: God wants to see all people morally prosperous, and then they will be materially prosperous. [emphasis in original]

Chernovet'skyi did indeed create such a party; in the spectacular elections of 2004 he was its candidate for president. In the runoff elections between Viktor Yushchenko and Viktor Yanukovych, Chernovet'skyi threw his support—and by extension that of his voters and a large part of the membership of the Embassy of God—to Yushchenko. In myriad ways, Chernovet'skyi's initiatives harness a religious basis for morality to propose specific economic goals and political reforms—all in the name of fulfilling

God's plan for Ukraine. As a highly successful and wealthy businessman and politician, Chernovet'skyi is a compelling illustration of the potential harvests that prosperity theology can yield. By advocating such an ideologically infused theology that endorses the capitalist ethic at a critical juncture of the country's development, he neatly equates his staggering wealth with moral purity. He found God, began to live a moral life as an observant Christian, and from that moment all blessings have flowed.[26]

On the other hand, this theology offers little guidance, solace, or explanation to other "good Christians" who live a moral life and yet are denied material comfort and financial stability. Specifically with regard to Ukraine, Chernovet'skyi does not address how a believer should navigate the harsh and corrupt world of business in which maximization of one's own interests is the overriding priority and in which violence is the dominant response to noncompliance of contractual agreements.[27] Doing business in Ukraine can present moral quandaries involving lying, cheating, and other forms of deceit that are supposedly not becoming of believers. Prosperity theology, as it is preached at the Embassy of God, suggests that if each believer individually resists corruption and goes against the current by adhering to a biblically based morality, eventually the course of the river will be reversed and it will flow as it should. The believer will be rewarded in this life with wealth and in the next with salvation.

Religious communities that preach prosperity theology and serve those who see themselves as impoverished confront frustrated consumer desires by providing an outlet for the desire to possess. Books, calendars, tapes, and other trinkets are for sale at many churches.[28] The Embassy of God conveniently has its own publishing house, Foros, where Pastor Sunday's forty-plus books have been published and where members work. Foros also publishes a wide range of religious instructional and inspirational materials in a variety of media packaged in an "infotainment" style that are offered for sale at every service.

## Business According to the Word

To help bring in the harvest of prosperity theology, one of the women pastors directs and singlehandedly finances the Transformations Business Center, a center designed to teach the basic principles of business from a Christian perspective. This means conducting business according to the Bible and according to the principles of social interaction and obligation as the pastors of the Embassy of God understand them to be outlined in the

Gospel. When the workplace is another site of missionizing and evangelizing, entrepreneurial and political engagement is done in the name of serving God.

The goal of the Transformations Business Center is to bridge the gap between the practices that actually govern economic life and those that believers feel *should* govern it. There is strength in numbers, and the center
attempts to unite Christian businesses for mutual support. Valentyna is a
"business pastor," and she traveled around Ukraine, Russia, and Belarus for
two years giving seminars on how religion should form the bedrock of
business ethics and offering practical tips on how to start a successful business. She explains her motivations for creating these seminars:

> Businessmen here don't sleep at night. I ask every worldly busi-
> nessman, "How do you sleep?" He says, "Badly." I say, "I know be-
> cause I also slept poorly when I was involved in business." I didn't
> deceive anyone. I didn't kill anyone. But I could look at someone and
> think, He's not what he appears to be. I knew how businessmen
> lived. . . . When you go into business you're always under pressure,
> pressure from your partners, from the laws, fear of failure. Is your
> partner loyal, moral? Will he betray you? But religion made me free,
> and for businessmen, that freedom means a lot, and it is Jesus that
> gives that freedom.[29]

As her faith deepened and she realized that she enjoyed these seminars,
she decided to become a pastor, specifically a "business pastor," merging
the Protestant ethic and the spirit of capitalism in a way that would surely
have pleased Max Weber. In 2002, her family became the sole sponsor of
the Transformations Business Center, which now occupies two rooms of a
renovated House of Culture. One of her daughters-in-law now works there
with her, along with five other women. One room serves as the office,
where six women have their desks, each equipped with a computer, and the
other is a sacred-profane site of services and business seminars. Business
seminars begin and end with prayer and incorporate other forms of worship. The services conducted at the Transformations Business Center include sermons that teach the strategic principles of marketing.

In order for modern forms of exchange to function, there must be some
level of trust, either in the individual trading partner or in those means (institutions, laws, intervening organizations, and so on) that provide recourse for compensation in the event that agreements are violated and
losses incurred. The thrust of many of the programs and teachings of this

center are aimed at helping individuals establish a trust in God that is then directed toward partners, employees, and clients. Above all, it is transformed into an abstract trust that these endeavors will succeed in spite of a multitude of obstacles.

To illustrate the level at which the center starts—and the degree of despair and fear among would-be entrepreneurs—when a person enters the seminar room, written on a placard hanging front and center on the wall are the words:

> This is my house.
> Here they:
> love me
> understand me
> support me
> wait for me
> nourish me with healthy food for thought
> wish that I become successful
> create a safe place for me
> accept me as I am.

As Valentyna explains, numerous people come to the center when their business has already fallen on hard times, after they are already in serious debt, so they are frequently very depressed and pessimistic about their chances for recovery. The first level of trust to be created, therefore, is between the visitors, many of whom are not believers, and the center's staff. The center offers free counseling for a variety of business-related needs, such as obtaining financing, dealing with government bureaucracies, marketing, advertising, and building distribution networks. The center keeps a file of other "Christian" businesses throughout Ukraine, positioning itself as the central node of a network that links Christian—meaning trustworthy—suppliers and buyers. They also sponsor an annual Christian business fair where Christian businesses present their services and products to other businesses and to the public. Participation in the seminar costs 75 hryvnia a month, or about 15 dollars, and the course runs for either seven or ten months. Approximately half of the participants are women.

By harnessing a new universe of discourse that includes religious frames, biblical citations, and doctrinal principles, the center reinterprets the meaning of established business practices and introduces new ones. God is positioned as the new business partner, meaning that no one is alone anymore. Businesspeople are encouraged to focus on what God has given them and, in recognition, to write a business plan that addresses first and foremost how they can fulfill God's plan. Salaries are no longer hard-earned income, but rather "blessings." These new orientations and commitments are reaffirmed in a special service held once a week at the center in which the entrepreneurs collectively pray for individual success.

In many ways, the center offers a program of applied theology. Some individual prayer groups are organized according to profession. A group of musicians, computer programmers, or journalists, for example, meet weekly to study the Bible, discuss their careers and business-related problems, and provide each other with opportunities to strengthen networks, an essential resource in postsocialist entrepreneurial life. The Embassy of God's Christian Business Leadership Fellowship tries to make a norm of "Christian principles" as a basis for doing business, as opposed to the common mode of mafia-like "understanding" (Rus. *po poniatiiam*), meaning independent of the law. In other words, religious belief and affiliation at the Embassy of God play a role in articulating where the boundaries lie between business practices that are acceptable and unacceptable, honorable and dishonorable.

The Weberian thesis that elements of ascetic Protestantism are particularly conducive to the flourishing of modern forms of capitalist enterprise is not lost on this business pastor. She condemns idleness and self-indulgent pitying and in its place encourages hard work as a religious imperative, profit as a sacred endeavor, and risk taking as means to glorify God by acting on one's god-given talents. With God as a business partner, a pastor as a business advisor, and a zealous conviction applied to work, a believer will not fail. Both this center and Steve Johnson's center, discussed in chapter 4, celebrate the virtues of making money and of understanding wealth as a blessing, as an indication of divine grace.

Steve's center is more concerned with teaching the moral implications of biblical principles that should be enacted in economic life. He brings in "successful" American businessmen on mission to Ukraine to evidence the application of these principles in a wealthier country where the embrace of evangelical religious doctrine has led to "blessings" for the individual and for the society as a whole. With greater knowledge of the local business climate and the particular challenges it presents, the Transformations Business pastor actually shows how to apply these principles in concrete situations, how to make moral decisions in the pursuit of wealth. In a hands-on way, she helps write the business plan. She creates networks of individual entrepreneurs who have announced their own commitments to upholding these principles in business transactions. The various structural supports the center offers aim for an ongoing mode of doing business among growing numbers of Ukrainian entrepreneurs.

Much as Weber outlined in his seminal work on the Protestant ethic and the spirit of capitalism, both of these centers stimulate not just a mode of doing business but a motivation for doing it, one that could be called an activist salvation ethic.[30] In other words, by linking salvation with financial success, a godly entrepreneur is empowered to seek profit for the sake of investment to better fulfill a god-given calling. An activist salvation ethic yields a moral vision that links entrepreneurship with God, generating wealth with developing virtue, and worldly rewards with heavenly rewards. In this vein, prosperity theology is merely the doctrinal extension of the mutual reinforcing potentialities Weber evoked to analyze the intersection of religion and capitalism in the West.

Although Chernovet'skyi is a living fulfillment of the ideals of prosperity theology, he is one of the exceptions. For the overwhelming majority of converts to evangelicalism, especially those who show up at the Business Transformations Center, the oft-repeated insight of Marx and Engels is more applicable: "Religious distress is at the same time the expression of real distress and the protest against real distress."[31] In the Marxian vein, of course, religion provides a source of comfort, a form of "opium." Marx criticized religion for offering an otherworldly explanation for suffering and promises of distant redemption, which divert attention from altering the source of one's suffering in the here and now. Evangelical communities around the world have proven themselves particularly successful at flourishing amid poverty, deprivation, and social instability.[32] By offering a passage from economic disenfranchisement to divine empowerment, individuals are released from ascribed categories and ushered into a transformative mode that promises healing and eventual salvation. Arguably, such a stance helps believers accommodate deplorable conditions rather than strive to change them. It also establishes an alternative means for evaluating self-worth independent of material success and social hierarchies and allows one to claim the moral high ground—which becomes especially important in the event of failure. These factors that facilitate accommodation to poverty exert appeal in Ukraine as well, where many are still reeling from the ongoing social and political changes that cost them their social status and profession.

But as this center shows, religious organizations can also offer a means to cope with and even overcome suffering by reordering relations of trust and by functioning as a magnet that holds a community of mutual assistance and reciprocal obligation together. The locus of change is firmly understood to be the individual in communion with God. This is the basis for the activist salvation ethic they promote. Yet by providing an economic infrastructure in the form of this center and by pushing for an activist political agenda, they recognize the need for structural change to realize their vision of moral renewal.

## The Embassy of God as Revitalization Movement

Many anthropological explanations of religious movements have taken inspiration from Anthony Wallace, who as early as 1956 suggested that many religious phenomena began as "revitalization movements."[33] By extension, he argued, organized religions are merely relics of old revitalization movements that managed to survive in a routinized form in stabilized cultures. Under the umbrella of "revitalization," Wallace includes cargo cults, nativist, millenarian, and other reformative movements that redefine or create new sacred symbols. Such movements usually emerge within a context of social stress brought on by sweeping and disorienting cultural change that has historically been brought on by colonialism. Revitalization movements aim to stem a sense of disintegration and demise of the familiar by revitalizing certain cultural elements to cope with change.

Wallace defined a revitalization movement as a deliberate attempt to create a "more satisfying culture" that usually begins with a vision of the supernatural appearing to a single individual under stress, revealing that person's own troubles, as well as those of society, to have resulted from the violation of certain rules. The supernatural force promises personal and social revitalization if ritual and moral purification are practiced and catastrophe if they are not. Feeling greater confidence thanks to divine sanction, this visionary figure embarks on a missionary or messianic quest to tell others of his experience and preaches that others will also gain a supernatural protector if they accept new values and practices. The visionary evolves into a prophet, even a charismatic one, when his authority is seen as sanctioned by the supernatural and his sense of morality is accepted as exemplary. The prophet gains converts who, like himself, undergo "revitalizing personality transformations" and pledge to perform duties to a higher power. As the movement grows, it naturally encounters resistance, so the specifics of the doctrine are modified to gain greater acceptance. When the new religious paradigm with its various injunctions becomes accepted, Wallace claims, "a noticeable social revitalization occurs, signalized by the reduction of the personal deterioration symptoms of individuals, by extensive culture changes and by an enthusiastic embarkation on some organized program of group action."[34] If these actions are successful in reducing individual and social stress, the religious movement advanced by the prophet is seen as viable and the practices and understandings of the sacred associated with it become "routinized," and a certain form of cultural transformation is accomplished. Wallace's theorizing about cultural revitalization and religious movements grew out of his research with the Seneca, a Native American tribe in North America that faced extinction but were revived by a prophet, Handsome Lake, who founded a religious movement by synthesizing concepts of the sacred from Iroquois belief and Christianity into a religion called the Old Way of Handsome Lake.

The key point is that revitalization movements prompt culture change that is distinct from the patterns of adaptation, appropriation, and acculturation, as evidenced, for example, by changes in congregational life and religious practice that were depicted in the last chapter and brought about through sustained interaction. The Embassy of God has followed a different pattern that mirrors the process of revitalizing cultural change. Recall Pastor Sunday's vision directing him to preach to white people. This served as the God-given motivation to found a church among Slavs even though as a Nigerian, and a young, rather short, self-taught Pentecostal preacher to boot, this represented formidable obstacles that only the most charismatic of leaders could surmount. As we have seen, his ambitions to revitalize and reform Ukrainian society are far from modest. Indeed, Ukraine is merely where he and his congregants have started. It is the preferred springboard from which they evangelize other parts of the world to offer their dual prescriptions for salvation in the form of cure and conversion.

I am not suggesting that the Embassy of God or evangelicalism is single-handedly revitalizing Ukrainian society or ever will. Rather, I wish to stress that although the Embassy of God draws on doctrinal elements of Pentecostalism that are widely practiced in the West, in Africa, and elsewhere, it is a distinctly Ukrainian church constituting a local response to immediate postsocialist circumstances. As a result, its activities are likely to yield changes in other local domains.

The emergence of liberation theology within Latin American Catholicism prompted Pentecostal churches there to take positions on political issues and address social ills, even as it split the ranks of Catholics. The efforts of the Embassy of God and other evangelical churches to inspire morally induced social transformation through various charitable initiatives and political visions places growing pressure on other religious organizations to become more publicly active in solving the problems of *this* world.[35] It has become increasingly difficult for the Orthodox Church to offer, as it has in the past, contemplation, prayer, and monastic withdrawal as solutions to social suffering in the face of the activist salvation ethic the Embassy of God advocates. Similarly, the success of the highly emotional and participatory nature of Pentecostalism helped fuel charismatic Catholicism in Latin America. In Ukraine, the significant role given to lay participants in governing local Protestant congregations—and specifically the prominent leadership positions neo-Pentecostals have repeatedly allocated to women—suggest that this will be a source of pressure to adjust the highly centralized, hierarchical, patriarchal leaderships of the national churches.

By being in the forefront of redefining the obligations individuals have to one another through its programs for the poor and the disenfranchised, the Embassy of God begins to shift the expectations individuals have for the state and for each other. They begin to relocate the locus of solutions to individual and social problems among believers in highly local, yet transnational, communities. Through its very public manifestations, such as the March for Life and the March for Jesus, this church recasts notions of engagement with the world, and especially the world of politics. When it makes specific pronouncements regarding how individuals of faith should realize their convictions politically and socially, they begin to dismantle the idea that faith and religiously inspired understandings of morality are private, "invisible" matters. This represents a radical departure from the sharp differentiation of distinct spheres of moral, religious activity and the very profane, often even immoral political world. In other words, the Embassy of God and other evangelical churches are rapidly reversing the "political quietism" and withdrawal from worldly activities that used to characterize most religious organizations, and especially evangelical ones, throughout twentieth-century Ukrainian history. The "compliant" part of the Soviet-era "defiant compliance" is shifting to include a defiant, morally charged challenge, to no longer just to resist social ills, but to reform them.

The religious pluralism that has been institutionalized in Ukraine since the fall of the Soviet Union has led to a flourishing of religious activity, and it has allowed religious communities in all of their guises to offer competing visions of a desired moral order. Churches like the Embassy of God play a key role in articulating the type of commitments one should have to others and what the reciprocal obligations should be between a state and its citizenry, thereby laying the foundation for remaking the social contract. When the twenty-five thousand members of the Embassy of God and other evangelical groups become vocal participants in a public dialogue of morality and polity, they prompt other religious organizations to do the same. Recall that virtually every religious organization took a stance during the Orange Revolution. All, save the Ukrainian Orthodox Church-Moscow Patriarchate, publicly declared *and* demonstrated their opposition to the falsified 2004 elections.

As the symbolic boundaries separating religion, politics, and morality fluctuate during this transformative period, religion is reentering the public sphere in Ukraine in a meaningful way and is increasingly accepted as a viable source of moral guidance. Religion holds sway over believers—and politicians—in that it offers a repertoire of moral values and sacred practices from which to foster collective action to realize a political worldview that has the potential to revitalize social transformation and deliver, as Wallace claimed, a reversal of the feelings of disintegration and demise.

Sharp economic differences remain not only within formerly socialist societies but also between the societies that experienced socialism and those that did not. Yet those differences remain largely misunderstood and are readily used to further structure the inequality between "new" and "old" Europe. Evangelicalism provides an institutional base from which believers can detach themselves from nations mired in economic distress and political turmoil and enter larger, transnational religious communities, in a sense claiming another sort of religious-based citizenship complete with alternative rights, obligations, and forms of belonging. This dynamic holds whether one speaks of a Nigerian establishing a church in Ukraine or Ukrainian missionaries establishing a church in the United Arab Emirates to preach to post-Soviet shuttle traders.

The dexterity and flexibility with which the Embassy of God and other religious institutions have identified and responded to social, emotional, spiritual, economic, and political needs suggests that even after seventy-four years of socialism and its aggressive espousal of atheist policies, religiously motivated engagement has become firmly rooted in Ukraine. As the wide range of activities at the Embassy of God shows, religion operates at multiple levels, forging meaningful intersections between cure and conversion, morality and money, local and transnational, and public and private. Their ambassadors of God are redefining individual agency as a partnership with God and repositioning the agents of social change as a joint venture between church and state. They seek to create the communal structural supports to shape basic political values and economic practices to be in accordance with biblical principles. In essence, by advocating and ultimately institutionalizing a public role for religion as a guiding force during this transformative period, the Embassy of God is attempting to revitalize Ukrainian society by making desecularization seem as inevitable and natural as secularization once did.

# Epilogue

## Religion as Portal to the World

In considering the encounter between Western and Soviet believers at the close of the twentieth century, I am reminded of Marshall Sahlins's critique of the anthropological propensity to see the arrival of Western capitalism with its accompanying moralities and mentalities as the beginning of indigenous history, one that inevitably progresses toward a ruinous end for indigenous cultures. Using the Eskimo as an example, he argues against this inherited tradition by claiming that in spite of the steady arrival of new forms of technology, exchange, and governance over the course of the twentieth century, "the Eskimo are still there—and they are still Eskimo."[1] If indigenous peoples have only been pseudo-beneficiaries of development initiatives, he asserts, they have also only been pseudo-victims. Neither they nor their cultures have been eradicated. Instead, Sahlins suggests, new technologies, knowledges, and capital have been used to enhance, broaden, and finance a "traditional" lifestyle that now includes snowmobiles and hunting and gathering.

Rather than thinking of the cultural encounter between the "West and the Rest" as one of homogenization (with "them" becoming like "us"), Sahlins claims that the encounter has led to an indigenization of modernity, meaning that the basic tenets of modernity, such as new ways of producing and classifying knowledge, technological advances, and new modes of transport, have been integrated into an indigenous cosmology. This interaction has, of course, ushered in substantial changes in Eskimo culture, but certainly not ruin and clearly not disappearance. As we have seen, after the Cold War and the arrival of eager American missionaries in Ukraine to save white Europeans from "godless communism," Ukrainians are still there, and they are still selecting the forms of religion they chose to adopt.

On the heels of Sahlins's Eskimo example, I am reminded of an anecdote that the Chukchi have been telling lately. The Chukchi are a native Siberian people living near the Arctic Circle. More than most, they stubbornly resisted Russian colonization and missionizing by Orthodox clergy. They became the butt of numerous "ethnic" anecdotes about stupidity in the Soviet Union. The experience of Soviet modernity, with its imposition of a vision of "progress" on native peoples, was brutal. The Chukchi now tell the following anecdote to comment on a more recent "civilizing mission" launched by Ukrainian believers:

> Three men are riding in a train, a Chukotkan, a Ukrainian, and an American. The Ukrainian is drinking vodka and eating *salo* (smoked pork fat, a Ukrainian specialty). At one point, the Ukrainian stands up and throws everything out the window. "Hey, what did you do that for?" asks the Chukotkan. "That was good food!" "Oh, we have a lot of that in my country," answers the Ukrainian. After a while the American stands up and throws his Pepsi and hamburger out the window. "Hey, what did you do that for?" asks the Chukotkan. "That was good food!" "Oh, we have a lot of that in my country," responds the American. After a while, the Chukotkan stands up and throws the Ukrainian out the window. "Hey, what did you do that for?" asks the American. "Oh, we have a lot of them in my country," responds the Chukotkan.[2]

When the Chukotkan claims to have a lot of "them" in his country, he is referring to Ukrainian missionaries who now evangelize in significant numbers in Russia. Their efforts have been successful to some degree, and evangelical faiths have made inroads among native peoples. Yet the Chukchi are still there and some have—metaphorically—thrown the Ukrainians out of the window.

Christianity is a religion of expansion, and its history has been a long series of encounters with different faith traditions. Prior to the arrival of Western missionaries, there was a developed sense of Soviet evangelicalism as it was practiced in Ukraine, which emerged from interaction with other ethnic and faith-based traditions, such as German Mennonite, Russian Molokan, and, of course, Slavic Orthodox believers. A fusion of beliefs, practices, and sensibilities occurred, which resulted neither in an eradication of Ukrainian faith traditions nor a mimetic replication of the Other's form of religious practice. The Western missionaries who began to arrive in Ukraine to proselytize in the late 1980s neither introduced nor imposed evangelicalism. Rather, they exposed Ukrainians to a global form of evangelical Christianity to which Ukrainians have been receptive because it coincided with a broad popular recognition of a need for moral renewal, for renewed commitment to certain understandings of right and wrong.

In discussing how and why individuals have converted to evangelicalism over time in Ukraine, I have illustrated the myriad ways that religion serves as a spearhead for broader cultural change by remaking aspects of the self and constituting new communities that sustain those changes and parlay them into a social phenomenon. Studies of conversion need to consider not just why individuals convert but also how particular socio-political contexts predispose people to be open to religious-based solutions to their problems and how cultures are transformed when there are significant changes in the religious landscape. Whether it is Ukrainians evangelizing Chukchi or Americans evangelizing Ukrainians, the view of cultural change I have presented here restores a measure of agency to the recipient of evangelizing efforts and reframes periods and zones of cultural contact as the spark for creative appropriation, selection, and discerning rejection of new cultural elements in spite of the clear power differentials that exist. The process of local adaptation places these global models of religious institutional organization, in Ukraine and elsewhere, in a permanent state of evolution because the models are constantly transformed as they are applied and indigenized. These processes of selection, rejection, and adaptation to local cultural practices occur alongside the embrace of sufficient similarities in doctrine and ritual practice so as to yield a common identifier—"believer," "Baptist," "charismatic" and the like—that allows converts to feel solidarity and a sense of communal membership with fellow believers, wherever they may be.

The idea of an encounter based on exchange also challenges linear or teleological models of cultural change. By likening the Embassy of God to the long anthropological tradition of "revitalization movements," I aim to show how a religious group can simultaneously reflect and affect the local and the global by synthesizing various cultural elements into qualitatively new concepts of self and community that prompt cultural transformation. Who could have predicted that in the wake of socialism, a Nigerian would create the largest European megachurch in Kyiv, evangelizing Americans and Europeans and even boldly moving into the "10/40 window," meaning the Middle East?[3]

This kind of religious innovation affects the religious organizations operating in many regions of the world. Evangelicals believe in cognitively choosing a faith based on an experiential, unmediated relationship with the divine, which challenges the privileges of a state church serving an "imagined national community" of automatically inherited believers. Doctrinal beliefs in an unmediated relationship with the divine for everyone throw into question established ecclesiastical relations of power and authority. With numerous women in clerical and other leadership positions, Pentecostal and charismatic churches challenge accepted notions of gender hierarchy and provide an arena where women can assume authority. And finally, the charitable endeavors of evangelical churches challenge individuals and other religious groups to accept a moral obligation to help the needy, rather than delegating that responsibility to the state. These represent some of the ways that established cultural practices in Orthodox Ukraine are refashioned by evangelical converts seeking moral renewal after socialism.

The "state religions" in the former Soviet Union are effective political players, influencing social, political, and religious policies on a number of levels. Already 41 percent of Ukrainians maintain that their president must be a religious person, as compared to 24 percent in Russia.[4] Serhii Plokhy points to the growing role of Protestant communities in Ukrainian politics. He suggests that the significant interest demonstrated by the various political parties in the Protestant vote and the participation of Protestants in Ukrainian politics at the highest levels of government indicate a general tolerance for and growing power of Protestant churches in predominantly Orthodox Ukraine.[5] The identities and allegiances that these new communities are forging are likely to prosper, as they have in Latin America and Africa.

Of course, it is imperative to note that processes of appropriation and revitalization are not entirely creative and benevolent, and they do not always yield conditions conducive to justice, tolerance and prosperity. One must ask: What perils does a revival of religion hold when it takes on an evangelical cast, as it has in Ukraine? Will the concern for the needy advocated by evangelicalism take inclusivist forms and promote tolerance? Or will that concern replicate sharp boundaries of exclusion between those judged capable of being saved and those it condemns? As we have seen, there are decisive limits to the evangelical embrace when it comes to homosexuality. Scholars have sharply divided opinions on these questions.[6] It is, in fact, this dual potential, what Peter Berger calls the "world making" and "world breaking" potentialities of religion, that makes the study of religion, the sacred and moralities so compelling.[7]

## Global Christianity and Movement

Since the late Soviet period, tactically and strategically, Western missionary organizations have been working to establish Ukraine as a base for clerical and missionary training. Quite simply, Ukraine was one of the few post-Soviet states that did not impede the development of religious pluralism through state regulation. Scholars studying religious conversion throughout the former Soviet Union increasingly allude to Ukrainian missionaries proselytizing evangelical Christianity, not only among the Chukchi in the Russian Far North but also among the Nenets in the circumpolar region and the Kyrgyz in Kyrgyzstan.[8] Ukrainians have the cultural and linguistic capital to evangelize in areas where Westerners would be unlikely to go, such as the Russian Far North or circumpolar regions, or unlikely to have much success, such as in Muslim Central Asia. Although the collapse of the USSR was a watershed year for the regulation of religion in the former Soviet Union, it would be a mistake to conclude that it was the beginning of something. All of these groups have been proselytized to before.

Western missionary organizations have reassessed their priorities after 9/11 to Muslim areas and to China in view of the growing access to 1.3 billion Chinese. Yet, in the fifteen short years since the collapse of the USSR, Western religious organizations have helped finance an educational and training infrastructure. This has not served to replicate patterns of communal worship and political engagement as they are found in the United States or in Europe. Rather, this assistance has, above all, advanced an understanding of evangelicalism particular to this region's historical experience, which Ukrainians are now harnessing to their own project of moral revitalization and healing after socialism.

The Ukrainian understanding of religiosity, piety, and evil, informed by such aspects of the Soviet experience as colonization, humiliation, repression, victimization, and demise, is selectively blended with Western media-based techniques and strategies of outreach to inform Eurasian missionizing endeavors. Misha, the Yakut former believer in shamanism, convert to the Baptist faith, and double convert to Pentecostalism, has since completed his pastoral training in Kyiv, thanks to financing from a Californian Pentecostal. He now preaches in rural Yakutia, explaining his understandings of theology, faith healing, and the power of prayer, which he has learned from a self-taught Nigerian who has now lived longer in his adopted Ukraine than he has in Nigeria. This is global Christianity at work. For evangelicals, Ukraine has now become a central node in multiple zones of contact, redirecting and reshaping new moral visions and new sacred practices.

The world's major religions were a force for cultural interconnectedness long before the term *globalization* was ever coined. The essential difference between the spread of global Christianity today and the spread of Christianity that occurred in the early modern period is that this time, the globalizing tendencies of religious affiliation cater to identities and allegiances that are much more deterritorialized. The local and transnational communities formed by the spread of global Christianity challenge traditional ties that link a particular religion to a certain ethnic group, social hierarchy, territory, or state. The process of deterritorialization is driven by intensifying cultural interconnectedness brought on by movement and migration more than a general unboundedness, as scholars such as Homi Bhabha and Arjun Appadurai have argued, or processes of homogenization, as Benjamin Barber's "McWorld" thesis suggests. In a word, global Christianity, as a religion of expansion, is embedded in modern forms of movement. Doctrinally, those who practice it see themselves as missionaries and accept the moral obligation to evangelize. Aspects of evangelical belief are easily localized through adaptation and inserted into various cultural repertoires. This movement of people, knowledges, and practices creates significant interconnections and even interdependencies between individuals and groups.

Movement frequently follows ethnic lines. Recall that Ukrainian immigrants to the United States cyclically return to Ukraine to missionize as well as to other destinations where Ukrainian economic migrants are relocating, such as Argentina. It also prompts Ukrainians in Ukraine to travel to proselytize among Ukrainians in Siberia and Berlin. But it would be a mistake to assume that missionizing exclusively follows ethnic lines. Rather, it provides a springboard, a point of departure, which is why Ukraine is emerging as a point from which to embark upon projects to missionize Eurasia.

Yet the movement and interconnections among global Christian communities dynamically crisscross in interesting ways. Joel Robbins challenges us to think of the "mechanics" and "range of dynamics" that characterize cultural globalization, particularly as it concerns the spread of Pentecostal and charismatic Christianity.[9] I have already highlighted the importance of movement and noted how this movement uses ethnicity even as it subverts and changes it. Concerning the "range of dynamics" driving the spread of evangelicalism, I suggest that the zones of contact of cultural interconnectedness are not as likely to come from the West as they have in the past. Philip Jenkins has recently pointed out that Christianity has quite literally gone south.[10] The majority of Christians, especially evangelical believers, are now in Africa and in Latin America. Evangelical communities in the southern hemisphere are growing rapidly and now dwarf American evangelicals demographically. The growing legions of evangelical communities in the southern hemisphere suggest that future influences in Ukraine and the former Soviet Union are not likely to come from Europe or the United States but rather from the so-called Third World.

In Latin America and Africa we see a phenomenon that has been called the "Pentecostalization of Christianity." In other words, the Catholic church in Latin America as well as the mission churches in Africa and African Independent Churches have all had to reckon with the appeal of Pentecostalism's experiential, non-creedal view of religiosity and its seeming elasticity to incorporate local cultural elements into its sacred practices and communal life. It is perhaps not surprising that Pentecostal expansion has been so significant in Africa, Latin America, and now, I am suggesting, Eurasia. David Martin suggests that its emphasis on morality and healing makes it a faith that appeals to "the insulted and the injured."[11]

Critical of secular attempts to deliver comfort and security, what Manuel Vasquez calls "a crisis of modern emancipatory projects," evangelicalism offers doctrines and practices that work with the ambiguity and heterogeneity of the present.[12] Evangelicals have been able to mobilize individuals in increasingly fragmented and complex societies by concretely addressing local concerns and personal predicaments, all the while offering ethereal and otherworldly rewards, such as salvation, redemption, and transcendence from a painful past. By addressing individual concerns in partnership with the divine using an inerrant text as a guide, evangelical communities are able to offer hope and restore a sense of order, predictability, and protection.

Evangelical communities the world over, and now in Ukraine too, have demonstrated an affinity for modern societies undergoing change and a powerful appeal to individuals experiencing isolation, disempowerment, or crisis. Evangelical practices have proven particularly adept at providing a means of remaking the self and reconstituting a sense of community on multiple levels, as individuals and as members of a national and global community of believers. The experience of being "born again" after socialism has allowed Ukrainian believers to redeem an unsavory past and to begin again, as self-disciplining moral individuals in this world and as saved souls in the next.

# Notes

## Introduction

1. William Fletcher, "The Soviet Bible Belt: World War II's Impact on Religion," in *The Impact of World War II on the Soviet Union,* ed. Susan J. Linz (New York: Rowan and Allanheld, 1985b), 91.

2. Mark Elliott and Robert Richardson, "Growing Protestant Diversity in the Former Soviet Union," in *Russian Pluralism—Now Irreversible?* eds. Uri Ra'anan, Keith Ames and Kate Martin (New York: St. Martin's Press, 1992), 200.

3. Nicholas Mitrokin, "Aspects of the Religious Situation in Ukraine," *Religion, State, and Society* 29, no. 3 (September 2001): 173–96.

4. There are already a number of books that analyze religious policy in the Imperial and Soviet periods. See Heather J. Coleman, *Russian Baptists and Spiritual Revolution, 1905–1929* (Bloomington: Indiana University Press, 2005); Gregory L. Freeze, *The Parish Clergy in Nineteenth-Century Russia: Crisis, Reform, Counter-Reform* (Princeton: Princeton University Press, 1983); Dimitry V. Pospielovsky's trilogy, *A History of Marxist-Leninist Atheism and Soviet Antireligious Policies* (New York: St. Martin's Press, 1987), *Soviet Antireligious Campaigns and Persecutions* (New York: St. Martin's Press, 1988), and *Soviet Studies on the Church and the Believer's Response to Atheism* (New York: St. Martin's Press, 1988); John Anderson, *Religion, State, and Politics in the Soviet Union and the Successor States* (Cambridge: Cambridge University Press, 1994); and Tatiana A. Chumachenko, *Church and State in Soviet Russia: Russian Orthodoxy from World War II to the Khrushchev Years,* trans. Edward E. Roslof (Armonk, NY: M. E. Sharpe, 2002).

5. *Anabaptist* literally means "rebaptizer" and connotes the belief in adult baptism. German Anabaptists were considered radical because of their antiestablishment views and practices, which included nonviolence, communal living, and charitable initiatives, especially toward the poor.

6. Other Protestant denominations, such as Lutheran, Adventist, and Mennonite, have also had a historical presence in tsarist Russia and especially in Ukraine, but they are not depicted here.

7. For a discussion of the similarities between the attitudes of the pre-1905 Imperial government and Soviet authorities with regard to "foreign faiths," see R. Beermann, "The Baptists and Soviet Society," *Soviet Studies* 20, no. 1 (1968): esp. 68–69.

8. John D. Rockefeller Sr. was a very devout Baptist who used his personal fortune to finance a variety of social and charitable initiatives.

9. Serhii Plokhy has argued that the fierce repression and outlaw in 1946 of the Ukrainian Greek Catholic Church was primarily motivated by Stalin's concerns over the Vatican exerting too much influence on post–World War II reconstruction. The Church was also accused of Nazi collaboration, providing assistance to the underground nationalist movement and of promoting sympathy for the Ukrainian nationalist project. See Serhii Plokhy, "In the Shadow of Yalta: International Politics and the Soviet Liquidation of the Ukrainian Greek Catholic Church," in Serhii Plokhy and Frank Sysyn, *Religion and Nation in Modern Ukraine* (Edmonton: Canadian Institute of Ukrainian Studies, 2003), 59.

10. Talal Asad, *Formations of the Secular: Christianity, Islam, Modernity* (Stanford: Stanford University Press, 2003).

11. Some dispute the secular nature of European society. Grace Davie has argued that secularization in Britain, and in Europe more broadly, has yielded a decline in public affiliation with a specific religious organization without a corresponding drop in religious belief, yielding a phenomenon she characterizes as "believing without belonging." The experience in Sweden, where individual financing for religious institutions remains significant but actual attendance is low, has prompted some to turn Davie's assessment around and claim that Swedes "believe in belonging." In short, secularization, however defined, is not unidimensional. See Grace Davie, "Europe: The Exception That Proves the Rule?" in *The Desecularization of the World,* ed. Peter Berger (Washington, DC: Ethics and Public Policy Center, 1999) and *Religion in Britain since 1945: Believing without Belonging* (Oxford: Blackwell, 1994).

12. José Casanova, *Public Religions in the Modern World* (Chicago: University of Chicago Press, 1996a), 29.

13. Nikolai Berdiaev, *The Origins of Russian Communism* (Ann Arbor: University of Michigan Press, 1960); James von Geldern, *Bolshevik Festivals, 1917–1920* (Berkeley: University of California Press, 1993); Nina Tumarkin, *Lenin Lives! The Lenin Cult in Soviet Russia* (Cambridge: Harvard University Press, 1997); Igal Halfin, *From Darkness to Light: Class, Consciousness, and Salvation in Revolutionary Russia* (Pittsburgh: University of Pittsburgh Press, 2000); and Oleg Kharkhordin, *The Collective and the Individual: A Study of Practices* (Berkeley: University of California, 1999).

14. Ruth Mandel and Caroline Humphrey, eds., *Markets and Moralities: Ethnographies of Postsocialism* (Oxford: Berg, 2002); Nancy Ries, "'Honest Bandits' and 'Warped People': Russian Narratives about Money, Corruption, and Moral Decay," in *Ethnography in Unstable Places,* ed. Carol Greenhouse, Kay Warren, and Elizabeth Metz

(Durham, NC: Duke University, 2003); Melissa Caldwell, *Not by Bread Alone: Social Support in the New Russia* (Berkeley: University of California Press, 2004); Michelle Rivkin-Fish, *Women's Health in Post-Soviet Russia: The Politics of Intervention* (Bloomington: Indiana University Press, 2005); Douglas Rogers, "Money, Moonshine, and the Politics of Liquidity in Rural Russia," *American Ethnologist* 32, no. 1 (February 2005): 63–81; and Jennifer Patico, "To Be Happy in a Mercedes: Tropes of Value and Ambivalent Visions of Marketization," *American Ethnologist* 32, no. 3 (August 2005): 479–96. None of these studies directly engages the relationship of morality to religion.

15. Signe Howell, ed., *The Ethnography of Moralities* (London: Routledge, 1997), 5.

16. Howell, *Ethnography of Moralities*, 3. In making this point, Howell takes inspiration from May and Abraham Edel, *Anthropology and Ethics* (Springfield, IL: Charles C. Thomas, 1959).

17. Catherine Wanner, "Money, Morality, and New Forms of Exchange in Postsocialist Ukraine," *Ethnos* 70, no. 4 (2005): 515–37.

18. Sally Falk Moore, "Explaining the Present: Theoretical Dilemmas in Processual Ethnography," *American Ethnologist* 14, no. 4 (November 1987): 727–36; Eric R. Wolf, "The Virgin of Guadalupe: A Mexican National Symbol," *Journal of American Folklore* 71 (January 1958): 34–39; and James C. Scott, *Domination and the Arts of Resistance: Hidden Transcripts* (New Haven: Yale University Press, 1990).

19. Emile Durkheim, *The Elementary Forms of Religious Life* (1912; repr. New York: Free Press, 1995). Some anthropological studies have challenged the universal centrality of morality in religious cosmologies that Durkheim asserts. While I recognize the merit of such critiques, morality is of such fundamental importance for evangelicals that their communities do indeed become "moral communities."

20. See Murray W. Dempster, Bryon D. Klaus, and Douglas Petersen, eds., *The Globalization of Pentecostalism: A Religion Made to Travel* (Oxford: Regnum Books, 1999).

21. Joel Robbins, *Becoming Sinners: Christianity and Moral Torment in a Papua New Guinea Society* (Berkeley: University of California Press, 2004a); Diane J. Austin-Broos, *Jamaica Genesis: Religion and the Politics of Moral Orders* (Chicago: University of Chicago Press, 1997); Jean Comaroff, *Body of Power, Spirit of Resistance: The Culture and History of a South African People* (Chicago: University of Chicago Press, 1985); and J. D. Y. Peel, "Conversion and Tradition in Two African Societies: Ijebu and Buganda," *Past and Present* 77, no. 1 (November 1977): 108–41.

22. Wilfred M. McClay, "Two Concepts of Secularism," in *Religion Returns to the Public Square: Faith and Policy in America*, ed. Hugh Heclo (Washington, D.C.: Woodrow Wilson Center Press, 2003), 33.

23. Susan Friend Harding, *The Book of Jerry Falwell: Fundamentalist Language and Politics* (Princeton: Princeton University Press, 2000).

24. Lila Abu-Lughod, *Veiled Sentiments: Honor and Poetry in a Bedouin Society* (Berkeley: University of California Press, 1986), 18–19.

25. Alexei D. Krindatch, "Religion in Postsoviet Ukraine as a Factor in Regional, Ethno-Cultural, and Political Diversity," *Religion, State, and Society* 31, no. 1 (March 2003): 43, 49, 50. A nationwide survey conducted by the Razumkov Center in Kyiv in 2003 found that 75.2 percent of Ukrainians consider themselves believers, with 21.9 percent claiming they do not believe in God. See www.state.gov/g/drl/rls/irf/2005/51588.htm, accessed 2 February 2007.

26. Lewis Rambo, *Understanding Religious Conversion* (New Haven: Yale University Press, 1993).

## Chapter 1. Spiritual Seekers in a Secularizing State

1. Robert P. Geraci, *Window on the East: National and Imperial Identities in Late Tsarist Russia* (Ithaca: Cornell University Press, 2001), esp. ch. 1; Robert P. Geraci and Michael Khodarkovsky, eds., *Of Religion and Empire: Missions, Conversion, and Tolerance in Tsarist Russia* (Ithaca: Cornell University Press, 2001); and Paul W. Werth, *At the Margins of Orthodoxy: Mission, Governance, and Confessional Politics in Russia's Volga-Kama Region, 1827–1905* (Ithaca: Cornell University Press, 2001).

2. *Bratskii Vestnik* no. 4 (1957), 9. These measures were intended for Baptists, Molokans, Dukhobors, Mennonites as well as Old Believers.

3. Studies of Baptist communities in Russia and the USSR include Heather J. Coleman, *Russian Baptists*; Sergei Zhuk, *Russia's Lost Reformation: Peasants, Millennialism, and Radical Religious Sects in Southern Russia and Ukraine, 1830–1905* (Baltimore, MD: Johns Hopkins University Press, 2004); Paul D. Steeves, "The Russian Baptist Union, 1917–35: Evangelical Awakening in Russia," Ph.D. dissertation, University of Kansas, 1976; and S. N. Savinskii, *Istoriia Evangel'skikh Khristian-Baptistov Ukrainy, Rossii, Belorussii, 1917–67* (St. Petersburg: Biblia dlia Vsekh, 2001); A. I. Klibanov, *Istoriia religioznogo sektantstva v Rossii* (Moscow: Izdatel'stvo Nauka, 1965) and *Religioznoe sektantstvo i sovremennost'* (Moscow: Izdatel'stvo Nauka, 1969); and A. V. Karev, "Russkoe Evangel'sko-baptistskoe dvizhenie," *Bratskii Vestnik*, no. 3 (1957), 5–51, and no. 4 (1957), 5–38.

Other studies written from the perspective of either insider evangelical and anticommunist or anti-evangelical and insider communist, include Walter Sawatsky, *Soviet Evangelicals since World War II* (Scottsdale, PA: Herald Press, 1981); G. S. Lialina, *Baptizm: Illiuzii i Real'nost'* (Moscow: Izdatel'stvo Politicheskoi Literatury, 1977); and Lev Nikolaevich Mitrokhin, *Baptizm* (Moscow: Izdatel'stvo Politicheskoi Literatury, 1974). Sawatsky's study is considered the best by the Independent Baptists, the successor group to the *Initiativniki*, and was published as *Evangelicheskoe Dvizhenie v SSSR Posle Vtoroi Mirovoi Voiny* (Moscow: ITs-Garant, 1995) and is pseudonymously available as Alexander De Chalandeau, "The Theology of the Evangelical Christians-Baptists in the USSR, as Reflected in the *Bratskii Vestnik*," Ph.D. dissertation, Faculté de Théologie Protestante de l'Université des Sciences Humaines de Strasbourg, 1978.

4. Mazaev, a wealthy sheep farmer originally from eastern Ukraine, led the Russian Baptist Union from 1886 to 1909 and again from 1911 to 1920. He undertook a number of ambitious initiatives, financing most of them himself, such as convening congresses, even though it was illegal to do so, and launching in 1890 a clandestine monthly journal called *Beseda* (Rus. Symposium). Extensive biographical information as well as several of D. I. Mazeev's key speeches can be found in Leonid Kovalenko, *Oblako Svidetelei Khristovykh dlia Narodov Rossii v XIX–XX Vekakh* (Sacramento, CA: 1996).

5. *Baptist*, no. 9 (1911), 69. Official statistics, however, measured their ranks as reaching that level two years later. By 1912 Baptists had added 21,140 new members, increasing the membership by a third and bringing the total number of Russian Baptists to 66,788.

Evangelical Christians added 9,175 new members for a 1912 total of 29,988. A. I. Klibanov notes that differing practices make an accurate census difficult: Some congregations counted anyone who attended services, whereas others counted only baptized members. Some congregations refused to provide numbers at all. And difficulties in communication and rapid growth at this time also surely compromised the accuracy of these statistics. See Klibanov, *Religioznoe sektantstvo i sovremennost'*, 224.

6. For a discussion of the role of Germans in spreading Protestant faiths in the Russian Empire, see *Bratskii Vestnik*, no. 3 (1927), esp. 5–17.

7. Zhuk, *Russia's Lost Reformation*, 49–50; and B. Liubashchenko, *Istoriia Protestantyzma v Ukraini* (Kyiv: Polis, 1996), 217, draw in an explicit and implicit manner, respectively, on the Weberian notion of a Protestant work ethic and contrast the moral superiority and more developed nature of Shtundist communities over the debauchery and drunkenness they claim beset the Orthodox.

8. For a detailed depiction of Voronin's life and his contribution to forging Baptist communities in the Russian Empire, see *Baptist Ukrainy*, no. 9 (1927), 2–4.

9. Kalveit had moved to Tbilisi to witness to his brother, who was serving in the army there. In 1891 he was sentenced to five years of internal exile beyond the Caucasus, followed by another three-year sentence. Sawatsky, *Soviet Evangelicals*, 13–16.

10. The Molokans were the largest sect in Imperial Russia. They split off from the Dukhobors in 1823 in a dispute over the assertion that the Bible was the foundation of doctrine. The Molokans never embraced the Dukhobor practice of communal land ownership, and they reject all sacraments, including the Orthodox practice of fasting. Although they originated in Ukraine, they were banished to the Caucasus in 1840. Many early evangelical converts came from Molokan communities.

11. By 1875 local Orthodox authorities in Kherson had already registered 1,546 Baptist believers; by 1881, it was up to 3,363. Just five years later, 95 Baptist communities were registered in this province. B. Liubashchenko, *Istoriia Protestantyzmy*, 240. The close ties among Mennonite, Shtundist, and Baptist believers leave open the possibility that these figures might represent a conflation of groups. Mitrokhin notes that Imperial and, later, Soviet authorities often failed to recognize the dogmatic and theological differences between different Protestant communities and would erroneously lump them together. Inaccuracies were compounded because communal leaders, who usually had an accurate sense of their membership size, were often reluctant to reveal it. See Mitrokhin, *Baptizm*, 59.

12. Coleman, *Russian Baptists*, 85.

13. Led by Vasilii Nikolaevich Ivanov, the British Bible Society regularly attracted Molokans, Shtundists, disciples of Tolstoy, and Baptists, some of whom Ivanov christened in his apartment. Ivanov returned to Tbilisi in 1882, just two years after founding the community, but Ivan Zhidkov took over the leadership and was credited with baptizing fifteen hundred converts, more than any other Baptist preacher at the time. For an overview of the development of evangelical communities in this city, see "Evangel'skoe dvizhenie v g. Khar'kove," *Baptist Ukrainy*, no. 11 (1927), 30–34.

14. *Bratskii Vestnik*, no. 4 (1957), 9.

15. Evangel'skoe dvizhenie v g. Khar'kove," *Baptist Ukrainy*, no. 11 (1927), 32–34; and I. I. Zhidkov, "Vozniknovenie Khar'kovskoi obshchiny evangeli'skikh Khristian-Baptistov," *Bratskii Vestnik*, no. 6 (1948), 59.

16. Datsko, *Tserkov' Preobrazhenie*, 9.

17. Coleman, *Russian Baptists*, 75.

18. *Prisutstviia*, 6 March 1913.

19. Coleman, *Russian Baptists*, 75.

20. Coleman, *Russian Baptists*, 76.

21. In 1914, 3,768 Orthodox believers converted to Baptism, 1,164 became Evangelical Christians, and 11 became Pashkovites. This contrasts sharply with the 1,265 apostates from evangelicalism to Orthodoxy. Coleman, *Russian Baptists*, 80.

22. Orlando Figes, *The People's Tragedy: The Russian Revolution, 1891–1924* (New York: Penguin, 1996), 352.

23. Stites, *Revolutionary Dreams*, 101–5.

24. Figes, "The Russian Revolution of 1917 and its Language in the Village," *Russian Review* 56 (July 1997): 323–45, 339. See also Mark Steinberg, "Workers on the Cross: Religious Imagination in the Writings of Russian Workers, 1910–1924," *Russian Review* 53 (April 1994): 213–39.

25. Coleman, *Russian Baptists*, 131.

26. Many religious minorities welcomed the Revolution as a means to escape oppressive and restrictive tsarist legislation, a fact sometimes overlooked since so much of the scholarship concerning religion and religious organizations after 1917 focuses on the adversarial relationship between the new Soviet state and the Orthodox Church. See especially Daniel Peris, *Storming the Heavens: The Soviet League of the Militant Godless* (Ithaca: Cornell University Press, 1998); William B. Husband, *"Godless Communists": Atheism and Society in Soviet Russia, 1917–32* (DeKalb: Northern Illinois University Press, 2000); David E. Powell, *Antireligious Propaganda in the Soviet Union: A Study of Mass Persuasion* (Cambridge, MA: MIT Press, 1975); and John Anderson, *Religion, State, and Politics.*

27. See William B. Husband, *"Godless Communists,"* 34. Husband also points out that Soviet publications later lauded the 1903 Bolshevik party program for its "militantly atheist stance," although none was apparent. Husband writes that "atheism did not occupy an important place in the Bolsheviks' pre-Revolutionary message, nor was it a central factor in their rise to power." *"Godless Communists,"* 35.

28. See Richard T. DeGeorge, *Soviet Ethics and Morality* (Ann Arbor: University of Michigan, 1969).

29. Figes, "The Russian Revolution," 331–32.

30. For an discussion of "communist morality" prescriptions on dress, manners, and dancing, all of which are reminiscent of evangelical moral codes, see Stites, *Revolutionary Dreams*, 115–19.

31. Heather J. Coleman, "Becoming a Russian Baptist: Conversion Narratives and Social Experience," *Russian Review* 61, no. 1 (2002): 94–112, 112.

32. For an overview of the secularization debate, see Steve Bruce, *Religion and Modernization: Sociologists and Historians Debate the Secularization Thesis* (Oxford: Clarendon Press, 1992) and David Martin, *A General Theory of Secularization* (New York: Harper and Row, 1978).

33. The full text is reproduced in Pospielovsky, *A History of Marxist-Leninist Atheism and Soviet Antireligious Policies*, 133.

34. Powell, *Antireligious Propaganda*, 22–34.

35. For a discussion of how celebrations and commemorations structure time and the relevance this has for individual and group identity formation, see Wanner, *Burden of Dreams*, 141–69.

36. For an overview of this period, see Husband, *"Godless Communists,"* 36–68; and Peris, *Storming the Heavens*, 19–46.

37. Gregory L. Freeze, "Counter-Reformation in Russian Orthodoxy: Popular Response to Religious Innovation, 1922–1925" *Slavic Review* 54, no. 2 (Summer 1995): 305–39, 309.

38. Frank Sysyn, "The Ukrainian Autocephalous Orthodox Church and the Traditions of the Kyiv Metropolitanate," in Serhii Plokhy and Frank Sysyn, *Religion and Nation in Modern Ukraine* (Toronto: University of Toronto Press, 2003), 36–39.

39. DAKhO, f. R-203, op. 1, d. 514–6, l. 4.

40. DAKhO, f. R-203, op. 1, d. 514–a, l. 7.

41. DAKhO, f. R-203, op. 1, d. 514–b, l. 107.

42. TsDAVOVU, f. 5, op. 1 d. 507, ll. 200–202.

43. TsGAOO, f. 1, op. 20, d. 2006, ll. 4–40b.

44. DAKhO, f. R-845, op. 2, d. 411, l. 5.

45. TsDAVOVU, f. 1, op. 5, d. 155, l. 172.

46. TsGAOO, f. 1, op. 20, d. 1772, l. 13.

47. DAKhO, f. 1, op. 1, d. 140, l. 20.

48. TsDAHOU, f. 17, op. 20, d. 2917, l. 82.

49. See Steeves, "The Russian Baptist Union," 159–60; and Stites, *Revolutionary Dreams*, 121.

50. TsDAHOU, f. 1, op. 20, d. 1839, ll. 37–38.

51. William C. Fletcher, *Soviet Charismatics: The Pentecostals in the USSR* (New York: Peter Lang, 1985a), 42.

52. One of the best studies of the early history of Pentecostalism is Grant Wacker, *Heaven Below: Early Pentecostals and American Culture* (Cambridge, MA: Harvard University Press, 2001).

53. Soviet sources frequently date the founding of Pentecostalism to Richard G. Spurling, who originally founded the Church of God in 1886, a church maintaining a pre-Pentecostal tradition that included glossolalic outbursts at worship meetings. Spurling's Church of God, however, did not formally accept the Pentecostal doctrine of Holy Ghost baptism until 1908.

54. The first recorded appearance of Pentecostalism in the Russian Empire occurred in 1911. A missionary named Urshan returned to Russia from America and founded a congregation in Vyborg in 1911. Among his recruits were N. P. Smorodin and A. I. Ivanov. Somorodin founded one of the three main branches of Pentecostalism in the USSR, the Smorodintsy. The other two are the Murashkovtsy and the Voronaevtsy; the most important, by far, were the Voronaevtsy. Smorodin relocated to Poland during the civil war. These eastern Polish lands were reincorporated into Soviet Belarussia during World War II, which helps explain why Pentecostalism is the second-largest faith in Belarus after Orthodoxy. See Fletcher, *Soviet Charismatics*, 27.

55. Smaller splinter groups also formed in Ukraine, such as the Pentecostal Zionists, founded by a woman, P. V. Kochenkova. Using the book of the prophet Isaiah, she created a doctrine of earthly Palestine whose center would be Mount Zion, where Christ will allegedly build the biblical millennial kingdom for the Pentecostal Zionists. The

absence of a Second Coming, predicted to occur in 1928, and the collectivization of agriculture decimated the group's ranks. During World War II missionary activity resumed and the Pentecostal-Zionists became the second largest branch of Pentecostalism. See Fletcher, *Soviet Charismatics,* 30–31, 43.

56. Fletcher, *Soviet Charismatics,* 43.

57. Fletcher, *Soviet Charismatics,* 87.

58. P. V. Pavlova, "Doklad," *Baptist,* no. 3 (1925), 7; cited in Steeves, "The Russian Baptist Union," 194.

59. These figures and all other membership figures cited here for 1925 are from DAKhO, f. R-845, op. 2, d. 411, l. 26.

60. DAKhO, f. R-845, op. 2, d. 623, ll. 95–96.

61. DAKhO, f. R-845, op. 2, d. 623, ll. 95–96.

62. *Baptist Ukrainy,* no. 1 (1926), 2. *Baptist Ukrainy* was published in Kharkiv from 1926 to 1929 in Russian with a Ukrainian-language section. It was introduced a year after *Baptist* began to be published in 1925.

63. See Steeves, "The Russian Baptist Union," 224 for an account of the variety of activities that were undertaken in Ukraine and were difficult or impossible to accomplish in Russia.

64. *Baptist Ukrainy,* no. 5 (1926), 43.

65. *Baptist Ukrainy,* no. 5 (1926), 43.

66. DAKhO, f. R-32, op. 1, d. 352, l. 71.

67. DAKhO, f. R-845, op. 2, d. 411, ll. 32–33.

68. DAKhO, f. R-845, op. 2, d. 1069, l. 35a.

69. DAKhO, f. R-845, op. 2, d. 1069, l. 37.

70. DAKhO, f. R-845, op. 2, d. 411, l. 2.

71. TsDAVOVU, f. 2, op. 6, d. 215, l. 214.

72. The commune "*Mir Vam*" was liquidated in 1925 because of the mixed social and property background of its ninety-three participants. In spite of its liquation, in January 1926, forty-nine members remained on the commune. DAKhO, f. R-947, op. 2, d. 14, ll. 73–74.

73. DAKhO, f. R-947, op. 2, d. 14, ll. 73–74.

74. DAKhO, f. R-947, op. 2, d. 14, ll. 73–74.

75. *Baptist Ukrainy,* no. 1 (1926), 48.

76. DAKhO, f. R-845, op. 2, d. 623, ll. 95–96.

77. DAKhO, f. R-947, op. 2, d. 14, ll. 10–11.

78. TsDAVOVU, f. 5, op. 2, d. 952, ll. 1, 35.

79. DAKhO, f. 845, op. 2, d. 1051, ll. 7–8.

80. TsDAHOU, f. 5, op. 1, d. 2185, l. 19.

81. Symon Petlyura was one of the leading figures of the Directorate of the Central Rada, a short-lived government that tried to secure Ukrainian independence. Petlyura led forces together with the Poles against the Bolsheviks during the civil war. He was assassinated in Paris in 1926. A. I. Denikin was a leader of the counterrevolutionary White Army that fought against the Bolsheviks. After his forces were defeated in 1919, Denikin left Russia and eventually settled in Ann Arbor, Michigan, where he died in 1947.

82. DAKhO, f. R-203, op. 1, d. 1981, l. 25.

83. TsDAHOU, f. 1, op. 20, d. 2006, l. 50.

84. TsDAHOU, f. 1, op. 20, d. 2006, l. 26.

85. DAKhO, f. R-845, op. 2, d. 411, ll. 32–33.

86. L. N. Mitrokhin's entire book is dedicated to the Baptist faith in the USSR. Yet, in a single sentence he transitions from the rapid growth of evangelical communities up until the early 1930s to the German attack on the USSR in 1941. See *Baptizm,* 75. There is no mention of 1929 as a turning point, nor of the repressions of the 1930s. He merely notes that the number of Baptist communities in one district of the Far East fell from 311 in 1929 to 86 in 1932. No explanation is offered other than to note that the sharp decline in Baptist growth was a trend throughout the USSR.

87. TsDAHOU, f. 1, op. 20, d. 1450, l. 104.

88. DAKhO, f. 7, op. 1., d. 1041, l. 32.

89. Coleman, *Russian Baptists,* 221; and Steeves, "The Russian Baptist Union," 257.

90. K. Ignatiuk, "Ko II Vsesoiuznomu S″ezdu Soiuza Bezbozhnikov," *Antireligioznik,* no. 5 (1929), 73.

91. TsDAHOU, f. 1, op. 20, d. 2006, l. 6.

92. DAKhO, f. R-203, op. 1, d. 514–a, l. 2a.

93. DAKhO, f. R-203, op. 1, d. 514, l. 2a.

94. DAKhO, f. 498, op. 1, d. 48, l. 57.

95. The other cathedrals closed on this day were Nikolaevskii Sobor, Panteleimonovskii Church, Staro-obriadcheskii Church, Nikolaevskii Church in Pavlovka, and the village church of Lipovaia Roshcha.

96. Those prayer houses were located at 40 Gordienkovskaia St., 136 Sverdlovskaia St., 7 Sakharozavodskaia St., 12 Kar′kovskaia St.

97. DAKhO, f. 845, op. 2, d. 1067, l. 17.

98. DAKhO, f. R-845, op. 2, d. 1069, l. 37.

99. Sawatsky, *Soviet Evangelicals,* 320.

100. Fletcher, *Soviet Charismatics,* 44–46. These claims were refuted by his wife after she arrived in the United States in 1960.

101. Peris, *Storming the Heavens,* 9

102. Danièle Hervieu-Léger, *Religion as a Chain of Memory* (New Brunswick, NJ: Rutgers University Press, 1993).

103. For a historical view, see Stephen P. Dunn and Ethel Dunn, *The Peasants of Central Russia* (New York: Holt, Reinhart, and Winston, 1967). Also see Dale Pesman, *Russia and Soul: An Exploration* (Ithaca: Cornell University Press, 2000).

104. Christopher Binns, "The Changing Face of Power: Revolution and Accommodation in the Development of a Soviet Ceremonial System," part I in *Man* 14, no. 4 (1979): 585–606, and part II in *Man* 15, no. 1 (1980): 170–87.

105. Sheila Fitzpatrick, *Stalin's Peasants: Resistance and Survival in the Russian Village after Collectivization* (New York: Oxford University Press, 1994), 204.

# Chapter 2. Enlightening the Faithful

1. *Bratskii Vestnik,* no. 1 (1945), 16.

2. Amir Weiner makes the argument that World War II actually fortified the legitimating mythology of Soviet rule in spite of the repressions of the 1930s and the massive

devastation incurred during the war. See his *Making Sense of War: The Second World War and the Fate of the Bolshevik Revolution* (Princeton, NJ: Princeton University Press, 2001).

3. Berkhoff also argues that in spite of increased religious freedoms under the Reichskommissariat, ultimately the wartime revival of Orthodoxy was modest in scope and primarily linked to the observance of life cycle rituals. The disillusionment with Orthodoxy, fueled by the anticlericalism that began in the late tsarist period and the hostility to the Church that nearly twenty-five years of Soviet rule had bequeathed, could not be overcome simply by opening more churches. Karel C. Berkhoff, "Was There a Religious Revival in Soviet Ukraine under the Nazi Regime?" *Slavic and East European Review* 78, no. 3 (2000): 536–67, 538–39.

4. The UAOC thrived in the post–World War II North American diaspora, where it played a meaningful role in forming communities and shaping political orientations. See Lubomyr Luciuk, *Searching for Place: Ukrainian Displaced Persons, Canada, and the Migrations of Memory* (Toronto: University of Toronto Press, 2000); Myron B. Kuropas, *The Ukrainian Americans: Roots and Aspirations* (Toronto: University of Toronto Press, 1991); and Vic Satzewich, *The Ukrainian Diaspora* (London: Routledge, 2002).

5. John Anderson, *Religion, State, and Politics*, 9.

6. For more on how World War II affected the Ukrainian churches, see Bohdan R. Bociurkiw, *The Ukrainian Greek Catholic Church and the Soviet State (1939–1950)* (Toronto: Canadian Institute of Ukrainian Studies Press, 1996) and "The Uniate Church in Soviet Ukraine: A Case Study in Soviet Church Policy," *Canadian Slavonic Papers* 7 (1995): 89–113; Serhii Plokhy, "In the Shadow of Yalta: International Politics and the Soviet Liquidation of The Ukrainian Greek Catholic Church," in *Religion and Nation in Modern Ukraine,* ed. Serhii Plokhy and Frank E. Sysyn (Toronto: Canadian Institute of Ukrainian Studies Press, 2003).

7. DAKhO, lf. 3858, op. 17, d. 92, l. 18. Eighty percent of the believers in Kharkiv oblast lived in rural areas. Given the loss of family and other bases of support, church communities quickly emerged as mutual aid societies, which accounts in part for the rapid growth in membership.

8. Shortly after its creation, the official name of the union was modified by replacing the *and* with a hyphen to illustrate the supposed unity between the two Protestant streams in the Soviet Union. The name of the council also changed in 1966 when it merged with the Council for Religious Affairs and adopted this name.

9. The "August Agreement" stipulating the terms under which the Pentecostals (Christians of Evangelical Faith) joined the AUCECB can be found in Fletcher, *Soviet Charismatics*, 92–93.

10. L. N. Mitrokhin, *Baptizm* (Moscow: Isdatel'stvo Politicheskoi Literatury), 77.

11. Michael Bourdeaux, *Religious Ferment in Russia: Protestant Opposition to Soviet Religious Policy* (London: Macmillan, 1968), 8.

12. *Glauben in der Zweiten Welt,* a Swiss-based religious rights activist organization, claimed that circulation was not more than one thousand and that *Bratskii Vestnik,* like all Christian literature in the USSR, was in tremendous short supply.

13. *Bratskii Vestnik,* no. 2–3 (1953), 110–11. See also *Bratskii Vestnik,* no. 5–6 (1954), 61, 99, for a discussion of the problem of theological and ritual ignorance among professed believers.

14. Little scholarly attention has focused on the Antireligious Campaign, which was widely viewed as reactionary and counterproductive. William Taubman's comprehensive biography, *Khrushchev: The Man and His Era* (New York: W.W. Norton, 2003), scarcely refers to it.

15. For an overview of Khrushchev's policies, see Anderson, *Religion, State, and Politics*; Joan Delaney Grossman, "Khrushchev's Anti-Religious Policy and Campaign of 1954," *Soviet Studies* 24, no. 3 (Jan. 1973): 374–86; and Donald A. Lowrie and William C. Fletcher, "Khrushchev's Religious Policy, 1959–1964," in *Aspects of Religion in the Soviet Union, 1917–67*, ed. Richard H. Marshall Jr. (Chicago, IL: University of Chicago Press, 1971).

16. For a comparative perspective on how Khrushchev's antireligious policies affected other faith groups in the USSR, see Z. Bartoshevich, "O Chem Govoriat Fakty," *Nauka i Religia* 5 (1963): 71–73, on Georgia; Yaacov Ro'i, "The Task of Creating the New Soviet Man: Atheistic Propaganda in the Soviet Muslim Areas," *Soviet Studies* 36, no. 1 (Jan. 1984): 26–44; Nathaniel Knight, "The Number of Orthodox Churches before and after the Khrushchev Antireligious Drive," *Slavic Review* 50, no. 3 (Autumn 1991): 612–20; and for an overview, see John Anderson, "The Council for Religious Affairs and the Shaping of Soviet Religious Policy," *Soviet Studies* 43, no. 4: 689–710.

17. Anderson, *Religion, State, and Politics*, 56.

18. Grossman, "Khrushchev's Anti-Religious Policy." For a broad overview of dissent during this period, see Jay Bergman, "Soviet Dissidents on the Russian Intelligentsia, 1956–1985: The Search for a Usable Past," *Russian Review* 51, no. 1 (Jan. 1992): 16–35.

19. Among the best are A. I. Klibanov, *Religioznoe sektantstvo i sovremennost' (sotsiologicheskie i istoricheskie ocherki)* (Moscow: Izdatel'stvo "Nauka," 1969); A. A. Eryshev, *Religioznoe Sektantsvo i ego Sushchnost'* (Kyiv: Izdatel'stvo Kievskovo Universiteta, 1959); and a special edition of A. F. Okulov, *Voprosy Nauchnogo Ateizma* (Moscow: Izdatel'stvo "Mysl," 1966). For a Marxist-Leninist perspective, see G. S. Lialina, *Baptizm: Illiuzii i Real'nost'* (Moscow: Isdatel'stvo Politicheskoi Literatury, 1977).

20. For the full text of the moral code and an analysis of its effects, see Richard T. De-George, *Soviet Ethics and Morality* (Ann Arbor: University of Michigan Press, 1969), 83.

21. Alexander Solzhenitsyn, *One Day in the Life of Ivan Denisovich* (New York: E. P. Dutton & Co., 1963), 157.

22. Jay Bergman argues that the success of dissident struggle was compromised by the excessively wide spectrum of solutions they offered, which implied a lack of consensus on the ethical principles society was supposed to protect. Bergman, "Soviet Dissidents," 18. The moral critique offered by evangelicals, while hardly uniform, nonetheless drew on particular interpretations of frequently cited Biblical passages and therefore endorsed certain ethical principles and prescriptions for how they should be respected.

23. Talal Asad, *Formations of the Secular: Christianity, Islam, Modernity* (Stanford, CT: Stanford University Press, 2003), 61–62.

24. I thank Paul Brodwin for his valuable comments on an earlier version of this section, which I presented at the American Anthropological Association.

25. There was also dismay among Orthodox clergy over the perceived passivity of their leadership to state interference. See Anderson, *Religion, State, and Politics*, ch. 4.

26. There are several books sympathetic to the objections of the reform Baptist group. See Michael Bourdeaux, *Religious Ferment in Russia: Protestant Opposition to Soviet Religious Policy* (London: MacMillan, 1968); and Walter Sawatsky, *Soviet Evangelicals since*

*World War II.* For a depiction of how evangelicals experienced antireligious policies, see Michael Bourdeaux, *Opium of the People: The Christian Religion in the U.S.S.R.* (London: Faber and Faber, 1965).

27. Fletcher speculates that many Pentecostals would have found the *Initsiativniki* movement "most congenial," given that large numbers of Pentecostals were already alienated from the AUCECB, had withdrawn their memberships, and were living an underground existence by 1961. See *Soviet Charismatics,* 99.

28. See Georgi Vins, *Three Generations of Suffering,* trans. Jane Ellis (London: Hodder and Stoughton, 1976); and *Testament from Prison,* trans. Jane Ellis, ed. Michael Bourdeaux (Elgin, IL: David C. Cook Publishing, 1975).

29. Z. Bartoshevich, "O Chem Govoriat Fakty," *Nauka i Religia* 5 (1963): 71–73.

30. Nancy Ries, *Russian Talk: Culture and Conversation during Perestroika* (Ithaca: Cornell University Press, 1997), 29–30.

31. Peris, *Storming the Heavens,* 179.

32. Some debates were declared spectacular public failures. Artem Borzenko counseled against staging debates, claiming that they were an ineffective method of propaganda. See "Nuzhno li Provodit' Disputy?" *Nauka i Religiia* 2 (1960): 84–85. Three years later, he reversed this argument and advocated staging them. Borzenko, "O Disputakh i Literaturnykh Sudakh," *Nauka i Religiia* 1 (1963): 70–72.

33. Interview conducted 16 February 2002.

34. Anderson, *Religion, State, and Politics,* 62.

35. In tsarist Russia, a common anti-Semitic charge was that Jews killed Christian children for their blood to use in rituals, harking back to the Old Testament parable of Abraham and his son, Isaac.

36. In 1968 Michael Bourdeaux published the first of several influential studies of Baptist communities in the USSR. An Anglican priest, Bourdeaux proved a very effective spokesperson for the plight of unregistered communities in the USSR. It was not his intention to discount the persecution of registered communities, but his focus on the confrontation between unregistered Baptists and Soviet authorities drew more attention to their plight.

37. Tatiana Chumachenko, *Church and State in Soviet Russia: Russian Orthodoxy from World War II to the Khrushchev Years* (Armonk, NY: M. E. Sharpe, 2002) documents how these dilemmas and dynamics played out for Orthodox clergy.

38. Interviews conducted May 2003 and May 2004.

39. Datsko, *Preoprazhenie,* 13. Technically, this threat hung over all churches, but most larger congregations had more than one person to lead it—for the smaller churches it usually meant closure.

40. Shoshana Felman and Dori Laub argue that the very essence of trauma is that it eludes articulation. The visceral nature of the experience makes articulation elusive. This does not mean, however, that one does not try. See Felman and Laub, *Testimony: Crises of Witnessing in Literature, Psychoanalysis, and History* (New York: Routledge, 1992).

41. Asad, *Formations of the Secular,* 83.

42. Interestingly, the fall harvest festival was originally introduced as a secular holiday in the 1920s to supplant the Orthodox Feast of the Intercession. See Stites, *Revolutionary Dreams,* 110.

43. I once witnessed a retrospective indictment of a Pentecostal pastor by Soviet Pentecostal refugees in Philadelphia for marrying a convert twenty-five years earlier. His wife was not a believer when he met her, but she converted before marrying him. She has since led the life of a believing pastor's wife but this was not good enough.

44. In the first half of the twentieth century, American Pentecostals were also criticized for inducing hysteria in believers.

45. Alexei Yurchak, *Everything Was Forever Until It Was No More: The Last Soviet Generation* (Princeton, NJ: Princeton University, 2005), 59–60.

46. Matthew C. Guttman, *The Romance of Democracy: Compliant Defiance in Contemporary Mexico* (Berkeley: University of California Press, 2002).

47. Such quietism was also characteristic of conservative evangelical groups in the United States. After the Scopes Trial and before the rise of Billy Graham, conservative Christians in the United States were also rather apolitical.

48. In the 1830s John Nelson Darby pioneered a novel interpretation of the Bible that was quickly embraced by believers who otherwise insisted on the inerrancy and literalness of the Bible. Darby argued that the prophecies in the books of Daniel in the Old Testament and Revelation in the New Testament have been fulfilled and that therefore the Second Coming is imminent. He posited that Jesus would return to rapture his church, meaning true believers, just prior to the "end times," the end of history. This kind of apocalyptic imagery was readily embraced by Soviet Evangelicals. His ideas were also endorsed by many evangelicals in the United States. For an analysis of how premillennial dispensationalism has shaped contemporary American evangelical views of history, see Susan Harding, "Imagining the Last Days: The Politics of Apocalyptic Language," in *Accounting for Fundamentalisms: The Dynamic Character of Movements,* ed. Martin E. Marty and R. Scott Appleby (Chicago, IL: University of Chicago Press, 1994).

49. Katherine Verdery, *What Was Socialism, and What Comes Next?* (Princeton, NJ: Princeton University Press, 1996).

50. Christel Lane, *Christian Religion in the Soviet Union: A Sociological Study* (London: George Allen and Unwin, 1978).

51. See James C. Scott, *Weapons of the Weak: Everyday Forms of Peasant Resistance* (New Haven, CT: Yale University Press, 1985); and *Domination and the Arts of Resistance: Hidden Transcripts* (New Haven, CT: Yale University Press, 1990).

52. *Nauka i Religiia* 7 (1966): 25.

53. The Zaochnyi Bibleiskii Institut was created in 1992 with fourteen students during a period of acute clerical crisis. Thanks to favorable American immigration laws, established clergy and lay leaders emigrated to America in droves, leaving most growing congregations without leadership.

54. Michael Rowe, "Christian Prisoners in the USSR, 1979–81," *Religion in Communist Lands* 10, no. 1 (Spring 1982): 81–82.

55. Yurchak, *Everything Was Forever.*

56. See Manuel Vasquez, *The Brazilian Popular Church and the Crisis of Modernity* (Cambridge: Cambridge University Press, 1998), 278.

57. The 1973 Arab-Israeli War and the growing awareness of the difficulties of life in Israel for Soviet Jews dampened enthusiasm to relocate to Israel. In 1977, one year after HIAS changed its policy, half of the Soviet Jews elected to go the United States over

Israel. In 1979 emigration peaked as fifty-one thousand Jews emigrated. Twenty-nine percent were from Ukraine. The most famous Soviet Jewish enclave, "Little Odessa," is Brighton Beach in Brooklyn, New York. Three-quarters of the residents are from Ukraine. For studies of Brighton Beach, see Fran Markowitz, *A Community in Spite of Itself: Soviet Jewish Émigrés in New York* (Washington, DC: Smithsonian, 1993); and Annelise Orleck, *The Soviet Jewish Americans* (Westport, CT: Greenwood Press, 1999).

58. For example, a British Pentecostal leader, Percy Brewster, was widely quoted as saying, "Regardless of where we live, we must be obedient to the laws of our own country. The church should be registered. In England registration is obligatory." Cited in Kent R. Hill, *The Soviet Union on the Brink: An Inside Look at Christianity and Glasnost* (Portland, OR: Multnomah, 1991), 182.

59. Jimmy Swaggart, "From Me to You," *The Evangelist,* January 1986, cited in Hill, *The Soviet Union on the Brink,* 182.

60. Fletcher, *Soviet Charismatics,* 136.

61. Thanks to direct intervention by Ronald Reagan, Boris Perchatkin emigrated to the United States in July 1988.

62. Rowe, "Christian Prisoners," 83.

## Chapter 3. The Rewards of Suffering

1. The only study of these communities is Susan Wiley Hardwick, *Russian Refuge: Religion, Migration, and Settlement on the North American Pacific Rim* (Chicago: University of Chicago Press, 1995).

2. Nina Glick-Schiller, *Georges Woke Up Laughing: Long-Distance Nationalism and the Search for Home* (Durham, NC: Duke University Press, 2001); and Erica Lee, *At America's Gates: Chinese Immigration during the Exclusion Era, 1882–43* (Chapel Hill: University of North Carolina Press, 2003).

3. Two edited volumes touch on the spectrum of experiences, R. Stephen Warner and Judith Witmer, eds., *Gatherings in Diaspora: Religious Communities and the New Immigration* (Philadelphia, PA: Temple University Press, 1998); and Helen Rose Ebaugh and Janet Saltzman Chafetz, eds., *Religion across Borders: Transnational Immigrant Networks* (Walnut Creek, CA: AltaMira Press, 2002). For a more detailed ethnographic study of the intersection of religion and migration, see Kenneth Guest, *God in Chinatown: Religion and Survival in New York's Evolving Immigrant Community* (New York: New York University Press, 2003).

4. Satzewich, *The Ukrainian Diaspora,* 89. See also Wsevolod W. Isajiw, Yury Roshyk, and Roman Senkus, eds., *The Refugee Experience: Ukrainian Displaced Persons after World War II* (Edmonton: Canadian Institute of Ukrainian Studies Press, 1992).

5. See www.census.gov/population/cen2000/phc-t20/tab05.pdf, accessed 26 March 2007. The 2000 U.S. census revealed that the number of Russian-speakers had climbed to 706,242.

6. Timothy L. Smith, "Religion and Ethnicity in America," *American Historical Review* 83 (1978): 1155–85.

7. In the Philadelphia area, there are thirteen Soviet evangelical congregations. All have regular exchanges with other immigrant congregations in the United States, usu-

ally from the same region. The two largest umbrella organizations uniting Russian and Ukrainian Baptist churches are the Pacific Coast Slavic Association and the Russian-Ukrainian Evangelical Baptist Union, which unites churches on the east coast. According to the head of the Russian-Ukrainian Evangelical Baptist Union, there are approximately eighteen thousand formal members of Russian-speaking Baptist congregations associated with this union. There are, of course, numerous autonomous churches as well. Interview conducted 9 March 2001.

8. Aihwa Ong, *Flexible Citizenship: Cultural Logistics of Transnationality* (Durham, NC: Duke University Press, 1999).

9. Even though I focus on legal migration of a mostly permanent nature, it is important to keep in mind that this pertains to fewer and fewer people. Since 1991, migration patterns from the former Soviet Union have radically changed; they are now dominated by entirely unregulated, haphazard border crossings for the purposes of "shuttle trade" (usually to Turkey, the United Arab Emirates, or China), contract work (to eastern European countries such as Poland and the Czech Republic and, increasingly, to Portugal and Italy) and forced migration (out of Chechnya, Georgia, or Nagorno-Karabakh).

10. Interview conducted 6 May 2001.

11. Soviet Evangelicals have settled extensively in Sacramento, California. Starting in the 1950s, a radio station based in Sacramento ran a Russian-language evangelical radio broadcast that was received in parts of the former Soviet Union. For the earliest evangelical refugees, this suggested that Sacramento might be a hospitable new home. Sacramento became the preferred relocation point for evangelicals and today has the largest Soviet evangelical community. Portland and Seattle are other key destinations.

12. See Catherine Wanner, "Missionaries of Faith and Culture: Evangelical Encounters in Ukraine," *Slavic Review* 63, no. 4: 732–55.

13. This becomes a problem in some Pacific Northwest regions, such as the city of Portland, where popular initiatives have significant legislative impact. When émigrés settle in residential clusters and then abstain from voting, governance is significantly compromised, if not impeded.

14. Fran Markowitz, "Criss-Crossing Identities: The Russian Jewish Diaspora and the Jewish Diaspora in Russia," *Diaspora* 4, no. 2 (1995): 201–11, 203. For studies of the settlement process, see Tanya Basok and Robert J. Brym, S*oviet-Jewish Emigration and Resettlement in the 1990s* (Toronto: York Lanes Press, 191); Rita J. Simon, ed., *New Lives: The Adjustment of Soviet Jewish Immigrants in the United States and Israel* (Lexington, MA: Lexington Books, 1985).

15. The construction brigades are a dramatic example of a mechanism that actually insulates immigrants from the need to speak English. The men order lunch at McDonald's by saying, "Number one," live at the job site among immigrants in specially rented apartments, and rely on a Russian-speaking foreman to explain their duties and negotiate their pay with a Russian-speaking owner.

16. Interview conducted 10 June 2001.

17. Laada Bilaniuk, *Contested Tongues: Language Politics and Cultural Correction in Ukraine* (Ithaca: Cornell University Press, 2005).

18. Interview conducted 12 June 2001.

19. The church is categorically against restricting aid to Baptists out of fear that people will convert for the sole purpose of gaining material rewards.

20. Interviews conducted February 2002.

21. See Catherine Wanner, "Advocating New Moralities: Conversion to Evangelicalism in Ukraine," *Religion, State, and Society* 31, no. 3 (2003): 273–87.

22. Interview conducted 16 February 2002.

23. William Safran, "Diasporas in Modern Societies: Myths of Homeland and Return," *Diaspora* 1, no. 1 (1991): 83–99, 85.

24. Two are in Poltava oblast, in the east. Three of the other missionaries serving in western Ukraine are in Lviv, two are in Volyn, and one each in Chernihiv, Zhitomyr, and Rivne oblasts.

25. Georges E. Fouron and Nina Glick Schiller, "The Generation of Identity: Redefining the Second Generation within a Transnational Social Field," in *Migration, Transnationalization, and Race in a Changing New York,* ed. Héctor R. Cordero-Guzmán, Robert C. Smith, and Ramón Grosfoguel (Philadelphia, PA: Temple University Press, 2001), 61.

26. Initially only the most anti-Soviet historians referred to the USSR as an empire. Since *perestroika* began in 1985, numerous scholars have begun to refer to the USSR as an empire. See Ronald Grigor Suny and Terry Martin, eds., *A State of Nations: Empire and Nation-Making in the Age of Lenin and Stalin* (Oxford: Oxford University Press, 2001).

27. Susanne Hoeber Rudolph and James Piscatori, eds., *Transnational Religion and Fading States* (Boulder, CO: Westview Press, 1997). The essays are primarily concerned with the intersection of religious organizations and the development of civil society. The activities of religious communities are pervasive, flexible, and difficult for states to inhibit; when they turn their attention to migration, they are obviously affecting multiple states at once

## Chapter 4. Missionizing, Converting, and Remaking the Moral Self

1. For a discussion of the impact of the Millennium celebrations on the growth of religious participation See esp. Michael Bourdeaux, "Glasnost and the Gospel: The Emergence of Religious Pluralism," in *The International Politics of Eurasia,* ed. Michael Bourdeaux (Armonk, NY: M.E. Sharpe, 1995). For Ukrainians, the fact that the anniversary was initially commemorated in Moscow, with only subsequent "regional" commemorations in Kyiv, underlined the colonial nature of the relationship of Ukrainians, their language, culture, and church, to Russians and simultaneously advanced religious and nationalist resurgence. See Catherine Wanner, *Burden of Dreams: History and Identity in Post-Soviet Ukraine* (University Park, PA: Pennsylvania State University Press, 1998), esp. 140–69.

2. For a discussion of this process, see Serhii Plokhy, "Kyiv vs. Moscow: The Autocephalous Movement in Independent Ukraine," *Harriman Review* 9, nos. 1–2 (Spring 1996): 32–37; Andrii Krawchuk, "Religious Life in Ukraine: Continuity and Change," *Journal of Ecumenical Studies* 33, no. 1 (Winter 1996): 59–68; and Geraldine Fagan and Aleksandr Shchipkov, "Rome Is Not Our Father, But Neither Is Moscow Our Mother: Will There Be a Local Ukrainian Orthodox Church?" *Religion, State, and Society* 29, no. 3 (September 2001): 197–205.

3. Jose Casanova, "Between Nation and Civil Society: Ethnolinguistic and Religious Pluralism in Independent Ukraine," in *Democratic Civility: The History and Cross-*

*Cultural Possibility of a Modern Political Ideal,* ed. Robert W. Hefner (New Brunswick, NJ: Transaction Publishers, 1998), 203–28, 215.

4. Taras Kuzio, "The Struggle to Establish the World's Largest Orthodox Church," *RFE/RL,* 5 September 2000. See also Krindatch, "Religion in Postsoviet Ukraine," 40.

5. For a complete breakdown of the number of registered communities as well as a listing of infractions against their rights, see the U.S. Department of State's "International Religious Freedom Report" at www.state.gov/g/drl/rls/irf/2005/51588pf.htm for Ukraine and www.state.gov/g/drl/rls/irf/2005/51576.htm for Russia, accessed 26 March 2007.

6. Vasyl Markus, "Politics and Religion in Ukraine: In Search of a New Pluralistic Dimension," in *The Politics of Religion in Russia and the New States of Eurasia,* ed. Michael Bourdeaux (Armonk, NY: M.E. Sharpe, 1995), 163.

7. Mitrokhin, "Aspects of the Religious Situation in Ukraine," 173.

8. http://www.risu.org.ua/eng/major.religions, accessed 28 September 2006.

9. Besides the "International Religious Freedom Report," see Peter Roudik, "Ukraine," in *Religious Liberty: The Legal Framework in Selected OSCE Countries* (Washington, DC, United States Congress, Commission on Security and Cooperation in Europe, 2001), 149–58. and Kevin Boyle and Juliet Sheen, eds., *Freedom of Religion and Belief: A World Report* (New York: Routledge, 1997).

For an in-depth comparison of the politics of religion in Ukraine and Russia, see Serhii Plokhy, "State Politics and Religious Pluralism in Russia and Ukraine: A Comparative Perspective," in *Protecting the Human Rights of Religious Minorities in Eastern Europe,* ed. P. G. Danchin and E. A. Cole (New York: Columbia University Press, 2002); Myroslaw Tataryn, "Russia and Ukraine: Two Models of Religious Liberty and Two Models for Orthodoxy," *Religion, State, and Society* 29, no. 3 (September 2001): 155–72; and Vasyl Markus, "Politics and Religion in Ukraine."

10. Russian Federal Law, "On Freedom of Conscience and Religious Organizations," No. 125–82 (26 September 1997). For an assessment of this law and its relation to the Russian Constitution, see the Winter 1998 issue of the *Emory International Law Review* 12, no. 1, which is entirely dedicated to analyzing the legal ramifications of this law for various religious denominations. See esp. T. Jeremy Gunn, "Caesar's Sword: The 1997 Law of the Russian Federation on Freedom of Conscience and Religious Associations," 98–99.

11. For a discussion of the use of registration procedures and other administrative mechanisms to discriminate or repress minority religious groups, see David Little, "Religious Minorities and Religious Freedom," in *Protecting the Human Rights.*

12. See Felix Corley, "Belarus: Europe's Most Repressive Religion Law Adopted," *Keston News Service,* 2 October 2002. The organization Forum 18 monitors violations of religious freedom in formerly socialist countries. See www.forum18.org, esp. "Belarus: Religion Law Stunts Church Growth," at www.forum18.org/Archive.php?article_id=162, accessed 26 March 2007.

13. Corley, "Belarus."

14. A spokesman for the Pentecostal Union claimed that of their 494 registered communities, 250 have already had their registration obstructed. See Corley, "Belarus."

15. See "International Religious Freedom Report 2002," 3.

16. Howard Biddulph, "Interconfessional Intolerance in Ukraine," *East-West Church Ministry Report* 10, no. 1 (Winter 2002). A career missionary with the Church of Jesus Christ of Latter-day Saints, Biddulph was in Kyiv from 1991 to 1994.

17. The Ukrainian Orthodox Church-Moscow Patriarchate is the only Orthodox church in Ukraine that is canonically recognized.

18. Several of these nontraditional religious groups, such as the White Brotherhood, gained international notoriety. See Eliot Borenstein, "Suspending Disbelief: 'Cults" and Postmodernism in Post-Soviet Russia," in *Consuming Russia: Popular Culture, Sex, and Society since Gorbachev*, ed. Adel Marie Barker (Durham, NC: Duke University Press, 1999).

19. Roudnik, *Religious Liberty*, 157.

20. In contrast, in 2001 there were over 2,200 missionaries working in Russia, but a little less than a third of them, 794, were American. In Belarus, of the 82 missionaries, 44 were American. Thirteen were Belarussian. Patrick Johnson and Jason Mandryk with Robyn Johnson, *Operation World: 21st Century Edition* (Waynesboro, GA: Paternoster Publishing, 2001), 645, 540, 100.

21. Catherine Wanner, "Advocating New Moralities: Conversion to Evangelicalism in Ukraine," *Religion, State, and Society* 31, no. 3 (September 2003): 273–87.

22. See esp. Robbins, *Becoming Sinners*; Austin-Broos, *Jamaica Genesis*; and Comaroff and Comaroff, *Of Revelation and Revolution*.

23. See Jeffers Engelhardt, "Right Singing and Orthodox Conversion in Estonia" and Galina Valtchinova, "Converting 'Back' to the 'Faith of our Ancestors,'" both papers presented at the Max Planck Institute conference on "Religious Conversion after Socialism," 7–9 April 2005.

24. Malcolm Ruel analyzes how the understanding of belief has evolved over time among Christians. He argues that the use of the term *believer*, as I am indicating Ukrainians employ it, is indeed the earliest meaning of Christian belief. This understanding of belief and of being a believer, he argues, has evolved in a highly individualistic way to the point that "belief as doctrine has *almost* become the honest opinion of anyone who declares himself to be a Christian." Malcolm Ruel, "Christians as Believers," in *Religious Organization and Religious Experience*, ed. John Davis (London: Academic Press, 1982), 9–31.

25. Elliott and Richardson, "Growing Protestant Diversity," 191.

26. Johnson and Mandryk, *Operation World*, 644–45.

27. This estimate was made as of 1 January 2002. The structural differences between Protestant and Orthodox congregations account for such a high proportion of overall Protestant congregations in Ukraine. While Protestant congregations might be numerous, they often serve a small group of highly active and committed believers, most of whom are official members of the church. This is in sharp contrast to Orthodox cathedrals, which serve a large and amorphous group of local believers who often have only nominal allegiance to a particular church. See www.lta.lviv.ua/irs, accessed 15 February 2007.

28. See www.risu.org.ua/eng/major.religions, accessed 26 March 2007.

29. As of 2005, almost half of all evangelical communities were meeting in rented space, indicating a lack of financial resources. See www.state.gov/g/drl/rls/irf/2005/51588.htm, accessed 26 March 2007.

30. Johnson and Mandryk, *Operation World*, 750.

31. Quoted from the SEND website at www.send.org/ukraine/lives.htm, accessed 26 March 2007.

32. See Mark C. Elliott, "Guidelines for Guest Preaching, Teaching, and Cross-Cultural Communication," *East-West Church and Ministry Report* 10, no. 2 (Spring

2002): 8–12; and Judith E. Lingenfelter and Sherwood G. Lingenfelter, "Teaching Cross-Culturally," *East-West Church and Ministry Report* 11, no. 4 (Fall 2003): 4–8.

33. See David Martin, *Tongues of Fire: The Explosion of Protestantism in Latin America* (Oxford: Blackwell, 1990); and Laura Nuzzi O'Shaughnessy, "Onward Christian Soldiers: The Case of Protestantism in Central America," in *Religious Resurgence and Politics in the Contemporary World,* ed. Emile Sahliyeh (Albany: State University of New York Press, 1990).

34. Personal communication, 8 April 2006; interviews conducted May 2004 and May 2005.

35. See www.readministries.org, accessed 26 March 2007.

36. Interviews conducted May 2003, May 2004, and May 2005.

37. Max Weber, *The Protestant Ethic and the "Spirit" of Capitalism and Other Writings* (New York: Penguin Books, 2002).

38. Perry L. Glazer, *The Quest for Russia's Soul: Evangelicals and Moral Education in Post-Communist Russia* (Waco, TX: Baylor University Press, 2002).

39. Wanner, "Money, Morality and New Forms of Exchange in Ukraine."

40. Interview conducted 26 December 2001.

41. Galina Linquist argues that in the absence of trust, Russian businessmen are left to play "a game without rules" in which the structural dimensions of individual agency are severely limited. The legal and moral sanctions that usually apply in the West in the event of a breach of contract are entirely absent in Russia. Hence, businessmen turn to magic to regain a sense of hope and control. *Conjuring Hope: Healing and Magic in Contemporary Russia* (Oxford: Berghahn Books, 2006), 210 and 223.

42. John Comaroff and Jean Comaroff, *Ethnography and the Historical Imagination* (Boulder: Westview Press, 1992), 246.

43. Ibid. 258.

44. Roman Catholic, Jewish, and Mormon communities still have foreign clergy leading at least half of their communities in Ukraine.

45. See www.state.gov/g/drl/rls/irf/2005/51588.htm, accessed 26 March 2007.

46. Johnson and Mandryk, *Operation World,* 750. Granted, this "ideal-type" congregational projection suffers from not taking into consideration membership size, but it does point to valid trends.

47. Johnson and Mandryk, *Operation World,* 750.

48. Clifford Geertz, *The Interpretation of Culture,* esp. ch. 4, 112.

49. Comaroff and Comaroff, *Of Revelation and Revolution*; and Van der Veer, ed., *Conversion to Modernities: The Globalization of Christianity* (New York: Routledge, 1996).

50. Peter van der Veer, "Introduction," in *Conversion to Modernities,* 7. Comaroff and Comaroff have made a similar point regarding the colonization of South Africa. They write, "The missionary encounter must be regarded as a two-sided historical process: as a dialectic that takes into account the social and cultural endowments of, and the consequences for, all the actors—missionaries no less than Africans." Comaroff and Comaroff, *Of Revelation and Revolution,* 54.

51. David Snow and Richard Machalek, "The Sociology of Conversion," *Annual Review of Sociology* 10 (1984): 167–90; and David Yamane, "Narrative and Religious Experience," *Sociology of Religion* 61, no. 2 (Summer 2000): 171–90.

52. Clifford L. Staples and Armand L. Mauss, "Conversion or Commitment? A Reassessment of the Snow Machalek Approach to the Study of Conversion," *Journal for the Scientific Study of Religion* 26, no. 2 (1987): 133–47, 137.

53. See esp. James T. Richardson, "The Active versus Passive Convert: Paradigm Conflict in Conversion/Recruitment Research," *Journal for the Scientific Study of Religion* 24 (1985): 199–236. Another key contribution has been the development of a schema of "motifs of conversion," meaning the type of sacred object with which the individual identifies; this is valuable in analyzing which aspect of the religious experience has enduring meaning for the convert. John Lofland and Norman Skonovd, "Conversion Motifs," *Journal for the Scientific Study of Religion* 20 (1981): 373–85.

54. Among the best studies are R. F. Paloutzian et al., "Religious Conversion and Personality Change," *Journal of Personality* 67, no. 6 (1999): 1047–79, esp. 1056; and Chana Ullman, *The Transformed Self: The Psychology of Religious Conversion* (New York: Plenum Press, 1989).

55. Interview conducted 14 May 2005.

56. Christ was dead for three days before his resurrection. Misha did not mention this, but I suspect that he would have found the parallel meaningful.

57. George Herbert Mead, *Mind, Self, and Society from the Standpoint of a Social Behaviorist*, ed. C. Morris (Chicago, IL: University of Chicago Press, 1934), 88–90.

58. David Snow and Richard Machalek, "The Convert as a Social Type," in *Sociological Theory*, ed. R. Collins (San Francisco, CA: Jossey-Bass, 1983) and "The Sociology of Conversion,"; and Susan Friend Harding, *The Book of Jerry Falwell: Fundamentalist Language and Politics* (Princeton, NJ: Princeton University Press, 2000). For a succinct summation of these issues, see David Yamane, "Narrative and Religious Experience."

59. Harding, *The Book of Jerry Falwell*, ch. 1.

60. Susan F. Harding, "Convicted by the Holy Spirit: The Rhetoric of Fundamental Baptist Conversion," *American Ethnologist* 4 (February 1987): 167–81, 179.

61. Serguei Oushakine, "Third Europe-Asia Lecture. In the State of Post-Soviet Aphasia: Symbolic Development in Contemporary Russia" *Europe-Asia Studies* 52, no. 6: 991–1016.

62. Oushakine, "In the State of Post-Soviet Aphasia," 1005–6.

63. Interview conducted 13 November 2001.

64. Harding, *The Book of Jerry Falwell*, 60.

65. Interview conducted 30 May 2004.

66. Eileen Barker, *The Making of a Moonie: Choice or Brainwashing?* (London: Basil, 1984), 244.

67. Interview conducted 16 December 2001.

68. Alena V. Ledeneva, *Russia's Economy of Favors: Blat, Networking, and Informational Exchange* (Cambridge: Cambridge University Press, 1998).

69. See Roger Finke and Rodney Stark, *Acts of Faith: Understanding the Human Side of Religion* (Berkeley: University of California Press, 2000).

70. Interview conducted 5 November 2001.

71. Melissa Caldwell, "A New Role for Religion in Russia's New Consumer Age: The Case of Moscow," *Religion, State, and Society* 33, no. 1 (2005): 43–58; and Lindquist, *Conjuring Hope*.

72. P. Ewick and S. Silbey, "Subversive Stories and Hegemonic Tales: Toward a Sociology of Narrative," *Law and Society Review* 29 (1995): 197–226.

73. See Ruth Mandel and Caroline Humphrey, eds. *Markets and Moralities*; and Signe Howell, ed., *The Ethnography of Moralities*.

74. Diane Austin-Broos, "The Anthropology of Conversion: An Introduction," in *The Anthropology of Religious Conversion*, ed. Andrew Buckser and Stephen D. Glazier (Lanham, MD: Rowman and Littlefield, 2003), 2.

75. J. Lofland and R. Stark, "Becoming a Worldsaver: A Theory of Religious Conversion," *American Sociological Review* 30 (1965): 862–74.

76. Ullman, *The Transformed Self*, xvi.

77. For an analysis of what conversion narratives reveal about attitudes toward the Soviet past, see Wanner, "Advocating New Moralities." Because conversion allows an individual to break with values and practices that are no longer considered appropriate, they can be read as a prescription for revolutionary change. For an analysis of conversion narratives of Russian Baptists in the 1920s, see Heather Coleman, "Becoming a Russian Baptist: Conversion Narratives and Social Experience," *Russian Review* 61, no. 1 (2002): 94–112. Birgit Meyer also found a level of motivation among Pentecostal converts in Ghana. See "Make a Complete Break with the Past."

## Chapter 5. God Is Love

1. Terence Ranger, "Religion, Development and African Christian Identity," in *Religion, Development and African Identity*, ed. K. Holst Petersen (Uppsala: Scandinavian Institute of African Studies, 1987), 31.

2. For an interesting comparison of Augustine and Foucault's writings on power, love, morality, and a variety of other issues, see J. Joyce Schuld, *Foucault and Augustine: Reconsidering Power and Love* (Notre Dame, IN: University of Notre Dame Press, 2003).

3. Interview conducted November 2001.

4. Interview conducted June 2000.

5. The importance of African believers supporting Christian churches worldwide should not be underestimated. Note that a third of the volunteers at the Moscow soup kitchen Melissa Caldwell studied were also Africans. They saw the soup kitchen as a means to recreate a sense of community in a society where racism rarely accorded them any form of communal membership. See Caldwell, *Not by Bread Alone*.

6. Interview conducted 29 October 2001.

7. Interview conducted 29 January 2002.

8. Birgit Meyer, "Christianity in Africa: From African Independent to Pentecostal-Charismatic Churches," *Annual Review of Anthropology* 33 (2004): 447–74, 468.

9. David Martin, *Pentecostalism: The World Their Parish* (Oxford: Blackwell, 2002).

10. Interview conducted 11 November 2001.

11. Ruth Marshall-Fratani, "Mediating the Global and Local in Nigerian Pentecostalism," in *Between Babel and Pentecost: Transnational Pentecostalism in Africa and Latin America*, ed. André Corten and Ruth Marshall-Fratani (Bloomington: Indiana University Press, 2001), 86.

12. Interview conducted 1 November 2001.

13. For an analysis of these types of activities, see Wanner, "Advocating New Moralities," 281–85.

14. Interview conducted 18 June 2001.

15. Interview conducted 30 January 2002.

16. See archives.cnn.com/2001/US/09/14/Falwell.apology/, last accessed 26 March 2007.

17. Susan Harding, "Imagining the Last Days: The Politics of Apocalyptic Language," in *Accounting for Fundamentalisms: The Dynamic Character of Movements,* ed. Martin E. Marty and R. Scott Appleby (Chicago, IL: University of Chicago Press, 1994).

18. Interview conducted 5 November 2001.

19. Anthony Giddens, *The Consequences of Modernity* (Stanford, CA: Stanford University Press, 1990), 53.

20. Ibid., 79.

21. Stephen Hunt, Malcolm Hamilton, and Tony Walter have characterized Charismatic Pentecostalism "an experience-led fundamentalism." See Hunt, Hamilton, and Walter, *Charismatic Christianity: Sociological Perspectives* (New York: St. Martin's Press, 1997), 6. While I agree that it is certainly experience-led, attaching the label "fundamentalist" to charismatic communities is a misnomer, both in this and in many other parts of the world. In Ukraine, it blurs critical distinctions between Soviet-era Pentecostal congregations and Charismatic ones, between moral mandates and other differences that distinguish them.

22. The word *charismatic* comes from the Greek *charismata,* meaning "gifts" and is justified Biblically by 1 Corinthians 12–14 and Acts 2.

23. For a depiction of faith healing ceremonies among Soviet-era Pentecostal believers and their justifications for preferring them to traditional, science-based medical services, see Klibanov, *Religioznoe Sektantsvo,* 160–63.

24. Some immigrant Pentecostal churches in the United States retain this custom.

25. Interview conducted 20 January 2002.

26. For a discussion of the role of the visual arts in religious practice, see David Morgan and Sally M. Promey, eds. *The Visual Culture of American Religions* (Berkeley: University of California Press, 2001), esp. introduction, ch. 1.

27. For an analysis of the effect of music on faith, see Robert Wunthrow, *All in Sync: How Music and Art Are Revitalizing American Religion* (Berkeley: University of California Press, 2003).

28. Roger N. Lancaster, *Thanks to God and the Revolution: Popular Religion and Class Consciousness in the New Nicaragua* (New York: Columbia University Press, 1988), 115.

## Chapter 6. Ambassadors of God

1. I have met Kyivans who came to the Embassy of God because friends in the United States recommended it.

2. See their website at www.godembassy.org, accessed 17 March 2007.

3. Peter Berger, The Sacred Canopy: Elements of a Sociological Theory of Religion (New York: Doubleday, 1969), 4–6.

4. Interview conducted 18 May 2005.

5. David Martin, *Pentecostalism: The World Their Parish* (Oxford: Blackwell, 2002).

6. For discussion of the social implications and consequences of certain aspects of

Pentecostal doctrine in Africa, see Birgit Meyer, *Translating the Devil: Religion and Modernity among the Ewe in Ghana* (Edinburgh: University of Edinburgh Press, 1999); and André Corten and Ruth Marshall-Fratani, eds. *Between Babel and Pentecost.*

7. See www.aa.org, accessed 26 March 2007.

8. "The Big Book" published by AA, the signature depiction of the program, generally uses gender-neutral language. However, it also has a chapter entitled "To Wives." This chapter was written in 1939, when it was assumed that alcoholics were overwhelmingly male. The 2001 edition of the book still carries the 1939 version of the chapter but adds in a footnote that a significant portion of alcoholics today are women. Approximately a third of all participants in AA programs and the Embassy of God's Love Rehabilitation Center are women.

9. Natalya Potopayeva, *The Way to Freedom for Your Family* (Kyiv: Bright Star Publishing House, 2004), 153. This book, like much of the vast library penned by Pastor Adelaja, has been translated into English. During the period of my fieldwork, the church had two full-time American missionaries in Kyiv assisting with translation and interpretation.

10. Henri J. M. Nouwen, *The Wounded Healer* (New York: Doubleday, 1972).

11. This is a tendency that all charismatic churches share. Many of the statistics they report are like Soviet production quotas—always overfulfilling the plan and overtaking the competition.

12. See www.aa.org, accessed 26 March 2007.

13. Within the U.S. context James Peacock and Thomas Csordas note a similar emphasis on the symbiotic adoption of a religious worldview and community membership as integral aspects of the healing process among, respectively, Pentecostals in the south and charismatic Catholics. See James Peacock, "Symbolic and Psychological Anthropology: The Case of Pentecostal Faith Healing," *Ethos* 12, no. 1 (Spring 1984): 37–53; and Thomas J. Csordas, "Elements of Charismatic Persuasion and Healing," *Medical Anthropology Quarterly* 2, no. 2 (1988): 121–42, 136.

14. Asad, *Formations of the Secular*, 79–85.

15. Frank Manning describes a Pentecostal service in Bermuda, which became a faith-healing ceremony when a drunk appeared and began vomiting. This was interpreted as the power of the Holy Spirit expelling the devil from his body and the first step in his being saved for Jesus. See Manning, "The Salvation of a Drunk," *American Ethnologist* 4, no. 3 (1977): 397–412.

16. George R. Saunders, "The Crisis of Presence in Italian Pentecostal Conversion," *American Ethnologist* 22, no. 2 (1995): 324–40, 336–37.

17. Another possibility is to volunteer at the halfway houses the Rehab Center offers in every city district. The largest one has up to thirty people living there.

18. Interview conducted 16 May 2004.

19. Interview conducted 21 May 2004.

20. Ram Cnaan, *The Invisible Caring Hand* (New York: New York University Press, 2002), 128.

21. Cnaan, *The Invisible Caring Hand,* 115.

22. Katrina Schwartz was one of the fewer than one hundred participants in Riga's first gay pride parade in 2005. The participants were heavily outnumbered by protesters, whose expression of aggressive homophobia were encouraged by a broad spectrum

of political and religious leaders. See her account of the march, "United in Hostility," at www.tol.cz/look/TOL/article.tpl?IdLanguage=1&IdPublication=4&NrIssue=134&Nr Section=3&NrArticle=14895, accessed 26 March 2007.

23. Personal communication from Pastor Sunday, 13 April 2006.

24. All quotations from L. M. Chernovet'skyi are cited from an interview published in the Embassy of God's own full-color magazine. This particular issue doubled as a ten-year anniversary commemorative publication. Vadim Chernets, "L. M. Chernovet'skyi: Blagodaria Bogy, . . ." *Posol* no. 1 (2004): 6–7.

25. Martin, *Pentecostalism,* 80.

26. Religious communities are vehicles for displaying inequalities, and their very survival depends on the ability and willingness of their members to tithe ten percent of their income. Believers who are in a position to financially sustain the community and its activities, such as Chernovet'skyi, gain status, of course, one that may or may not elude them in the wider society. Sascha Goluboff's study of a Moscow synagogue is a particularly poignant illustration of these tensions. She documents how synagogue life changed when significant class divisions emerged among members after 1991 that over-lapped with ethnic differences, conflating the two sources of tension. See *Jewish Russians: Upheavals in a Moscow Synagogue* (Philadelphia: University of Pennsylvania Press, 2002).

27. For an account of the myriad ways that state institutions and the law become re-sources to be exploited in the pursuit of wealth, see Catherine Wanner, "Money, Moral-ity, and New Forms of Exchange in Ukraine."

28. The popular churches in Latin America, for example, tend to downplay con-sumption, celebrating instead discipline, responsibility, and trust. The reaction to American goods advertised on television has been to equate them with "the evils of moral chaos, family break-up, and consumer hedonism." Martin, *Pentecostalism,* 35.

29. Interview conducted 12 May 2005.

30. Max Weber, *The Protestant Ethic and the "Spirit" of Capitalism.*

31. Karl Marx and Friedrich Engels, *On Religion* (New York: Schocken, 1964), 42.

32. The following studies conducted in Latin America illustrate this point: Manuel Vasquez, *The Brazilian Popular Church and the Crisis of Modernity* (Cambridge: Cam-bridge University Press, 1998); John Burdick, *Looking for God in Brazil* (Berkeley: Uni-versity of California Press, 1993); David Martin, *Tongues of Fire* and *Pentecostalism.*

33. Anthony Wallace, "Revitalization Movements," *American Anthropologist* 58, no. 2 (1958): 264–81.

34. Wallace, "Revitalization Movements," 275.

35. David Stoll, *Is Latin America Turning Protestant? The Politics of Evangelical Growth* (Berkeley: University of California Press, 1990).

# Epilogue

1. Marshall Sahlins, "What is Anthropological Enlightenment? Some Lessons of the Twentieth Century," *Annual Review of Anthropology* 28 (1999): i–xxiii, vii.

2. I am indebted to Virginia Vaté for this anecdote.

3. The 10/40 window is the least evangelized part of the globe, between 10 and 40 de-grees of latitude spanning from West Africa to East Asia and including the Middle East.

4. Krindatch, "Religion in Postsoviet Ukraine," 37.

5. Plokhy, "State Politics and Religious Pluralism," 310.

6. For more optimistic assessments of the likelihood of evangelical communities to foster positive social transformation, see David Martin, *Pentecostalism*; and Paul Gifford, *African Christianity: Its Public Role* (Bloomington: Indiana University Press, 1998). For a more skeptical view of the role of evangelicalism to promote tolerance, see Philip Jenkins, *The Next Christendom: The Rise of Global Christianity* (Oxford: Oxford University Press, 2002).

7. Peter Berger, *The Sacred Canopy: Elements of a Sociological Theory of Religion* (New York: Doubleday, 1969), 4–6.

8. Mathjis Pelkmans, ed., *Conversion after Socialism: Disruptions, Modernities, and the Technologies of Faith* (Oxford: Berghahn, forthcoming).

9. Joel Robbins, "The Globalization of Pentecostal and Charismatic Christianity," *Annual Review of Anthropology* 33 (2004b): 117–43.

10. Jenkins, *The Next Christendom*.

11. Martin, *Pentecostalism*, 9.

12. Vasquez, *The Brazilian Popular Church and the Crisis of Modernity*.

# REFERENCES

## Archival Sources

DAKhO        Derzhavnyi Arkhiv Kharkivs'koyi Oblasti
TsDAVOVU     Tsentral'nyi Derzhavnyi Arkhiv Vyshchykh Orhaniv Vlady ta Upravlinnia Ukrainy
TsDAHOU      Tsentral'nyi Derzhavnyi Arkhiv Hromads'kykh Obyednan' Ukrainy

## Journals

Antireligioznik
Baptist
Baptist Ukrainy
Bratskii Listok
Bratskii Vestnik
Khristianin
Nauka i Religiia
Prisutstviia
Voprosy Nauchnogo Ateizma

**Books and Articles**

Abu-Lughod, Lila. 1986. *Veiled Sentiments: Honor and Poetry in a Bedouin Society.* Berkeley: University of California Press.

Anderson, John. 1991. "The Council for Religious Affairs and the Shaping of Soviet Religious Policy," *Soviet Studies* 43, no. 4: 689–710.

——. 1994. *Religion, State, and Politics in the Soviet Union and Successor States.* New York: Cambridge University Press.

Anderson, Robert Mapes. 1979. *Vision of the Disinherited.* Oxford: Oxford University Press.

Appadurai, Arjun, and Carol Breckenridge. 1989. "On Moving Targets," *Public Culture* 2, no. 1: i–iv.

Asad, Talal. 1993. *Genealogies of Religion: Discipline and Reasons of Power in Christianity and Islam.* Baltimore, MD: Johns Hopkins University Press.

——. 2003. *Formations of the Secular: Christianity, Islam, Modernity.* Stanford, CA: Stanford University Press.

Austin-Broos, Diane J. 1997. *Jamaica Genesis: Religion and the Politics of Moral Orders.* Chicago, IL: University of Chicago Press.

——. 2003. "The Anthropology of Conversion: An Introduction." In *The Anthropology of Religious Conversion*, edited by Andrew Buckser and Stephen D. Glazier. Lanham, MD: Rowman & Littlefield.

Barker, Eileen. 1984. *The Making of a Moonie: Choice or Brainwashing?* London: Basil Blackwell.

Basch, Linda, Nina Glick Schiller, and Christina Szanton Blanc. 1994. *Nations Unbound: Transnational Projects, Postcolonial Predicaments, and Deterritorialized Nation-States.* Langhorne, PA: Gordon and Breach.

Baskok, Tanya, and Brym, Robert, eds. 1991. *Soviet-Jewish Emigration and Resettlement in the 1990s.* Toronto: York Lanes Press.

Basova, Irina G. 1998. "Freedom under Fire: The New Russian Religious Law," *Temple International and Comparative Law Journal* 14, no. 1:181–208.

Batalden, Stephen. 1993. *Seeking God: The Recovery of Religious Identity in Orthodox Russia, Ukraine, and Georgia.* DeKalb: Northern Illinois University Press.

Beermann, R. 1968. "The Baptists and Soviet Society," *Soviet Studies* 20, no. 1 (1968):67–80.

Berdiaev, Nicolas. 1972. *The Origin of Russian Communism.* Ann Arbor: University of Michigan Press.

Berger, Peter. 1969. *The Sacred Canopy: Elements of a Sociological Theory of Religion.* Garden City, NJ: Anchor Press.

——, ed. 1999. *The Desacralization of the World: Resurgent Religion and World Politics.* Grand Rapids, MI: William B. Eerdmans Publishing Company.

Bergman, Jay. 1992. "Soviet Dissidents on the Russian Intelligentsia, 1956–1985: The Search for a Usable Past," *Russian Review* 51, no. 1: 16–35.

Berkhoff, Karel. C. 2000. "Was There a Religious Revival in Soviet Ukraine under the Nazi Regime?" *Slavic and East European Review.* 78 no. 3: 536–67.

Biddulph, Howard. 2002. "Interconfessional Intolerance in Ukraine," *East-West Church Ministry Report* 10, no. 1.

Bilaniuk, Laada. 2005. *Contested Tongues: Language Politics and Cultural Correction in Ukraine.* Ithaca: Cornell University Press.

Binns, Christopher. 1979. "The Changing Face of Power: Revolution and Accommodation in the Development of a Soviet Ceremonial System Part I," *Man* 14, no. 4:585–606.

——. 1980. "The Changing Face of Power: Revolution and Accommodation in the Development of a Soviet Ceremonial System Part II" *Man* 15(1): 170–87.

Bociurkiw, Bohdan R. 1995. "The Uniate Church in Soviet Ukraine: A Case Study in Soviet Church Policy," *Canadian Slavonic Papers.* 7:89–113.

——. 1996. *The Ukrainian Greek Catholic Church and the Soviet State (1939–1950).* Toronto: Canadian Institute of Ukrainian Studies Press.

Borenstein, Eliot. 1999. "Suspending Disbelief: 'Cults' and Postmodernism in Post-Soviet Russia." In *Consuming Russia: Popular Culture, Sex and Society Since Gorbachev,* edited by Adele Marie Barker. Durham, NC: Duke University Press.

Bourdeaux, Michael. 1965. *Opium of the People: The Christian Religion in the U.S.S.R.* London: Faber and Faber.

——. 1968. *Religious Ferment in Russia: Protestant Opposition to Soviet Religious Policy.* New York: St. Martin's Press.

——, ed. 1995. "Glasnost and the Gospel: The Emergence of Religious Pluralism." In *The Politics of Religion in Russia and the New States of Eurasia.* Armonk, NY: M.E. Sharpe.

Boyle, Kevin, and Juliet Sheen, eds. 1997. *Freedom of Religion and Belief: A World Report.* New York: Routledge.

Bruce, Steve. 1992. *Religion and Modernization: Sociologists and Historians Debate the Secularization Thesis.* Oxford: Clarendon Press.

Burdick, John. 1993. *Looking for God in Brazil.* Berkeley: University of California Press.

Caldwell, Melissa. 2004. *Not By Bread Alone: Social Support in the New Russia.* Berkeley: University of California Press.

——. 2005. "A New Role for Religion in Russia's New Consumer Age: The Case of Moscow," *Religion, State and Society* 33, no. 1:43–58.

Casanova, José. 1996a. *Public Religions in the Modern World.* Chicago, IL: University of Chicago Press.

——. 1996b. "Incipient Religious Denominationalism in Ukraine and Its Effects on Ukrainian-Russian Relations," *Harriman Review* 9, nos. 1/2: 38–42.

——. 1998. "Between Nation and Civil Society: Ethnolinguistic and Religious Pluralism in Independent Ukraine." In *Democratic Civility: The History and Cross-Cultural Possibility of a Modern Political Ideal,* edited by Robert W. Hefner. New Brunswick, NJ: Transaction Publishers.

Chernets, Vadim. 2004. "L.M. Chernovet'skyi: Blagodaria Bogy . . . ," *Posol* 1:6–7.

Chumachenko, Tatiana A. 2002. *Church and State in Soviet Russia: Russian Orthodoxy from World War II to the Khrushchev Years,* translated by Edward E. Roslof. Armonk, NY: M.E. Sharpe.

Cnaan, Ram. 2002. *The Invisible Caring Hand*. New York: New York University Press.

Coleman, Heather J. 2000. "Becoming a Russian Baptist: Conversion Narratives and Social Experience," *The Russian Review* 61, no. 1:94–112.

———. 2005. *Russian Baptists and Spiritual Revolution, 1905–1929*. Bloomington: Indiana University Press.

Comaroff, Jean. 1985. *Body of Power, Spirit of Resistance: The Culture and History of a South African People*. Chicago, IL: University of Chicago Press.

Comaroff, Jean, and John Comaroff. 1991. *Of Revelation and Revolution: Christianity, Colonialism, and Consciousness in South Africa*. Vol. I. Chicago, IL: University of Chicago Press.

———. 1992. *Ethnography and the Historical Imagination*. Boulder, CO: Westview Press.

———. 1997. *Of Revelation and Revolution: The Dialectics of Modernity on a South African Frontier*. Vol. 2. Chicago, IL: University of Chicago Press.

Corley, Felix. 2002. "Belarus: Europe's Most Repressive Religion Law Adopted," *Keston News Service*, 2 October 2002.

Corten, André, and Ruth Marshall-Fratani. 2001. *Between Babel and Pentecost: Transnational Pentecostalism in Africa and Latin America*. Bloomington: Indiana University Press.

Csordas, Thomas J. 1988. "Elements of Charismatic Persuasion and Healing," *Medical Anthropology Quarterly* 2, no. 2 (June 1988): 121–42.

Cucchiari, Salvatore. 1990. "Between Shame and Sanctification: Patriarchy and Its Transformation in Sicilian Pentecostalism," *American Ethnologist* 17 (1990): 687–707.

Davie, Grace. 1994. *Religion in Britain since 1945: Believing without Belonging*. Oxford: Blackwell.

———. 1999. "Europe: The Exception that Proves the Rule?" In *The Desecularization of the World*, edited by Peter Berger. Washington, DC: Ethics and Public Policy Center.

DeGeorge, Richard T. 1969. *Soviet Ethics and Morality*. Ann Arbor: University of Michigan Press.

Dempster, Murray W., Bryon D. Klaus, and Douglas Petersen, eds. 1998. *The Globalization of Pentecostalism: A Religion Made to Travel*. Oxford: Regnum Books.

Dunn, Stephen P., and Ethel Dunn. 1967. *The Peasants of Central Russia*. New York: Holt, Reinhart and Winston.

Durkheim, Emile. 1995. *The Elementary Forms of Religious Life*. New York: Free Press.

Ebaugh, Helen Rose, and Janet Saltzman Chafetz, eds. 2000. *Religion and the New Immigrants: Continuities and Adaptations in Immigrant Congregations*. Walnut Creek, CA: Altamira Press.

———. eds. 2002. *Religion across Borders: Transnational Immigrant Networks*. Walnut Creek, CA: Altamira Press.

Edel, May, and Abraham Edel. 1959. *Anthropology and Ethics*. Springfield, IL: Charles C. Thomas.

Elliott, Mark C. 2002. "Guidelines for Guest Preaching, Teaching, and Cross-Cultural Communication," *East-West Church and Ministry Report* 10, no. 2:8–12.

Elliott, Mark, and Robert Richardson. 1992. "Growing Protestant Diversity in the Former Soviet Union." In *Russian Pluralism—Now Irreversible?* edited by Uri Ra'anan, Keith Ames, and Kate Martin. New York: St. Martin's Press.

Engelhardt, Jeffers. 2005. "Right Singing and Orthodox Conversion in Estonia." Paper presented at the Max Planck Institute conference on "Religious Conversion after Socialism," 7–9 April 2005.

Eryshev, A. A. 1959. *Religioznoe Sektantsvo i ego Sushchnost'*. Kyiv: Izdatel'stvo Kievskogo Universiteta.

Ewick, Patricia, and Susan S. Silbey. 1995. "Subversive Stories and Hegemonic Tales: Toward a Sociology of Narrative," *Law and Society Review* 29:197–226.

Fagan, Geraldine, and Aleksandr Shchipkov. 2001. "Rome Is Not Our Father, but Neither Is Moscow Our Mother: Will There Be a Local Ukrainian Orthodox Church?" *Religion, State & Society* 29, no. 3: 197–205.

Felman, Shoshana, and Dori Laub. 1992. *Testimony: Crises of Witnessing in Literature, Psychoanalysis, and History*. New York: Routledge.

Figes, Orlando. 1975. "The Russian Revolution of 1919 and Its Language in the Village." *Russian Review* 56, no. 3 (July 1997):323–45.

——. 1996. *A People's Tragedy: The Russian Revolution, 1891–1924*. New York: Penguin Books.

Filatov, Sergei, ed. 2002. *Religiya i Obshchestvo: Ocherki Sovremennoi Religioznoi Zhizni Rossii*. Moscow: Letnyi Sad.

Fitzpatrick, Sheila. 1994. *Stalin's Peasant's: Resistance and Survival in the Russian Village after Collectivization*. New York: Oxford University Press.

Fletcher, William C. 1985a. *Soviet Charismatics: The Pentecostals in the USSR*. New York: Peter Lang.

——. 1985b. "The Soviet Bible Belt: World War II's Impact on Religion." In *The Impact of World War II on the Soviet Union*, edited by S. J. Linz. New York: Rowan and Allanheld.

Fouron, Georges E., and Nina Glick Schiller. 2001. "The Generation of Identity: Redefining the Second Generation within a Transnational Social Field," In *Migration, Transnationalization, and Race in a Changing New York*, edited by Héctor R. Cordero-Guzmán, Robert C. Smith, and Ramón Grosfoguel. Philadelphia, PA: Temple University Press.

Freeze, Gregory L. 1983. *The Parish Clergy in Nineteenth Century Russia: Crisis, Reform, Counter-Reform*. Princeton, NJ: Princeton University Press.

——. 1995. "Counter-Reformation in Russian Orthodoxy: Popular Response to Religious Innovation, 1922–1925," *Slavic Review* 54, no. 2 (Summer 1995):305–39.

Geertz, Clifford. 1973. *The Interpretation of Cultures*. New York: Basic Books.

Geraci, Robert P. 2001. *Window on the East: National and Imperial Identities in Late Tsarist Russia*. Ithaca: Cornell University Press.

Geraci, Robert P., and Michael Khodarkovsky, eds. 2001. *Of Religion and Empire: Missions, Conversion, and Tolerance in Tsarist Russia*. Ithaca: Cornell University Press.

Giddens, Anthony. 1990. *The Consequences of Modernity*. Stanford, CA: Stanford University Press.

Gifford, Paul. 1998. *African Christianity: Its Public Role*. Bloomington: Indiana University Press.

Glazer, Perry L. 2002. *The Quest for Russia's Soul: Evangelicals and Moral Education in Post-Communist Russia*. Waco, TX: Baylor University Press.

Glick-Schiller, Nina. 2001. *Georges Woke Up Laughing: Long-Distance Nationalism and the Search for Home*. Durham, NC: Duke University Press.

Goluboff, Sascha. 2003. *Jewish Russians: Upheavals in a Moscow Synagogue*. Philadelphia: University of Pennsylvania Press.

Grazhdan, V. D. 1966. "Piatidesiatnichestvo i Sovremennost'." In *Voprosy Nauchnogo Ateizma*. Moscow: AN SSSR.

Grossman, Joan Delaney. 1973. "Khrushchev's Anti-Religious Policy and Campaign of 1954," *Soviet Studies* 24, no. 3: 374–86.

Guest, Kenneth. 2003. *God in Chinatown: Religion and Survival in New York's Evolving Immigrant Community*. New York: New York University Press.

Gunn, T. Jeremy. 1998. "Caesar's Sword: The 1997 Law of the Russian Federation on Freedom of Conscience and Religious Associations," *Emory International Law Review* 12 no. 1: 43–99.

Guttman, Matthew C. 2002. *The Romance of Democracy: Compliant Defiance in Contemporary Mexico*. Berkeley: University of California Press.

Halfin, Igal. 2000. *From Darkness to Light: Class, Consciousness, and Salvation in Revolutionary Russia*. Pittsburgh, PA: University of Pittsburgh Press.

Harding, Susan Friend. 1987. "Convicted by the Holy Spirit: The Rhetoric of Fundamental Baptist Conversion," *American Ethnologist* 4:167–79.

——. 1994. "Imagining the Last Days: The Politics of Apocalyptic Language." In *Accounting for Fundamentalisms: The Dynamic Character of Movements*, edited by Martin E. Marty and R. Scott Appleby. Chicago, IL: University of Chicago Press.

——. 2000. *The Book of Jerry Falwell: Fundamentalist Language and Politics*. Princeton, NJ: Princeton University Press.

Hardwick, Susan Wiley. 1993. *Russian Refuge: Religion, Migration, and Settlement on the North American Pacific Rim*. Chicago, IL: University of Chicago Press.

Hervieu-Léger, Danièle. 2000. *Religion as a Chain of Memory*, translated by Simon Lee. Cambridge: Polity Press.

Hill, Kent R. 1991. *The Soviet Union on the Brink: An Inside Look at Christianity and Glasnost*. Portland, OR: Multnomah.

Howell, Signe, ed. 1997. *The Ethnography of Moralities*. London: Routledge.

Hunt, Stephen, Malcolm Hamilton, and Tony Walter, eds. 1996. *Charismatic Christianity: Sociological Perspectives*. New York: St. Martin's Press.

Husband, William B. 2000. *"Godless Communists": Atheism and Society in Soviet Russia, 1917–1932*. DeKalb: Northern Illinois University Press.

Isajiw, Wsevolod W., Yury Roshyk, and Roman Senkus, eds. 1992. *The Refugee Experience: Ukrainian Displaced Persons after World War II*. Edmonton: Canadian Institute of Ukrainian Studies Press.

Jenkins, Philip. 2002. *The Next Christendom: The Rise of Global Christianity*. New York: Oxford University Press.

Johnston, Patrick, and Jason Mandryk. 2001. *Operation World: 21st Century Edition.* Waynesboro, GA, Paternoster Publishing.

Klibanov, A. I. 1950. "Sektanstvo v Proshlom i v Nastoiashchem," In *Voprosy Istorii Religii i Ateizma.* Vol. IX. Moscow: Academy of Sciences of the USSR.

——. 1965. *Istoriia religioznogo sektantstva v Rossii.* Moscow: Izdatel'stvo Nauka.

——. 1969. *Religioznoe Sektantstvo i Sovremennost'.* Moscow: Nauka Press.

Knight, Nathaniel. 1991. "The Number of Orthodox Churches before and after the Khrushchev Antireligious Drive," *Slavic Review* 50, no. 3:612–620.

Krawchuk, Andrii. 1996. "Religious Life in Ukraine: Continuity and Change," *Journal of Ecumenical Studies* 33, no. 1:59–68.

Krindatch, Alexei D. 2003. "Religion in Postsoviet Ukraine as a Factor in Regional, Ethnocultural and Political Diversity," *Religion, State, and Society* 31, no. 1:37–73.

Kuropas, Myron B. 1991. *The Ukrainian Americans: Roots and Aspirations.* Toronto: University of Toronto Press.

Kuzio, Taras. 2000. "The Struggle to Establish the World's Largest Orthodox Church," *RFE/RL* 5 September 2000.

Lancaster, Roger. 1988. *Thanks to God and the Revolution.* New York: Columbia University Press.

Lane, Christel. 1978. *Christian Religion in the Soviet Union: A Sociological Study.* London: George Allen & Unwin.

Ledeneva, Alena. V. 1998. *Russia's Economy of Favours: Blat, Networking and Informational Exchange.* Cambridge: Cambridge University Press.

Lee, Erica. 2003. *At America's Gates: Chinese Immigration during the Exclusion Era, 1882–43.* Chapel Hill: University of North Carolina Press.

Lialina, G. C. 1977. *Baptizm: Illiuzii i Real'nost'.* Moscow: Isdatel'stvo politicheskoi literatury.

Lindquist, Galina. 2006. *Conjuring Hope: Healing and Magic in Russia.* Oxford: Berghahn.

Lingenfelter, Judith E., and Sherwood G. Lingenfelter. 2003. "Teaching Cross-Culturally," *East-West Church Ministry Report* 11, no. 4:4–8.

Little, David. 2002. "Religious Minorities and Religious Freedom." In *Protecting the Human Rights of Religious Minorities in Eastern Europe*, edited by R. G. Danchin and E. A. Cole. New York: Columbia University Press.

Liubashchenko, V. I. 1996. *Istoriia Protestantyzma v Ukraini.* Kyiv: Polis.

Lofland, J., and N. Skonovd. 1981. "Conversion Motifs," *Journal for the Scientific Study of Religion* 20:373–85.

Lofland, J., and R. Stark. 1965. "Becoming a Worldsaver: A Theory of Religious Conversion," *American Sociological Review* 30:862–74.

Luciuk, Lubomyr. 2000. *Searching for Place: Ukrainian Displaced Persons, Canada, and the Migrations of Memory.* Toronto: University of Toronto Press.

Mandel, Ruth, and Caroline Humphrey, eds. 2002. *Markets and Moralities: Ethnographies of Postsocialism.* Oxford: Berg.

Manning, Frank. 1977. "The Salvation of a Drunk," *American Anthropologist* 4, no. 3:397–412.

Markowitz, Fran. 1993. *A Community in Spite of Itself: Soviet Jewish Émigrés in New York*. Washington, DC: Smithsonian Institution Press.

———. 1995. "Criss-Crossing Identities: The Russian Jewish Diaspora and the Jewish Diaspora in Russia," *Diaspora* 4, no. 2: 201–11.

Markus, Vasyl. 1995. "Politics and Religion in Ukraine: In Search of a New Pluralistic Dimension." In *The Politics of Religion in Russia and the New States of Eurasia,* edited by Michael Bourdeaux. Armonk, NY: M. E. Sharpe.

Marshall-Fratini, Ruth. 2001. "Mediating the Global and Local in Nigerian Pentecostalism." In *Between Babel and Pentecost: Transnational Pentecostalism in Africa and Latin America,* edited by André Corten and Ruth Marshall-Fratini. Bloomington: Indiana University Press.

Martin, David. 1978. *A General Theory of Secularization.* New York: Harper and Row.

———. 1990. *Tongues of Fire: The Explosion of Protestantism in Latin America.* Oxford: Basil Blackwell.

———. 2002. *Pentecostalism: The World Their Parish.* Oxford: Blackwell.

Marx, Karl, and Friedrich Engels. 1964. *On Religion.* New York: Schocken.

McClay, Wilfred M. 2003. "Two Concepts of Secularism." In *Religion Returns to the Public Square: Faith and Policy in America,* edited by Hugh Heclo. Washington, DC: Woodrow Wilson Center Press.

Mead, George Herbert. 1934. *Mind, Self and Society from the Standpoint of a Social Behaviorist,* edited by C. Morris. Chicago, IL: University of Chicago Press.

Meyer, Brigit. 1996. "Make a Complete Break with the Past: Memory and Postcolonial Modernity in Ghanaian Pentecostal Discourse," *Journal of Religion in Africa* 28, no. 3 (Aug. 1998):316–49.

———. 1997. *Translating the Devil: Religion and Modernity among the Ewe in Ghana.* Edinburgh: University of Edinburgh Press.

———. 2004. "Christianity in Africa: From African Independent to Pentecostal-Charismatic Churches," *Annual Review of Anthropology* 33 (2004):447–74.

Meyer, Brigit, and Peter Geschiere, eds. 1999. *Globalization and Identity: Dialectics of Flow and Closure.* Oxford.

Mitrokhin, L. N. 1966. *Baptizm.* Moscow: Politizad.

———. 1974. *Baptizm.* Moscow: Isdatel'stvo politicheskoi literatury.

Mitrokhin, Nikolai. 2001. "Aspects of the Religious Situation in Ukraine," *Religion, State, and Society* 29, no. 3:173–96.

Moore, Sally Falk. 1987. "Explaining the Present: Theoretical Dilemmas in Processual Ethnography," *American Ethnologist* 14, no. 4 (Nov. 1987):727–36.

Morgan, David, and Sally Promey, eds. 2001. *The Visual Culture of American Religions.* Berkeley: University of California Press.

Moskalenko, Aleksei Trovimovich. 1966. *Piatidesiatniki.* Moscow: Isdatel'stvo politicheskoi literatury.

Nouwen, Henri J. M. 1972. *The Wounded Healer.* New York: Doubleday.

Ong, Anna. 1999. *Flexible Citizenship: The Cultural Logics of Transnationality.* Durham, NC: Duke University Press.

Orleck, Annelise. 1999. *The Soviet Jewish Americans.* Westport, CT: Greenwood Press.

O'Shaughnessy, Laura Nuzzi. 1990. "Onward Christian Soldiers: The Case of Protestantism in Central America." In *Religious Resurgence and Politics in the Contemporary World*, edited by Emile Sahliyeh. Albany: State University of New York Press.

Oushakine, Serguei. 2000. "In the State of Post-Soviet Aphasia: Symbolic Development in Contemporary Russia." *Europe-Asia Studies* 52, no. 6:991–1016.

Paloutzian, R. F., J. T. Richardson, and L. R. Rambo. 1999. "Religious Conversion and Personality Change." *Journal of Personality* 67, no. 6:1047–79.

Patico, Jennifer. 2005. "To Be Happy in a Mercedes: Tropes of Value and Ambivalent Visions of Marketization." *American Ethnologist* 32, no. 3 (Aug. 2005): 479–96.

Peacock, James. 1984. "Symbolic and Psychological Anthropology: The Case of Pentecostal Faith Healing." *Ethos* 12, no. 1 (Spring 1984):37–53.

Peel, J. D. Y. 1975. "Conversion and Tradition in Two African Societies: Ijebu and Buganda." *Past and Present* 77:108–41.

Pelkmans, Mathijs, ed. Forthcoming. *Conversion after Socialism: Disruptions, Modernities, and the Technologies of Faith*. Oxford: Berghahn.

Peris, Daniel. 1992. "The 1929 Congress of the Godless." *Soviet Studies* 43, no. 4:711–32.

———. 1998. *Storming the Heavens: The Soviet League of the Militant Godless*. Ithaca: Cornell University Press.

Pesman, Dale. 2000. *Russia and Soul: An Exploration*. Ithaca: Cornell University Press.

Peterson, Anna, Manuel Vásquez, and Philip Williams, eds. 2001. *Christianity, Social Change, and Globalization in the Americas*. New Brunswick, NJ: Rutgers University Press.

Plokhy, Serhii. 1996. "Kyiv vs. Moscow: The Autocephalous Movement in Independent Ukraine." *Harriman Review* 9, nos. 1–2: 32–37.

———. 2002. "State Politics and Religious Pluralism in Russia and Ukraine: A Comparative Perspective." In *Protecting the Human Rights of Religious Minorities in Eastern Europe*, edited by P. G. Danchin and E. A. Cole. New York: Columbia University Press.

Plokhy, Serhii, and Frank Sysyn. 2003. *Religion and Nation in Modern Ukraine*. Edmonton, Canada: Canadian Institute of Ukrainian Studies Press.

Pospielovsky, Dimitry V. 1987a. *A History of Marxist-Leninist Atheism and Soviet Antireligious Policies*, Vol. 1. New York: St. Martin's Press.

———. 1987b. *Soviet Antireligious Campaigns and Persecutions*. Vol. 2. New York: St. Martin's Press.

———. 1988. *Soviet Studies on the Church and the Believer's Response to Atheism*. Vol. 3. New York: St. Martin's Press.

Potopayeva, Natalya. 2004. *The Way to Freedom for Your Family*. Kyiv: Bright Star Publishing House.

Powell, David E. 1975. *Antireligious Propaganda in the Soviet Union: A Study of Mass Persuasion*. Cambridge, MA: MIT Press.

Ra'anan, Uri, Keith Armes, and Kate Martin, eds. 1992. *Russian Pluralism—Now Irreversible?* New York: St. Martin's Press.

Rambo, Lewis R. 1993. *Understanding Religious Conversion.* New Haven, CT: Yale University Press.

Ranger, Terence. 1987. *Religion, Development and African Christian Identity.* In *Religion, Development and African Identity,* edited by K. Holst Petersen. Uppsala: Scandinavian Institute of African Studies.

Richardson, James T. 1985. "The Active versus Passive Convert: Paradigm Conflict in Conversion/Recruitment Research," *Journal for the Scientific Study of Religion* 24:199–236.

Ries, Nancy. 2002. " 'Honest' Bandits and 'Warped People': Russian Narratives about Money, Corruption, and Moral Decay." In *Ethnography in Unstable Places: Everyday Lives in Contexts of Dramatic Political Change,* edited by Carol J. Greenhouse, Elizabeth Mertz, and Kay B. Warren. Durham, NC: Duke University Press.

———. 1997. *Russian Talk: Culture and Conversation during Perestroika.* Ithaca: Cornell University Press.

Rivkin-Fish, Michelle. 2005. *Women's Health in Post-Soviet Russia: The Politics of Intervention.* Bloomington: Indiana University Press.

Robbins, Joel. 2004a. *Becoming Sinners: Christianity and Moral Torment in a Papua New Guinea Society.* Berkeley: University of California Press.

———. 2004b. "The Globalization of Pentecostal and Charismatic Christianity," *Annual Review of Anthropology* 33:117–43.

Rogers, Douglas. 2005. "Money, Moonshine and the Politics of Liquidity in Rural Russia," *American Ethnologist* 32, no. 1 (Feb. 2005):63–81.

Ro'i, Yaacov. 1984. "The Task of Creating the New Soviet Man: Atheistic Propaganda in the Soviet Muslim Areas," *Soviet Studies* 36, no. 1:26–44.

———. 1996. *Jews and Jewish Life in Russia and the Soviet Union.* New York: Frank Cass.

Roudik, Peter. 2001. "Ukraine." In *Religious Liberty: The Legal Framework in Selected OSCE Countries.* Washington, DC: United States Congress, Commission on Security and Cooperation in Europe.

Rowe, Michael. 1982. "Christian Prisoners in the USSR 1979–81," *Religion in Communist Lands* 10, no. 1:81–82.

Rudolph, Susanne Hoeber, and James Piscatori, eds. 1997. *Transnational Religion and Fading States.* Boulder, CO: Westview Press.

Ruel, Malcolm. 1982. "Christians as Believers." In *Religious Organization and Religious Experience,* edited by John Davis. London: Academic Press.

Safran, William. 1991. "Diasporas in Modern Societies: Myths of Homeland and Return," *Diaspora* 1, no. 1:83–99.

Sahlins, Marshall. 1998a. "Two or Three Things that I Know about Culture," *The Journal of the Royal Anthropological Institute* 5(3): 399–421.

———. 1998b. "What is Anthropological Enlightenment? Some Lessons of the Twentieth Century." *Annual Review of Anthropology* 28:i–xxiii.

Satzewich, Vic. 2002. *The Ukrainian Diaspora: Global Diasporas*. London: Routledge.

Saunders, George R. 1995. "The Crisis of Presence in Italian Pentecostal Conversion," *American Ethnologist* 22, no. 2:324–40.

Savinsky, S. N. 2000. *Istoriya Yevangel'skikh Khristian—Baptistov Ukrainy, Rossii, Belorussii (1917–1967)*. St. Petersburg: Bibliya dlya vsekh.

Schiller, Nina Glick, and Georges Eugene Fouron. 2001. *Georges Woke Up Laughing: Long-Distance Nationalism and the Search for Home*. Durham, NC: Duke University Press.

Schuld, J. Joyce. 2003. *Foucault and Augustine: Reconsidering Power and Love*. Notre Dame, IN: University of Notre Dame Press.

Scott, James C. 1985. *Weapons of the Weak: Everyday Forms of Peasant Resistance*. New Haven: Yale University Press.

——. 1990. *Domination and the Arts of Resistance: Hidden Transcripts*. New Haven, CT: Yale University Press.

Shterin, Marat S., and James T. Richardson. 1998. "Local Laws Restricting Religion in Russia: Precursors of Russia's New National Law," *Journal of Church and State* 40, no. 2:319–341.

Simon, Rita J., ed. 1985. *New Lives: The Adjustment of Soviet Jewish Immigrants in the United States and Israel*. Lexington, MA: Lexington Books.

Smith, Timothy L. 1978. "Religion and Ethnicity in America," *American Historical Review* 83:1155–85.

Snow, David, and Richard Machalek. 1983. "The Convert as a Social Type." In *Sociological Theory*, edited by R. Collins. San Francisco, CA: Jossey-Bass.

——. 1984. "The Sociology of Conversion," *Annual Review of Sociology* 10:167–90.

Solzhenitsyn, Alexander. 1963. *One Day in the Life of Ivan Denisovich*. New York: E. P. Dutton.

Staples, Clifford L., and Armand L. Mauss. 1987. "Conversion or Commitment? A Reassessment of the Snow and Machalek Approach to the Study of Conversion," *Journal for the Scientific Study of Religion* 26:133–47.

Stark, Rodney, and Roger Finke. 2000. *Acts of Faith: Explaining the Human Side of Religion*. Berkeley: University of California Press.

Steeves, Paul D. 1976. "The Russian Baptist Union, 1917–35: Evangelical Awakening in Russia," Ph.D. dissertation, University of Kansas.

Stites, Richard. 1989. *Revolutionary Dreams: Utopian Visions and Experimental Life in the Russian Revolution*. Oxford: Oxford University Press.

Stoll, David. 1990. *Is Latin America Turning Protestant? The Politics of Evangelical Growth*. Berkeley: University of California Press.

Stromberg, P. 1993. *Language and Self-Transformation: A Study of the Christian Conversion Narrative*. Cambridge: Cambridge University Press.

Suny, Ronald Grigor, and Terry Martin, eds. 2001. *A State of Nations: Empire and Nation-Making in the Age of Lenin and Stalin* Oxford: Oxford University Press.

Swatsky, Walter. 1981. *Soviet Evangelicals Since World War II*. Scotsdale, PA: Herald Press.

Tataryn, Myroslaw. 2001. "Russia and Ukraine: Two Models of Religious Liberty and Two Models for Orthodoxy," *Religion, State and Society* 29, no. 3:155–72.

Taubman, William. 2003. *Khrushchev: The Man and His Era*. New York: W.W. Norton.

Tumarkin, Nina. 1983. *Lenin Lives! The Lenin Cult in Soviet Russia*. Cambridge, MA: Harvard University Press.

Ullman, Chana. 1989. *The Transformed Self: The Psychology of Religious Conversion*. New York: Plenum Press.

Valchinova, Galina. 2005. "Converting 'Back' to the 'Faith of our Ancestors.' " Paper presented at the Max Planck Institute Conference "Religious Conversion after Socialism," 7–9 April 2005.

Van der Veer, Peter, ed. 1996. *Conversion to Modernities: The Globalization of Christianity*. New York: Routledge.

Vasquez, Manuel C. 1998. *The Brazilian Popular Church and the Crisis of Modernity*. Cambridge: Cambridge University Press.

Verdery, Katherine. 1996. *What Was Socialism, and What Comes Next?* Princeton, NJ: Princeton University Press.

Vins, Georgi. 1975. *Testament from·Prison*, translated by Jane Ellis, edited by Michael Bourdeaux. Elgin, IL: David C. Cook Publishing.

———. 1976. *Three Generations of Suffering*, translated by Jane Ellis. London: Hodder and Stoughton.

von Geldern, James. 1993. *Bolshevik Festivals, 1917–1920*. Berkeley: University of California Press.

Vornovolkov, Oleg. 2002. "Faktory, povliiavshie na rasprostranenie Piatidesiatnicheskogo Dvizheniia na iuge Ukrainy," *Khristianskaia Mysl'* no. 1 (Aug. 2002):41–75.

Wacker, Grant. 2001. *Heaven Below: Early Pentecostals and American Culture*. Cambridge, MA: Harvard University Press.

Wallace, Anthony F. C. 1956. "Revitalization Movements," *American Anthropologist* 58, no. 2:264–81.

Wanner, Catherine. 1998. *Burden of Dreams: History and Identity in Post-Soviet Ukraine*. University Park: Pennsylvania State University Press.

———. 2003. "Advocating New Moralities: Conversion to Evangelicalism in Ukraine," *Religion, State, and Society* 31, no. 3 (September 2003):173–87.

———. 2004. "Missionaries of Faith and Culture: Evangelical Encounters in Ukraine," *Slavic Review* 63, no. 4 (Winter 2004):732–55.

———. 2005. "Money, Morality and New Forms of Exchange in Postsocialist Ukraine," *Ethnos* 71, no. 4 (Winter 2005):515–37.

Warner, R. Stephen, and Judith Witmer, eds. 1998. *Gatherings in Diaspora: Religious Communities and the New Immigration* Philadelphia, PA: Temple University Press.

Weber, Max. 2002. *The Protestant Ethic and the "Spirit" of Capitalism and Other Writings*. New York: Penguin Books.

Weiner, Amir. 2001. *Making Sense of War: The Second World War and the Fate of the Bolshevik Revolution*. Princeton, NJ: Princeton University Press.

Werth, Paul W. 2001. *At the Margins of Orthodoxy: Mission, Governance and Confessional Politics in Russia's Volga-Kama Region, 1827–1905.* Ithaca: Cornell University Press.

Wolf, Eric R. 1958. "The Virgin of Guadalupe: A Mexican National Symbol," *Journal of American Folklore* 71, no. 279 (Jan. 1958):34–39.

Wunthrow, Robert. 2003. *All in Sync: How Music and Art Are Revitalizing American Religion.* Berkeley: University of California Press.

Yamane, David. 2000. "Narrative and Religious Experience," *Sociology of Religion* 61, no. 2:171–90.

Yurchak, Alexei. 2005. *Everything Was Forever Until It Was No More: The Last Soviet Generation.* Princeton, NJ: Princeton University.

Zhuk, Sergei Ivanovich. 2002. *Russia's Lost Reformation: Peasants and Radical Religious Sects in Southern Russia and Ukraine, 1830–1917.* Baltimore, MD: Johns Hopkins University Press.

# INDEX

Page numbers in italics refer to photographs.